TO

MY FATHER

GEORGE WILLIAM EVANS

THESE LECTURES ARE AFFECTIONATELY

DEDICATED

AMERICAN MATHEMATICAL SOCIETY
COLLOQUIUM LECTURES, VOLUME V

---

# THE CAMBRIDGE COLLOQUIUM

## 1916

### PART I

### FUNCTIONALS AND THEIR APPLICATIONS
### SELECTED TOPICS, INCLUDING
### INTEGRAL EQUATIONS

BY

GRIFFITH CONRAD EVANS

NEW YORK
PUBLISHED BY THE
AMERICAN MATHEMATICAL SOCIETY
501 WEST 116TH STREET
1918

PRESS OF
THE NEW ERA PRINTING COMPANY
LANCASTER, PA.

# PREFACE

The American Mathematical Society held its Eighth Colloquium in connection with the Twenty-Third Summer Meeting at Harvard University during the week of September 3–9, 1916. At this Colloquium the following lectures were delivered:

I. Functionals and their Applications. Selected Topics, including Integral Equations. By Professor Griffith C. Evans of the Rice Institute.

II. Analysis Situs. By Professor Oswald Veblen of Princeton University.

The present volume, which is issued as Part I, contains Professor (now Captain) Evans's lectures. Professor (now Captain) Veblen has been prevented by national service from preparing his manuscript for publication. The Committee hopes that, in the not too distant future, his lectures may appear as Part II of a single volume. It seems best, however, to issue Professor Evans's lectures promptly, even though a certain discontinuity may thereby result.

LUTHER P. EISENHART,
WILLIAM F. OSGOOD,
R. G. D. RICHARDSON,
*Committee on Publication.*

# AUTHOR'S PREFACE.

Most mathematicians are familiar with that development of the subject of integral equations which is epitomized by the name Hilbert. There are however other domains whose description is not so completely available in book form, which represent nevertheless an expansion of the same circle of fundamental notions, implied in the central theory of integral equations. Volterra's genial concepts, developed during the last thirty years, and outlined in his treatise of 1913, have by contact with the ideas of Hadamard, Stieltjes, Lebesgue, Borel and others, given rise to many new points of view. It is the purpose of the Lectures to select for discussion some of those which appear most to promise further rapid expansion.

A word may be necessary as to the arrangement. In order to make the subject matter accessible to as large a circle of readers as possible, the text in large type has been devised to be intelligible to those who approach the subject for the first time, and may be read by itself. The text in small type comes, on the other hand, closer to the present state of the subject, and may be more suggestive. The author thus hopes to fulfil the avowed purpose of the Colloquium.

Commas in formulæ are omitted when not necessary for clearness; thus $r(\lambda, t)$ is written $r(\lambda t)$ if the meaning is clear from the context.

The author has given references to American mathematicians freely, in order that familiarity with names may stimulate conversation at meetings of the Society, and thereby increase interest in the subject itself.

Houston, Texas,
February, 1918.

# CONTENTS

## LECTURE I

### Functionals, Derivatives, Variational Equations



## LECTURE II

### Complex Functionals

## LECTURE III

### Implicit Functional Equations

## LECTURE IV

### Integro-Differential Equations of Bôcher Type



## LECTURE V

### Direct Generalizations of the Theory of Integral Equations

## ERRATA CORRIGE.

On page 35 in equation (9′) change $\gamma$ to $\alpha$. In all the formulæ and equations following on page 35 change $\gamma$ to $\beta$ and $\beta$ to $\alpha$.

On page 37 in equation (12) change $\gamma$ to $\beta$ and $\beta$ to $\alpha$.

On page 39 in the second equation there should be an $i$ as a factor of each of the last two terms of the integrand.

### *Note to Art.* 27 *Lecture* II.

The approach to the analog of Green's theorem is more clear if done in the following way, and bears more relation to the development with which we are familiar in calculus. The meaning of equations (17) to (20) is perhaps not clear, as the equations stand. But the invariant $H_{\Phi_1\Phi_1'}$ defined by (21):

$$(21) \qquad (V_1 \times V_2)H_{\Phi_1\Phi_1'} = W_1 \times W_2'$$

which may be rewritten in the new forms:

$$\begin{aligned} H_{\Phi_1\Phi_1'} &= (\beta . W_1)\,(\beta \cdot W_1') + (\alpha \cdot W_1)\,(\alpha \cdot W_1') \\ &= -\,(\beta \cdot W_1)\,(\alpha \cdot W_2') + (\alpha \cdot W_1)\,(\beta \cdot W_2') \end{aligned}$$

as we see below, bears a noticeable relation to the scalar product of two gradients which is subjected to the familiar analysis of Green's theorem.

The forms just written however do not lend themselves to the customary integration by parts. Let us then in these formulæ replace the part which refers to say $W_1$ and $W_2$ by functions $\varphi_1$ and $\varphi_2$ which depend on them (retaining meanwhile the quantities $W_1'$ and $W_2'$) and seek to write $H_{\Phi_1\Phi_1'}$ in the form:

$$H_{\Phi_1\Phi_1'} = W_1' \cdot \nabla\varphi_1 + W_2' \cdot \nabla\varphi_2$$

or more generally, introducing an arbitrary point function $k(x, y, z)$,

$$(22) \qquad kH_{\Phi_1\Phi_1'} = W_1' \cdot \nabla\varphi_1 + W_2' \cdot \nabla\varphi_2$$

Green's theorem is merely the result of integrating both sides of

(22) over a three dimensional region, and reducing the right hand member by an integration by parts.

What conditions must $\varphi_1$, $\varphi_2$ satisfy in order to make possible the equation (22)? A short analysis shows that a necessary and sufficient condition is given by equation (17), which may be deduced directly, starting from this point of view.

The analysis follows. In the first place, by making use of the identities (see (8) page 34)

$$W_1 = V_1\,\alpha\cdot W_1 + V_2\,\beta\cdot W_1,\; W_2' = V_1\alpha\cdot W_2' + V_2\,\beta\cdot W_2'$$

we have

$$W_1 \times W_2' = (V_1 \times V_2)\{(\alpha\cdot W_1)\,(\beta\cdot W_2') - (\beta\cdot W_1)\,(\alpha\cdot W_2')\}$$

whence, from the definition (21),

$$H_{\Phi_1\Phi_1'} = -\,(\beta\cdot W_1)\,(\alpha\cdot W_2') + (\alpha\cdot W_1)\,(\beta\cdot W_2')$$

By the condition of isogeneity (10″), we get the other new form mentioned for $H_{\Phi_1\Phi_1'}$, as well as additional ones of the same character.

The equation just written, by comparison with (22), gives us the equation

$$k[(\alpha\cdot W_1)\,(\beta\cdot W_2') - (\beta\cdot W_1)\,(\alpha\cdot W_2')] = W_1'\cdot\nabla\varphi_1 + W_2'\cdot\nabla\varphi_2.$$

In the right hand member the following substitutions may be made, to make the two members similar in construction:

$$W_1'\cdot\nabla\varphi_1 = \nabla\varphi_1\cdot(V_1\beta - V_2\alpha)\cdot W_2' = (V_1\cdot\nabla\varphi_1)\,(\beta\cdot W_2') - (V_2\cdot\nabla\varphi_1)\,(\alpha\cdot W_2')$$

$$W_2'\cdot\nabla\varphi_2 = \nabla\varphi_2\cdot(V_1\alpha + V_2\beta)\cdot W_2' = (V_1\cdot\nabla\varphi_2)\,(\alpha\cdot W_2') + (V_2\cdot\nabla\varphi_2)\,(\beta\cdot W_2').$$

Hence the equation becomes

$$(\nabla\varphi_1\cdot V_1 + \nabla\varphi_2\cdot V_2 - k\alpha\cdot W_1)\,(\beta\cdot W_2') + {} + (\nabla\varphi_2\cdot V_1 - \nabla\varphi_1\cdot V_2 + k\beta\cdot W_1)\,(\alpha\cdot W_2') = 0.$$

By hypothesis, $\varphi_1$, $\varphi_2$, $k$ are independent of $W_1'$, $W_2'$; hence by putting $W_2' = V_2$ and $V_1$ successively the following equations are deduced

$$k\alpha\cdot W_1 = \nabla\varphi_1\cdot V_1 + \nabla\varphi_2\cdot V_2$$
$$k\beta\cdot W_1 = \nabla\varphi_1\cdot V_2 - \nabla\varphi_2\cdot V_1$$

which with the identity $W_1 = V_1\alpha \cdot W_1 + V_2\beta \cdot W_1$ yield the result:

$$kW_1 = (V_1V_1 + V_2V_2)\cdot\nabla\varphi_1 + (V_1V_2 - V_2V_1)\cdot\nabla\varphi_2$$

which is merely (17). Vice versa, from (17) may be deduced (22). Equation (18) is equivalent to (17) by the relation of isogeneity.

In a similar manner equation (19) or (20) is seen to be a necessary and sufficient condition for the functions $\varphi_1'$ and $\varphi_2'$ to satisfy in order that $H_{\Phi_1\Phi_1'}$ may be written in the form (22').

Equation (17) is equivalent to two independent differential equations on the functions $\varphi_1$, $\varphi_2$ to be determined, as is seen in the equivalence of that equation to the two preceding (i. e., the conditions in the plane $V_1V_2$). Hence the function $k$ remains entirely arbitrary, and may if we choose be taken everywhere positive.

# LECTURE I

## FUNCTIONALS, DERIVATIVES AND VARIATIONAL EQUATIONS*

### § 1. Fundamental Notions; Functionals of Plane Curves

**1. Continuity of a Functional.** If we have two sets of values $x$ and $y$, we say that $y$ is a function of $x$ if to every value of $x$ in its set corresponds a value of $y$. Similarly, if we have a set of functions $\varphi(x)$ given between limits $a$ and $b$, and a set of values $y$, we say that $y$ is a functional of $\varphi(x)$ if to every $\varphi(x)$ of the set corresponds one of the values $y$. This relation we may write in some such form as the following:

$$y = y[\overset{b}{\underset{a}{\varphi(x)}}]. \tag{1}$$

It is an obvious generalization if instead of a functional of $\varphi(x)$, we speak of a functional of a curve (in a plane, or in space), or of a surface. Of special interest are the closed curves. The area inside a closed plane curve, the Green's function of which the point arguments are fixed, and the solutions of boundary value problems in physics are ready examples of functionals of curves or surfaces. The maximum of a function is a functional of that function.

* This lecture is based upon the following references:

Volterra, Sopra le funzioni che dipendono da altre funzioni; Sopra le funzioni dipendenti da linee, *Rendiconti della Reale Accademia dei Lincei,* vol. 3 (1887), five notes;

*Leçons sur les fonctions de lignes,* Paris (1913), chapters I, II, III.

Hadamard, Sur l'équilibre des plaques élastiques encastrées, *Mémoires présentées à l'Académie des Sciences,* vol. 33.

P. Lévy, Sur les équations intégro-differentielles définissant des fonctions de lignes, *Théses présentées à la Faculté des Sciences de Paris,* no. d'ordre 1436;

Sur les équations aux dérivées fonctionelles et leur application à la Physique mathématique, *Rendiconti del Circolo Matematico di Palermo,* vol. 33 (1912);

Sur l'intégration des équations aux dérivées fonctionelles partielles, *Rendiconti del Circolo Matematico di Palermo,* vol. 37 (1914).

The argument of a functional, if a curve or a surface, may be regarded as having sense; and the value of a functional of a curve will depend therefore generally on the direction in which the curve is taken, and the value of a functional of a surface upon which choice we make for the positive aspect of the surface.

A variable $y$ which depends upon all the values of a continuous function $\varphi(x)$, in a range $a \leq x \leq b$, that is, by means of a relation of the form (1), may for many purposes be considered as a function of an infinite number of variables, e. g., of the values of $\varphi$ which correspond to the rational values of $x$. In fact, since this infinity is a denumerable one, the properties of functionals of a continuous function may in a measure be foretold by considering the properties of functions depending upon a finite number of variables and letting that number become infinite.

As an instance, consider the definition of continuity. A function $f(x_1 \cdots x_n)$ is said to be continuous at a point $(x_1^0 \cdots x_n^0)$ if the quantity $|f - f_0|$ can be made as small as desired by taking the quantities $|x_i - x_i^0|$, $i = 1, 2, \cdots, n$, all less than $\delta$, with $\delta$ small enough. A similar conception applies to a function of an infinite number of variables,* and therefore to a functional. We shall therefore say that $y[\overset{b}{\underset{a}{\varphi(x)}}]$ is continuous in $\varphi$ for $\varphi = \varphi_0$ if the limit as $\delta$ vanishes of $y[\varphi(x)]$ is $y[\varphi_0(x)]$, where $|\varphi(x) - \varphi_0(x)| < \delta$, $a \leq x \leq b$; in other words, as $\varphi$ approaches $\varphi_0$ uniformly.

**2. Derivative of a Functional.** The same generalization is not serviceable directly in the extension of the idea of *derivative.* It is therefore from this point of view more convenient to generalize the idea of *differential*—a linear continuous function of the increments of the infinite number of variables thus leading to a linear continuous functional of the increment $\theta(x)$ of $\varphi(x)$. The functional derivative is however itself a natural conception.

In the neighborhood of a value $x_0$, let $\varphi(x)$ be given a continuous increment $\theta(x)$ which does not change sign: let us write

* It may be desirable to replace, in some cases, the quantity $\delta$ by $\sigma_i\delta$, $i = 1, 2, \cdots, n$, where the $\sigma_i$ are given "scale" values (in accordance with E. H. Moore's concept of relative uniformity).

$|\theta(x)| < \epsilon$, in the interval $x_0 - h \leq x \leq x_0 + h$, setting $\theta(x) = 0$ otherwise, and let us form the ratio $\Delta y/\sigma$, where $\sigma = \int_a^b \theta(x)dx$. If this ratio approaches a limit as $\epsilon$ and $h$ approach zero in an arbitrary manner, the limit is defined as the functional derivative of $y[\overset{b}{\underset{a}{\varphi(x)}}]$ at the point $x_0$:

$$y'[\overset{b}{\underset{a}{\varphi(x)}} | x_0] = \lim_{\epsilon=0,\, h=0} \frac{\Delta y}{\sigma}. \tag{2}$$

A similar definition applies for the derivative of a functional of a plane curve, as the accompanying diagram shows; the derivative may be denoted by the symbol $y'[C | M]$, or even $y'(M)$,

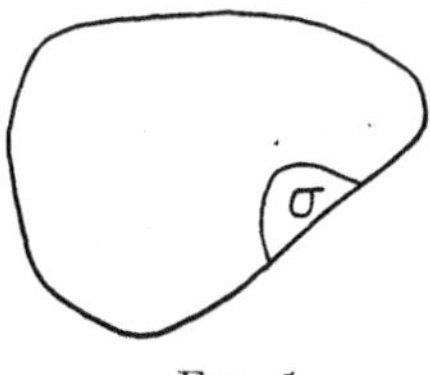


FIG. 1

if there is no ambiguity. The point $M$ denotes in this connection a point on the curve $C$. The quantity $\sigma$ is considered as positive or negative according as it lies on the same side of the curve, or not, as the positive normal (which we take on a closed curve as directed towards the interior).*

**3. Additive and Non-Additive Functionals of Plane Curves.** Let $C_1$ and $C_2$ be two closed plane curves exterior to each other except for a common portion $C'$, with directions such that $C'$ is traversed in opposite ways on the two curves; and let $C_3$ be the curve composed of $C_1$ and $C_2$ with the omission of $C'$, the

* It is not desirable, for what follows, to consider any curves whose running point co-ordinates are not functions of finite variation of a parameter $t$; in fact we need consider only "standard" curves (see Art. 49). For simplicity of geometrical treatment, we thus make a distinction with respect to generality when the argument of a functional is a curve, instead of a function (see, for instance, Lecture III). The case where the curves have vertices involves no special consideration.

direction following that on the original curves. If now for every such case the relation

(3) $$y[C_1] + y[C_2] = y[C_3]$$

is satisfied, the functional $y[C]$ is said to be *additive.*

If $y$ is an additive functional, $\Delta y$ will depend merely upon the contour $\sigma$, without regard to the rest of the curve $C$, of which $\sigma$ represents the distortion. Evidently then, $y'[C|M]$ will not depend upon $C$, but upon the point $M$ alone: *the derivative of an additive functional is merely a point function in the plane.*

Let us give to the points of $C$ a displacement along the normal, of amount $\delta n(M) = \epsilon\psi(M)$, where $\psi(M)$ represents a continuous function of the arc distance along $C$. Denote by $\delta y$ the principal part of the infinitesimal change of $y$, i. e., the quantity $\epsilon[dy/d\epsilon]_{\epsilon=0}$. From the definition of functional derivative, we should expect, for an additive functional:

(4) $$\delta y = \int_C y'(M)\delta n(M)ds$$

and for a non-additive functional:

(5) $$\delta y = \int_C y'[C|M]\delta n(M)ds,$$

and therefore, for an additive functional:

(6) $$y[C_2] - y[C_1] = \int\int y'(M)d\sigma,$$

where the region of integration is the region between $C_1$ and $C_2$, $d\sigma$ being given the proper sign at each point; and for a non-additive functional:

(7) $$y[C_2] - y[C_1] = \int\int y'[C|M]d\sigma,$$

where the region is the same as before, and the curves $C$ form a continuous one-parameter family containing $C_1$ and $C_2$.

The formulæ (4) and (5) are still valid if the significance of $\delta n(C)$ is slightly generalized, and it is used to denote the variation of $C$ in the sense of the calculus of variations, that is, a quantity of the type $\epsilon\left[\dfrac{\partial\psi(M, \epsilon)}{\partial\epsilon}\right]_{\epsilon=0}$.

If the curve $C_1$ may be shrunk down to zero without going outside the region of definition, we shall have, for an additive functional, the equation:

$$y[C] = \iint_{(C)} y'(M)d\sigma. \tag{6'}$$

The formulæ (4) to (7) may fail to hold in cases where the derivative does not remain finite, or when the functional itself depends in a special manner upon certain points. These important special cases will be treated, as need arises. But meanwhile it is perhaps desirable to point out sufficient conditions under which formulæ (4) to (7) may be deduced.

**4. Existence of a Derivative, Additive Functionals vs. Functions of Point Sets.** An additive functional of a curve, $y[C]$, is said to be a *functional of finite variation* if the inequality

$$\Sigma_i \mid y[\overline{C}_i] \mid < M$$

is satisfied, in which $M$ is a constant, and the closed curves $\overline{C}_i$ are squares (or, with equal generality, rectangles) mutually exterior (except for possible common boundaries), finite or denumerably infinite in number, and all contained in a given finite region. The functional is *absolutely continuous* if the quantity $M$ can be made as small as desired, $< \epsilon$, by taking the sum of the areas of the squares small enough, $< \delta$, irrespective of their position.

It is also convenient to be able to speak of a restricted derivative, and this we define as $\lim_{\overline{C}=0} y[\overline{C}]/(\text{area inside } \overline{C})$, the curve $\overline{C}$ being restricted to a square. In some cases it may be desirable to restrict the curves to circles instead of squares.

We notice at once the relation of the theory of additive functionals to that of functions of point sets. In fact if we define a function $f(\omega)$ of the points in any cell of a square network as the value of $y[\overline{C}]$ for the contour of that square, the value of the function of point sets $f(e)$ will be defined for any point set $e$ which is measurable according to Borel, and if the frontier of $e$ is a standard curve $C$, we shall have $f(e) = y[C]$. To paraphrase a theorem of De la Vallée-Poussin:*

*Every additive functional which is continuous and of finite variation defines a continuous additive function of point sets, for point sets measurable according to Borel; the restricted derivatives of the functional and the function are the same wherever they exist.*

Hence it follows that *an additive continuous functional of finite variation has a finite derivative* (*in the restricted sense*) *at all points except possibly those of a set of measure zero.*

* De la Vallée-Poussin, *Transactions of the American Mathematical Society*, vol. 16 (1915), p. 493.

If the functional is *absolutely continuous*, the corresponding function of point sets $f(e)$ will be absolutely continuous for all sets measurable $(B)$. But any set measurable $(L)$ is a set measurable $(B)$ of the same measure plus a set measurable $(L)$ of zero measure. And thus by defining $f(e) = 0$ when $e$ is a set of zero measure $(L)$, $f(e)$ will be defined uniquely for all sets measurable $(L)$, and will be additive and absolutely continuous. It will then have a summable restricted derivative at all points except those of a set of measure zero, and will be itself the integral of that derivative over the set $e$.* As such, however, it will have a generalized derivative at all points except possibly those of a null set. *Hence if* $y[C]$ *is an absolutely continuous additive functional it will have a derivative (unrestricted), independent of* $C$, *at all points except possibly those of a null set; moreover equation* (6′) *is satisfied:*

$$y[C] = \iint_{(C)} y'(M)d\sigma.$$

Equations (4) and (6) are obvious consequences of (6′).

In the case when the additive functional is merely continuous, there appear in the above equation other terms beside the integral, corresponding to points where the inferior restricted derivative becomes positively infinite, or the superior restricted derivative negatively infinite.

**5. Examples of Functional Derivatives.** The theorem just enunciated has application in showing the existence of certain differential operators, of which perhaps one example will be sufficient illustration. Consider a function $u(x, y)$ continuous, with its first partial derivatives. The quantity $\int_C \partial u/\partial n\, ds$ will be an additive functional; let us denote its functional derivative, where it exists, by $\Delta u$.

If the function $f(x, y)$ is summable, and $u(x, y)$ satisfies the equation

$$\int_C \frac{\partial u}{\partial n} ds = \iint_{(C)} f(x, y) dx dy \tag{8}$$

for all standard curves, or even for all rectangles, it follows that the functional which we are investigating is absolutely continuous; and therefore $\Delta u$ exists and satisfies the equation

$$\Delta u = - f(x, y)$$

except at a point set of zero measure. The existence of $\Delta u$ does not imply the existence of $\partial^2 u/\partial x^2$ or $\partial^2 u/\partial y^2$; and yet, as we shall see in Lecture IV, where $f(x, y)$ is assumed to be continuous, the equation (8), which is equivalent to Poisson's equation, still lends itself to solution.

**6. Non-Additive Functionals.** The functional derivative of a non-additive functional will not in general be independent of the curve $C$, and therefore the extension (7) of the result expressed in equation (6) must be obtained.

* De la Vallée-Poussin, Cours d'analyse infinitésimale, Louvain, 1912, vol. 2, p. 102.

Sufficient conditions for this generalization are given by Volterra; it is possible however to reduce them somewhat in extent.*

Consider a functional $F$ depending on all the values of $\varphi(x)$ between $a$ and $b$. The following theorem may be proved directly. *If for a certain continuous function $\varphi_0(x)$, the functional $F[\varphi(x)]$, continuous in $\varphi(x)$, has a derivative $F'[\varphi(x) \mid \xi]$ for every value of $\xi$ in a certain closed subinterval $a'b'$ of $ab$ (which may be $ab$ itself) that derivative remains limited and continuous throughout $a'b'$.*

To prove this theorem, write $F'[\varphi_0(x) \mid \xi] = t$, and let $\xi_1, \xi_2, \cdots$ be an infinite set of values having $\xi_0$ as a limiting point, such that

$$\lim_{n=\infty} F'[\varphi_0(x) \mid \xi_n] = t'.$$

We shall assume that $t'$ is finite; the case where $t'$ is infinite occasions an obvious modification of the proof. Let $\mid t - t' \mid = p$, and suppose momentarily $p \neq 0$.

Give to $\varphi_0(x)$ a variation of one sign $\theta_1(x)$, of the kind specified in the definition of the derivative, and take $\epsilon_1$ and $h_1$ so small that we have the inequality

$$\mid F[\varphi_0(x) + \theta_1(x)] - F[\varphi_0(x)] - t\sigma_1 \mid < \tfrac{1}{2} \mid p\sigma_1 \mid .$$

We may, however, by taking a variation $\theta_2$, small enough, and about a point $\xi_n$ near enough to $\xi_0$, and adding to it a variation $\theta_3$, small enough everywhere, yet different from zero at $\xi_0$, obtain a variation $\theta_1$ for which is satisfied the inequality:

$$\mid F[\varphi_0(x) + \theta_2(x) + \theta_3(x)] - F[\varphi_0(x) - t'(\sigma_2 + \sigma_3) \mid < \tfrac{1}{2} \mid p(\sigma_2 + \sigma_3) \mid .$$

For since $F$ is assumed to be continuous, the increment $\theta_3$ may be made so small as to affect the difference $F[\varphi_0 + \varphi_2] - F[\varphi_0]$ as little as we please.

But from these two inequalities it follows that

$$\mid (t - t')(\sigma_2 + \sigma_3) \mid < \mid p \mid (\sigma_2 + \sigma_3) \mid ,$$

which is a contradiction. Hence $p = 0$, and the theorem is proved.

In order now to obtain the formulæ (5) and (7) we consider as a region for the argument $\varphi(x)$ that included between two given continuous functions $\Phi_1(x)$ and $\Phi_2(x)$, where $\Phi_1(x) < \Phi_2(x)$, in the interval $a \leqq x \leqq b$, and assume that $F[\varphi]$ is defined for every continuous function in that region, and is continuous. This we call the assumption $(\alpha)$.

In addition to $(\alpha)$ we assume the conditions $(\lambda)$ $(\mu)$, as follows:

$(\lambda)$ The functional derivative $F'[\varphi(x) \mid \xi]$ exists for every function in the region, and every $\xi$, $a \leqq x \leqq b$.

$(\mu)$ The ratio $\Delta F/\sigma$ approaches its limit uniformly with respect to all possible functions $\varphi(x)$ and values $\xi$.

From $(\alpha)$ $(\lambda)$ $(\mu)$ it may be deduced that $F'$ is *continuous in $\xi$* uniformly for all points $\xi$ and functions $\varphi$ in the region; and that it is *continuous in $\xi$ and $\varphi$* uniformly with respect to $\xi$ and $\varphi$, provided that $\varphi$ is restricted to a family of continuous functions, closed in the sense that the limiting functions are uniform limits.

* Evans, *Bulletin of the American Mathematical Society*, vol. 21 (1915), pp. 387–397.

For convenience we denote by $(\mu_1)$ that part of the assumption $(\mu)$ which requires uniformity with respect to the functional argument alone. From $(\alpha)$ $(\lambda)$ $(\mu_1)$ can be deduced a theorem analogous to Rolle's theorem in the differential calculus:

Let $F[\varphi_1] = F[\varphi_2] = 0$, where $\varphi_1 - \varphi_2$ is a function which does not change sign in the interval $ab$ and is different from zero only in the interval $a'b'$. Then there is a function $\varphi_0$, of the pencil determined by $\varphi_1$ and $\varphi_2$ and a value $\xi_0$, $a' \leqq \xi_0 \leqq b'$, such that $F'[\varphi_0(x) \mid \xi_0] = 0$.

From this theorem follows the law of the mean, in the same way as in the differential calculus:

Law of the Mean. *Let $\varphi_1 - \varphi_2$ not change sign in the interval $ab$, and be different from zero in the sub-interval $a'b'$ (which may be $ab$ itself). There is a function $\varphi_0$ of the pencil determined by $\varphi_1$ and $\varphi_2$, and a value $\xi_0$, $a' \leqq \xi_0 \leqq b'$, such that*

$$F[\varphi_2(x)] - F[\varphi_1(x)] = F'[\varphi_0(x) \mid \xi] \int_a^b (\varphi_2(x) - \varphi_1(x))dx. \tag{9}$$

Let us consider now functions $\varphi(x)$ and $\varphi(x) + \omega\psi(x)$, in the given range, $\omega$ being an arbitrary parameter whose values are restricted to the neighborhood of $\omega = 0$, and make the assumptions $(\alpha)$ $(\lambda)$ $(\mu)$. We can find an explicit expression for $[dF/d\omega]_{\omega=0}$. In fact, this is easily shown to be of the form

$$\left(\frac{dF}{d\omega}\right)_{\omega=0} = \int_a^b F'[\varphi(x) \mid \xi]\psi(\xi)d\xi, \tag{10}$$

of which equation (5) is an obvious consequence. Hence also we have:

$$\left(\frac{dF}{d\omega}\right)_{\omega=\omega} = \int_a^b F'[\varphi(x) + \omega\psi(x) \mid \xi]\psi(\xi)d\xi. \tag{11}$$

From (11) may be deduced the equation

$$F[\varphi(x) + \psi(x)] - F[\varphi(x)] = \int_a^b F'[\varphi(x) + \theta\psi(x) \mid \xi]\psi(\xi)d\xi, \tag{12}$$

where $0 < \theta < 1$. And from (12) follows the equation (7), already given.

## § 2. Functionals of Curves in Space

**7. Introduction.** We are interested in this lecture not so much in the character of the curve, which is the argument of the functional, as in the character rather of the functional relation itself. And so we shall assume without statement, or with slight statement, whatever properties may be needed from time to time in order to make possible the differential and geometric transformations used in the analysis of the functionals. The curves are to be closed, and in particular, each one must be capable of being capped by at least two surfaces which have no points in common except points on the curve, and which enclose a region lying entirely within the region of definition of the functional. Moreover we must be able to pass from one curve of the class to any other by means of a family of curves depending upon a parameter $\lambda$, such that the co-ordinates $(xyz)$ of a point on the variable curve will be continuous functions of $\lambda$ with continuous derivatives up to the second order. We shall consider, of course, only rectifiable curves, since we shall use as a variable the distance $s$ along the curve.

In this lecture we consider merely real functionals of space curves. Lecture II is devoted to their theory as complex numbers.

**8. Functional Derivatives and Functional Fluxes.** If we take in the neighborhood of a point $M$, a small portion $\Delta s$ of the curve $C$, and give to every point of it a displacement $\Delta x$ parallel to the $x$-axis, thus forming a new curve $C'$, the quantity

$$X[C|M] = \lim_{\Delta s=0,\ \Delta x=0} \frac{\Delta F[C]}{\Delta s \Delta x}, \tag{13}$$

if it exists, is called the derivative of $F[C]$ at the point $M$ in the direction $X$. Under the conditions of uniform continuity analogous to those specified in the case of plane curves, if we make a displacement of the given curve $C$ by an amount of which the projections on the three axes are respectively $\epsilon\xi(s)$, $\epsilon\eta(s)$, $\epsilon\zeta(s)$, we find for the rate of change of $F$ the value

$$\left(\frac{\partial F}{\partial \epsilon}\right)_{\epsilon=0} = \int_C (X\xi + Y\eta + Z\zeta)ds. \tag{14}$$

In fact if the points of the curve first take on a displacement parallel to the $x$-axis of amount $\epsilon\xi(s)$, there will result to $F[C]$ an increment of amount $\Delta F_1 = \epsilon \int_C X\xi ds$, etc. The above formula (14) may be written in the alternate form

$$\delta F[C] = \int_C (X\delta x + Y\delta y + Z\delta z)ds. \tag{14'}$$

2

If the functional derivatives fail to exist at special points of the curve $C$, terms corresponding to these special points may be introduced into the formula for the variation of $F[C]$, as in the case of functionals of plane curves.

Since the true argument of the functional $F[C]$ is understood to be the curve $C$, and not the three functions of $s$ which define the co-ordinates of any point of $C$, it follows that the three derivatives $X$, $Y$, $Z$ are not entirely independent. In fact, if we make $\delta x$, $\delta y$, $\delta z$ such that at every point of the curve they define a direction tangent to it, we have

$$\int_C (X\delta x + Y\delta y + Z\delta z)ds = 0$$

or

$$\int_C K(X \cos x, s + Y \cos y, s + Z \cos z, s)ds = 0,$$

where $K$ is an arbitrary function of $s$. Hence

(15) $$X \cos x, s + Y \cos y, s + Z \cos z, s = 0.$$

According to the formulæ (14) or (14′), the derivative of $F[C]$ in any direction $n$ is the projection $R_n$ of the vector $R$, with components $X$, $Y$, $Z$, in that direction. Hence for new axes $x'$, $y'$, $z'$ through the point, we have the usual formulæ for transformation of co-ordinates:

(16) $$X' = X \cos x, x' + Y \cos y, x' + Z \cos z, x', \text{ etc.}$$

From (15) we see moreover that the vector $R[C|M]$ is normal to the curve $C$ at $M$.

The vector $R$ has the advantage that it is uniquely defined for every point of the curve $C$ for a given functional. It is not, however, the only functional vector which may be defined, and for additive functionals, especially, not the most convenient one.

Consider a curve $C$, and two planes at right angles which contain the tangent line to $C$ at a point $M$. Let $V_1$ and $V_2$ be defined as

(17) $$V_1 = \lim_{\sigma_1=0} \frac{\Delta F}{\sigma_1}, \qquad V_2 = \lim_{\sigma_2=0} \frac{\Delta F}{\sigma_2},$$

due respectively to small displacements of area $\sigma_1$ and $\sigma_2$, of an element $ds$ of the curve, in the two planes. Consider each $V_i$ as directed normally to its plane in such a way as to make the direction around $\sigma_i$ positive, looking down this normal. Let $V$ be the vector perpendicular to $C$ whose components are $V_1$ and $V_2$.

If $V[C|M]$ is continuous in $C$ and $M$ in the neighborhood of the point and curve in question, we can deduce in the same way as for the corresponding theorem about directional derivatives in the differential calculus, that the rate of change of $F[C]$ for a displacement $\sigma$ in any plane containing the curve is the component of $V$ perpendicular to that plane.

From the fact that, except for infinitesimals of higher order, we have the equation:

$$\Delta F = V_n d\sigma = (X\delta x + Y\delta y + Z\delta z)ds$$

we may deduce the equations

$$(18) \qquad \begin{aligned} X &= V_z \cos s, y - V_y \cos s, z, \\ Y &= V_x \cos s, z - V_z \cos s, x, \\ Z &= V_y \cos s, x - V_x \cos s, y, \end{aligned}$$

which may be expressed in the shorter form

$$(18') \qquad R = \tau \times V,$$

where $\tau$ is a unit vector in the direction of the curve, and $\tau \times V$ stands for the vector product of the two vectors $\tau$ and $V$ (the vector area of the parallelogram of which they are the two sides). In fact if the element of arc $ds$ has an arbitrary vector displacement $\delta\rho$ we shall have

$$d\sigma = (\delta\rho \times \tau)ds$$

and

$$\Delta F = V \cdot d\sigma = V \cdot (\delta\rho \times \tau)ds,$$

where $V \cdot d\sigma$ stands for the scalar product of the vectors $V$ and $d\sigma$.* But $V \cdot (\delta\rho \times \tau) = \delta\rho \cdot (\tau \times V)$, and therefore, since

* If $\alpha$ and $\beta$ are two vectors, $\alpha \cdot \beta$ is defined as $\alpha_x\beta_x + \alpha_y\beta_y + \alpha_z\beta_z$. The quantity $\alpha \cdot (\beta \times \gamma)$ is thus seen to be the volume of the parallelopiped of

$V \cdot d\sigma = R \cdot \delta\rho ds$, $R = \tau \times V$. We may therefore rewrite equation (7) in the form

$$(19) \qquad F[C_2] - F[C_1] = \iint V_n d\sigma = \iint V \cdot d\sigma.$$

If we change $V$ by adding to it any component in the direction $\tau$ of the curve $C$ at $M$, the rate of change of $F[C]$, for a small variation about $M$ in a plane containing the direction of the curve, will still be given by the projection of $V$ in a direction perpendicular to this plane. *The formulæ* (18), (18′), (19) *will all remain valid,* since the terms due to this extra component all are seen to have the value zero. We can regard the functional vector $V[C|M]$ therefore as containing an arbitrary component along the curve $C$; in contradistinction to the vector $R[C|M]$, which is uniquely determined.

Following P. Lévy, we call $V[C|M]$ the *flux of the functional.*

**9. Additive Functionals of Curves in Space.** We can speak of additive functionals of curves in space, as well as additive functionals of plane curves. For additive functionals of space curves, the *flux* $V$ acquires special importance. *We can so choose* $V$ *as to make it independent of* $C$:

$$(20) \qquad V[C|M] = V(M) = V(xyz).$$

In fact, we notice that $V_n[C|M]$, the component of $V$ perpendicular to the element of surface $\sigma$ at $M$, depends merely on the orientation and position of $\sigma$, and not on the curve $C$, of which it forms the local variation; for, since $F$ is additive, we have

$$(20') \qquad V_n = \lim_{\sigma=0} \frac{F[C_\sigma]}{\sigma},$$

where $C_\sigma$ is the boundary of $\sigma$. Moreover, if at a point $M$ we determine the quantities $V_x$, $V_y$, $V_z$ in this way, by taking $\sigma$ perpendicular to the $x$, $y$, and $z$ directions respectively, the

sides $\alpha$, $\beta$, $\gamma$, taken with the positive or negative sign according as the vectors have the same order as the axes, or the opposite. If we denote this triple product by $[\alpha\beta\gamma]$, we have obviously

$$[\alpha\beta\gamma] = \alpha \cdot (\beta \times \gamma) = (\alpha \times \beta) \cdot \gamma = [\beta\gamma\alpha] = [\gamma\alpha\beta].$$

construction familiar in the case of hydrodynamics shows us that $V_n$ is merely the component in the direction $N$ of the vector $(V_x, V_y, V_z)$.

On account of (20′), Volterra uses the symbols $\partial F/\partial(yz)$, $\partial F/\partial(zx)$, $\partial F/\partial(xy)$ to denote the three components of $V$, and the symbol $dF/d\sigma$ to denote the vector $V$ itself.

**10. The Condition of Integrability for Additive Functionals.** For any closed surface we must have the equation

$$\iint V_n d\sigma = 0, \tag{21}$$

since it may be regarded as forming a double cap for a closed curve lying on it. Hence at every point in the region we are considering, the relation

$$\frac{\partial V_x}{\partial x} + \frac{\partial V_y}{\partial y} + \frac{\partial V_z}{\partial z} = 0 \tag{21′}$$

must hold; *the divergence of $V$ must everywhere vanish.*

On the other hand, it is evident, that if the relation (21′) holds everywhere for the vector point function $V$, it will define an additive functional of space curves by (19), of which $V$ will be the vector flux. Equation (21) will hold in fact for any closed surface, and $V$ will satisfy (20′).

**11. Change of Variable.** If we make a one-one point transformation of space $x = x(\bar{x}\bar{y}\bar{z})$, $y = y(\bar{x}\bar{y}\bar{z})$, $z = z(\bar{x}\bar{y}\bar{z})$, where $x(\bar{x}\bar{y}\bar{z})$, $y(\bar{x}\bar{y}\bar{z})$, $z(\bar{x}\bar{y}\bar{z})$ are continuous functions with continuous first derivatives, with $[\partial(xyz)/\partial(\bar{x}\bar{y}\bar{z})] \neq 0$, the closed curve $C$ will go over into a closed curve $\bar{C}$, and the additive functional $F[C]$ will go over into an additive functional $\bar{F}[\bar{C}]$, which will have a flux vector $\bar{V}$.

If $(u, v)$ are the curvilinear co-ordinates of corresponding points on the caps $\Sigma$ and $\bar{\Sigma}$ of $C$ and $\bar{C}$ respectively, then

$$\begin{aligned} \bar{F}[\bar{C}] = F[C] &= \iint V_x dydz + V_y dzdx + V_z dxdy \\ &= \iint \left\{ V_x \frac{\partial(yz)}{\partial(uv)} + V_y \frac{\partial(zx)}{\partial(uv)} + V_z \frac{\partial(xy)}{\partial(uv)} \right\} dudv. \end{aligned}$$

But

$$\frac{\partial(yz)}{\partial(uv)} = \frac{\partial(yz)}{\partial(\bar{y}\bar{z})}\frac{\partial(\bar{y}\bar{z})}{\partial(uv)} + \frac{\partial(yz)}{\partial(\bar{z}\bar{x})}\frac{\partial(\bar{z}\bar{x})}{\partial(uv)} + \frac{\partial(yz)}{\partial(\bar{x}\bar{y})}\frac{\partial(\bar{x}\bar{y})}{\partial(uv)}, \text{ etc.}$$

Hence if we write

$$\overline{V}_{\bar{x}} = V_x\frac{\partial(yz)}{\partial(\bar{y}\bar{z})} + V_y\frac{\partial(zx)}{\partial(\bar{y}\bar{z})} + V_z\frac{\partial(xy)}{\partial(\bar{y}\bar{z})},$$

(22)
$$\overline{V}_{\bar{y}} = V_x\frac{\partial(yz)}{\partial(\bar{z}\bar{x})} + V_y\frac{\partial(zx)}{\partial(\bar{z}\bar{x})} + V_z\frac{\partial(xy)}{\partial(\bar{z}\bar{x})},$$

$$\overline{V}_{\bar{z}} = V_x\frac{\partial(yz)}{\partial(\bar{x}\bar{y})} + V_y\frac{\partial(zx)}{\partial(\bar{x}\bar{y})} + V_z\frac{\partial(xy)}{\partial(\bar{x}\bar{y})},$$

we obtain, by substitution in the equation for $\overline{F}[\overline{C}]$, the equations

$$\overline{F}[\overline{C}] = \int\int\left\{\overline{V}_{\bar{x}}\frac{\partial(\bar{y}\bar{z})}{\partial(uv)} + \overline{V}_{\bar{y}}\frac{\partial(\bar{z}\bar{x})}{\partial(uv)} + \overline{V}_{\bar{z}}\frac{\partial(\bar{x}\bar{y})}{\partial(uv)}\right\} dudv$$

$$= \int\int \overline{V}_{\bar{x}}d\bar{y}d\bar{z} + \overline{V}_{\bar{y}}d\bar{z}d\bar{x} + \overline{V}_{\bar{z}}d\bar{x}d\bar{y}.$$

Hence the vector whose components are defined by (22) is the transformation of $V$, that is, the vector flux of $F[C]$ in the new space.

If the functional $F[C]$ is not additive, the formulæ of transformation will be best given for the functional derivatives $X[C \mid M]$, $Y[C \mid M]$, $Z[C \mid M]$; since the vector flux is not uniquely defined. We have at once:

(23) $$\overline{X}[\overline{C} \mid \overline{M}] = \left\{X[C \mid M]\frac{\partial x}{\partial \bar{x}} + Y[C \mid M]\frac{\partial y}{\partial \bar{x}} + Z[C \mid M]\frac{\partial z}{\partial \bar{x}}\right\}\frac{ds}{d\bar{s}}, \text{ etc.,}$$

where $ds$ and $d\bar{s}$ are corresponding elements of arc.

**12. Functionals of Surfaces and Hypersurfaces.** The main elements of the theory of functionals have been generalized by Volterra to apply to functionals of $r$-spaces which are immersed in an $n$-space, mostly for the purpose of an extension to the field of complex functionals.

The theory of functionals of hyperspaces of $n - 2$ dimensions in the $n$-space corresponds closely to that of functionals of curves in three dimensions. Still simpler, of course, is the theory of functionals of hyperspaces of dimension $n - 1$, except for the consideration of the singular manifolds for the functional.

Fischer* has considered the exceptional points and curves of functionals of surfaces in ordinary space, and connected his results, by examples, with the calculus of variations.

## § 3. Variational Equations in Functionals of Plane Curves

**13. The Dependence of the Green's Function on the Boundary.** The Green's function for Laplace's equation in two dimensions, denoted by $g[C|P, B]$ or $g[C|xy, x_B y_B]$, is, except for the point $B$, single valued and harmonic in $P$ within the closed curve $C$, becomes logarithmically infinite as $P$ approaches $B$:

$$g = \log\frac{1}{r} + \omega$$

and vanishes if $P$ is on $C$. As is well known, it is symmetrical:

$$g[C|PB] = g[C|BP].$$

We wish to consider it now as a functional of the curve $C$, and express its dependence upon $C$.

If we take two curves $C$ and $C'$, the latter supposed momentarily to be entirely inside the former, and two points $A$ and $B$, both inside $C'$, which we surround with small circles, an application of Green's theorem to the complete boundary of the region between the circles and the curve $C'$ yields the result

$$2\pi(g[C'|AB] - g[C|AB]) = -\int_{C'} g[C|AM]\frac{\partial g[C'|MB]}{\partial n}ds,$$

upon shrinking the circles down to zero. Here $n$ denotes the interior normal, and $M$ a point on $C$ corresponding to the variable of integration.

But for a small variation in $C$ of amount $\delta n(M)$ the function $g[C|AM]$ is an infinitesimal whose principal part is $(\partial g/\partial n)\delta n$. We have therefore, upon substitution, the result:

$$(24)\quad \delta g[C|AB] = -\frac{1}{2\pi}\int_{C}\frac{\partial g[C|AM]}{\partial n}\frac{\partial g[C|MB]}{\partial n}\delta n(M)ds.$$

Since any variation of $C$ can be written as one which is wholly

* Fischer, *American Journal of Mathematics*, vol. 38 (1916), p. 259.

internal plus one which is wholly external, the above formula (24) applies to any variation $\delta n(M)$, continuous with continuous derivative. It was first given by Hadamard.*

The equation (24) is called an *equation in functional derivatives*; in fact, by means of (5), it may be written in the form:

$$(24') \qquad g[C|ABM] = -\frac{1}{2\pi}\frac{\partial g[C|AM]}{\partial n}\frac{\partial g[C|MB]}{\partial n},$$

in which $g'[C|ABM]$ denotes the functional derivative of $g[C|AB]$ at $M$. It may also be called, more shortly, a *variational equation.*

If we take a family of curves of which one and only one curve passes through each point of the region, and denote by $n_A$ and $n_B$ the normals to the curves at $A$ and $B$ respectively, it follows at once, as was pointed out by Hadamard, that the quantity

$$\Phi[C|AB] = 2\pi\frac{\partial^2 g[C|AB]}{\partial n_A \partial n_B}$$

satisfies the important equation

$$(25) \qquad \delta\Phi[C|AB] = \int_C \Phi[C|AM]\Phi[C|MB]\delta n(M)ds$$

or, as it may be written,

$$(25') \qquad \Phi'[C|ABM] = \Phi[C|AM]\Phi[C|MB].$$

Hadamard's equation is also satisfied by other important differential parameters.

P. Lévy has constructed an extensive theory of these equations. They may be considered as the limits of total differential equations as the number of independent variables is allowed to become infinite. In fact, if in the equation

$$dz = \sum_1^n {}_i f_i(x_1 \cdots x_n, z)dx_i$$

we take

$$x_i = x(t_i), \qquad dx_i = \delta x(t_i)\Delta t,$$

where $\Delta t = t_{i+1} - t_i = (b - a)/n$, and write

$$f_i(x_1 \cdots x_n, z) = f(x(t_1), x(t_2), \cdots, x(t_n); z|t_i)$$

letting then $n$ become infinite, the quantity $z(x_1 \cdots x_n)$ becomes

* *Comptes Rendus*, vol. 136 (1903), p. 353.

$z[x(\overset{b}{\underset{a}{t}})]$, and we obtain the equation

$$dz = \delta z[x(\overset{b}{\underset{a}{t}})] = \int_a^b f\,[x(t),\, z\,|\,t]\delta x(t)dt,$$

or

$$z'[x(t)\,|\,M] = f\,[x(\overset{b}{\underset{a}{t}}),\, z\,|\,M],$$

in which $z'[x(t)\,|\,M]$ denotes the functional derivative of $z$.

In the total differential equation there are certain *conditions of integrability* on the $f_i$ which must be satisfied in order to make the $f_i$ possible partial derivatives of some function $z(x_1\cdots x_n)$. Similar conditions must therefore be expected for these new equations. Their nature can be best described in terms of an additional concept.

**14. Adjoint Linear Functionals.** Consider a closed curve $C$ and let $E_1[u\,|\,M]$ and $E_2[v\,|\,M]$ be two linear functionals* of the functional arguments $u$ and $v$, defined on $C$; functionals which depend also on the point argument $M$, on $C$. The functionals $E_1$ and $E_2$ will be said to be *adjoint* (with respect to $M$ or $s$) if for every pair of functions $u(M)$, $v(M)$ in the field considered the relation

(26) $$\int_C v(M)E_1[u\,|\,M]ds = \int_C u(M)E_2[v\,|\,M]ds$$

is satisfied. The field of functions $u$, $v$ will be that of all continuous functions, or continuous with their first $k$ derivatives, as the conditions of the problem demand. It follows from (26) that the linear functionals must be homogeneous (i. e., $E[0\,|\,M] \equiv 0$) if they are to have adjoints.

From (26) it follows immediately that no linear functional admits more than one adjoint. If, in particular, $E_1[u\,|\,M]$ is merely a differential expression in $u$ with regard to the variable $s$, on the curve, the equation (26) yields the well-known relations between the coefficients of the given and adjoint expressions.†

* $E[u]$ is a linear functional if $E[c_1u_1 + c_2u_2] = c_1E[u_1] + c_2E[u_2]$, where $c_1$ and $c_2$ are arbitrary constants.

† If $C$ is not a closed curve there will be involved relations among the end values of $u$ and its derivatives.

If our expression is of the form

$$(27)\quad E_1[u|s] = \int_C f(ss_1)u(s_1)ds_1 + A_0(s)u(s) + \sum_{i=1}^{p} A_i(s)\frac{d^iu(s)}{ds^i},$$

where $s$ and $s_1$ replace $M$ and $M_1$, the adjoint expression has the form

$$(27')\quad \begin{aligned} E_2[v|s] = \int_C f(s_1s)v(s_1)ds_1 + A_0(s)v(s) \\ + \sum_{i=1}^{p}(-1)^i\frac{d^i}{ds^i}(A_i(s)v(s)). \end{aligned}$$

If $E_1[u|s]$ and $F_1[u|s]$ have for adjoints $E_2[v|s]$ and $F_2[v|s]$ respectively, then $E_1[F_1[u]]$ (that is, $E_1[F_1[u|s']|s]$) has for adjoint $F_2[E_2[v]]$ (that is, $F_2[E_2[v|s']|s]$). In fact, by (26),

$$\begin{aligned} \int_C v(s)E_1[F_1[u|s']|s]ds &= \int_C F_1[u|s]E_2[v|s]ds \\ &= \int_C F_2[E_2[v|s']|s]u(s)ds. \end{aligned}$$

Similarly, more than two expressions can be compounded, and $G_2[F_2\{E_2[v]\}]$ shown to be the adjoint of $E_1[F_1\{G_1[u]\}]$. In particular, if $E[u|M]$ is self adjoint, and $F_2$ is the adjoint of $F_1$, then the expression $F_1[E\{F_2[u]\}]$ is also self adjoint. This fact we shall make use of, later.

**15. The Conditions of Integrability.** We wish to find the functional $\Phi[C|A, B\cdots]$ which will satisfy an equation of the type

$$(28)\quad \delta\Phi[C|AB\cdots] = \int_C F[C, \Phi|A, B\cdots M]\delta n(M)ds,$$

where $F$ depends upon $C$ and perhaps also $\Phi$, as functional arguments (i. e., for instance upon all the values of $\Phi$ when $A$, $B$, $\cdots$ range independently over the curve $C$*), and on $M$ as a point argument. According to (28) we should expect that given $\Phi[C_0|AB\cdots]$ the functional $\Phi$ would be determined for all other curves $C$. This existence theorem will be considered later;

* In (25) $F$ depends upon the particular values of $\Phi$ when $A$ and $B$ take the position $M$ on $C$.

we must insure now however that $\Phi$ shall be really a functional of $C$, and not depend on the manner in which $C$ is approached by the summing of successive variations from $C_0$.

Let $C_{\lambda\mu}$ be any two parameter family of curves containing $C_0$ and $C$, in such a way, say, that $C_{00} = C_0$, and $C_{11} = C$. In order that $\Phi$ shall not be dependent on the path that $(\lambda\mu)$ traces in going from (0, 0) to (1, 1) it is necessary and sufficient that

$$\frac{\partial}{\partial\mu}\frac{\partial\Phi}{\partial\lambda} = \frac{\partial}{\partial\lambda}\frac{\partial\Phi}{\partial\mu}.$$

This condition must hold for every two parameter family which can be formed from the class of curves we are considering.

If we write $\delta^2 = \delta(\delta\Phi)$, we shall have for it the value

$$\frac{\partial^2\Phi}{\partial\lambda\partial\mu}\,d\lambda d\mu$$

and the test for integrability, corresponding to the possibility of interchanging the order of differentiation in regard to $\lambda$ and $\mu$, lies in the possibility of interchanging the two variations $\delta n$ and $\delta_1 n$ of $C$ without changing $\delta^2\Phi$.

The variation of $\delta\Phi$, as given by (28), due to the new variation $\delta_1 n(M_1)$, depends upon the variation of $F$, which we may write as some linear functional $E[\delta_1 n \mid M]$ of $\delta_1 n$, upon the variation of $\delta n$ itself (i. e., $\partial/\partial\mu(\partial n/\partial\lambda)d\lambda d\mu$), which we call $\delta^2 n$, and on the variation of $ds$. The last is obviously given by the formula

$$-\,k\delta_1 n\delta s,$$

where $k$ is the curvature, counted positively if the center of curvature lies on the positive direction of $n$. We have, then:

$$\delta^2\Phi = \int_C E[\delta_1 n \mid M]\delta n(M)ds \qquad (29)$$
$$+ \int_C F[C, \Phi \mid M](\delta^2 n - k\delta n\delta_1 n)ds.$$

In order to investigate more closely the quantity $\delta^2 n$ consider the special equation

$$\Psi[C] = \iint_{(C)} f(M)dxdy,$$

which defines $\Psi$ as a functional of curves. We have

$$\delta\Psi[C] = \int_C f(M)ds$$

and

$$\delta^2\Psi[C] = \int_C \frac{\partial f}{\partial n}\delta_1 n\delta n ds + \int_C f(M)(\delta^2 n - k\delta n\delta_1 n)ds,$$

provided that we define (as a permanent convention) the path of the point $M$ as normal to $C$, as $C$ varies. But in this equation $\delta^2\Psi$ is independent of the order of making the variations $\delta n$, $\delta_1 n$, since $\Psi$ is a functional of $C$; also, obviously, are the first and third terms of the right-hand member. Hence the same property holds for $\int_C f(M)\delta^2 n ds$, whatever the function $f(M)$ may be. *Hence $\delta^2 n$ itself is independent of the order of making the variations $\delta n$ and $\delta_1 n$.*

With reference to the original equation (29) therefore, we see that the necessary and sufficient condition for integrability is that the functional $E[\delta_1 n \mid M]$ be self adjoint. But this functional is merely the variation of $\Phi'[C \mid AB \cdots M]$. Hence *the necessary and sufficient condition for the integrability of* (28) *is that*

$$\delta\Phi'[C \mid AB \cdots M]$$

*be a self adjoint functional of $\delta n$.*

If $E[\delta n \mid M]$ is identically self adjoint, that is, for every $\Phi$ and $C$, the equation (28) is said to be *completely integrable.*

In calculating the functional $E$ we must not expect to find it in the simple form (5), since the variation of the point $M$ with $C$ as $C$ varies is usually going to introduce new terms into the expression.

**16. Special Equations.** In the case of Hadamard's equation, we have

$$\begin{aligned}\delta\Phi'[C \mid ABM] &= \Phi[C \mid AM]\delta\Phi[C \mid MB] + \delta\Phi[C \mid AM]\Phi[C \mid MB] \\ &= \int_C \{\Phi[C \mid AM]\Phi[C \mid MM_1]\Phi[C \mid M_1 B] \\ &\quad + \Phi[C \mid AM_1]\Phi[C \mid M_1 M]\Phi[C \mid MB]\}\delta_1 n(M_1)ds_1 \\ &\quad + \frac{\partial}{\partial n}\{\Phi[C \mid AM]\Phi[C \mid MB]\}\delta_1 n(M).\end{aligned}$$

As a functional of $\delta_1 n$, this expression, according to (27), is its own adjoint; for the integral is symmetrical in $M$ and $M_1$, and the term outside the integral is merely of the form of a function of $M$ multiplied into $\delta_1 n(M)$. *Hadamard's equation is therefore completely integrable.*

On the other hand, the condition of integrability for the somewhat similar equation

$$\Phi'[C|ABM] = \Phi[C|AM]\Phi[C|BM] \tag{30}$$

reduces by (27) to the condition:

$$\Phi(AM)\Phi(MM_1)\Phi(BM_1) + \Phi(AM_1)\Phi(MM_1)\Phi(BM)$$
$$= \Phi(AM_1)\Phi(M_1M)\Phi(BM) + \Phi(AM)\Phi(M_1M)\Phi(BM_1)$$

or

$$\{\Phi(AM)\Phi(BM_1) + \Phi(AM_1)\Phi(BM)\}\{\Phi(MM_1) - \Phi(M_1M)\} = 0. \tag{30'}$$

In these equations the $C$ is omitted for brevity; it must be remembered that the points $M$ and $M_1$ are however restricted to lying on the curve $C$.

If the first factor of (30′) is identically zero, we find $\Phi[C|AM] \equiv 0$, by putting $B = A$. Hence by (30), $\Phi'[C|ABM]$ vanishes identically, and therefore, by (7),

$$\Phi[C|AB] \equiv \text{const.} \equiv 0.$$

If on the other hand, the second factor vanishes identically (which is the alternative if we restrict ourselves to functionals $\Phi$ which are analytic in their point arguments) we have

$$\Phi[C_0|AB] = \Phi[C_0|BA]$$

provided that $C_0$ goes through both $A$ and $B$. But since from (30), for every $C$, $A$, $B$,

$$\Phi'[C|ABM] \equiv \Phi'[C|BAM],$$

it follows by (7) that the function $\Phi[C|AB] - \Phi[C|BA]$ is independent of the curve $C$. Hence, identically:

$$\Phi[C|AB] = \Phi[C|BA],$$

which is a sufficient condition for integrability.

Consider as a third equation

$$(31) \qquad \delta\Phi[C] = \int_C f(\Phi, M)\delta n(M)ds,$$

for which we have

$$\delta\Phi'[C\,|\,M] = \frac{\partial f(\Phi, M)}{\partial\Phi}\delta\Phi + \frac{\partial f(\Phi, M)}{\partial n}\delta_1 n(M)$$

$$= \int_C \frac{\partial f(\Phi, M)}{\partial\Phi} f(\Phi, m_1)\delta_1 n(M_1)ds_1 + \frac{\partial f(\Phi, M)}{\partial n}\delta_1 n(M).$$

By (27) the condition of integrability is the following:

$$(31') \qquad \frac{\partial f(\Phi, M)}{\partial\Phi} f(\Phi, M_1) = \frac{\partial f(\Phi, M_1)}{\partial\Phi} f(\Phi, M).$$

If the equation is to be completely integrable, this condition must be satisfied for all functionals $\Phi$ and points $M$ and $M_1$ on $C$. This is the same as saying that $\partial \log f(\Phi M)/\partial\Phi$ shall be independent of $M$, $M$ on $C$. Hence, for $M$ on $C$, $f$ must be of the form:

$$f(\Phi, M) = g(\Phi)\varphi(M),$$

and since the function does not involve $C$ it must have this form always. Therefore, by (30)

$$\frac{\delta\Phi}{g(\Phi)} = \int_C \varphi(M)\delta n ds.$$

The right-hand member of this equation is merely $\delta\Psi[C]$, where

$$\Psi[C] = \iint_{(C)} \varphi(M)d\sigma$$

is an arbitrary additive functional. But the relation

$$\delta\Phi/g(\Phi) = \delta\Psi$$

merely tells us that the quantities $\Phi$ and $\Psi$ are functionally dependent, i. e., that $d\Phi/d\Psi$ exists and is given by $g(\Phi)$. Hence *the functionals defined by* (30), *if* (30) *is completely integrable, are merely functions of additive functionals of curves* $C$.

As a last example, consider the equation

$$\delta\Phi[C] = \int_C \Phi'[C\,|\,M]\delta n(M)ds,$$

which is an identity for any given functional $\Phi[C]$, under the conditions described for (7). Let us suppose that $\Phi'[C\,|\,M]$ has itself an integrable derivative $\Phi''[C\,|\,MM_1]$. We shall have then for $\delta\Phi'$ the expression

$$\int_C \Phi''[C\,|\,MM_1]\delta_1 n(M_1)ds,$$

plus possibly other terms which are not integrals. The condition

$$\Phi''[C\,|\,MM_1] = \Phi''[C\,|\,M_1M]$$

must therefore be included in the condition of integrability, a result which was originally stated by Volterra. *The second functional derivative must be symmetrical in its point arguments.*

**17. The Integrability of the Equation for the Green's Function.** For the equation

$$\Phi'[C\,|\,ABM] = -\frac{\partial\Phi[C\,|\,AM]}{\partial n}\frac{\partial\Phi[C\,|\,MB]}{\partial n}, \tag{32}$$

which is equivalent except for a constant to (24), we have

$$\begin{aligned}\delta\Phi'(ABM) = -\int\Bigg[&\frac{\partial\Phi(AM)}{\partial n}\frac{\partial\Phi(M_1B)}{\partial n_1}\frac{\partial^2\Phi(MM_1)}{\partial n\partial n_1}\\ &+\frac{\partial\Phi(AM_1)}{\partial n_1}\frac{\partial\Phi(MB)}{\partial n}\frac{\partial^2\Phi(M_1M)}{\partial n\partial n_1}\Bigg]\delta_1 n(s_1)ds_1\\ &-\frac{\partial}{\partial n}\left(\frac{\partial\Phi(AM)}{\partial n}\frac{\partial\Phi(MB)}{\partial n}\right)\delta_1 n(s)\\ &+\left(\frac{\partial\Phi(AM)}{\partial s}\frac{\partial\Phi(MB)}{\partial n}+\frac{\partial\Phi(MB)}{\partial s}\frac{\partial\Phi(AM)}{\partial n}\right)\delta_1 n'(s),\end{aligned}$$

in which the last two terms represent the variation of the right-hand member of (32) due to the displacement of the point $M$, the last term arising from the change of direction of $n$. The notation $\delta_1 n'(s)$ stands for the derivative with respect to $s$ of the quantity $\delta_1 n$.

In order for this expression to be self adjoint, we have, by (27):

$$\frac{\partial\Phi(AM)}{\partial s}\frac{\partial\Phi(MB)}{\partial n}+\frac{\partial\Phi(MB)}{\partial s}\frac{\partial\Phi(AM)}{\partial n} = 0 \tag{33}$$

for all curves $C$, all points $A$ and $B$, and all points $M$ on $C$. *Equation (32) is therefore not completely integrable.* Since (30) is an identity, its variation also must vanish. This will be constituted by an integral, a term in $\delta n$ and a term in $\delta n'$. By choosing particular types of functions $\delta n(s)$ it is easily seen that each of these terms must vanish separately.

The coefficient of $\delta n'$ is called by Lévy the *derivative with respect to* $\delta n'$. Thus the derivative with respect to $\delta n'$ of $\partial\Phi(AM)/\partial n$ is $-\partial\Phi(AM)/\partial s$, and the derivative of $\partial\Phi(AM)/\partial s$ is $+\partial\Phi(AM)/\partial n$. Hence we can write down at once the derivative with respect to $\delta n'$ of the left-hand member of (33), and since this must vanish, we have the further identity

$$(33') \qquad \frac{\partial\Phi(AM)}{\partial n}\frac{\partial\Phi(MB)}{\partial n} - \frac{\partial\Phi(AM)}{\partial s}\frac{\partial\Phi(MB)}{\partial s} = 0.$$

Consider functionals $\Phi$ which as far as concerns the point arguments, are continuous with continuous derivatives in the neighborhood of the curve $C$. It can be shown quite simply that this requires either (*a*), that $\Phi$ shall be independent of $C$ and shall be a function merely of a single point argument $A$ or $B$, or (*b*), that if it depends upon $C$, it shall, as far as its point arguments are concerned, be an analytic function of $x + iy$ and $x_1 - iy_1$, where $A = (xy)$, $B = (x_1y_1)$, and $i = \pm\sqrt{-1}$. In fact, in this last case, from the equations (33), (33′) follow the equations:

$$\frac{\partial\Phi(AM)}{\partial n} = i\frac{\partial\Phi(AM)}{\partial s}, \qquad \frac{\partial\Phi(MB)}{\partial n} = -i\frac{\partial\Phi(MB)}{\partial s},$$

from which the above conclusion can be shown to follow.

The value of the functional may be chosen arbitrarily for one curve $C_0$, and is then determined by the equation for the other curves $C$.

The Green's function does not remain continuous when $A$ and $B$ approach the same point $M$ on the curve, and hence is not subject to the above analysis. Lévy has the following theorem:

*Consider a functional* $\Phi[C \mid AB]$, *equal to the function* $(1/2\pi)g[C \mid AB]$ *plus a function which remains analytic when the point arguments lie in the neighborhood of the curve. A necessary and sufficient condition that there exist such a functional which satisfies* (32) *and takes on, for a given curve* $C_0$ *given arbitrary values* $\Phi_0[C \mid AB]$, *is that*

$$(33') \qquad \frac{\partial\Phi_0(AM)}{\partial s} = \frac{\partial\Phi_0(MB)}{\partial s} = 0;$$

*that is, that* $\Phi_0$ *shall remain constant if one point argument is held fast and the other allowed to travel around the curve* $C_0$.

**18. Variational vs. Integro-Differential Equations.** If equation (28) is completely integrable, we can obtain its solution by means of any particular family of curves we please, which leads to the curve $C$. In this way, by introducing a quantity $\lambda$ as a parameter which determines the curve of the family, the equation under consideration becomes an integro-differential equation, or perhaps reduces to a degenerate form of such an equation.

Consider the equation

$$(34) \qquad \delta\Phi[C] = \int_C F[C \mid \Phi, M]\delta n(M)ds,$$

in which the functional $\Phi[C]$ has no point arguments. If we introduce a second parameter $t$ for the set of orthogonal trajectories to the $\lambda$-curves, we may write $\delta n(M)ds = r(\lambda t)d\lambda dt$, where $r(\lambda t)$ is a known function, so that (34) takes the form

$$(34') \qquad \frac{d\Phi}{d\lambda} = \int_{T_0}^{T_1} F(\lambda, \Phi, t) r(\lambda t) dt.$$

This equation may reduce to a differential equation; in any case, however, if we integrate with respect to $\lambda$ from $\lambda_0$ to $\lambda$ we have an implicit functional equation of the type which is described in Art. 36, Lecture III. Hence the theorem: *Within a certain range $R$ of the $xy$ plane, and a range of values $\Phi_0 - L \leqq \Phi \leqq \Phi_0 + L$, there is one and only one continuous solution $\Phi[C]$ of* (34), *for $C$ in $R$, which takes on the value $\Phi_0$ for the curve $C_0$; provided that $F[C \mid \Phi, M]$ is continuous in its three arguments, and there is a constant $A$ (independent of $C$ and $M$) such that:*

$$(34'') \qquad | F[C \mid \Phi_2, M] - F[C \mid \Phi_1, M] | \leqq A \, | \Phi_2 - \Phi_1 | .$$

If we consider the more general equation (28) we must replace the point arguments $A, B, \cdots$ by their curvilinear co-ordinates $(\lambda_1 t_1)$, $(\lambda_2 t_2)$, $\cdots$. If the functional $F$, which now depends upon all the values of $\Phi$, for $t_1, t_2, \cdots$ moving independently over their common range, satisfies still a Cauchy-Lipschitz condition of the type (34″), the treatment of the equation depends merely upon the same theorem about implicit functional equations. If on the other hand, the functional $F$ depends upon $\Phi$ in such a way as to bring in its derivatives with respect to one or more of the arguments, the theory of the equation must be a generalization of the theory of partial differential equations. The two equations (25) and (32), respectively, offer examples of these two types.

## § 4. Partial Variational Equations

**19. Volterra's Equation for the Dirichlet Integral.** Upon the convention that we have already made, that as $C$ varies, the point $M$ is understood to move in the direction of the normal to $C$ at $M$, we shall speak of a functional $u[C \mid M]$ as being independent of $C$ if it remains invariant as $M$ changes with $C$. We are thus able to consider functionals $\Phi$ which depend upon a curve $C$ and a function $u(M)$ on the curve $C$, each varying independently of the other; and we can consider the partial functional derivatives of such functionals with respect to $C$ and $u$, and the possible relations that may hold between them.

Dirichlet's integral

$$(35) \qquad \Phi[C, u] = \iint_{(C)} \left\{ \left( \frac{\partial u}{\partial x} \right)^2 + \left( \frac{\partial u}{\partial y} \right)^2 \right\} dxdy,$$

where $u(x, y)$ is a solution of Laplace's equation inside $C$, is a functional of the contour $C$ and the values $u(M)$ which are assigned to $u(x, y)$ on $C$. If we change $u(M)$ without changing $C$, we have:

$$\delta_u \Phi = 2 \iint_{(C)} \left\{ \frac{\partial u}{\partial x} \delta \frac{\partial u}{\partial x} + \frac{\partial u}{\partial y} \delta \frac{\partial u}{\partial y} \right\} dxdy$$

which reduces by an integration by parts and the setting of $\nabla^2 u = 0$, to the form

$$\delta_u \Phi = -2 \int_C \frac{\partial u}{\partial n} \delta u \, ds.$$

By means of the definition of functional derivative, this yields:

$$\Phi_u'[C, u \mid M] = -2\frac{\partial u(M)}{\partial n}. \tag{36}$$

On the other hand, if we vary $C$, and vary $u(M)$ on $C$ at the same time in such a way that $u(xy)$ remains unchanged inside $C$, that is so that $\delta u = \partial u/\partial n\ \delta n$, we have for the new quantity

$$\delta\Phi = \int_C \{\Phi_u'(M)\delta u(M) + \Phi_C'(M)\delta n(M)\}ds$$

$$= \int_C \left\{\Phi_u'(M)\frac{\partial u}{\partial n} + \Phi_C'(M)\right\}\delta n(M)ds$$

the formula

$$\delta\Phi = -\int_C \left\{\left(\frac{\partial u}{\partial x}\right)^2 + \left(\frac{\partial u}{\partial y}\right)^2\right\}\delta n\ ds$$

$$= -\int_C \left\{\left(\frac{\partial u}{\partial n}\right)^2 + u'^2\right\}\delta n\ ds,$$

where $u'$ denotes $\partial u/\partial s$. Hence:

$$\Phi_u'(M)\frac{\partial u}{\partial n} + \Phi_C'(M) = -\left(\frac{\partial u}{\partial n}\right)^2 - u'^2.$$

By means of (36) this yields the equation

$$\Phi_C'[C, u \mid M] = \tfrac{1}{4}\{\Phi_u'[C, u \mid M]\}^2 - \{u'(M)\}^2, \tag{37}$$

which is a partial equation in the functional derivatives of $\Phi[C \mid u]$ involving only the independent arguments $C$, and $u(M)$ on $C$ (since $\partial u/\partial s$ is known when $u$ is known on $C$).

Equations of the type (37) may be called partial variational equations, or equations in partial functional derivatives. We may expect to find them for such functionals as are related to partial differential equations by means of the Calculus of Variations; for some such connection is necessary in order to eliminate the interior values of $u(xy)$ from explicit connection with the quantities considered. Quantities like the area of minimal surfaces, the energy in a changing system, etc., will therefore satisfy such equations. In particular, to give another special example, if within the closed curve $C$, the quantity $u(xy)$ is a solution of the equation

$$\frac{\partial^2 u}{\partial x^2} + \frac{\partial^2 u}{\partial y^2} = \lambda u,$$

the quantity

$$\Psi[C, u] = \iint_{(C)} \left\{\left(\frac{\partial u}{\partial x}\right)^2 + \left(\frac{\partial u}{\partial y}\right)^2 + \lambda u^2\right\}dxdy$$

satisfies the partial variational equation

$$\Psi_C'[C, u \mid M] = \tfrac{1}{4}\{\Psi_u'[C, u \mid M]\}^2 - u'(M)^2 - \lambda u(M)^2. \tag{38}$$

**20. The Condition of Integrability.** The equation to be considered is of the form

$$\Phi_C'[C, u \mid M] = F[C, u, \Phi_u' \mid \Phi, M]. \tag{39}$$

We have already considered the second variation of a functional $u[C]$. of $C$ alone. If the functional depends also on $M$, its second variation takes on a more complicated form. This can be arrived at in the following manner,

Consider two separate variations $\delta n$ and $\delta_1 n$ depending on parameters $\lambda$ and $\mu$; the final position of a point $M$ will be $M_1$ or $M_2$ according to which of the variations is executed first, and the corresponding difference between the values of $u[C \mid M]$ will be $M_1M_2\, \partial u/\partial s$. Accordingly, if $\partial u/\partial s$ vanishes identically on $C$, the quantity $\delta^2 u[C \mid M]$ will be independent of the order of making the variations $\delta n$ and $\delta_1 n$, from that particular curve $C$.

Given now any functional $u[C \mid M]$ we can write it in the neighborhood of $C$ as $u_1[C \mid M] + u_2(xy)$, taking for the first term a functional which remains constant on the particular curve $C$, and for the second, a function of $x$, $y$ independent of the curve $C$. The second variation of $u_2(xy)$ will involve a differentiation with respect to $\delta n'$, according to the method of Art. 17, and we shall therefore have:

$$\delta^2 u_2 = \frac{\partial^2 u_2}{\partial n \partial n_1}\, \delta n \delta n_1 - \frac{\partial u_2}{\partial s}\, \delta_1 n' \delta n + \frac{\partial u_2}{\partial n}\, \delta^2 n,$$

and accordingly, since $\partial^2 u_2/\partial n\, \partial_1 n$ and $\delta^2 n$ are independent of the order of making $\delta n$ and $\delta_1 n$, the quantity $\delta^2 u_2 + u_2' \delta_1 n' \delta n$ must be also. But the same property holds for the quantity $\delta^2 u_1 + u_1' \delta_1 n' \delta n$, and therefore we have the result that *the expression*

$$\delta^2 u + u' \delta_1 n' \delta n$$

*is symmetrical in $\delta n$ and $\delta_1 n$.*

Return now to the condition of integrability for (39). The variations of $\Phi_C'$ and $\Phi_u'$ will be linear functionals of $\delta_1 n$ and $\delta_1 u$. If we write them in the form

$$\begin{aligned} \delta\Phi_u'[C, u \mid M] &= E[\delta_1 u] + F[\delta_1 n] + k\Phi_u'[C, u \mid M]\delta_1 n \\ \delta\Phi_C'[C, u \mid M] &= \bar{F}[\delta_1 u] + G[\delta_1 n] + \Phi_u'[C, u \mid M] u' \delta_1 n', \end{aligned} \tag{40}$$

the last term in each expression being inserted merely for convenience, we find, in the same way as in (29), for the second variation of $\Phi$:

$$\begin{aligned} \delta^2\Phi[C, u] = &\int_C \{E[\delta_1 u]\delta n + F[\delta_1 n]\delta u + \bar{F}[\delta_1 u]\delta n + G[\delta_1 n]\delta n\} ds \\ &+ \int_C \{\Phi_u'(M)(\delta^2 u + u'\delta_1 n'\delta n) + \Phi_C'(M)(\delta^2 n - k\delta_1 n \delta n)\} ds. \end{aligned} \tag{41}$$

The second integral is already independent of the order of making the successive variations. In order to produce the same result in the first integral, and therefore, *in order to make $\delta\Phi$ an exact differential, it is necessary and sufficient that the functionals $E[\delta u]$ and $G[\delta n]$ be self adjoint, and that the functionals $\bar{F}[\delta u]$ and $F[\delta n]$ be mutually adjoint.*

Let us apply this result to equation (39). We are assuming that $\Phi[C, u]$ is such a functional that:

$$\delta\Phi = \int_C \{\Phi_C'[C, u \mid M]\delta n + \Phi_u'[C, u \mid M]\delta u\} ds,$$

and we may therefore substitute this value for $\delta\Phi$ when we find the variation of $\delta\Phi'$ in (39). We have then:

$$(42) \qquad \delta\Phi_C'[C, u \mid M] = H[\delta\Phi_u'] + L[\delta u] + L_1[\delta n]$$

where the functionals $H$, $L$ and $L_1$ depend upon the arguments indicated, and on $\Phi$, $C$, $M$, $u(M)$, $\Phi_u'[C, u \mid M]$ and the derivatives of $\delta u$ and $\delta n$.

From (40) and (42) we have:

$$\delta\Phi_C'[C, u \mid M] = H[E[\delta u]] + H[F[\delta n]] + H[k\Phi_u'\delta n] + L[\delta u] + L_1[\delta n]$$

whence

$$\overline{F}[\delta u] = H[E[\delta u]] + L[\delta u]$$

$$G[\delta n] + \Phi_C'u'\delta n' = H[F[\delta n]] + H[k\Phi_u'\delta n] + L_1[\delta n].$$

Denote by $\overline{H}$ and $\overline{L}$ the adjoints respectively of $H$ and $L$. If $E$ is self adjoint and $\overline{F}$ is the adjoint of $F$, we must have, by Art. 14:

$$F[\delta n] = E[\overline{H}[\delta n]] + \overline{L}[\delta n]$$

and therefore

$$G[\delta n] = H[E[\overline{H}[\delta n]]] + H[\overline{L}[\delta n]] + H[k\Phi_u'\delta n] + L[\delta n] - \Phi_u'u'\delta n'.$$

Hence if $G[\delta n]$ is to be self adjoint, and thus $\delta\Phi$ an exact differential, it is necessary that the expression

$$(43) \qquad H[\overline{L}[\delta n]] + H[k\Phi_u'\delta n] + L_1[\delta n] - \Phi_u'u'\delta n'$$

be self adjoint.

*If the expression* (43) *is self adjoint identically, that is, for all curves $C$ and quantities $\Phi$, $u(M)$ and $\Phi_u'$, the equation* (39) *is said to be completely integrable.*

With reference to equation (37), we have

$$\begin{aligned}\delta\Phi_C'[C, u \mid M] &= \tfrac{1}{2}\Phi_u'\delta\Phi_u' - 2u'\delta\{u'(M)\} \\ &= \tfrac{1}{2}\Phi_u'\delta\Phi_u' - 2u'(\delta u)' - 2ku'^2\delta n\end{aligned}$$

since

$$\delta\{u'(M)\} = \delta\frac{du}{ds} = \frac{d\delta u}{ds} - \frac{du}{ds}\frac{d\delta s}{ds} = (\delta u)' + ku'\delta n.$$

Hence

$$\begin{aligned}H[\delta\Phi_u'] &= \tfrac{1}{2}\Phi_u'\delta\Phi_u', \\ L[\delta u] &= -\,2u'(\delta u)', \\ L_1[\delta n] &= -\,2ku'^2\delta n,\end{aligned}$$

and from the second of these equations it follows that:

$$\overline{L}[\delta n] = 2u'\delta n' + 2u''\delta n$$

so that (43) takes the form

$$u'\Phi_u'\delta n' + u''\Phi_u'\delta n + \tfrac{1}{2}k\Phi_u'^2\delta n - 2ku'^2\delta n - u'\Phi_u'\delta n',$$

which is identically self adjoint, since the terms in $\delta n'$ annul each other. *Hence equation* (37) *is completely integrable.*

The same fact is true of equation (38).

By a process analogous to that which we have already discussed in Art. 13, in describing the generalization of a system of partial differential equations in one dependent function to a variational equation in a corresponding functional, we may (with Lévy) arrive at equations of the type of (39); only in this case we must separate the independent variables into two sets, $x_1 \cdots x_n$, corresponding to the argument $u$, and $y_1 \cdots y_n$, corresponding to the argument $C$. The related system of differential equations will then be the following:

$$\text{(44)} \quad \frac{\partial z}{\partial y_i} = f_i\left(x_1 \cdots x_n, y_1 \cdots y_n, z, \frac{\partial z}{\partial x_1} \cdots \frac{\partial z}{\partial x_n}\right), \qquad i = 1, 2, \cdots, n.$$

The conditions of integrability have been deduced for (39) in the same way as the more familiar conditions are deduced for (44); in fact the condition that (43) be self adjoint is merely the analog of the relations

$$\text{(45)} \quad \begin{aligned} &\frac{\partial f_i}{\partial y_j} + f_j \frac{\partial f_i}{\partial z} + \sum_{k=1}^{n} \frac{\partial f_i}{\partial p_k}\left(\frac{\partial f_j}{\partial x_k} + p_k \frac{\partial f_j}{\partial z}\right) \\ &= \frac{\partial f_j}{\partial y_i} + f_i \frac{\partial f_j}{\partial z} + \sum_{k=1}^{n} \frac{\partial f_j}{\partial p_k}\left(\frac{\partial f_i}{\partial x_k} + p_k \frac{\partial f_i}{\partial z}\right), \qquad i, j = 1, 2, \cdots, n, \end{aligned}$$

in which $p_k$ stands for $\partial z / \partial x_k$.

The equation (39) and its treatment are thus seen to be the result of the same significant and fruitful process of generalization which lies at the basis of the theory of functionals and the theory of integral equations.

Fundamental problems for (44) are $(a)$ the determination of a solution which for $y_1 = y_2 = \cdots = y_n = 0$ takes on values which are given analytic functions of $x_1 \cdots x_n$, and $(b)$ the determination of a solution which when

$$x_i = \xi_i(y_1 \cdots y_n), \qquad i = 1, 2, \cdots, n,$$

takes on the values $z = \zeta_0(y_1 \cdots y_n)$. Their analogs in the present case are $(a)$ the determination of a solution of (39) which for $C = C_0$ takes on assigned values $\Phi[C_0, u]$, and $(b)$ the determination of a solution of (39) which reduces to assigned values $\Psi[C, v]$ when $u(M)$ is put equal to some function $v(M)$, given on each $C$ (i. e., when $u(M) = v[C \mid M]$).

The theory of the second problem, as developed by Lévy, involves the solution of implicit functional equations, as treated in our Lecture III, and an extension of the concept of *characteristic*, as applied to the equations (44). This new concept seems to be necessary for any use of these equations in applied mathematics.

# LECTURE II.

## COMPLEX FUNCTIONALS.*

### § 1. The Relation of Isogeneity

**21. Isogeneity and Complex Vector Fluxes.** Our survey of the theory of functionals of curves in space, as taken up in Lecture I, cannot be complete without a study of the possible relations that may hold between them as complex quantities. This study serves to generalize some of the basic properties of analytic functions. It is not impossible that there should be more than one direction of investigation to carry out this purpose; the present theory, which is due to Volterra, has as its basis the relation of *isogeneity*, which is the generalization to functionals of curves, in space, of the relation which holds between two complex point functions on a surface, when one is an analytic function of the other. The relation between conjugate functions has, however, a different generalization (see Art. 48). In this lecture Volterra's theory is presented in terms of the linear vector function, and the analysis thus somewhat simplified.

Consider the two complex functionals $F[C] = F_1[C] + iF_2[C]$ and $\Phi[C] = \Phi_1[C] + i\Phi_2[C]$, and make a small continuous variation of $C$ in the neighborhood of $P$, of area $\sigma\Sigma$, of the sort used for defining a vector flux. If the ratio of the increments of $\Phi$ and $F$, namely the quantity:

$$\frac{\Delta\Phi_1 + i\Delta\Phi_2}{\Delta F_1 + i\Delta F_2},$$

* This lecture is based upon the following references:

V. Volterra: Sur une généralisation de la théorie des fonctions d'une variable imaginaire, *Acta Mathematica*, vol. 12 (1889), pp. 233–286;

The generalization of analytic functions, *Book of the Opening*, Rice Institute (1917), vol. 3, pp. 1036–1084.

Poincaré, Sur les résidus des intégrales doubles, *Acta Mathematica*, vol. 9 (1887), pp. 321–384.

P. Lévy, Sur les équations intégro-differentielles définissant des fonctions de lignes, *Thèses présentées à la Faculté des Sciences de Paris*, no. d'ordre 1436.

approaches a limit, as $\sigma$ approaches zero, independent of the surface on which the variation takes place, we denote the value of this limit by

$$\frac{d\Phi}{dF} = \lim_{\sigma=0} \frac{\Delta\Phi_1 + i\Delta\Phi_2}{\Delta F_1 + i\Delta F_2}, \tag{1}$$

and say that $\Phi$ is *isogenous* to $F$. The relation is obviously reciprocal; moreover, if two functionals are isogenous to a third they are isogenous to each other. The relation of isogeneity may be expressed in terms of the vector fluxes of $F$ and $\Phi$.

Denote by $V_1$, $V_2$, $W_1$ and $W_2$ the components of the vector fluxes of $F_1$, $F_2$, $\Phi_1$ and $\Phi_2$ respectively, normal to the curve $C$ at the point $P$. Denote by $W_1'$ and $W_1''$ the vector components (or their algebraic values, as the context in any particular case will determine) of $W_1$ in the directions $V_1$ and $V_2$ respectively; similarly for $W_2$. If now we make in the neighborhood of the point $P$ two variations of the curve $C$, of areas $\sigma_1$ and $\sigma_2$, the first containing $V_1$ in its plane of variation, thus contributing nothing as an increment of $F_1$, and the second containing $V_2$ in its plane of variation and therefore not changing $F_2$, we obtain two expressions for $d\Phi/dF$. As a necessary condition for isogeneity these must be equal:

$$\frac{(W_1'' + iW_2'')\cdot d\sigma_1}{iV_2\cdot d\sigma_1} = \frac{(W_1' + iW_2')\cdot d\sigma_2}{V_1\cdot d\sigma_2},$$

or

$$\frac{W_1'' + iW_2''}{i|V_2|} = \frac{W_1' + iW_2'}{|V_1|}, \tag{2}$$

where $|V_1|$ and $|V_2|$ denote the absolute values of the respective vectors.

The deduction just given is no longer valid if $V_1$ and $V_2$ happen to have the same direction. But in this case $W_1$ and $W_2$ are also co-directional and have the same direction as $V_1$ and $V_2$, as we see by taking a variation which contains this vector in its plane. If, on the other hand, $V_1$ and $V_2$ are equal in magnitude and at right angles, equation (2) shows that $W_1$ and $W_2$ will be similarly related. In fact, as P. Lévy has pointed out, the equation (2) implies that if an ellipse is constructed with conjugate semidiameters $V_1$ and $V_2$, $W_1$ and $W_2$ will be conjugate semidiameters in an ellipse similar to this and similarly placed.

**22. Summary of the Properties of the Linear Vector Function.** For the purpose of expressing the condition (2) in convenient form, it is desirable to have at hand a few of the important formulæ for the manipulation of linear vector functions. They are for convenience summarized in this section.

A vector $W$ is a *linear vector function* of a vector $V$ if when $V = c_1V_1 + c_2V_2$, where $c_1$ and $c_2$ are constants, it follows that $W = c_1W_1 + c_2W_2$. The properties of this relation can be briefly and conveniently expressed in terms of the Gibbs concept of *dyadic*.

A dyadic is the sum of symbolic products of the form

$$A = \alpha_1\beta_1 + \alpha_2\beta_2 + \cdots + \alpha_k\beta_k,$$

the nature of the product being defined merely by the fact that when the dyadic is combined with a vector $\rho$ on the right (notation $A\cdot\rho$) a new vector $\rho'$ is produced, which is given by the equation

$$\rho' = A\cdot\rho = \alpha_1(\beta_1\cdot\rho) + \alpha_2(\beta_2\cdot\rho) + \cdots + \alpha_k(\beta_k\cdot\rho). \tag{3}$$

Obviously, according to this equation, the vector $\rho'$ is a linear vector function of the vector $\rho$. Two dyadics are said to be equal if they represent the same transformation, that is, if when combined right-handedly with an arbitrary $\rho$, the same vector $\rho'$ in both cases is produced.

Similarly we can define multiplication on the left of a dyadic by a vector, and show that the resulting vector is uniquely determined, that is, that two equal dyadics produce the same vector by multiplication on the left, although of course generally a different vector from that produced by multiplication on the right.

The following properties of dyadics follow immediately from the definition:

(*a*) $$\rho'\cdot(A\cdot\rho) = (\rho'\cdot A)\cdot\rho,$$

so that the notation $\rho'\cdot A\cdot\rho$ has no ambiguity.

(*b*) $$\alpha(\beta + \gamma) = \alpha\beta + \alpha\gamma.$$

(*c*) If

$$A_1 = \alpha_1'\beta_1' + \alpha_2'\beta_2' + \cdots + \alpha_k'\beta_k',$$

$$A_2 = \alpha_1''\beta_1'' + \alpha_2''\beta_2'' + \cdots + \alpha_n''\beta_n'',$$

and $A_3$ is the dyadic such that $A_3\cdot\rho = A_2\cdot(A_1\cdot\rho)$, then it may be expressed in the form

$$A_3 = A_2\cdot A_1 = \Sigma_{ij}\,\alpha_i''(\beta_i''\cdot\alpha_j')\beta_j', \tag{4}$$

whence it is called the product of $A_1$ by $A_2$. In general $A_2\cdot A_1$ is not the same as $A_1\cdot A_2$.

(*d*) If $A_3$ is the dyadic such that $A_3\cdot\rho = A_1\cdot\rho + A_2\cdot\rho$ it may be expressed in the form

$$A_3 = \Sigma_i\,\alpha_i'\beta_i' + \Sigma_j\,\alpha_j''\beta_j'',$$

whence it is called the sum of $A_1$ and $A_2$. Obviously:

$$A_1 + A_2 = A_2 + A_1.$$

(e) If $A_c$ is the dyadic such that $\rho \cdot A_c = A \cdot \rho$, then $A_c$ is called the conjugate of $A$, and we have for it the expression

(5) $$A_c = \Sigma_i \beta_i \alpha_i.$$

The vectors in any dyadic may be resolved into components, and the resulting products expanded according to the distributive law. If we take three unit vectors $i$, $j$, $k$, mutually normal, any dyadic may be expressed in the form

$$a_{11}ii + a_{12}ij + a_{13}ik + a_{21}ji + \cdots + a_{33}kk,$$

and represented by the matrix

$$\begin{pmatrix} a_{11} & a_{12} & a_{13} \\ a_{21} & a_{22} & a_{23} \\ a_{31} & a_{32} & a_{33} \end{pmatrix}.$$

The multiplication of dyadics is, as we have seen, equivalent to the succession of two linear transformations, and this again is well known to be equivalent to the multiplication of the corresponding matrices. In other words, to multiply two dyadics $A_1$ and $A_2$ according to (c) is the same thing as multiplying their respective matrices; the algebra of dyadics is the same as the algebra of matrices.

The familiar fact that the matrix of transformation of the element of area is the matrix of cofactors from the matrix of transformation of the lineal elements may be expressed by the formula

(6) $$(A \cdot V_1) \times (A \cdot V_2) = B \cdot (V_1 \times V_2),$$

where $B$ is the matrix of cofactors of the elements of $A$. If further, $K$ is the matrix whose cofactors form the elements of $A$, and if $D$ is its determinant, a fundamental theorem of algebra enables us to rewrite the above equation in the form

(6′) $$(A \cdot V_1) \times (A \cdot V_2) = DK \cdot (V_1 \times V_2).$$

The matrices (or dyadics) $A$, $B$, $K$ are in fact connected by the following simple algebraic relations:

(6″) $$B = DK, \qquad AK_c = DI, \qquad A = DK_c^{-1}$$
$$B_c = D^2 A^{-1},$$

where $I$ is the idemfactor (the dyadic corresponding to the identical transformation), and $A^{-1}$ is the dyadic reciprocal to $A$ (the inverse transformation).

Given any three non-coplanar vectors $\alpha$, $\beta$, $\gamma$ we define a *reciprocal system* $\alpha'$, $\beta'$, $\gamma'$ in order to simplify the expression of certain vector formulæ. The vector $\alpha'$ is taken as normal to the two vectors $\beta$, $\gamma$ in direction, and in value such that $\alpha \cdot \alpha' = 1$. Similarly, $\beta'$ and $\gamma'$ are defined so that $\beta' \cdot \alpha = 0$, $\beta' \cdot \beta = 1$, $\beta' \cdot \gamma = 0$, and $\gamma' \cdot \alpha = 0$, $\gamma' \cdot \beta = 0$, $\gamma' \cdot \gamma = 1$. A system of mutually normal unit vectors is self reciprocal.

Consider the resolution of a vector $\rho$ on the three vectors $\alpha$, $\beta$, $\gamma$. Such vector components themselves are linear vector functions of $\rho$, and therefore the dyadic of transformation in each case will be determined if its action on three non-coplanar vectors is known. Let $E_1$, $E_2$, $E_3$ be the three dyadics of transformation. We must have for $E_1$ the equations

$$E_1 \cdot \alpha = \alpha, \qquad E_1 \cdot \beta = 0, \qquad E_1 \cdot \gamma = 0,$$

which we obtain by considering its action on $\alpha$, $\beta$, $\gamma$ themselves. These equations are however satisfied by the dyadic $E_1 = \alpha\alpha'$. Hence the formulæ:

$$E_1 = \alpha\alpha', \qquad E_2 = \beta\beta', \qquad E_3 = \gamma\gamma'. \tag{7}$$

Moreover, since any vector will be the sum of the three components obtained by resolving it in three non-coplanar directions, we have the identity

$$\rho = (E_1 + E_2 + E_3) \cdot \rho = (\alpha\alpha' + \beta\beta' + \gamma\gamma') \cdot \rho, \tag{8}$$

which is merely another way of saying that the dyadic in parenthesis is the idemfactor $I$.

**23. The Condition of Isogeneity.** Let $\tau$ be the unit vector in the direction of the curve $C$ at $P$, and let $\alpha$, $\beta$, $\tau$ be the reciprocal system to $V_1$, $V_2$, $\tau$. From (7) and (8) we have

$$E_1 = V_1\alpha, \qquad E_2 = V_2\beta, \tag{7'}$$

$$W_i = (V_1\alpha + V_2\beta) \cdot W_i, \qquad i = 1, 2. \tag{8'}$$

From (2) we have

$$\frac{W_2''}{|V_2|} = \frac{W_1'}{|V_1|}, \qquad \frac{W_1''}{|V_2|} = -\frac{W_2'}{|V_1|},$$

whence

$$W_2'' = W_1' \frac{|V_2|}{|V_1|}, \qquad W_2' = -W_1'' \frac{|V_1|}{|V_2|}.$$

Making use of the fact that $E_1 \cdot W_1$ is a vector in the direction of $V_1$, and that therefore its algebraic magnitude is given by the formula

$$W_1' = \frac{V_1 \cdot E_1 \cdot W_1}{|V_1|},$$

we may rewrite the first of the above equations in the form:

$$W_2'' = \frac{V_1 \cdot E_1 \cdot W_1}{V_1 \cdot V_1} |V_2|,$$

whence, since $E_2 \cdot W_2$ is a vector in the direction $V_2$, and with reference to the direction of $V_2$ of algebraic magnitude $W_2''$, we get:

$$E_2 \cdot W_2 = \frac{V_1 \cdot E_1 \cdot W_1}{V_1 \cdot V_1} V_2.$$

By (7′) this reduces at once to the value $E_2 \cdot W_2 = (\alpha \cdot W_1)V_2$.

Similarly $E_1 \cdot W_2 = -(\beta \cdot W_1)V_1$ and therefore by (8′) we have the equation

$$W_2 = -(\beta \cdot W_1)V_1 + (\alpha \cdot W_1)V_2,$$

which, in dyadic notation, may be rewritten in the form:

$$W_2 = -(V_1\beta - V_2\alpha) \cdot W_1. \tag{9}$$

In the same way, or by multiplying both sides of (9) left-handedly by the dyadic $V_1\beta - V_2\alpha$, we get the inverse relation

$$W_1 = (V_1\beta - V_2\gamma) \cdot W_2. \tag{9′}$$

These are the vector forms of the relation (2). *That either* (9) *or* (9′) *hold at a given point P and for a given curve C is a necessary and sufficient condition that* $\Phi[C]$ *and* $F[C]$ *be isogenous at P for C.*

We have just shown the necessity of the condition. Let us now show the sufficiency, by calculating directly the quantity $d\Phi/dF$. If we replace $\Delta F_1 + i\Delta F_2$ by $(V_1 + iV_2)\cdot\sigma$ and $\Delta\Phi_1 + i\Delta\Phi_2$ by $(W_1 + iW_2)\cdot\sigma$, we have, from (9) and (8′), the equation

$$(W_1 + iW_2)\cdot\sigma = \sigma\cdot(V_1\beta + V_2\gamma - iV_1\gamma + iV_2\beta)\cdot W_1,$$

of which however the dyadic term factors into two, so that we have the expression

$$\sigma\cdot(V_1 + iV_2)(\beta - i\gamma)\cdot W_1,$$

which is nothing but the product of the two scalar quantities $(V_1 + iV_2)\cdot\sigma$ and $(\beta - i\gamma)\cdot W_1$. We have then the result

$$\frac{d\Phi}{dF} = (\beta - i\gamma)\cdot W_1, \tag{10}$$

which does not involve the manner in which $\sigma$ has been allowed to approach zero.

In terms of $W_2$, instead of $W_1$, we have the result:

$$\frac{d\Phi}{dF} = i(\beta - i\gamma)\cdot W_2. \tag{10′}$$

In fact, $W_1$ and $W_2$ are connected by the relations:

$$\begin{aligned} \beta\cdot W_1 - \gamma\cdot W_2 &= 0, \\ \beta\cdot W_2 + \gamma\cdot W_1 &= 0. \end{aligned} \tag{10″}$$

## § 2. The Theory of Isogeneity for Additive Functionals

**24. The Condition of Isogeneity.** We saw in Art. 9 that in the case of additive functionals the vector flux could be chosen as a vector point function, independent of the curve $C$. Let us assume that $V_1$, $V_2$, $W_1$, $W_2$ are so chosen, and find the conditions on them in order that $\Phi$ and $F$ shall be isogenous complex functionals.

If we take for $C$ a curve which at $P$ is tangent to the plane of $V_1$ and $V_2$, the components of these two vectors perpendicular to the curve will lie on the same line. Hence the components of $W_1$ and $W_2$ perpendicular to the curve will, as we saw in Art. 21, lie on this same line, and the vectors $W_1$ and $W_2$ themselves will lie in the plane of $V_1$ and $V_2$. If we indicate with the subscript $x$ the component of a vector in the direction $x$, and denote the components of the vector product of $V_1$ and $V_2$ by $D_x$, $D_y$, $D_z$, i. e.,

$$D_x = V_{1y}V_{2z} - V_{2y}V_{1z}, \text{ etc.,}$$

this condition may be written in the form

$$(11) \qquad \begin{aligned} D_xW_{1x} + D_yW_{1y} + D_zW_{1z} &= 0, \\ D_xW_{2x} + D_yW_{2y} + D_zW_{2z} &= 0, \end{aligned}$$

or in the equivalent vector form

$$(11') \qquad [V_1V_2W_1] = [V_1V_2W_2] = 0.$$

If now we take a new curve, normal at $P$ to the plane of $V_1$ and $V_2$, we may apply the analysis of Art. 23, and we find therefore that $W_1$ and $W_2$ must satisfy the relation (9). The vectors $\alpha$, $\beta$ are now vectors in this common plane of all the vector fluxes, and such that $\alpha \cdot V_1 = 1$, $\alpha \cdot V_2 = 0$, etc. With this understanding, the conditions (9) or (9′) with (11) or (11′) are sufficient, and the formulæ (10) and (10′) give the value of $d\Phi/dF$.

**25. The Analog of Laplace's Equation.** The question arises as to how much of the functional $\Phi[C]$, isogenous to $F[C]$, is arbitrary, when $F[C]$ is given in advance. It is necessary that the condition of integrability (Lecture I, equation (21′)) be satisfied for both $W_1$ and $W_2$. *If $R$ is a vector point function, a necessary and sufficient condition that it be the vector flux of the real or pure imaginary part of a functional $\Phi[C]$, isogenous to $F[C]$, is that it satisfy the equations*

$$[V_1V_2R] = 0,$$
$$\text{Div } R = 0, \tag{12}$$
$$\text{Div } (V_1\gamma - V_2\beta)\cdot R = 0.^*$$

In fact if we take $R$ as a $W_1$, the $W_2$ defined by (9) will satisfy the condition of integrability and lie in the plane of $V_1$ and $V_2$. Likewise, if we take $R$ as a $W_2$, the $W_1$ defined by (9′) will satisfy the condition of integrability and lie in the plane of $V_1$ and $V_2$.

**26. A Special Case Connected with the Theory of Laplace's Equation.** Consider the case when $V_1$ and $V_2$ are unit vectors parallel to the $X$ and $Y$ axes, and therefore independent of $x$, $y$, $z$. For the sake of conciseness in the resulting formulæ, we shall take $V_1$ in the negative direction of the $Y$-axis, and $V_2$ in the positive direction of the $X$-axis:

$$V_1 = (0, -1, 0), \qquad V_2 = (1, 0, 0). \tag{13}$$

We have therefore

$$\alpha = (0, -1, 0), \qquad \beta = (1, 0, 0), \tag{13′}$$

and so the equations (12), which $W_1$ must satisfy, become:

$$W_{1z} = 0, \tag{14}$$

$$\frac{\partial W_{1x}}{\partial x} + \frac{\partial W_{1y}}{\partial y} = 0, \tag{14′}$$

$$\frac{\partial W_{1y}}{\partial x} - \frac{\partial W_{1x}}{\partial y} = 0. \tag{14″}$$

In fact $\alpha\cdot W_1$ is $-W_{1y}$ and $\beta\cdot W_1$ is $W_{1x}$.

* The notation Div $R$ denotes the quantity $(\partial R_x/\partial x) + (\partial R_y/\partial y) + (\partial R_z/\partial z)$, the divergence of $R$.

The last equation tells us that there is a function $G_1(xyz)$ such that $\partial G_1/\partial x = W_{1x}$ and $\partial G_1/\partial y = W_{1y}$. From (14′) we have

$$\frac{\partial^2 G_1}{\partial x^2} + \frac{\partial^2 G_1}{\partial y^2} = 0. \tag{15}$$

In the same way, corresponding to $W_2$, there is a function $G_2(xyz)$ which also satisfies Laplace's equation, with respect to the variables $x$, $y$.

The relation between $G_1$ and $G_2$ is given to us by means of the relation of isogeneity; in fact, from (9) we have:

$$W_{2x} = -W_{1y}, \qquad W_{2y} = W_{1x},$$

whence

$$\frac{\partial G_2}{\partial x} = -\frac{\partial G_1}{\partial y}, \qquad \frac{\partial G_2}{\partial y} = \frac{\partial G_1}{\partial x}, \tag{15'}$$

which are the Cauchy-Riemann equations in the variables $x$, $y$.

We may now calculate explicitly the functionals $F[C]$ and $\Phi[C]$. We have:

$$F = \int\int (V_1 + iV_2)\cdot d\sigma$$

where $\sigma$ is an arbitrary cap of the closed curve $C$. Hence,

$$F = \int\int - \cos y, n\, d\sigma + i\int\int \cos x, n\, d\sigma.$$

In this expression the positive direction of the normal is taken as the one which stands to positive motion along the curve $C$ in the same relation as that in which the $z$-axis stands to rotation from the $x$-axis to the $y$-axis. Since the direction of positive rotation in the $xz$-plane is from the $z$-axis to the $x$-axis, we have:

$$F = -\int\int_{(\sigma)} dzdx + i\int\int_{(\sigma)} dydz = \int_C dz \int_{(z=\text{const.})} [dx + idy]$$

and finally:

$$F[C] = \int_C (x + iy)dz. \tag{16}$$

In order to calculate $\Phi[C]$, we have

$$\Phi = \int\int \left\{ \frac{\partial G_1}{\partial x} \cos x, n + \frac{\partial G_1}{\partial y} \cos y, n \right\} d\sigma$$
$$+ i \int\int \left\{ \frac{\partial G_2}{\partial x} \cos x, n + \frac{\partial G_2}{\partial y} \cos y, n \right\} d\sigma,$$

which by (15′) is the same as the equation

$$\Phi = \int\int \left\{ \frac{\partial G_2}{\partial y} \cos x, n - \frac{\partial G_2}{\partial x} \cos y, n - i \frac{\partial G_1}{\partial y} \cos x, n \right.$$
$$\left. + i \frac{\partial G_1}{\partial x} \cos y, n \right\} d\sigma,$$

which again reduces to the following equation:

$$\Phi = \int dz \int \left\{ \frac{\partial G_2}{\partial x} dx + \frac{\partial G_2}{\partial y} dy - i \left( \frac{\partial G_1}{\partial x} dx + \frac{\partial G_1}{\partial y} dy \right) \right\}.$$

But since each of the interior integrals, $z$ being constant, is a curvilinear integral independent of the path, we have

$$\Phi = \int_C \{ G_2(xyz) - iG_1(xyz) \} dz.$$

On account of the relations (15′), however, the function $G_1 + iG_2$ for a constant value of $z$ is an analytic function of the complex variable $x + iy$. Hence if we write

$$\begin{aligned} G(x + iy, z) &= - i\{ G_1(xyz) + iG_2(xyz) \} \\ &= G_2(xyz) - iG_1(xyz), \end{aligned}$$

$G(x + iy, z)$ will be an analytic function of $x + iy$, and *the most general functional isogenous to*

$$F[C] = \int_C (x + iy) dz$$

*will be*

$$\Phi[C] = \int_C G(x + iy, z) dz. \tag{16′}$$

**27. The Analog of Green's Theorem, and Theorems of Determinateness.** Consider two complex functionals $\Phi[C]$ and $\Phi'[C]$, both isogenous to the complex functional $F[C]$, and the differential equations

(17) $kW_1 = (V_1V_1 + V_2V_2)\cdot\nabla\varphi_1 + (V_1V_2 - V_2V_1)\cdot\nabla\varphi_2,$

(18) $kW_2 = -(V_1V_2 - V_2V_1)\cdot\nabla\varphi_1 + (V_1V_1 + V_2V_2)\cdot\nabla\varphi_2,$

(19) $kW_1' = (V_1V_1 + V_2V_2)\cdot\nabla\varphi_1' + (V_1V_2 - V_2V_1)\cdot\nabla\varphi_2',$

(20) $kW_2' = -(V_1V_2 - V_2V_1)\cdot\nabla\varphi_1' + (V_1V_1 + V_2V_2)\cdot\nabla\varphi_2',$

which are to be satisfied by certain point functions $\varphi_1, \varphi_1', \varphi_2, \varphi_2'$, as yet undetermined. In these equations $W_1$, $W_2$ and $W_1'$, $W_2'$ are the vector fluxes of $\Phi$ and $\Phi'$ respectively, $\nabla\varphi_1$ denotes the vector $(\partial\varphi_1/\partial x, \partial\varphi_1/\partial y, \partial\varphi_1/\partial z)$, etc., and $k$ is a point function $k(xyz)$, at present not further specified.

If we multiply both sides of (17) left-handedly by the dyadic $-(V_1\beta - V_2\alpha)$, the resulting equation reduces to (18). Similarly (20) is a consequence of (19).

If $\alpha, \beta, \gamma$ are any three vectors, a much used formula in vector analysis gives us the equations*

$$\alpha \times (\beta \times \gamma) = -(\beta \times \gamma) \times \alpha$$
$$= \alpha\cdot\gamma\beta - \alpha\cdot\beta\gamma = (\beta\gamma - \gamma\beta)\cdot\alpha.$$

Hence we can rewrite equations (17) to (20) in the form:

(17′) $kW_1 = (V_1V_1 + V_2V_2)\cdot\nabla\varphi_1 + \nabla\varphi_2 \times (V_1 \times V_2),$

(18′) $kW_2 = -\nabla\varphi_1' \times (V_1 \times V_2) + (V_1V_1 + V_2V_2)\cdot\nabla\varphi_2',$

etc.

In connection with the equations (17) to (20) or (17′) to (20′), we consider a certain scalar invariant $H_{\Phi_1\Phi_1'}$ defined by the equation

(21) $$(V_1 \times V_2)H_{\Phi_1\Phi_1'} = W_1 \times W_2',$$

where the left- and right-hand members represent, of course, in virtue of (11) or (11′), collinear vectors. If in this equation we substitute for $W_1$ its value as given by (17′), we obtain the relation

$$k(V_1 \times V_2)H_{\Phi_1\Phi_1'} = (V_1 \times W_2')(V_1\cdot\nabla\varphi_1)$$
$$+ (V_2 \times W_2')(V_2\cdot\nabla\varphi_1) + \{\nabla\varphi_2 \times (V_1 \times V_2)\} \times W_2'.$$

* Gibbs-Wilson, Vector analysis, New York (1901), p. 74.

The above quoted vector formula gives us for the last term of this equation the equivalent form

$$- W_2' \times \{\nabla\varphi_2 \times (V_1 \times V_2)\} = - \{W_2' \cdot (V_1 \times V_2)\}\nabla\varphi_2 + (W_2' \cdot \nabla\varphi_2)(V_1 \times V_2).$$

and in this expression the first term vanishes, since $W_2'$ lies in the plane of $V_1$ and $V_2$. Moreover from (9) we have

$$V_1 \times W_2' = (V_1 \times V_2)\alpha \cdot W_1',$$

$$V_2 \times W_2' = - (V_2 \times V_1)\beta \cdot W_1' - (V_1 \times V_2)\beta \cdot W_1',$$

since $V_1 \times V_1 = 0$ and $V_2 \times V_2 = 0$. Hence our equation becomes

$$k(V_1 \times V_2)H_{\Phi_1\Phi_1'} = (V_1 \times V_2)\{(\alpha \cdot W_1')(V_1 \cdot \nabla\varphi_1) + (\beta \cdot W_1')(V_2 \cdot \nabla\varphi_1) + W_2' \cdot \nabla\varphi_2\},$$

or

$$kH_{\Phi_1\Phi_1'} = \nabla\varphi_1 \cdot (V_1\alpha + V_2\beta) \cdot W_1' + W_2' \cdot \nabla\varphi_2.$$

By means of the identity (8′), however, this reduces to the formula

$$kH_{\Phi_1\Phi_1'} = W_1' \cdot \nabla\varphi_1 + W_2' \cdot \nabla\varphi_2. \tag{22}$$

Also, in the same way, eliminating $W_2'$ instead of $W_1$, from 21, we have

$$kH_{\phi_1\Phi_1'} = W_1 \cdot \nabla\varphi_1' + W_2 \cdot \nabla\varphi_2'. \tag{22'}$$

The function $H_{\Phi_1\Phi_1'}$, from its definition in (21), is seen to be the ratio of the areas of the two parallelograms, one with sides $W_1$ and $W_2'$, the other with sides $V_1$ and $V_2$.

If we take $\Phi_1' = \Phi_1$, denoting $H_{\Phi_1\Phi_1'}$ by $\Theta_{\Phi_1}$, we have the equation

$$(V_1 \times V_2)\Theta_{\Phi_1} = W_1 \times W_2. \tag{23}$$

It is not hard to see that the quantity $\Theta_{\Phi_1}$ is essentially positive. In fact, from (9) we have

$$W_1 \times W_2 = - (W_1 \times V_1)(\beta \cdot W_1) + (W_1 \times V_2)(\alpha \cdot W_1)$$

and this, by means of the identity (8′), becomes

$$(V_1 \times V_2)(\beta \cdot W_1)^2 + (V_1 \times V_2)(\alpha \cdot W_1)^2$$

so that we have

$$\Theta_{\Phi_1} = (\alpha \cdot W_1)^2 + (\beta \cdot W_1)^2$$

a quantity that is essentially not negative.

It is worth while perhaps to rewrite the formulæ (22), (22′) without the use of vectors. They may in fact be written as follows:

$$kH_{\Phi_1\Phi_1'} = W_{1x}'\frac{\partial \varphi_1}{\partial x} + W_{1y}'\frac{\partial \varphi_1}{\partial y} + W_{1z}'\frac{\partial \varphi_1}{\partial z}$$

$$+ W_{2x}'\frac{\partial \varphi_2}{\partial x} + W_{2y}'\frac{\partial \varphi_2}{\partial y} + W_{2z}'\frac{\partial \varphi_2}{\partial z}$$

$$= W_{1x}\frac{\partial \varphi_1'}{\partial x} + W_{1y}\frac{\partial \varphi_1'}{\partial y} + W_{1z}\frac{\partial \varphi_1'}{\partial z}$$

$$+ W_{2x}\frac{\partial \varphi_2'}{\partial x} + W_{2y}\frac{\partial \varphi_2'}{\partial y} + W_{2z}\frac{\partial \varphi_2'}{\partial z}.$$

If we integrate both sides of these equations over a region $S$ enclosed in a surface $\sigma$, and perform the suggested integration by parts we obtain the formulæ ($d\sigma$ as a vector having the direction of the interior normal):

$$(24) \qquad \iiint kHdS = -\iint [\varphi_1 W_1' \cdot d\sigma + \varphi_2 W_2' \cdot d\sigma]$$

$$= -\iint [\varphi_1' W_1 \cdot d\sigma + \varphi_2' W_2 \cdot d\sigma],$$

$$(25) \qquad \iiint k\Theta dS = -\iint [\varphi_1 W_1 \cdot d\sigma + \varphi_2 W_2 \cdot d\sigma].$$

These are the analogs of Green's theorem, for the operator of Laplace.

From these equations, Vòlterra is able to obtain certain theorems of determinateness analogous to the well-known facts about the uniqueness of harmonic functions which take on given values along closed curves. He assumes that (17), equivalent to two linear partial differential equations of the first order in $\varphi_1$ and $\varphi_2$, admits solutions, continuous with their first partial derivatives, within a given region, when the function $k(xyz)$ has been chosen continuously of one sign; this sign without loss of generality, being taken as positive. By writing then

$\Phi_1' = \Phi_1$, in equations (17) to (20), he is able to deduce the following theorem.

*Let* $\Phi[C] = \Phi_1[C] + i\Phi_2[C]$ *be isogenous to* $F[C] = F_1[C] + iF_2[C]$, *and without singularities within a closed surface* $\sigma$.* *Then, if the values of* $\Phi[C]$ *are known for all the closed curves which lie on* $\sigma$, *the functional* $\Phi[C]$ *will be determined for all the closed curves of the region* $S$, *enclosed by* $\sigma$.

In fact, suppose there were two such functionals, and let $\Phi''[C]$ be their difference. The quantities $W_1''\cdot d\sigma$ and $W_2''\cdot d\sigma$ will vanish at every point of $\sigma$. Hence if we apply the equation (25) to $\Phi''[C]$, the right-hand member will vanish, and we shall have

$$\iiint k\Theta dS = 0,$$

where the integration is carried out over the region $S$. But since $k$ is positive and $\Theta$ is nowhere negative, $\Theta$ must be identically zero. This implies however (provided that $V_1$ and $V_2$ are not collinear) that $W_1''$ and $W_2''$ vanish identically, and hence $\Phi''[C]$ must vanish identically.

**28. Transformation of the Variables** $x, y, z$. Make a transformation of coordinates $x = x(\bar{x}\bar{y}\bar{z})$, $y = y(\bar{x}\bar{y}\bar{z})$, $z = z(\bar{x}\bar{y}\bar{z})$, whose Jacobian $D = \partial(xyz)/\partial(\bar{x}\bar{y}\bar{z})$ does not vanish; denote by $K$ the matrix and dyadic corresponding to $D$:

$$K = \begin{bmatrix} \frac{\partial x}{\partial \bar{x}} & \frac{\partial y}{\partial \bar{x}} & \frac{\partial z}{\partial \bar{x}} \\ \frac{\partial x}{\partial \bar{y}} & \frac{\partial y}{\partial \bar{y}} & \frac{\partial z}{\partial \bar{y}} \\ \frac{\partial x}{\partial \bar{z}} & \frac{\partial y}{\partial \bar{z}} & \frac{\partial z}{\partial \bar{z}} \end{bmatrix}, \tag{26}$$

and by $A$ the matrix of the cofactors of the elements of $K$, that is, the matrix of the quantities $\partial(yz)/\partial(\bar{y}\bar{z})$, etc.

According to (6″) we have $A = DK_c^{-1}$, and according to (22), Lecture I, any vector flux $V$ is transformed by the formula

$$\bar{V} = A\cdot V. \tag{27}$$

* The vector $W_1$ is assumed to be continuous within and on the surface $\sigma$ and its components to have continuous partial derivatives of the first order at all points inside $\sigma$.

*The relation of isogeneity is preserved by the transformation.* In fact, coplanar vectors, transformed by any linear vector function, remain coplanar; and therefore $\overline{W}_1$ and $\overline{W}_2$ are coplanar with $\overline{V}_1$ and $\overline{V}_2$. Moreover the condition (9) is satisfied. To see this let $\overline{\alpha}$ and $\overline{\beta}$ be the plane system reciprocal to $\overline{V}_1$ and $\overline{V}_2$. We have then

(28) $$\overline{\alpha} = \alpha \cdot A^{-1}, \qquad \overline{\beta} = \beta \cdot A^{-1},$$

whence $\overline{\beta} \cdot \overline{W}_1 = \beta \cdot W_1$ and $\overline{\alpha} \cdot \overline{W}_1 = \alpha \cdot W_1$, and therefore, with the aid of (27),

$$-(\overline{V}_1\overline{\beta} - \overline{V}_2\overline{\alpha}) \cdot \overline{W}_1 = A \cdot \{-(V_1\beta - V_2\alpha) \cdot W_1 = A \cdot W_2 = \overline{W}_2,$$

and the condition of isogeneity is satisfied. This fact may also be established by means of P. Lévy's geometrical interpretation.

*The quantity* $H_{\Phi_1\Phi_1'}$ *is absolutely invariant of the transformation.* If we multiply left-handedly both members of (21), which defines $H_{\Phi_1\Phi_1'}$, by the dyadic $B = DK$, the equation reduces by (6′) to the result:

$$(\overline{V}_1 \times \overline{V}_2)H_{\Phi_1\Phi_1'} = \overline{W}_1 \times \overline{W}_2'.$$

But this is the equation which defines $\overline{H}_{\Phi_1\Phi_1'}$; and therefore

$$\overline{H}_{\Phi_1\Phi_1'} = H_{\Phi_1\Phi_1'}.$$

We may also investigate the covariance of the equations (17) to (20). The vector elements of arc in the two spaces, $d\rho$ and $d\rho'$, are connected by the relation

(29) $$d\rho = d\overline{\rho} \cdot K = K_c \cdot d\overline{\rho}.$$

Let $\varphi(xyz)$ be any scalar point function; since

$$d\varphi = \nabla\varphi \cdot d\rho = \overline{\nabla}\varphi \cdot d\overline{\rho},$$

it follows from (29) that:

(29′) $$\overline{\nabla}\varphi = \nabla\varphi \cdot K_c = K \cdot \nabla\varphi.$$

If we apply these results to the equations (17) to (20), we see that these equations will remain satisfied in the transformed space by the functions $\varphi_1$, $\varphi_1'$, $\varphi_2$, $\varphi_2'$, provided that we take

(30) $$\overline{k} = \frac{\partial(xyz)}{\partial(\overline{x}\overline{y}\overline{z})} k.$$

An interesting result is connected with the total differential equation

(31) $$D_x dx + D_y dy + D_z dz = 0,$$

or

$$[d\rho V_1 V_2] = 0.$$

We have,

$$[d\bar{\rho}\bar{V}_1\bar{V}_2] = d\bar{\rho}\cdot(\bar{V}_1 \times \bar{V}_2) = Dd\bar{\rho}\cdot K\cdot(V_1 \times V_2) = Dd\rho\cdot(V_1 \times V_2),$$

and therefore, from (29), we have the equation

(32) $$[d\bar{\rho}\bar{V}_1\bar{V}_2] = \frac{\partial(xyz)}{\partial(\overline{xyz})}[d\rho V_1 V_2].$$

If then the equation (31) is satisfied, it remains satisfied after the transormation. Hence if (31) is integrable, it is transformed into an integrable equation.

In this case, that is, if $F[C]$ is such a complex functional that (31) is integrable, Volterra shows that the equations (17) to (20) can be satisfied in a specially simple manner; namely, by taking $\varphi_1 \equiv \varphi_1' \equiv 0$, and choosing $\varphi_2$ and $\varphi_2'$ to satisfy the thus simplified equations, or vice versa, by putting $\varphi_2 \equiv \varphi_2' \equiv 0$. *A transformation may then be found which changes $F[C]$ into the form discussed in Art.* 26.

**29. Functional Integration and Cauchy's Theorem.** Let $\Phi[C]$ be isogenous to $F[C]$. This relation may be stated in the form

(32) $$W = fV,$$

where $f = f_1(xyz) + if_2(xyz)$ is some scalar point function. Since the divergence of $W$ must vanish, it follows that we must have

(33) $$\nabla f\cdot V = 0.$$

*If the relation* (33) *is satisfied, the functional $F[C]$ and the function $f$ are said to be isogenous.*

If any functional $\Phi'$ is isogenous to $F$, it is also isogenous to $f$, for in this case there will be an $f'$ such that $W' = f'V$, whence

$$\nabla f\cdot W' = f'\nabla f\cdot V = 0.$$

Let us denote by $dF/d\sigma$ the vector $V = V_1 + iV_2$, and consider the quantity

(34) $$\Phi[C] = \iint_{(C)} f\frac{dF}{d\sigma}\cdot d\sigma,$$

where $\sigma$ is a cap of the closed curve $C$, and $F[C]$ and $f(xyz)$ are isogenous. Equation (34) really defines a functional of $C$, as is implied by the notation. For this, it is sufficient that

$$\text{Div}\ [fdF/d\sigma] \equiv 0.$$

This condition is satisfied since we have

$$\text{Div}\left(f\frac{dF}{d\sigma}\right) = f\ \text{Div}\ V + \nabla f\cdot V.$$

The notation

(35) $$\Phi[C] = \int fdF$$

is used by Volterra to denote the integral (34). If the field of integration is a closed surface, or a complete surface boundary to a region, we have the result:

(36) $$\int fdF = 0,$$

which is a generalization of Cauchy's theorem for functions of a single complex variable.

## § 3. Isogenous Non-Additive Functionals

**30. The Condition of Isogeneity.** The condition of isogeneity for non-additive functionals has already been obtained in terms of the vector flux $V$, or rather, in terms of its component normal to the curve. It is desirable to express the same condition in terms of the functional derivative vectors, which are uniquely determined in terms of the curve and the point where the differentiation takes place.

Denote by $R_1[C \mid M]$, $R_2[C \mid M]$ the vector derivatives of $F_1[C]$ and $F_2[C]$ respectively, and by $U_1[C \mid M]$ and $U_2[C \mid M]$ the vector derivatives of $\Phi_1[C]$ and $\Phi_2[C]$; so that we have

(37) $$R = R_1 + iR_2, \qquad U = U_1 + iU_2.$$

If we denote by $\tau$ the unit vector in the direction of the curve, and let $V$ and $W$ be the normal components of the vector fluxes, we shall, as we saw in Lecture I, have the relations

(38) $$R = \tau \times V, \qquad U = \tau \times W.$$

Form now the vector product, multiplying $\tau$ left-handedly on to the equation (9); we have

$$U_2 = -(R_1\beta - R_2\alpha)\cdot W_1.$$

Let us denote by $\beta'$ a vector perpendicular to $\tau$, such that $\beta = \beta' \times \tau$ and by $\alpha'$ a similar vector such that $\alpha = \alpha' \times \tau$. We have

$$\beta\cdot W_1 = \beta' \times \tau\cdot W_1 = [\beta'\tau W_1] = \beta'\cdot\tau\times W_1 = \beta'\cdot U_1,$$

and therefore, treating $\alpha\cdot W_1$ in the same way,

(39) $$U_2 = -(R_1\beta' - R_2\alpha')\cdot U_1.$$

*The equation* (39) *is the condition of isogeneity. The vectors* $\alpha'$, $\beta'$, $\tau$ *form the reciprocal system to the vectors* $R_1$, $R_2$, $\tau$, *and* $\alpha'$, $\beta'$ *are given by the formulæ*

$$(40)\qquad \begin{aligned} \alpha' &= \tau \times \alpha, \qquad & \beta' &= \tau \times \beta, \\ \alpha &= \alpha' \times \tau, \qquad & \beta &= \beta' \times \tau. \end{aligned}$$

In fact, if $\beta = \beta' \times \tau$, we have $\tau \times \beta = \tau \times (\beta' \times \tau)$ which may be expressed in the form $\tau \cdot \tau\beta' - \tau \cdot \beta'\tau$ (see Art. 27, footnote). This last expression reduces however to $\beta'$, since $\tau$ is normal to $\beta'$, and therefore $\tau \cdot \beta' = 0$. Hence $\tau \times \beta = \beta'$. Conversely, if $\tau \times \beta = \beta'$ it follows that $\beta = \beta' \times \tau$; and similar relations may be shown in the same way to hold between $\alpha$ and $\alpha'$.

In order to show that $\alpha'\ \beta'\ \tau$ is the reciprocal system to $R_1\ R_2\ \tau$, we must show that $R_1 \cdot \alpha' = 1$, $R_1 \cdot \beta' = 0$, $R_2 \cdot \alpha' = 0$, $R_2 \cdot \beta' = 1$, the other necessary relations being obvious. We have $R_1 \cdot \alpha' = (\tau \times V_1) \cdot (\tau \times \beta)$ and this, by a formula in vector analysis,* is $(\tau \cdot \tau)(V_1 \cdot \beta) - (\tau \cdot \beta)(V_1 \cdot \tau)$, which is $V_1 \cdot \beta$, which is 1. Similarly, the other relations are established. Thus the theorem is proved.

The equation (39) may be established geometrically, in the same way as (2) was established.

**31. Transformation of the Variables** $x$, $y$, $z$. According to equation (23) of Lecture I, we have

$$(41)\qquad \bar{R} = K \cdot R \frac{ds}{d\bar{s}},$$

where $K$ is the matrix or dyadic $K$ already defined, and $ds$ and $d\bar{s}$ are corresponding elements of arc. It follows that the relation of isogeneity is invariant of the transformation. In fact, multiplying (39) left-handedly by the dyadic $K$, we have

$$\bar{U}_2 = -(\bar{R}_1\beta' - \bar{R}_2\alpha') \cdot U_1.$$

If we define the quantities

$$\bar{\alpha}' = \alpha' \cdot K \frac{ds}{d\bar{s}}, \qquad \bar{\beta}' = \beta' \cdot K \frac{ds}{d\bar{s}},$$

they will be reciprocal to $\bar{R}_1$ and $\bar{R}_2$, in the new reciprocal system. Moreover

$$\alpha' = \bar{\alpha}' \cdot K^{-1} \frac{d\bar{s}}{ds}, \qquad \beta' = \bar{\beta}' \cdot K^{-1} \frac{d\bar{s}}{ds},$$

so that $\bar{\alpha}' \cdot \bar{U}_1 = \alpha' \cdot U_1$ and $\bar{\beta}' \cdot \bar{U}_1 = \beta' \cdot U_1$, and finally:

$$\bar{U}_2 = -(\bar{R}_1\bar{\beta}' - \bar{R}_2\bar{\beta}') \cdot U_1,$$

which is the relation of isogeneity in the transformed space.

**32. Functional Integration and Cauchy's Theorem.** A real vector functional $R[C \mid M]$ can represent the vector derivative of a functional $F[C]$ only if certain *conditions of integrability* are satisfied. In case each of the three components of $R[C \mid M]$ has itself at every point $M_1$ of $C$ a true derivative (e. g., $S_x[C \mid MM_1]$ is the vector derivative of the $x$-component of $R[C \mid M]$, taken at the point $M_1$), the conditions of integrability are given by Volterra as follows:†

* Gibbs-Wilson, Vector analysis, New York (1901), p. 76.

$$(42)\quad \begin{cases} R[C \mid M] \cdot \tau = 0, \\ S_x[C \mid MM_1] \cdot \tau_1 = 0, \quad S_y[C \mid MM_1] \cdot \tau_1 = 0, \quad S_z[C \mid MM_1] \cdot \tau_1 = 0, \end{cases}$$

where $\tau$ represents the unit vector in the direction of the curve at $M$, and $\tau_1$ the same quantity at $M_1$;

$$(43)\qquad S_{xx}[C \mid MM_1] = S_{xx}[C \mid M_1M],$$

$$(44)\qquad S_{yz}[C \mid MM_1] = S_{zy}[C \mid M_1M], \qquad \text{etc.},$$

where $S_{yz}$ represents the $z$-component of $S_y$, etc.

A complex vector functional $R = R_1 + iR_2$ can represent the vector derivative of a complex functional $F = F_1 + iF_2$, only if $R_1$ is the derivative of $F_1$ and $R_2$ is the derivative of $F_2$. In the special case just considered, the relations (42), (43), (44) will be satisfied for both real vectors $R_1$ and $R_2$, if they are satisfied for the complex vector $R$, and vice versa.

Let us speak of a scalar functional $\Theta[C \mid M]$ as an *integrand* for a scalar functional $F[C]$, if the vector $\Theta[C \mid M]R[C \mid M]$ satisfies the conditions of integrability. In the special case mentioned in the preceding paragraph, the equations (42) are automatically satisfied, so the conditions of integrability refer merely to (43) and (44).

If $\Theta[C \mid M]$ is an integrand for $F[C]$, there is a functional $\Phi[C]$ whose vector derivative is $\Theta[C \mid M]R[C \mid M]$. In fact:

$$(45)\qquad \Phi[C] = \iint \Theta[C \mid M]R[C \mid M] \cdot d\sigma + h,$$

where the integration is extended over a cap of $C$, or over a cap joining a fixed curve $C_0$ to the variable curve $C$, and $h$ is an arbitrary constant.

The equation (45) may be written in the form

$$(45')\qquad \Phi[C] - \Phi[C_0] = \iint \Theta[C \mid M]\frac{dF}{d\sigma} \cdot d\sigma = \int \Theta dF,$$

where $dF/d\sigma$ denotes $R[C \mid M]$. If we define:

$$\frac{d\Psi}{dF} = \frac{\dfrac{d\Psi}{d\sigma}}{\dfrac{dF}{d\sigma}},$$

where $\Psi[C]$ and $F[C]$ are any two isogenous functionals, we shall have $d\Psi/dF$ a scalar functional of $C$, $M$. Hence we have the formula

$$(46)\qquad \int \Theta dF = \int \Theta \frac{dF}{d\Psi} d\Psi.$$

*If $\Theta$ is an integrand for $F$, and $\Psi$ and $F$ are isogenous, then $\Theta(dF/d\Psi)$ will be an integrand for $\Psi$.*

The relations (45′), (46) are invariant of a transformation of spaces. For a closed surface, which does not contain singularities:

$$(47)\qquad \int \Theta dF = 0.$$

† Volterra, *Rendiconti della R. Accademia dei Lincei*, vol. III (1887), 2e semestre, p. 229.

## § 4. Additive Complex Functionals of Hyperspaces

**33. Elementary Functionals.** Volterra develops the theory of additive complex functionals of which the arguments are $r$-dimensional hyperspaces immersed in an $n$-space. For $r = n - 2$, the theory is a direct generalization of the theory of complex functionals of curves in 3-space; but for $r < n - 2$ the problem of finding a functional isogenous to a given one involves solving a system of partial differential equations where there are more equations than unknowns. That problem must then be replaced by this other: what conditions must be satisfied by $F[C]$ in order that

$$d\Phi_1 + id\Phi_2 = f(dF_1 + idF_2)$$

may be the differential of an additive functional of hyperspaces $\Phi[S_r]$, with $f$ a point function?

This condition is expressed by a certain system of linear partial differential equations, of which the coefficients depend on $F$, in the dependent variable $f$. These equations may be incompatible, and admit no solution other than a constant. If the functional $F[S_r]$ has been chosen however in such a way as to make the system *completely integrable*, the functional $F[S_r]$ is said to be *elementary*. Elementary functionals are not the only ones which can have functionals related to them isogenously, since every functional is isogenous to a constant times itself.

**34. Integrals of Analytic Functions of Two Complex Variables.** The case $n = 4$, $r = 1$ is interesting, because it is related to the theory of integrals of functions of two complex variables.* Consider in fact a surface integral:

$$\iint F[\xi, \eta] d\xi d\eta, \tag{48}$$

which is defined as

$$\iint \{(P + iQ)dxdz + (iP - Q)dxdt + (iP - Q)dydz + (P + iQ)dydt\}, \tag{49}$$

* For a summary of this subject see Osgood: Madison Colloquium, New York (1914), p. 136. There are questions of analysis situs which are fundamental.

the result obtained by carrying out in formal fashion the multiplication indicated when we put $\xi = x + iy$, $\eta = z + it$. In order to make our intuition clear, we can imagine the two-dimensional locus as enclosed in a three-dimensional space, and the integration as carried out over a surface in that 3-space. Further considerations are necessary to determine the *sense* of the integration; these can be arrived at by making precise the relations to the enclosing 3-space (Poincaré) or by considering the continuity properties of Jacobians relating to curvilinear coordinates on the surface (Volterra).

Poincaré showed that the necessary and sufficient condition that the integral (49) be independent of the surface, i. e., depend merely upon the closed curve of which it is the cap, is that $P + iQ$ be an analytic function of $x + iy$ and $z + it$. In this case, therefore, the quantities defined by (49) represent additive complex functionals of curves in 4-space. Singular surfaces (or singular curves as cut from them by the Poincaré 3-space) may be cut or looped by these curves.

*Any two additive complex functionals of the type just defined will be isogenous.* In fact, if $F[C]$ is one such functional and $F'[C]$ another, the condition to be satisfied is:

$$\frac{dF'}{dF} = f(xyzt),$$

in which the function $f$ does not depend upon the manner of letting the change $\sigma$, given to $C$, approach zero. But as we see from (49), we have always

$$\frac{dF'}{dF} = \frac{P' + iQ'}{P + iQ}.$$

It may be deduced in an equally simple manner that $F[C]$ is *elementary*. If in (49) we substitute $fP$ and $fQ$ for $P$ and $Q$ respectively, where $f = f_1(xyzt) + if_2(xyzt)$, it is merely necessary to write the condition that the new integral be independent of the surface. This gives us the relations

$$\frac{\partial}{\partial x}\{f(iP - Q)\} - \frac{\partial}{\partial y}\{f(P + iQ)\} = 0,$$

$$-\frac{\partial}{\partial x}\{f(P + iQ)\} - \frac{\partial}{\partial y}\{f(iP - Q)\} = 0,$$

$$\frac{\partial}{\partial t}\{f(P + iQ)\} - \frac{\partial}{\partial z}\{f(iP - Q)\} = 0,$$

$$\frac{\partial}{\partial t}\{f(iP - Q)\} + \frac{\partial}{\partial z}\{f(P + iQ)\} = 0.$$

Two of these are of course redundant. On account of the fact that $P + iQ$ is analytic in $\xi$ and $\eta$, the other two reduce, upon expansion, to the form

$$\frac{\partial f}{\partial x} + i\,\frac{\partial f}{\partial y} = 0,$$

$$\frac{\partial f}{\partial z} + i\,\frac{\partial f}{\partial t} = 0,$$

and yield the result that $f$ must be an analytic function of $\xi$ and $\eta$. But since, for their solution, no condition is imposed on $F[C]$, it follows that $F[C]$ is already elementary.

The theory of isogenous additive functionals of curves in 4-space includes more however than the theory of surface integrals of analytic functions of two complex variables; for the integral (49) contains no terms in $dx\,dy$ or $dz\,dt$. The theory thus will provide an extension of these properties to the general class of elementary functionals of curves in 4-space.

In general, for the consideration of $r$-functionals in $n$-space, we may enclose them in spaces of dimension $r + 2$; and in the $(r + 2)$-space apply the theory of functionals of curves in 3-space. When the functionals are elementary there will be important properties (like the generalization of Cauchy's theorem) which will be invariant of the $(r + 2)$-space in which the $r$-spaces may be enclosed.

# LECTURE III.

## IMPLICIT FUNCTIONAL EQUATIONS*

### § 1. The Method of Successive Approximations

**35. An Introductory Theorem.** An implicit functional equation which is easily solvable is the following:

$$\varphi(x) = F[\overset{b}{\underset{a}{\varphi(s)}}\,|\,x], \tag{1}$$

where, besides depending on the function $\varphi$ and the variable $x$, the functional constituting the right-hand member may depend upon other functions $f, g, \cdots$ and other variables $y, z, \cdots$, appearing parametrically. The equation (1) may be solved immediately by the method of successive approximations, and in fact serves, with the conditions imposed upon it, rather as a convenient formulation of that method than as a theorem of explicit value.

Consider a class $L$ of limited functions $\varphi(x)$, which contains the limit function of any uniformly convergent sequence of its functions $\varphi_n(x)$. Such a class is for instance the totality of continuous functions, in numerical value less than or equal to a given constant.

In regard to the functional $F$ we assume:

(*i*) If $\varphi(x)$ is a function of $L$, then $F[\varphi|x]$ is a function of $L$.

(*ii*) The functional $F$ satisfies a Cauchy-Lipschitz condition:

* This lecture is based on the following references:

Volterra, Leçons sur les fonctions de lignes, Paris (1913), chapter 4.

Hadamard, Leçons sur le calcul des variations, Paris (1910), chapter 7, Book II.

Riesz, Les opérations fonctionelles linéaires, *Annales Scientifiques de l'École Normale Supérieure*, vol. 31 (1914), pp. 9–14.

Lebesgue, Sur l'intégrale de Stieltjes et sur les opérations fonctionelles linéaires, *Comptes Rendus*, vol. 150 (1910), pp. 86–88.

Evans, Some general types of functional equations, *Proceedings of the Fifth International Congress of Mathematicians*, Cambridge (1912), vol. 1, pp. 385–396.

namely, if $\varphi_1$ and $\varphi_2$ are any two functions of $L$, then a constant $M$ can be found, $M < 1$, such that the following condition holds:

$$(2)\quad \max_a^b \left| F[\varphi_1(\overset{b}{\underset{a}{s}}) | x] - F[\varphi_2(\overset{b}{\underset{a}{s}}) | x] \right| \leq M \max_a^b \left| \varphi_1(x) - \varphi_2(x) \right|,$$

where $\max\limits_a^b |\varphi(x)|$ denotes the upper bound of a function $\varphi(x)$ in the range $ab$.

*Under these conditions, the class L contains one and only one solution of equation* (1).

To construct this solution we take $\varphi_0$, any particular function in $L$, and write

$$\varphi_n(x) = F[\varphi_{n-1} | x], \qquad n = 1, 2, 3, \cdots.$$

Then the function

$$\varphi(x) = \lim_{n=\infty} \varphi_n(x)$$

is in $L$, as is seen at once from the uniform convergence of the series

$$\varphi_0 + (\varphi_1 - \varphi_0) + (\varphi_2 - \varphi_1) + \cdots,$$

and is a solution of (1), since

$$\max_a^b |\varphi - F[\varphi | x]| \leq \max_a^b |\varphi - \varphi_{n+1}| + \max_a^b |F[\varphi_n | x] - F[\varphi | x].$$

If there were two solutions $\varphi$ and $\varphi'$ we should have, by equation (2):

$$\max_a^b |\varphi - \varphi'| \leq M \max_a^b |\varphi - \varphi'|,$$

which is a contradiction, since $M < 1$.

We have the corollary, that if $L$ contains a continuous function, and if $F[\varphi | x]$ represents a continuous function of $x$ when its argument $\varphi(x)$ represents a continuous function of $x$, then the unique solution of (1) is continuous.

**36. The Case of a Variable Upper Limit.** If the functional $F[\varphi | x]$ depends upon $\varphi$ only for values between $a$ and $x$, we are able to make use of a property of *prolongation*, which, speaking generally, makes less restrictive the convergence condition (*ii*) imposed on $M$ in Art. 35. In particular, if $F$ consists of terms independent of $\varphi$ plus a term whose variation is of the form

$$\int_a^x F'[\overset{x}{\underset{a}{\varphi(s)}} \mid x'x]\delta\varphi(x')dx'$$

the variation of $F$ due to a change of $\varphi$ can be made as small as we please by taking $x$ close enough to $a$.

Consider then the equation

$$\varphi(x) = F[\overset{x}{\underset{a}{\varphi(s)}} \mid x] \tag{3}$$

and in connection with it a class $L'$ of limited functions $\varphi(x)$. We shall assume that if $\varphi_n(x)$ ($\varphi_n$ being of $L'$) approaches a function $\varphi(x)$ uniformly in an interval $x_1x_2$, open or closed, then $\varphi(x)$ is of $L'$. It may not be defined outside of $x_1x_2$; we shall assume, however, that we can find another function over the rest of $ab$ so that $\varphi(x)$ as extended by this function will be for the whole interval $ab$ a member of $L'$.

In regard to the functional $F$ we assume that a finite number of points $a = a_0, a_1, a_2 \cdots a_k = b$ can be found so that the following conditions hold:

(*i*) If $\varphi(x)$ is a function of $L'$ in the interval $a \leqq x < a_{i+1}$, and satisfies equation (3) in the interval $a \leqq x < a_i$, then in the interval $a \leqq x < a_{i+1}$ the quantity $F[\varphi \mid x]$ represents a function in $L'$.

(*ii*) If $\varphi_1(x)$ and $\varphi_2(x)$ are functions of $L'$ in the interval $a \leqq x < a_{i+1}$, and satisfy the equation

$$\varphi_1(x) = \varphi_2(x) = F[\varphi_1 \mid x]$$

in the interval $a \leqq x < a_i$, then in the interval $a \leqq x < a_{i+1}$, we have the Cauchy-Lipschitz condition:

$$\max_a^x \mid F[\overset{x}{\underset{a}{\varphi_1(s)}} \mid x] - F[\overset{x}{\underset{a}{\varphi_2(s)}} \mid x] \mid \leqq M \max_a^x \mid \varphi_1(x) - \varphi_2(x) \mid, \tag{4}$$

in which $M$ is some constant, less than unity.

*Under these conditions, the class $L'$ contains one and only one solution of* (3), *in the interval $a \leqq x < b$.* The proof of this theorem is the same as that of Art. 35.

We have a true theorem if throughout (*i*), (*ii*) and the above conclusion we change the sign $<$ wherever it occurs, to the sign $\leqq$. We can deduce directly the corollary of this last theorem, that if $L'$ contains a function which is continuous $a \leqq x \leqq a_1$, and a function which, when $\varphi$ is given as continuous $a \leqq x \leqq a_i$, extends it continuously through the interval $a \leqq x \leqq a_{i+1}$, and if $F$ represents a continuous function of $x$ when its argument $\varphi$ is a continuous function of $x$, then the unique solution of (3) is continuous through the interval $a \leqq x \leqq b$.

The theorems of this article and the preceding one serve to establish the existence of the solutions of differential equations and integral equations of general types, without a restriction of linearity. More general theorems than these may easily be obtained, by replacing the functional *max* by some such thing as $\int \mid \varphi_1 - \varphi_2 \mid dx$, or by some more general functional such as the *norm* of A. A. Bennett,* or the *modulus* of E. H. Moore.† Gain of generality

* A. A. Bennett, *Proceedings of the National Academy of Sciences*, vol. 2 (1916), pp. 592–598.

† See Lecture V, General Analysis.

usually implies less immediate applicability to special cases, and the above theorems are sufficient for the cases which we are to consider. They supplant the repetition of the analysis of successive approximations in those cases.

## § 2. The Linear Functional

**37. Hadamard's Representation.** The resolution of an implicit equation in several variables for the purpose of determining one variable as a function of the others depends in the non-special case upon the linear relation which holds between the differentials of the variables involved. Likewise for the study of implicit equations in *functionals* in general, a study of the linear functional is first necessary. It is the purpose of this section to show that under very general conditions the restriction of linearity implies that the functional can be written explicitly, in terms of the limit of an integral, as found by Hadamard; a Stieltjes integral, as found by F. Riesz; a Lebesgue integral, as rewritten by Lebesgue. Of these forms the first is slightly more general than the others; although here the same hypotheses are used for all three.

We consider a functional

$$T\overset{b}{\underset{a}{[\varphi(x)]}} \tag{5}$$

operating on any function continuous, $a \leq x \leq b$, and assume that the functional is linear, that is, such that:

$$T[c_1\varphi_1 + c_2\varphi_2] = c_1 T[\varphi_1] + c_2 T[\varphi_2], \tag{6}$$

and also that it is continuous in regard to its argument $\varphi$, or what, on account of the postulate of linearity, evidently amounts to the same thing, satisfies a condition of the form:

$$| T[\varphi] | \leq M \overset{b}{\underset{a}{\max}} | \varphi(x) | \tag{7}$$

in which $M$ is some constant.*

There is no gain in generality in considering complex functionals. It may be seen directly that the real and imaginary parts

* The field of functions to which this representation applies is slightly extended by Fréchét, *Transactions of the American Mathematical Society*, vol. 5 (1904), p. 493. Conditions of convergence are also investigated.

of such complex functionals are real linear functionals satisfying similar conditions, and if they are real linear functionals of complex arguments, they are also real linear functionals of real arguments.

Hadamard's representation is as follows:*

THEOREM. *The linear continuous functional $T$ may be written in the form*

$$T[\overset{b}{\underset{a}{\varphi(x)}}] = \lim_{\mu=\infty} \int_a^b \varphi(x)\Psi(x, \mu)dx, \tag{8}$$

*where for a given value of $\mu$ the function $\Psi(x, \mu)$ is continuous in $x$, $a \leqq x \leqq b$, does not involve $\varphi(x)$, and depends merely upon the form of the operation $T$.*

To prove this theorem we take the function†

$$F(x) = \frac{1}{\sqrt{\pi}} e^{-x^2} \tag{9}$$

and form the integral

$$v(x, \mu) = \frac{\mu}{\sqrt{\pi}} \int_a^b \varphi(u) e^{-\mu^2(u-x)^2} du. \tag{10}$$

As is well known, if $\varphi(u)$ is continuous, $a \leqq x \leqq b$, then $v(x, \mu)$ is continuous in $x$ throughout the same interval, for every value of $\mu$, and for that interval approaches $\varphi(x)$ uniformly as a limit, as $\mu$ becomes infinite.

Consider now the quantity $T[v(x, \mu)]$, and in relation with it the quantity

$$\Psi(u, \mu) = T\left[\frac{\mu}{\sqrt{\pi}} e^{-\mu^2(u-x)^2}\right] = T[\mu F\{\mu(u - x)\}], \tag{11}$$

the functional operation still having reference to its argument as a function of $x$, the variable $u$ being a parameter.

We have

$$\sum_1^n \varphi(u_i)\Psi(u_i, \mu)\Delta u = T\left[\sum_1^n \varphi(u_i) \frac{\mu}{\sqrt{\pi}} e^{-\mu^2(u_i-x)^2}\Delta u\right]$$

* Sur les opérations fonctionelles, *Comptes Rendus des Sciences*, vol. 136 (1903), pp. 351–354.

† Instead of this particular function, which is also used in connection with the equation for the flow of heat, other functions may be taken for $F(x)$. The conditions that $F(x)$ must satisfy are given in the citation from Hadamard.

from the linearity property (6). Moreover as $n$ becomes infinite, the sum in the right-hand member of this last equation becomes an integral, and approaches that integral uniformly for all values of $x$. Hence from the continuity property of $T$ it follows that:

$$\int_a^b \varphi(u)\Psi(u, \mu)du = T\left[\frac{\mu}{\sqrt{\pi}}\int_a^b \varphi(u)e^{-\mu^2(u-x)^2}du\right.$$
$$= T[v(x, \mu)].$$

But since $v(x, \mu)$ approaches $\varphi(x)$ uniformly, this gives us

$$T[\overset{b}{\underset{a}{\varphi(x)}}] = \lim_{\mu=\infty}\int_a^b \varphi(u)\Psi(u, \mu)du, \tag{12}$$

where $\Psi(u, \mu)$ depends merely on the form of $T$ and does not involve $\varphi$.

In particular, if we take for $\varphi(x)$ the function

$$\frac{\mu'}{\sqrt{\pi}}e^{-\mu'^2(u-x)^2}$$

we get an identity which is satisfied by the function $\Psi(u, \mu')$, namely

$$\Psi(u, \mu') = \lim_{\mu=\infty}\frac{\mu'}{\sqrt{\pi}}\int_a^b e^{-\mu'^2(u-x)^2}\Psi(x, \mu)dx, \tag{12'}$$

which may also be written in the form

$$\begin{aligned}\lim_{\mu=\infty}\frac{\mu}{\sqrt{\pi}}\int_a^b \Psi(x, \mu')e^{-\mu^2(x-u)^2}dx \\ = \lim_{\mu=\infty}\frac{\mu'}{\sqrt{\pi}}\int_a^b e^{-\mu'^2(u-x)^2}\Psi(x, \mu)dx.\end{aligned} \tag{12''}$$

**38. The Stieltjes Integral.** The theory of the Stieltjes integral is based upon the properties of *functions of finite variation*; i. e., functions $\alpha(x)$ such that if we divide up the given interval $ab$ by points $x_0 = a, x_1, \cdots, x_n, x_{n+1} = b$, arbitrarily spaced, the sum

$$\sum_{i=0}^{n}|\alpha(x_{i+1}) - \alpha(x_i)| \tag{13}$$

for the given function $\alpha(x)$ remains finite, irrespective of the value of $n$. A function of finite variation may be written as the difference of two non-decreasing functions

$$(13') \qquad \alpha(x) = p(x) - n(x),$$

in which, for definiteness, we write $p(a) = \alpha(a)$. If $p(x)$ and $n(x)$ are, for each value of $x$, the least possible functions so definable, the function

$$(14) \qquad t(x) = p(x) - p(a) + n(x)$$

is called the *total variation* of $\alpha(x)$, and is the upper limit of the sum (13) formed for the interval $ax$, instead of the interval $ab$.

We may if we like in (13′) replace the two non-decreasing functions by functions which actually increase without remaining constant in any interval, although for these functions the equation (14) will no longer hold.

On account of (13′) it is immediately seen that the discontinuities which a function of finite variation may have are limited in nature. In fact if $x'$ is a point of discontinuity of $\alpha(x)$, both of the limits $\alpha(x' + 0)$ and $\alpha(x' - 0)$ must exist if $x'$ is an interior point of the interval, and one of them, if $x'$ is an end point of the interval. Moreover, *the number of these so-called discontinuities of the first kind is restricted*; they must be denumerable, though not necessarily countable in some preassigned order, say from left to right.

The number of intervals through which a function may remain constant is restricted in the same way.

By means of a function $\varphi(x)$ which is continuous, and a function $\alpha(x)$ which is of finite variation, in the interval $a \leq x \leq b$, form the expression

$$(15) \qquad \sum_{1}^{n+1}{}_i \varphi(\xi_i)\{\alpha(x_i) - \alpha(x_{i-1})\},$$

where the points $x_i$ are the same as before, and the points $\xi_i$ are arbitrary also except for the restrictions $x_{i-1} \leq \xi_i \leq x_i$. The expression (15) approaches a limit as $n$ becomes infinite, and the maximum sub-interval approaches zero; this limit is called the *Stieltjes integral* and written

$$(15') \qquad \int_a^b \varphi(x)d\alpha(x).$$

The importance of this integral depends upon the ease with which it may be handled, and the directness of its geometric interpretation.

It is not difficult to obtain a measure of convergence of the integral. If $\psi(x)$ is a function such that $|\varphi(x)| \leq \psi(x)$, and if $p(x)$ is a non-decreasing function, we have obviously:

$$\left|\int_a^b \varphi(x)dp(x)\right| \leq \int_a^b |\varphi(x)|dp(x) \leq \int_a^b \psi(x)dp(x).$$

Also,

$$\left|\int_a^b \varphi(x)d\alpha(x) - \sum_1^{n+1}{}_i\varphi(\xi_i)\{\alpha(x_i) - \alpha(x_{i-1})\}\right|$$

$$= \left|\sum_1^{n+1}{}_i\left[\int_{x_{i-1}}^{x_i} \varphi(x)dp(x) - \varphi(\xi_i)\{p(x_i) - p(x_{i-1})\}\right.\right.$$

$$\left.\left. - \int_{x_{i-1}}^{x_i} \varphi(x)dn(x) - \varphi(\xi_i)\{n(x_i) - n(x_{i-1})\}\right]\right|$$

and by the above inequality, this expression is

$$\leq \omega_\delta \sum_1^{n+1}{}_i\{p(x_i) - p(x_{i-1}) + n(x_i) - n(x_{i-1})\},$$

where $\delta$ is the maximum length of any sub-interval, and $\omega_\delta$ is the maximum oscillation of $\varphi(x)$ in any sub-interval. *Hence we have the inequality*

$$(16) \qquad \left|\int_a^b \varphi(x)d\alpha(x) - \sum_1^{n+1}{}_i\varphi(\xi_i)\{\alpha(x_i) - \alpha(x_{i-1})\}\right| \leq \omega_\delta t(b),$$

*in which $t(x)$ represents the total variation of $\alpha(x)$, as a measure of the convergence of the sum* (15) *to the integral* (15').

**39. Regular and Irregular Parts of the Stieltjes Integral.** Consider the integral

$$\int_a^b \varphi(x)dR(x),$$

in which $R(x)$ is an absolutely continuous function of $x$. We may write

$$R(x) - R(a) = \int_a^x r(x)dx,$$

where $r(x)$ is the derivative of $R(x)$ and is summable.

*Under these conditions we have the equation*

$$(17)\qquad \int_a^b \varphi(x)dR(x) = \int_a^b \varphi(x)r(x)dx$$

*the integral in the right-hand member being taken in the sense of Lebesgue.*

To prove this theorem, we make use of the definition of a Stieltjes integral, and write:

$$\int_a^b \varphi(x)d\int_a^x r(x)dx = \lim_{n=\infty} \sum_1^{n+1} {}_i\varphi(\xi_i)\int_{x_{i-1}}^{x_i} r(x)dx = \lim_{n=\infty} \int_a^b \varphi_n(x)r(x)dx,$$

where $\varphi_n(x) = \varphi(\xi_i)$, $x_{i-1} \leqq x < x_i$, and where therefore $\lim_{n=\infty} \varphi_n(x) = \varphi(x)$ uniformly. We now introduce the theorem:*

If the sequence of summable functions $\{f_n(x)\}$ converges as $n$ becomes infinite to a function $f(x)$, and there is a positive summable function $\psi(x)$ which is at least as great as each $|f_n(x)|$, then $f(x)$ will itself be summable, and we shall have the equation:

$$\int_{x_1}^{x_2} f(x)dx = \lim_{n=\infty} \int_{x_1}^{x_2} f_n(x)dx.$$

We take

$$f_n(x) = \varphi_n(x)r(x), \qquad f(x) = \varphi(x)r(x)$$

and notice the inequality

$$|f_n(x)| \leqq \max_a^b |\varphi(x)| \, |r(x)|,$$

in which the right-hand member denotes a summable function. Hence we have the equation

$$\lim_{n=\infty} \int_a^b \varphi_n(x)r(x)dx = \int_a^b \varphi(x)r(x)dx,$$

and the theorem is proved.

Fréchét has given a representation of the integral (15′), in the general case, in terms of a series of discrete terms involving the function $\varphi(x)$ at special points, a Lebesgue integral, and a particular Stieltjes integral involving a function which has a vanishing derivative except at points of a set of measure zero.† The representation is as follows:

THEOREM. *We have*

$$(18)\quad \int_a^b \varphi(x)d\alpha(x) = \sum_{a \leqq x_n \leqq b} A_n\varphi(x_n) + \int_a^b \varphi(x)\beta(x)dx + \int_a^b \varphi(x)d\lambda(x),$$

*where $A_n$ is the jump of $\alpha(x)$ at the point of discontinuity $x_n$, $\beta(x)$ is the derivative of the function $\alpha(x) - \alpha_1(x)$, $\alpha_1(x)$ being given by the definition:*

$$\alpha_1(x) = \sum_{a < x_n \leqq x} \{\alpha(x_n) - \alpha(x_n - 0)\} + \sum_{a \leqq x_n < x} \{\alpha(x_n + 0) - \alpha(x_n)\}, \qquad a < x \leqq b,$$

$$\alpha_1(a) = 0,$$

* De la Vallée-Poussin, *Transactions of the American Mathematical Society*, vol. 16 (1915), p. 447.

† Fréchét, *Comptes rendus du Congrès des Sociétés Savantes tenu à Grenoble* (1913), also *Transactions of the American Mathematical Society*, vol. 15 (1914), p. 152.

*and* $\lambda(x)$ *equals* $\alpha(x) - \alpha_1(x) - \int_a^x \beta(x)dx$, *a continuous function of finite variation which has a null derivative everywhere except at the points of a set of measure zero.*

It may be seen without difficulty that the representation is essentially unique.

In this theorem, the function $\alpha_1(x)$ is called the function of discontinuities. Its discontinuities are precisely the quantities

$$A_n = \alpha(x_n + 0) - \alpha(x_n - 0)$$

and its contribution to the Stieltjes integral constitutes, as may be briefly verified, the first term of the expansion (18). The summation is understood to extend over all the discontinuities $x_n$ indicated, even though these values of $x$ may not be denumerable in the usual order. For $x = a$ no values $x_n$ are included in either summation, and the definition of $\alpha_1(a)$ is therefore necessary.

**40. Representation of a Linear Functional by a Stieltjes Integral.** We may now state the representation given by F. Riesz:

THEOREM. *The linear continuous functional* $T[\varphi]$ *may be written in the form:*

$$T\overset{b}{\underset{a}{[\varphi(x)]}} = \int_a^b \varphi(x)d\alpha(x), \tag{19}$$

*where* $\alpha(x)$ *is a function of finite variation, depending upon the form of* $T$, *but independent of* $\varphi(x)$.

In order to build up the integral (19) it is desirable to extend the field of functions to which the operation $T$ applies. We consider a set of continuous functions $\{f_n(x)\}$, such that for every value of $x$ in $ab$ we have

$$f_1(x) \leq f_2(x) \leq f_3(x) \cdots,$$

and such that for every value of $x$ in $ab$ the quantity

$$\varphi(x) = \lim_{n=\infty} f_n(x)$$

exists. We can show immediately from (7), by considering the absolute convergence of the series

$$T[f_1] + (T[f_2] - T[f_1]) + (T[f_3] - T[f_2]) + \cdots,$$

that $\lim_{n=\infty} T[f_n]$ exists, and we define

$$T[\varphi] = \lim_{n=\infty} T[f_n]. \tag{20}$$

It is necessary to show that this limit is independent of the choice of the sequence of functions $f_n$ which approach $\varphi$.

Let the functions $f_n$ and $g_n$ form two such sequences, and consider with them the sequences $\bar{f}_n = f_n - 1/n$ and $\bar{g}_n = g_n - 1/n$. We have, since $f_n \leqq f_{n+1}$ and $g_n \leqq g_{n+1}$, the inequalities $\bar{f}_n < \bar{f}_{n+1}$, $\bar{g}_n < \bar{g}_{n+1}$, and also, as follows by an obvious calculation:

$$\lim_{n=\infty} T[\bar{f}_n] = \lim_{n=\infty} T[f_n], \qquad \lim_{n=\infty} T[\bar{g}_n] = \lim_{n=\infty} T[g_n].$$

Given $\bar{f}_m$ we can take $n$ great enough so that $\bar{g}_n > \bar{f}_m$. In fact, since $\bar{f}_m$ and $\bar{g}_n$ are continuous functions of $x$, the values of $x$ for which $\bar{g}_n \leqq \bar{f}_m$ form a closed set $E_n$, and $E_{n'}$ is included in $E_n$ if $n' > n$. Hence if we cannot find $n$ great enough so that there are no points in $E_n$, there will be a point $x_0$ such that*

$$\lim_{n=\infty} \bar{g}_n(x_0) \leqq \bar{f}_m(x_0),$$

which is a contradiction, since $\bar{f}_m(x_0) < \varphi(x_0)$.

We can then form a sequence of functions $\bar{f}_{m_1}(x) < \bar{g}_{m_1}(x) < \bar{f}_{m_2}(x) < \bar{g}_{m_2}(x) \cdots$, approaching $\varphi(x)$ as a limit. If we form the functional $T$ for this sequence, it will approach a limit which cannot be different from $\lim_{n=\infty} T[\bar{f}_n]$ or $\lim_{n=\infty} T[\bar{g}_n]$ and will therefore be the functional $T[\varphi]$ already defined.

The functional $T$ is linear in these functions, i. e.,

$$T[c_1\varphi_1 + c_2\varphi_2] = c_1 T[\varphi_1] + c_2 T[\varphi_2]$$

if $c_1$ and $c_2$ are restricted to positive constants. In order to make $T$ completely distributive we need to define

$$(21) \qquad T[\varphi_1 - \varphi_2] = T[\varphi_1] - T[\varphi_2],$$

a definition whose uniqueness is directly verifiable. We should however prove also the inequality (7):

$$| T[\varphi_1 - \varphi_2] | \leqq M \max_a^b | \varphi_1 - \varphi_2 |.$$

* If we have a sequence of point sets, each contained in the preceding, and none of them a null set, then there will be a point common to all of them, provided they are all closed sets.

Let us denote max $|\varphi_1 - \varphi_2|$ by $G$, and let $f_n$ and $g_n$ be two sequences which have as limits $\varphi_1$ and $\varphi_2$ respectively. Define a new function $h_n$ as follows:

$$
\begin{aligned}
&h_n(x) = f_n(x) && \text{wherever} && |f_n(x) - g_n(x)| \leq G, \\
(22)\quad &h_n(x) = g_n(x) + G && \text{wherever} && f_n - g_n > G, \\
&h_n(x) = g_n(x) - G && \text{wherever} && g_n - f_n > G.
\end{aligned}
$$

By this definition we have, as may be directly verified,

$$h_{n+1}(x) \geq h_n(x)$$

and also

$$\lim_{n=\infty} h_n(x) = \varphi_1(x).$$

We have however by the definition (21):

$$
\begin{aligned}
|T[\varphi_1 - \varphi_2]| &= \lim_{n=\infty} |T[f_n] - T[g_n]| \\
&= \lim_{n=\infty} |T[h_n - g_n]|
\end{aligned}
$$

which by (22) is $\leq MG$.

Our field as now extended is such that if $\varphi_1, \cdots, \varphi_k$ belong to it, any linear combination of them will belong to it, and will satisfy the inequality (7). With this, we are in a position to construct the Stieltjes integral.

The function which is unity in the sub-interval $c < x < h$, and zero otherwise, is the limit of a sequence of continuous functions $f_n(x)$, increasing with $n$. Hence the function

$$
(23)\quad
\begin{aligned}
f_{cd} &= 1, && c < x \leq d \qquad (c > a), \\
&= 0, && \text{otherwise},
\end{aligned}
$$

is the difference of two such functions, and therefore a member of the field of definition of the functional $T$. The function which we denote by $f_{ad}$ and define as:

$$
(23')\quad
\begin{aligned}
f_{ad} &= 1, && a \leq x \leq d, \\
&= 0, && \text{otherwise},
\end{aligned}
$$

is the limit of a decreasing sequence, and is also of the field of $T$.

The function $\alpha(x)$ defined by the equations

$$(24)\qquad \begin{aligned} \alpha(a) &= 0, \\ \alpha(x) &= T[f_{ax}], \qquad x \neq a, \end{aligned}$$

is a function of limited variation; for, from the equation

$$\sum_{1}^{n+1}{}_i \left| \alpha(x_i) - \alpha(x_{i-1}) \right| = \sum_{1}^{n} \left| T[f_{x_{i-1}x_i}] \right|$$

and the inequality (7), it follows that

$$\sum_{1}^{n+1}{}_i \left| \alpha(x_i) - \alpha(x_{i-1}) \right| \leqq M.$$

In order to form $T[\varphi(x)]$ we build up the continuous function $\varphi(x)$ out of the functions $f_{cd}$, and define

$$\varphi_n(x) = \sum_{1}^{n+1} \varphi(\xi_i) f_{x_{i-1}x_i}(x),$$

which is a member of the field of $T$, and approaches $\varphi(x)$ uniformly as $n$ becomes infinite, for $a \leqq x \leqq b$. Hence

$$T[\varphi(x)] = \lim_{n=\infty} T[\varphi_n(x)].$$

But

$$T[\varphi_n] = \sum_{1}^{n+1}{}_i \varphi(\xi_i)[\alpha(x_i) - \alpha(x_{i-1})],$$

and therefore, from the definition of a Stieltjes integral, we get (19).

**41. Representation of $T[\varphi]$ as a Lebesgue Integral.** Not only is it possible to split up the Stieltjes integral into three parts, of which the middle term is a Lebesgue integral of simple form, but also, as Lebesgue himself has shown, the Stieltjes integral can as a whole be replaced by a single Lebesgue integral, thus getting an essentially new representation of the linear functional. Although the representation loses in directness, it gains in the extension of the field of functions to which it may be applied.

In order to make this transformation it is necessary to make a change of independent variable which will smooth out the discontinuities in $\alpha(x)$, leaving it everywhere the integral of its derivative function. And in removing the discontinuities, gaps are created which it is necessary to fill by more or less artificial definitions of the functions involved in the integrand.

Following Lebesgue we make the transformation

$$t = t(x),$$

where $t(x)$ is the total variation function of $\alpha(x)$. In order to make the inverse of this function single valued, we must make a special definition of $x(t)$ in the intervals where $\alpha(x)$, and therefore $t(x)$, is constant. If $t(x)$ has the value $t_0$ in an interval $lm$, we take as $x(t_0)$, only one of the values in $lm$, say $l$, the least value. We thus make $\varphi(x(t))$ discontinuous at a denumerable infinity of points.

If $t(x)$ is discontinuous for a certain value of $x$, say $x = x_n$, $x(t)$ will not be defined in the interval $\{t(x_n - 0),\ t(x_n + 0)\}$ except for the value $t(x_n)$. Throughout the whole of this interval we write

$$x(t) = x_n$$

$$\varphi(x(t)) = \varphi(x_n),$$

and define $\alpha(x(t))$ as a linear function of $t$ in the partial intervals

$$\{t(x_n - 0),\ t(x_n)\}, \qquad \{t(x_n),\ t(x_n + 0)\},$$

thus obtaining a continuous function $\gamma(t)$ of $t$, for which

$$\int_a^b \varphi(x)d\alpha(x) = \int_0^{t(b)} \varphi(x(t))d\gamma(t), \tag{25}$$

as a direct inspection of the limiting sums will show.*

The function $\gamma(t)$ is still a function of limited variation, and possesses therefore a finite derivative $\theta(t)$, except at the points of a set of zero measure, integrable in the Lebesgue sense, considered at the points where it is finite. Moreover the total variation of $\gamma(t)$ in an interval 0 is $t$ itself, and therefore $\gamma(t)$ is an absolutely continuous function of $t$. Hence it is itself the integral of $\theta(t)$,

$$\int_0^t \theta(t)dt = \gamma(t),$$

and an application of the first theorem of Art. 39 yields the result

$$\int_0^{t(b)} \varphi(x(t))d\gamma(t) = \int_0^{t(b)} \varphi(x(t))\theta(t)dt. \tag{26}$$

The function $\theta(t)$ takes on merely the values $+ 1$ and $- 1$.

We have then Lebesgue's result:

Theorem. *The linear continuous functional $T[\varphi]$ may be written in the form*

$$T[\overset{b}{\underset{a}{\varphi(x)}}] = \int_0^{t(b)} \varphi(x(t))\theta(t)dt, \tag{27}$$

*where $x(t)$ and $\theta(t)$ are functions depending only on the form of $T$, but independent of the argument $\varphi$. The function $\theta(t)$ takes on merely the values $+ 1$ and $- 1$, and $x(t)$ is a non-decreasing, but not necessarily continuous function of $t$.*

The transformation, just described, may be carried through in various ways, such as by writing $\alpha(x)$ as the difference of two non-decreasing functions. More general transformations of this kind exist which have no special reference

* This involves, on account of the discontinuities of $\varphi(x(t))$, a slight, but obvious extension of the definition of the Stieltjes integral, $\gamma(t)$ being continuous.

to a function of finite variation, but deal with the parametric representation of a continuous curve.*

In this respect, the present case corresponds to that where the curve is rectifiable.

The equation (27) provides for a further generalization of the linear operation $T$. We have already seen, in F. Riesz's representation, that if the functional $T$ applies to all continuous functions it also applies to certain discontinuous functions which can be built up from the limits of increasing sequences of functions. Lebesgue notices that the right-hand member of (27) is defined and distributive when $\varphi$ is any limited summable function, providing thus an extension of the field of definition of $T[\varphi]$; moreover that the representation has the property:

$$\lim_{n=\infty} \int_a^b \varphi_n(x(t))\theta(t)dt = \int_a^b \varphi(x(t))\theta(t)dt$$

if the functions $\varphi_n(x)$ are summable and limited in their set, and

$$\varphi(x) = \lim_{n=\infty} \varphi_n(x).$$

The equation (27) may therefore be used to provide an extension of the definition of the Stieltjes integral to the case where the integrand $\varphi(x)$ is limited and summable, an extension which however departs from the geometric interpretation.†

Direct extensions of the field and the analysis of the Stieltjes integral have been given by Radon, *Wiener Sitzungsberichte*, vol. 122 (1913), pp. 1295–1438, and by Daniell, *Bulletin of the American Mathematical Society*, vol. 23 (1917), p. 211.

## § 3. The Linear Functional for Restricted Fields

**42. Continuity of Order $k$.** In general, the more limited the field of the functional $T[\varphi]$, the more unrestricted may be the character of the operation $T$ itself; and vice versa. We may, for instance, expect to find functionals which apply only to analytic functions. On the other hand, functionals which apply to a certain field may by definition, as we have already seen, sometimes be extended to more general fields.

We say that a functional $\Phi[\varphi]$ has continuity of order $k$, if, when the argument $\varphi$ is continuous with its first $k$ derivatives,

* Jackson, *Bulletin of the American Mathematical Society*, vol. 24 (1917), p. 77; see also Fréchét, Thèse, Note 1, *Rendiconti del Circolo Matematico di Palermo*, vol. 22 (1906), pp. 1–74.

† Integrals somewhat analogous in form to the Stieltjes integral have been treated by Hellinger, Dissertation, Göttingen (1907), Habilitationschrift, *Journal für Mathematik*, vol. 136; H. Hahn, *Monatshefte der Mathematik und Physik*, vol. 23 (1912), p. 161.

the increment of $\Phi[\varphi]$ can be made to approach zero, by making the increment of $\varphi$ together with its first $k$ derivatives approach zero uniformly and simultaneously; that is, we can make

$$|\Phi[\varphi + \theta] - \Phi[\varphi]| < \epsilon$$

by taking

$$|\theta(x)| < \eta, \cdots, |\theta^{(k)}(x)| < \eta.$$

The usual continuity is of order zero, and the forms of $T[\varphi]$ already obtained are deduced by processes valid only under this hypothesis.

A brief examination suffices to show that we cannot extend functionals which have continuity merely of order $k$, by definition over other fields so that they have continuity of order less than $k$; thus if $T[y] = dy/dx$, $T[y]$ will become infinite with $dy/dx$, and therefore cannot be applied to functionals which are merely the uniform limits of functions continuous with continuous first derivatives. The functionals used so extensively in Lecture I are not in general special cases of those treated in § 2.

**43. The Linear Functional, Continuous of Order $k$.** An explicit formula for a functional which has continuity merely of order $k$ has been given lately by Fischer.* He points out that if $\varphi(x)$ is of class $k$ it can be written in the form

$$\varphi(x) = \int_a^x dx_1 \int_a^{x_1} dx_2 \cdots \int_a^{x_{k-1}} \varphi^{(k)}(x_k)dx_k + \sum_{i=1}^{k} \frac{\varphi^{(k-i)}(a)}{(k-i)!}(x-a)^{k-i}, \tag{28}$$

and if $T[\varphi]$ is linear it will consequently have the form:

$$T[\overset{b}{\underset{a}{\varphi}}] = T_k[\overset{b}{\underset{a}{\varphi^{(k)}(x)}}] + \sum_1^k \frac{\varphi^{(k-i)}(a)}{(k-i)!} T[(\overset{b}{\underset{a}{x}} - a)^{k-i}], \tag{29}$$

where the functional

$$T_k[\overset{b}{\underset{a}{\varphi^k(x)}}] = T \int_a^x dx_1 \cdots \int_a^{x_{k-1}} \varphi^{(k)}(x_k)dx_k]$$

* Fischer, *Bulletin of the American Mathematical Society*, vol. 23 (1916), pp. 88–90. An extension to functionals of surfaces is also given.

is linear and continuous of the zeroth order in its argument $\varphi^{(k)}(x)$, and the $T[\overset{b}{\underset{a}{(x}} - a)^{k-i}]$, $i = 1, 2, \cdots$, are certain constants. Conversely, any functional of the form

$$(30) \qquad T_k[\varphi^{(k)}(x)] + \sum_{1}^{k} A_i\varphi^{(k-i)}(a) = T[\varphi(\overset{b}{\underset{a}{x}})]$$

where $T_k$ has continuity of order zero in its argument, and the $A_i$ are arbitrary constants, has continuity of order $k$. There is however no reason for preferring the point $a$ over the point $b$ or over any interior point.

A more natural form, obviously redundant, but possibly useful, is the following:

$$(31) \qquad T[\varphi(\overset{b}{\underset{a}{x}})] = \sum_{i=0}^{k} T_i[\varphi^{(i)}(\overset{b}{\underset{a}{x}})],$$

in which each of the functionals $T_i[\varphi^{(i)}(x)]$ has continuity of order zero.

An interesting form is also obtained by consideration of Hadamard's representation. By a proper choice of $\Psi(x, \mu)$ various particular functionals may be obtained with continuity of assigned order—for instance the representation of $\varphi^{(k)}(x)$. The functional represented depends upon the manner of convergence of the integral to its limit as $\mu$ becomes infinite, and what conditions must be imposed on $\varphi(x)$ to insure that convergence. It is therefore desirable to remove, if possible, the condition of continuity of order zero, which was used in the deduction of (8).

If $T[\varphi]$ has continuity merely of order $k$, it may be written as:

$$(32) \qquad T[\varphi(\overset{b}{\underset{a}{x}})] = \lim_{n=\infty} \int_{a-\epsilon}^{b+\epsilon} \varphi(x)P(x, n)dx,$$

where $\varphi(x)$ is extended continuously with its first $k$ derivatives beyond the interval $ab$ to the interval $\{a - \epsilon, b + \epsilon\}$, $\epsilon$ being a quantity arbitrarily small, and positive. For $P(u, n)$ we may take the function

$$\Psi(u, n) = T\left[\frac{n}{\sqrt{\pi}} e^{-n^2(u-x)^2}\right]$$

of Hadamard, and show that $v(x, n)$ approaches $\varphi(x)$ with its first $k$ derivatives, as $n$ becomes infinite, uniformly for $x$ in $ab$, or we can take such a function as

$$P(u, n) = \sqrt{\frac{n}{\pi}}\ \overset{b}{\underset{a}{T}}[\{1 - (u - x)^2\}^n],$$

and make use of the familiar theorems for polynomial approximation.*

## § 4. Volterra's Theorem for Implicit Functional Equations

**44. The Differential of a Functional.** Form the expression

$$(33) \qquad \Delta F = F[\varphi + \Delta F] - F[\varphi],$$

where the functional $F[\varphi]$ is continuous in its argument $\varphi(x)$. According to Fréchét,† the differential of $F$ for a given $\varphi$ is a linear functional $T[\Delta\varphi]$ of the arbitrary continuous increment $\Delta\varphi$ of $\varphi$, such that the inequality

$$(34) \qquad |\Delta F - T[\Delta\varphi]| < \epsilon \max_a^b |\Delta\varphi|$$

is satisfied. The quantity $\epsilon$ in (34) is assumed to approach zero with $\max |\Delta\varphi|$.

If for a given function $\varphi$ no linear functional $T[\Delta\varphi]$ can be found to satisfy (34), $F[\varphi]$ does not have a differential for the function $\varphi$. From (34) and the linearity of $T$, it follows that $T$ must be a continuous functional of its argument $\Delta\varphi$. Hence $T[\Delta\varphi]$ must be expressible in terms of the formulæ developed in § 2.‡ We shall consider in what follows only particular cases of those general expressions.

* De la Vallée-Poussin, Traité d'analyse infinitésimale, vol. II, Paris (1912), p. 132.

† *Transactions of the American Mathematical Society*, vol. 15 (1914), p. 139.

‡ If $F[\varphi]$ has continuity merely of order $k$, we restrict $\Delta\varphi$ to functions which approach zero uniformly, together with their first $k$ derivatives. It follows that the linear functional $T[\Delta\varphi]$ has continuity of order $k$, and it will therefore be expressible according to the formulæ of § 3.

**45. Volterra's Theorem.** Volterra considers the functional equation

$$H[\overset{b}{\underset{a}{\varphi(s)}}, \overset{b}{\underset{a}{f(s)}} \,|\, x] = 0, \tag{35}$$

in which the left-hand member is continuous in its three arguments, namely, the functions $\varphi$ and $\psi$ and the parameter $x$; the equation is assumed to be satisfied by the function $\varphi(x) = 0$, when $f(x)$ is itself put identically equal to zero, and the problem is to determine $\varphi(x)$ in terms of $f(x)$ in the functional neighborhood of $f = 0$, $\varphi = 0$, that is, in the neighborhood $|f(x)| < N$, $|\varphi(x)| < N$, $N$ small enough.

To take the definite case considered by Volterra, let the differential of $H$ due to a change of $\varphi$ alone be given by the special formula

$$d_\phi H = \Delta\varphi(x) - \int_a^b H_\phi[\overset{b}{\underset{a}{\varphi(s)}}, \overset{b}{\underset{a}{f(s)}} \,|\, x, x']\Delta\varphi(x')dx', \tag{36}$$

where

$$|\Delta_\phi H - d_\phi H| < \epsilon \max_a^b |\Delta\varphi(x)|, \tag{37}$$

and $H_\phi[\varphi, f|x, x']$ is limited and continuous with respect to its four arguments; and let (36) take on the form

$$d_\phi H = \Delta\varphi(x) - \int_a^b G(xx')\Delta\varphi(x')dx', \tag{38}$$

when $f$ and $\varphi$ are made to vanish identically.

THEOREM. *In the given neighborhood for $\varphi$ and $f$, and the given interval for $x$, let $H[\varphi, f|x]$ have a differential of form* (36) *where*

*(i) the quantity $\epsilon$ in* (37) *approaches zero with* max $|\varphi(x)|$ *uniformly for all functions $\varphi$, $f$ and all values $x$ in the domain considered, and*

*(ii) the Fredholm determinant of the kernel $G(xx')$ in* (38) *is unequal to zero.**

*Then there is a neighborhood of $f = 0$, $\varphi = 0$, namely, $\{|f| \leq N'$, $|\varphi| \leq N'\}$, $N'$ some value $\leq N$, in which* (35) *has one and only one solution $\varphi(x)$ for a given continuous function $f(x)$.*

The proof of this theorem is not difficult. Write (35) in the form

* That is, unity is not a characteristic value for the kernel $G(x, x')$.

$$\varphi(x) - \int_a^b G(xx')\varphi(x')dx' \tag{39}$$
$$= \varphi(x) - \int_a^b G(xx')\varphi(x')dx' - H[\varphi, f|x]$$

and denote the right-hand member by $\Theta[\varphi, f|x]$. The differential of $\Theta$,

$$d_\phi\Theta[\varphi, f|x] = -\int_a^b \{G(xx') - H_\phi[\varphi, f|xx']\}\Delta\varphi(x')dx', \tag{39'}$$

may be written for brevity in the form

$$\int_a^b R[\varphi, f|xx']\Delta\varphi(x')dx',$$

and satisfies the inequality

$$|\Delta_\phi\Theta - d_\phi\Theta| < \epsilon \max_a^b |\Delta\varphi(x)|,$$

where the $\epsilon$ is the $\epsilon$ of (37).

Equation (39) may be taken as an integral equation in $\varphi(x)$, the right-hand member being regarded for the moment as a known function of $x$. It yields then the result

$$\varphi(x) = \Phi[\varphi, f|x] \tag{40}$$

where

$$\Phi[\varphi, f|x] = \Theta[\varphi, f|x] - \int_a^b \Gamma(xx')\Theta[\varphi, f|x']dx', \tag{40'}$$

and $\Gamma(xx')$ is the kernel resolvent for $G(xx')$. Moreover, we can deduce (39) from (40) by the resolution of the inverse integral equation, so that (39) and (40) are fully equivalent. Equation (40) is however of the form of (1) Art. 1, and satisfies the conditions there imposed.

We have in fact for $d_\phi\Phi$ the formula

$$d_\phi\Phi = \int_a^b dx'\Delta\varphi(x')\{R[\varphi, f|xx'] \tag{41}$$
$$- \int_a^b \Gamma(x, x'')R[\varphi, f|x''x']dx''\}$$

and for $\Delta_\phi\Phi$ the inequality

$$|\Delta_\phi\Phi - d_\phi\Phi| < \epsilon \max_a^b |\Delta\varphi(x)|\{1 + \int_a^b |\Gamma(xx')|dx'\},$$

since $\Phi$ is itself linear in $\Theta$. This yields the inequality

$$(41') \qquad |\Delta_\phi \Phi - d_\phi \Phi| < \eta \max_a^b |\Delta\varphi(x)|,$$

where $\eta$ approaches zero with $\max |\Delta\varphi(x)|$, uniformly for all functions $\varphi, f$ and all values $x$ in the domain considered.

The functional $R[\varphi, f|xx']$ can be made uniformly as small as we please by restricting $\varphi$ and $f$ to a neighborhood (say $< M'$) small enough; and therefore by taking a proper value of $M'$, the restriction

$$|R[\varphi f|xx']| + \int_a^b |\Gamma(xx'')R[\varphi f|x''x']|dx' < \frac{r}{b-a}$$

will hold, where $r$ is given arbitrarily in advance, and this, with the aid of (41) and (41′), yields the inequality

$$(42) \qquad \Delta_\phi \Phi < (r + \eta) \max_a^b |\Delta\varphi(x)|.$$

Let $M''$ be small enough so that if $\max |\Delta\varphi| \leq M''$, $\eta$ will be less than $\frac{1}{2}$, let $M'$ be small enough so that $r < \frac{1}{2}$, and take $N''$ as the smaller of the two numbers $M'$, $M''/2$ (so that if $|\varphi_1|$ and $|\varphi_2|$ are $< N''$, their difference may be less than $M''$).

For a given function $f(x)$, the class $L$ of the theorem of Art. 1 is defined as the totality of continuous functions $\varphi(x)$ for which

$$(42'') \qquad |\varphi(x) - \Phi[0, f|x]| \leq N''.$$

In virtue of (42), since $r + \eta < 1$, both (*i*) and (*ii*) of Art. 1 will be satisfied, and there will be one and only one continuous function $\varphi(x)$ which for a given $f(x)$ satisfies the equation (35).

If we introduce $N'$, taking $N' < N''/2$, the neighborhood specified in the enunciation of Volterra's theorem will be such that (42″) is satisfied, and the theorem will be proved.

This is not of course the only possible theorem on the solution of implicit functional equations. More general theorems may be obtained, and other particular theorems also, depending upon what form we assume for the quantity $d_\phi H$ in (36), and what the solution of the resulting linear integral equation may be.*

* Certain forms of these linear equations are considered in Lecture V.

# LECTURE IV

## INTEGRO-DIFFERENTIAL EQUATIONS OF THE BÔCHER TYPE*

### § 1. THE GENERALIZATION OF LAPLACE'S EQUATION

**46. Hypothetical Experiments as a Basis of Physics.** It is regarded as experimental knowledge that in a dielectric the field of force due to electric charges, distributed arbitrarily, is conservative; and also that the total electric induction over a closed surface in a dielectric is $4\pi$ multiplied into the charge of electricity inside the surface. In what sense are these laws experimental? Obviously no experiment has ever yet been performed in which the total work was null; and no measurements upon total induction could be taken with such accuracy as to fix the multiplicative factor absolutely as $4\pi$, or even to show that it was constant.

And yet these laws are not entirely the results of more general laws of nature, nor are they implied wholly in definitions of such things as " charge," " dielectric," etc. It was only after Coulomb had made his direct (and inaccurate) experiments that he was able to state the proposition: that two point charges $m$ and $m'$ repel each other with a force $mm'/r^2$. At least in some way therefore, although there are no such things as point charges, Coulomb's law is an experimental law.

The characteristic terms of physics—point charges, electric density, dielectrics, conductors,—are as ideal as the points, lines, and numbers of pure mathematics. The basic laws of any branch of physics are stated as hypothetical experiments carried out upon these ideal elements; e. g., " if two point charges are at

* This lecture is based on the following references:

M. Bôcher, On harmonic functions in two dimensions, *Proceedings of the American Academy of Science*, vol. 41 (1905–06).

G. C. Evans, On the reduction of integro-differential equations, *Transactions of the American Mathematical Society*, vol. 15 (1914), pp. 477–496;

Sul calcolo della funzione di Green, *Rendiconti della R. Accademia dei Lincei*, vol. 22 (1913), first semester, pp. 855–860.

C. W. Oseen; cf. p. 136, note.

distance $r$ and have masses of electricity $m$ and $m'$, they will repel each other with a force $mm'/r^2$." The characteristic elements are suggested by approximately invariant processes in phenomena, and the postulates which frame the hypothetical experiments are arrived at by a process of successive approximation in the carrying out of actual experiments: "If charges of masses $m$ and $m'$ are concentrated on smaller and smaller pith balls, the force of repulsion can be made as near $mm'/r^2$ as the accuracy of measurement will allow." This is the same sort of experimentation which justifies the postulate of parallels, and distinguishes between Euclidean and Non-euclidean spaces, as far at least as this distinction, even in actual space, is not a matter of the definition of characteristic elements.

In order to make satisfactory any branch of theoretical physics, the basic elements should be chosen, and hypothetical experiments given in scope sufficient to determine completely the properties of those elements. The results of these experiments, stated as postulates, should be sufficient to develop, by their logical combination, all the details of the subject. In other words, *in the mathematical treatment of the subject there should be no new elements introduced, or new properties made use of.*

In some cases, this general proposition suggests an immediate modification of the existing theory. To take an example, in the theory of electricity, the potential and its first derivatives correspond to possible physical elements, namely, work and force; also certain differential parameters of the second order, such as the Laplacian of the potential, have physical interpretation in terms of electric density, etc.; but in order to introduce the second partial derivatives, by themselves, we must make new hypotheses sufficient to insure their existence. These hypotheses, however, are not the results of hypothetical experiments and have apparently no physical meaning inherent in the subject itself. To show the existence of the second derivative of $\int\int\int f/r dxdydz$ it is necessary to demand more than the mere integrability, or even continuity, of $f(xyz)$.

This difficulty disappears if instead of considering the differential equations, which are the results of limiting processes and involve assumptions about the existence of the limits, we consider the equations which express in integral form the results of our experiments. Thus, the equations

$$(1) \qquad \int_C \varphi_s ds = 0,$$

$$(2) \qquad \int\int \varphi_n d\sigma = \int\int\int f(xyz) dS,$$

$\varphi$ being a vector point function, represent the postulate of a conservative field of force, and the law of total induction in a medium of inductivity unity. The usual process is to pass from (1) and (2) to the consideration of Poisson's equation.

**47. Bôcher's Treatment of Laplace's Equation.** Professor Bôcher considers the relation

$$(3) \qquad \int_C \frac{\partial u(xy)}{\partial n} ds = 0,$$

assumed to hold merely for all circles within a given two dimensional region, and shows that when we assume merely the existence and continuity of $u$ and its first derivatives, the equation is nevertheless entirely equivalent to Laplace's equation provided that the region is restricted to that of the customary analysis (that is, one in which analytic continuation is possible; called by Borel, a Weierstrass region). By means of a two-way evaluation of the double integral

$$(3') \qquad \int\int \frac{1}{r} \frac{\partial u}{\partial r} d\sigma = \int\int \frac{\partial u}{\partial r} dr d\theta$$

extended over the interior of the circle, we can pass directly from (3) to the mean value theorem*

$$(3'') \qquad u_0 = \frac{1}{2\pi} \int_0^{2\pi} u d\theta.$$

In this way the uniqueness of the solution of (3) for given continuous boundary values on a closed curve is easily established.

* Bôcher, *Bulletin of the American Mathematical Society*, (2), 1 (1895), p. 205.

In fact, suppose that $u_1(xy)$ and $u_2(xy)$ were two functions which on the regular boundary of a simply connected region took on continuously the same values $h(M)$, and satisfied, for every circle contained within that region, the equation (3). Then their difference would also satisfy (3), and take on zero values on the boundary. This would imply, if the difference were not identically zero, that at some point $P$, in the interior, it would have a positive maximum or a negative minimum value. But if this point $P$ were surrounded by a circle small enough to lie entirely within the region, the value at $P$ would not be the mean of the values on the circumference. Therefore the value of the difference must be identically zero.

On the other hand, as is well known, there is a harmonic function $\bar{u}(x, y)$ which takes on the given boundary values $h(M)$; since it is harmonic, however, it satisfies the equation (3). The unique solution of (3) must therefore be harmonic: its second derivatives must exist at all interior points, and the equation

$$\frac{\partial^2 u}{\partial x^2} + \frac{\partial^2 u}{\partial y^2} = 0$$

must be satisfied. The equation (3), then, throughout regions in which $u$, $\partial u/\partial x$ and $\partial u/\partial y$ are continuous defines the same class of functions as that defined by Laplace's equation.

I have called equations of the type of (3) *integro-differential equations of Bôcher type.* This lecture is devoted to the treatment of the general equation of that type involving derivatives of the first order, corresponding therefore to the general linear partial differential equation of the second order: in the general equation, unlike the case of (3), the second derivatives will not even exist.

**48. Poisson's Equation.** If we write down the equations (1) and (2) for two dimensions, the first one tells us that there is a function

$$(4) \qquad u(xy) = \int_{(x_0y_0)}^{(x,\,y)} \varphi_s ds$$

such that $\partial u/\partial s$ is $\varphi_s$. The second equation thereupon gives us the relation

$$\int_C \frac{\partial u}{\partial n} ds = \int\int f(xy) dx dy \tag{5}$$

for an arbitrary contour $C$ in the given region. Equation (5) corresponds to Poisson's equation

$$\frac{\partial^2 u}{\partial x^2} + \frac{\partial^2 u}{\partial y^2} = - f(xy). \tag{6}$$

The latter has in general no solution if $f(xy)$ is merely continuous; the former however has one, and it is uniquely determined by given continuous boundary values. The uniqueness of the solution comes from the fact that the difference of two solutions of (5) is a solution of (3). The existence of the solution is demonstrated by showing that the function

$$\frac{1}{2\pi} \int\int g(xy|x'y') f(x'y') dx'dy'$$

where $g(xy|x'y')$ represents the usual Green's function for Laplace's equation, satisfies (5) and takes on null boundary values. This function then, plus the harmonic function which takes on the desired boundary values, will be the desired unique solution of (5).

The equation (5), and the corresponding equation for three dimensions

$$\int\int \frac{\partial u}{\partial n} d\sigma = \int\int\int f(xyz) dx dy dz, \tag{7}$$

may also be treated by a direct generalization of Bôcher's method of double integration, considering orthogonal systems of curves, and the expression of the integral in curvilinear co-ordinates, in case we do not restrict the closed surfaces of integration in (7) to spheres. The integration over the enclosed volume may be expressed as the iteration of a surface and a simple integral, and performed in two ways. In the case where spheres are used the element of surface integration is the solid angle; in the case where the closed surface in (7) is unrestricted, the element of surface integration is a functional of closed curves on that surface which bears to the function $\varphi(xyz) = c$, which defines the family of surfaces corresponding to the concentric spheres, a relation which is the generalization of the relation, in two dimensions, between a harmonic function and its conjugate; viz., the flux of the functional is the gradient of $\varphi$. This relation, holding between a harmonic function, which defines a family of isothermal surfaces, and a certain functional of curves on those surfaces, has been treated in a different connection by Volterra.* It has nothing to do with the relation between the real and imaginary parts of the functionals of Lecture II, although it is in one direction a generalization of the properties of analytic functions.

Rather than follow through this analysis we shall turn to the more generally applicable method of Green's theorem.

## § 2. Green's Theorem for the General Linear Integro-Differential Equation of Bôcher Type

**49. Adjoint Integro-Differential Equations.** We shall consider the integro-differential expression

$$(8)\quad \Lambda[C, u_s] = \int_C \left\{ \alpha_{11}\frac{\partial u}{\partial x} + \alpha_{12}\frac{\partial u}{\partial y} + \alpha_1 u \right\} dy - \left\{ \alpha_{21}\frac{\partial u}{\partial x} + \alpha_{22}\frac{\partial u}{\partial y} + \alpha_2 u \right\} dx,$$

and form the equation

$$(9)\qquad \Lambda[C|u_s] = \iint_\sigma (f - \alpha u)dxdy,$$

where $\sigma$ is the area enclosed by $C$. In case derivatives of sufficient order exist of $u$, and of the coefficients $\alpha_{ij}$, $\alpha_i$, $\alpha$, the equation (9) may be written as a partial differential equation; namely

$$(9')\quad a_{11}\frac{\partial^2 u}{\partial x^2} + 2a_{12}\frac{\partial^2 u}{\partial x \partial y} + a_{22}\frac{\partial^2 u}{\partial y^2} + a_1\frac{\partial u}{\partial x} + a_2\frac{\partial u}{\partial y} + au = f,$$

* Volterra, Leçons sur l'intégration des équations différentielles aux dérivées partielles; professées à Stockholm, Paris (Reprint 1912).

in which the coefficients are defined by the equations

$$a_{11} = \alpha_{11}, \qquad a_{22} = \alpha_{22}, \qquad 2a_{12} = \alpha_{12} + \alpha_{21},$$

$$(9'') \quad a_1 = \frac{\partial \alpha_{11}}{\partial x} + \frac{\partial \alpha_{21}}{\partial y} + \alpha_1, \qquad a_2 = \frac{\partial \alpha_{12}}{\partial x} + \frac{\partial \alpha_{22}}{\partial y} + \alpha_2,$$

$$a = \frac{\partial \alpha_1}{\partial x} + \frac{\partial \alpha_2}{\partial y} + \alpha.$$

Additional derivatives would be involved in the definition of the adjoint expression to (9′). The assumptions we shall use are, however, given below.

With (8) and (9) we consider the expression

$$(10) \quad \Gamma[C, v_s] = \int_C \left\{ \beta_{11} \frac{\partial v}{\partial x} + \beta_{12} \frac{\partial v}{\partial y} + \beta_1 v \right\} dy - \left\{ \beta_{21} \frac{\partial v}{\partial x} + \beta_{22} \frac{\partial v}{\partial y} + \beta_2 v \right\} dx$$

and *the equation*

$$(11) \qquad \Gamma[C, v_s] = \int\int_\sigma (g - \beta v) dx dy$$

*which we call the adjoint of* (9), *provided that the relations*

$$(12) \qquad \begin{aligned} \beta_{ij} &= \alpha_{ji}, \qquad i, j = 1, 2, \\ \beta_i &= -\alpha_i, \qquad i = 1, 2, \\ \beta &= \alpha + \frac{\partial \alpha_1}{\partial x} + \frac{\partial \alpha_2}{\partial y}, \end{aligned}$$

*are satisfied.* If the last of these equations is written in the symmetrical form

$$(12') \qquad 2\alpha + \frac{\partial \alpha_1}{\partial x} + \frac{\partial \alpha_2}{\partial y} = 2\beta + \frac{\partial \beta_1}{\partial x} + \frac{\partial \beta_2}{\partial y},$$

it is seen at once that the relation between an equation and its adjoint is symmetrical: if (11) is the adjoint of (9) then (9) is the adjoint of (11).

The curve $C$ is to be restricted to what may be called a *standard curve.* A standard curve is a closed curve which does not cut itself at any point, composed of a finite number of portions; for each portion, the co-ordinates of any point are given by two functions $\varphi(q)$ and $\psi(q)$, throughout a finite interval for a parameter $q$; the functions $\varphi(q)$ and $\psi(q)$ are assumed to be continuous throughout the closed interval, and therefore finite, with their derivatives of the first order. It is assumed that $\varphi'(q)$ and $\psi'(q)$ vanish only at a finite number of points unless they vanish identically, and do not both vanish at the same value of $q$. Hence no line parallel to either of the axes can cut the curve in more than a finite number of points, unless it includes itself a portion of the curve.

A standard curve *approaches a point P uniformly*, if, given an arbitrarily small circle with center at $P$, the curve comes and remains within that circle.

We consider a simply connected region $\Sigma$ and assume that at every point of it, the functions $u$, $v$ and their first partial derivatives, also $f$, $g$, $\alpha_{ij}$, $\alpha_1$, $\alpha_2$, $\partial\alpha_1/\partial x$, $\partial\alpha_2/\partial y$ and $\alpha$ remain finite and continuous. We form the expression

$$(13)\quad H[C, u_s, v_s] = \int_C \left\{ \left[ \alpha_{11}\left( v\frac{\partial u}{\partial x} - u\frac{\partial v}{\partial x}\right) + \left(\alpha_{12}v\frac{\partial u}{\partial y} - \alpha_{21}u\frac{\partial v}{\partial y}\right) + \alpha_1 uv \right] dy - \left[ \left(\alpha_{21}v\frac{\partial u}{\partial x} - \alpha_{12}u\frac{\partial v}{\partial x}\right) + \alpha_{22}\left( v\frac{\partial u}{\partial y} - u\frac{\partial v}{\partial y}\right) + \alpha_2 uv \right] dx \right\},$$

and state:

GREEN'S THEOREM. *If for every standard curve $C$ lying wholly within the region $\Sigma$ the equations*

$$(9)\qquad \Lambda[C, u_s] = \iint_\sigma (f - \alpha u)dxdy,$$

$$(11)\qquad \Gamma[C, v_s] = \iint_\sigma (g - \beta v)dxdy$$

*are satisfied, then the equation*

$$(14) \qquad H[C, u_s, v_s] = \int\int_\sigma (vf - ug)dxdy$$

*will also be satisfied.**

This theorem contains as a special case the usual Green's theorem for the differential expression (9′). If equation (9) is to be investigated, the function $g(xy)$ in (11) may be regarded as arbitrary, and will be chosen so as best to make the equation (9) integrable, in order that a convenient function $v(xy)$ may then be utilized in connection with (9) and (14).† If $g(xy)$ is taken identically null, the function $v(xy)$ is an *integrating multiplier* for the equation (9).

**50. Proof of Green's Theorem.** In order to prove this theorem we follow a method worked out by C. A. Epperson,‡ the integro-differential expressions being now however somewhat simplified in comparison with his, and establish first a lemma. For this purpose the curves $C$ are restricted to small squares about arbitrary points $P$ as center, which are made to approach $P$ as a limit; for convenience, the values of a function at $P$ and at a point on $C$ are designated by subscripts $P$ and $s$ respectively. The lemma follows:

LEMMA. *With the above restrictions upon the curves $C$, the relations*

$$(15) \qquad (f - \alpha u)_P = \lim_{\sigma = P} \frac{1}{\sigma} \Lambda[C, u_s],$$

$$(16) \qquad (g - \beta v)_P = \lim_{\sigma = P} \frac{1}{\sigma} \Gamma[C, v_s]$$

* Special cases of this form of Green's theorem were proved independently by C. W. Oseen, *Rendiconti del Circolo Matematico di Palermo*, vol. 38 (1914), pp. 167–179; and G. C. Evans, *Transactions of the American Mathematical Society*, vol. 15 (1914), pp. 477–496. A similar theorem has been proved for hydrodynamics by C. W. Oseen (see the footnote to the title of Lecture IV).

The theorem also holds if the curves $C$ are restricted to rectangles or even to circles (see the second method of proof).

† Such for instance as the *Parametrix*, defined by Hilbert.

‡ Epperson, *Bulletin of the American Mathematical Society*, vol. 22 (1915), pp. 17–26. In the demonstration referred to there is an error in the formula corresponding to (18) below.

holding for every point $P$ within $\Sigma$, imply the relation

$$(17)\qquad (vf - ug)_P = \lim_{\sigma=P} \frac{1}{\sigma} H[C, u_s, v_s].$$

Form the function

$$(vf - ug)_P = \lim_{\sigma=P} \frac{1}{\sigma} \left\{ v_P\Lambda[C, u_s] - u_P\Gamma[C, v_s] - \left(\left(\frac{\partial\alpha_1}{\partial x} + \frac{\partial\alpha_2}{\partial y}\right) uv\right)_P \right\}$$

from (15) and (16), with the aid of (12). If we write now the difference of the expression just given and that given by (17), we note that it consists of the quantities:

$$(i)\qquad -\left[\left(\frac{\partial\alpha_1}{\partial x} + \frac{\partial\alpha_2}{\partial y}\right) uv\right]_P,$$

$$(ii)\qquad \frac{1}{\sigma}\int \left\{ \alpha_{11}\left[(v_P - v_s)\frac{\partial u_s}{\partial x} - (u_P - u_s)\frac{\partial v_s}{\partial x}\right] + \alpha_{12}(v_P - v_s)\frac{\partial u_s}{\partial y} - \alpha_{21}(u_P - u_s)\frac{\partial v_s}{\partial y} + \alpha_1[(v_P - v_s)u_s + u_Pv_s] \right\} dy,$$

and a similar integral (*iii*), taken with regard to the variable $x$.

In the expression (*ii*), we have by the law of the mean:

$$v_P - v_s = \frac{\partial v_{P'}}{\partial x}(x_P - x_s) + \frac{\partial v_{P'}}{\partial y}(y_P - y_s),$$

where $P'$ is some point on the line connecting $P$ and $s$. Since these derivatives are uniformly continuous throughout the square $\sigma$, we may write

$$\left|(v_P - v_s) - \left\{\frac{\partial v_s}{\partial x}(x_P - x_s) + \frac{\partial v_s}{\partial y}(y_P - y_s)\right\}\right| < 2\epsilon\delta,$$

where $\delta$ is the length of one side of $\sigma$, and $\epsilon$ may be made small with $\delta$, uniformly for all points in $\sigma$. On account of the uniformity of this condition, since we are interested only in the limit of expression (*ii*), the $2\epsilon\delta$ contributes nothing to the value of $1/\sigma$ times the integral, and we may replace everywhere in (*ii*) the quantity $(v_P - v_s)$ by the quantity

$$\frac{\partial v_s}{\partial x}(x_P - x_s) + \frac{\partial v_s}{\partial y}(y_P - y_s),$$

with a similar substitution for the quantity $(u_P - u_s)$.

If now we denote the two opposite vertices of the square by $(x_1y_1)$ and $(x_2y_2)$ the expression (*ii*) becomes the difference of two integrals of the same expression, one along $x = x_1$, the other along $x = x_2$, and we have for it the value

$$\begin{aligned}\frac{1}{\sigma}\int_{y_1}^{y_2}\Bigg\{&\left[\alpha_{11}\left(\frac{\partial v}{\partial y}\frac{\partial u}{\partial x} - \frac{\partial u}{\partial y}\frac{\partial v}{\partial x}\right)\right]_{x_1}^{x_2}(y_P - y) \\ &+\left[\left(\alpha_{12}\frac{\partial v}{\partial x}\frac{\partial u}{\partial y} - \alpha_{21}\frac{\partial u}{\partial x}\frac{\partial v}{\partial y}\right)(x_P - x)\right]_{x_1}^{x_2} \\ &+\left[(\alpha_{12} - \alpha_{21})\frac{\partial v}{\partial y}\frac{\partial u}{\partial y}\right]_{x_1}^{x_2}(y_P - y) + \left[\alpha_1\frac{\partial v}{\partial x}u(x_P - x)\right]_{x_1}^{x_2} \\ &+\left[\alpha_1\frac{\partial v}{\partial y}u\right]_{x_1}^{x_2}(y_P - y) + \Big[\alpha v\Big]_{x_1}^{x_2}u_P\Bigg\}dy,\end{aligned}$$

where the quantities $x_2$ and $x_1$, above and below the bracket, indicate that the value of the expression within, when the arguments are $(x_1y)$, is to be subtracted from its value when the arguments are $(x_2y)$.

If we apply the law of the mean to the above integral, we notice that the terms which are multiplied into $y_P - y$ will disappear in the limit as we divide by $\sigma$ and let $\sigma$ approach zero, since, on account of the uniform continuity of the quantities involved, the integration will in each case yield an infinitesimal of higher order than $\sigma$. If in addition we make use of our special hypothesis that $x_P - x_1$ is equal to $x_2 - x_P$ we obtain for the limit of the whole expression (*ii*) the quantity

$$\begin{aligned}(18)\qquad &-\left(\alpha_{12}\frac{\partial v}{\partial x}\frac{\partial u}{\partial y} - \alpha_{21}\frac{\partial u}{\partial x}\frac{\partial v}{\partial y}\right)_P \\ &\qquad - \left(\alpha_1\frac{\partial v}{\partial x}u\right)_P + \left(\frac{\partial(\alpha_1 v)}{\partial x}u\right)_P,\end{aligned}$$

which is

$$(18') \qquad -\left(\alpha_{12}\frac{\partial v}{\partial x}\frac{\partial u}{\partial y}-\alpha_{21}\frac{\partial u}{\partial x}\frac{\partial v}{\partial y}\right)_P-\left(uv\frac{\partial \alpha_1}{\partial x}\right)_P.$$

In a precisely similar manner we find for the limit of the expression (*iii*) the quantity

$$-\left(\alpha_{21}\frac{\partial v}{\partial y}\frac{\partial u}{\partial x}-\alpha_{12}\frac{\partial u}{\partial y}\frac{\partial v}{\partial x}\right)_P+\left(uv\frac{\partial \alpha_2}{\partial y}\right)_P.$$

Hence the sum of (*i*), (*ii*) and (*iii*) has the limit zero, and the lemma is proved.

We see that all the limits involved in the proof of the lemma just given are uniform with respect to the point $P$. Hence we have the further lemma that *the limit specified in equation* (17) *is uniform with respect to the point* $P$, *for all points* $P$ *in a region enclosed by any standard curve* $C$ *lying wholly within* $\Sigma$, *and therefore that*

$$(19) \qquad \left|(vf-ug)_P-\frac{1}{\sigma}H[\bar{C}, u_s, v_s]\right| \leqq \eta\sigma,$$

*where* $\eta$ *is independent of* $P$, *and* $C$ *is the boundary of the square* $\sigma$.

If now we return to the original theorem, the proof is immediate. For if we divide up the region $\sigma$, bounded by the curve $C$, by a square grating, each square being of size $\sigma_r$, and denote by $S_r$ the outside boundary of the collection of squares entirely enclosed within $\sigma$, we shall have

$$\left|\int\!\!\int_{\sigma_r}(vf-ug)d\sigma-(vf-ug)_P\sigma_r\right| \leqq \epsilon\sigma_r,$$

where $P$ is the center of the square $\sigma_r$, and $\epsilon$ can be made uniformly as small as we please with $\sigma_r$, for all squares $\sigma_r$. Hence we have the equation

$$\left|\int\!\!\int_{S_r}(vf-ug)d\sigma-H[S_r, u_s, v_s]\right| \leqq (\eta+\epsilon)\Sigma\sigma_r,$$

and, since we can make the grating as minute as we please, by further subdivision, without changing the outside boundary $S_r$, the equation

$$\int\int_{S_r} (vf - ug)d\sigma = H[S_r, u_s, v_s].$$

If, having found this equation, we now change $S_r$ as we again decrease $\sigma_r$, keeping however $S_r$ the largest possible boundary of squares enclosed in $C$, and take the limit of both sides as $\sigma_r$ approaches zero, we have

$$\int\int_{\sigma} (vf - ug)d\sigma = H[C, u_s, v_s],$$

since the integrands in the curvilinear integrals constituting the right-hand member are uniformly continuous functions of their arguments. This completes the proof.

**51. A Proof by Approximating Polynomials.** An interesting method of proof of this same theorem is afforded by the method of approximating polynomials. In what follows only a special case is treated. Let $u$, $v$ and their first partial derivatives, and $f$ and $g$ be limited and continuous within and on the boundary of a rectangular region $D$: $a \leqq x \leqq b$, $a \leqq y \leqq b$, and consider the theorem with special reference to Poisson's equation:

THEOREM. *If for every standard curve enclosed entirely within the region D the two equations*

$$\int_C \frac{\partial u}{\partial n} ds = \int\int f(xy)dxdy, \tag{20}$$

$$\int_C \frac{\partial v}{\partial n} ds = \int\int g(xy)dxdy \tag{21}$$

*are satisfied, then the equation*

$$\int_C \left( v\frac{\partial u}{\partial n} - u\frac{\partial v}{\partial n} \right) ds = \int\int (vf - ug)dxdy \tag{22}$$

*will also be satisfied.**

Denote by $k_\mu$ the quantity

$$k_\mu = 2\frac{(2\mu)!!}{(2\mu + 1)!!},$$

and by $D'$ the region $a' \leqq x \leqq b'$, $a' \leqq y \leqq b'$, where $a'$ and $b'$ are fixed so that $a < a' < b' < b$. We shall prove the theorem first for the region $D'$. For the sake of convenience in notation we assume that $0 < a < b < 1$.

* A different method of considering $\nabla^2 u$ as a single differential operator has been developed by H. Petrini, *Acta Matematica*, vol. 31 (1908), see p. 181. Green's theorem may also be proved for this operator.

The polynomial

$$(23) \qquad P_\mu[u] = \frac{1}{k_\mu{}^2}\int\int_D u(\theta\psi)\{1 - (\theta - x)^2\}^\mu\{1 - (\psi - y)^2\}^\mu d\theta d\psi$$

converges uniformly, as $\mu$ becomes infinite, to the function $u(xy)$ throughout the square $D'$; moreover its first partial derivatives are polynomials which converge uniformly to the first partial derivatives of $u(xy)$, throughout the same region.*

*If the equation* (20) *is satisfied the polynomial* $\nabla^2 P_\mu[u]$ *converges uniformly throughout* $D'$ *to the function* $-f(xy)$, *as* $\mu$ *becomes infinite.*

To prove this, notice that as $C$ approaches $(x_0y_0)$ uniformly, we have

$$\lim_{\sigma=0} \frac{1}{\sigma}\int\int f(\theta\psi)d\theta d\psi = f(x_0y_0)$$

and

$$\lim_{\sigma=0} \frac{1}{\sigma}\int_C \frac{\partial P_\mu[u]}{\partial n} ds = -\nabla^2 P_\mu[u],$$

where $(x_0y_0)$ is any point in $D'$. Also:

$$P_\mu[u] = \int_{a-x}^{b-x} d\theta \int_{a-y}^{b-y} u(\theta + x, \psi + y)\frac{(1-\theta^2)^\mu(1-\psi^2)^\mu}{k_\mu{}^2}d\psi$$

and

$$(24) \quad \lim_{\mu=\infty} P_\mu[u] = \lim_{\mu=\infty}\int_{-\epsilon}^{\epsilon} d\theta \int_{-\epsilon}^{\epsilon} u(\theta + x, \psi + y)\frac{(1-\theta^2)^\mu(1-\psi^2)^\mu}{k_\mu{}^2}d\psi$$

uniformly for all points in $D'$ provided that $\epsilon$ is taken less than both $a' - a$ and $b' - b$. It is well known moreover that

$$(25) \quad \lim_{\mu=\infty} \frac{\partial}{\partial x} P_\mu[u]$$

$$= \lim_{\mu=\infty}\int_{-\epsilon}^{\epsilon} d\theta \int_{-\epsilon}^{\epsilon} \frac{\partial u(\theta + x, \psi + y)}{\partial x}\frac{(1-\theta^2)^\mu(1-\psi^2)^\mu}{k_\mu{}^2}d\psi,$$

and similarly for $\partial P_\mu[u]/\partial y$.

If the integral in the right-hand member of (24) is denoted by $\overline{P}_\mu[u]$ the integral in the right-hand member of (25) will be $\partial\overline{P}_\mu[u]/\partial x$. Further, the quantity

$$Q_\mu[u] = P_\mu[u] - \overline{P}_\mu[u]$$

will be a function of $x$, $y$ which, on account of the hypothesis made in regard to $\epsilon$, will have continuous limited derivatives of the first and second orders, which as we see by calculation, all uniformly approach zero, as $\mu$ becomes infinite. Hence from (25) follows the equation

$$(26) \qquad \nabla^2 P_\mu[u] = -\lim_{\sigma=0}\frac{1}{\sigma}\int_C \frac{\partial\overline{P}_\mu[u]}{\partial n} ds + \nabla^2 Q_\mu[u],$$

where $\nabla^2 Q_\mu[u]$ approaches zero uniformly as $\mu$ becomes infinite.

* De la Vallée-Poussin, Cours d'analyse infinitésimale, Louvain (1912), vol. 2, p. 131. The idea of this proof is suggested by the very short proof of the theorem of vol. 2, p. 24.

But we have

$$\int_C \frac{\partial \overline{P}_\mu}{\partial n} ds = \int_{-\epsilon}^{\epsilon} d\theta \int_{-\epsilon}^{\epsilon} d\psi \frac{(1-\theta^2)^\mu(1-\psi^2)^\mu}{k_\mu{}^2} \int_C \frac{\partial u(\theta+x, \psi+y)}{\partial n} ds,$$

in which the differentiation and the inner integration are carried out on the variables $x$, $y$. Hence, by (20), we have

$$\frac{1}{\sigma}\int_C \frac{\partial \overline{P}_\mu}{\partial n} ds = \int_{-\epsilon}^{\epsilon} d\theta \int_{-\epsilon}^{\epsilon} d\psi \frac{(1-\theta^2)^\mu(1-\psi^2)^\mu}{k_\mu{}^2} \frac{1}{\sigma}\int\int f(\theta+x, \psi+y)dxdy.$$

Here, however, since $f$ is continuous in both arguments, the quantity

$$\frac{1}{\sigma}\int\int f(\theta+x, \psi+y)dxdy$$

differs from $f(\theta + x_0, \psi + y_0)$ by an amount which is numerically less than a certain infinitesimal $\eta$, which approaches zero uniformly with $\sigma$ for all values of $\theta$ and $\psi$ in the range $\{-\epsilon, \epsilon\}$. Therefore, finally, we have

$$(27)\quad \lim_{\sigma=0}\frac{1}{\sigma}\int_C \frac{\partial \overline{P}_\mu}{\partial n} ds = \int_{-\epsilon}^{\epsilon} d\theta \int_{-\epsilon}^{\epsilon} f(\theta+x_0, \psi+y_0)\frac{(1-\theta^2)^\mu(1-\psi^2)^\mu}{k_\mu{}^2} d\psi.$$

By combining now (27) and (26), it follows that

$$-\lim_{\mu=\infty} \nabla^2 P_\mu[u] = \lim_{\mu=\infty}\int_{-\epsilon}^{\epsilon} d\theta \int_{-\epsilon}^{\epsilon} f(\theta+x_0, \psi+y_0)\frac{(1-\theta^2)^\mu(1-\psi^2)^\mu}{k_\mu{}^2} d\psi$$

uniformly for all values of $x_0y_0$ in $D'$. But this last limit is precisely $f(x_0y_0)$, so that the lemma is proved.

It is now easy to complete the main theorem. In fact, since $P_\mu[u]$ and $P_\mu[v]$ are polynomials, Green's theorem applies directly to them, as usually stated; viz.,

$$\int_C\left\{P_\mu[v]\frac{\partial P_\mu[u]}{\partial n} - P_\mu[u]\frac{\partial P_\mu[v]}{\partial n}\right\}ds$$
$$= -\int\int_\sigma \{P_\mu[v]\nabla^2 P_\mu[u] - P_\mu[u]\nabla^2 P_\mu[v]\}d\sigma.$$

Since, however, by (20) and (21), $P_\mu[u]$, $P_\mu[v]$, $\nabla^2 P_\mu[u]$, $\nabla^2 P_\mu[v]$ converge uniformly throughout $D'$ to the functions $u$, $v$, $f$, $g$ respectively, the limits of the integrals in the last equation will be the integrals of the limits; and for any curve $C$ in $D'$ the result will follow:

$$\int_C\left\{v\frac{\partial u}{\partial n} - u\frac{\partial v}{\partial n}\right\}ds = \int\int\{vf - ug\}dxdy.$$

But this result holds also for any standard curve lying wholly inside of $D$; for a region $D'$ may be drawn so as to contain this curve, since it has a nearest point to each boundary of $D$.

**52. Change of Variable.** With regard to the equations (9) and (11) let us make a transformation

$$(28)\qquad \xi = \varphi(xy), \qquad \eta = \theta(xy),$$

where $\varphi$ and $\theta$ are two functions continuous with their first derivatives in the given (simply connected) region, and let the Jacobian, $J = d(\xi\eta)/d(xy)$, not vanish in this region.

If we consider $\Lambda[C, u_s]$ and $\int\int (f - \alpha u)dxdy$ as functionals of $C$, and $u$, $a$, $\cdots$ as functions of $(x, y)$, leaving them unchanged in value as they are moved to the corresponding curves and points of the transformed plane, the integro-differential equation (9) is transformed into a similar equation, with $\bar{u} = u$, and

$$
(29) \quad \begin{aligned}
J\bar{\alpha}_{11} &= \alpha_{11}\left(\frac{\partial\varphi}{\partial x}\right)^2 + (\alpha_{12} + \alpha_{21})\frac{\partial\varphi}{\partial x}\frac{\partial\varphi}{\partial y} + \alpha_{22}\left(\frac{\partial\varphi}{\partial y}\right)^2, \\
J\bar{\alpha}_{12} &= \alpha_{11}\frac{\partial\varphi}{\partial x}\frac{\partial\theta}{\partial x} + \alpha_{12}\frac{\partial\varphi}{\partial x}\frac{\partial\theta}{\partial y} + \alpha_{21}\frac{\partial\varphi}{\partial y}\frac{\partial\theta}{\partial x} + \alpha_{22}\frac{\partial\varphi}{\partial y}\frac{\partial\theta}{\partial y}, \\
J\bar{\alpha}_{21} &= \alpha_{11}\frac{\partial\varphi}{\partial x}\frac{\partial\theta}{\partial x} + \alpha_{12}\frac{\partial\varphi}{\partial y}\frac{\partial\theta}{\partial x} + \alpha_{21}\frac{\partial\varphi}{\partial x}\frac{\partial\theta}{\partial y} + \alpha_{22}\frac{\partial\varphi}{\partial y}\frac{\partial\theta}{\partial y}, \\
J\bar{\alpha}_{22} &= \alpha_{11}\left(\frac{\partial\theta}{\partial x}\right)^2 + (\alpha_{12} + \alpha_{21})\frac{\partial\theta}{\partial x}\frac{\partial\theta}{\partial y} + \alpha_{22}\left(\frac{\partial\theta}{\partial y}\right)^2, \\
J\bar{\alpha}_1 &= \alpha_1\frac{\partial\varphi}{\partial x} + \alpha_2\frac{\partial\varphi}{\partial y}, \qquad J\alpha_2 = \alpha_1\frac{\partial\theta}{\partial x} + \alpha_2\frac{\partial\theta}{\partial y}, \\
J\bar{\alpha} &= \alpha, \qquad\qquad J\bar{f} = f.
\end{aligned}
$$

The expression

$$(30) \qquad I = (\alpha_{12} + \alpha_{21})^2 - 4\alpha_{11}\alpha_{22}$$

is an invariant of this transformation. In fact we have $\bar{I} = I$. The expression

$$(31) \qquad T(dx, dy) = \alpha_{11}dy^2 - (\alpha_{12} + \alpha_{21})dydx + \alpha_{22}dx^2$$

is a covariant; in fact,

$$\bar{T}(d\xi, d\eta) = JT(dx, dy).$$

This same transformation of the plane transforms the adjoint equation in a similar manner, every $\alpha$ and $\bar{\alpha}$ in (29) being replaced by the corresponding $\beta$ or $\bar{\beta}$. Moreover the relation of adjointness is preserved by the transformation. To insure this, however, it is necessary to assume the existence of the second derivatives of the functions $\varphi$ and $\psi$, since otherwise the coefficients in the transformation of the adjoint equation will not be defined.* To prove this fact, the only difficulty is connected with the last of the equations (12). This can be written in the equivalent form:

$$\int\int (\beta - \alpha)dxdy = \int_C \alpha_1 dy - \alpha_2 dx, \tag{32}$$

which is an invariant relation, since each member is a functional of $C$, which is seen to be unchanged in value by the transformation, on account of the formulae (29). Hence the equation (32) will be satisfied by the transformed quantities.

We can make a transformation

$$u = \psi(xy)\bar{u} \tag{33}$$

of the dependent variable. The function $\bar{u}$ will satisfy a new integro-differential equation of the same kind as before, with

$$\begin{gathered}\bar{\alpha}_{ij} = \psi\alpha_{ij}, \qquad \bar{\alpha} = \psi\alpha, \qquad \bar{f} = f,\\ \bar{\alpha}_1 = \alpha_{11}\frac{\partial\psi}{\partial x} + \alpha_{12}\frac{\partial\psi}{\partial y} + \alpha_1\psi,\\ \bar{\alpha}_2 = \alpha_{21}\frac{\partial\psi}{\partial x} + \alpha_{22}\frac{\partial\psi}{\partial y} + \alpha_2\psi.\end{gathered} \tag{34}$$

The quantity $I$ will be an invariant, and the quantity $T$ a covariant of this new transformation.

The relation of adjointness will be preserved if at the same time we make a transformation of the adjoint equation given by the formulæ:

$$\bar{v} = v, \qquad \bar{g} = g, \qquad \bar{\beta}_{ij} = \psi\beta_{ij},$$

$$\bar{\beta}_1 = -\beta_{11}\frac{\partial\psi}{\partial x} - \beta_{21}\frac{\partial\psi}{\partial y} + \beta_1\psi,$$

* It is possible, however, to use less restrictive conditions if the analysis is based on (32) instead of the last of the equations (12). This would demand a slightly different treatment of Green's theorem, breaking thereby from the theory of the Riemann integral.

$$\beta_2 = -\beta_{12}\frac{\partial\psi}{\partial x} - \beta_{22}\frac{\partial\psi}{\partial y} + \beta_2\psi, \tag{34'}$$

$$\bar{\beta} = \beta\psi - \beta_1\frac{\partial\psi}{\partial x} - \beta_2\frac{\partial\psi}{\partial y} + \frac{\partial}{\partial x}\left(\beta_{11}\frac{\partial\psi}{\partial x} + \beta_{21}\frac{\partial\psi}{\partial y}\right)$$
$$+ \frac{\partial}{\partial y}\left(\beta_{12}\frac{\partial\psi}{\partial x} + \beta_{22}\frac{\partial\psi}{\partial y}\right).$$

The expressions $I$ and $T$ will also of course be respectively invariant and covariant of this transformation.

For this last transformation to be defined it is necessary that the second derivatives of $\psi$ exist.

**53. The Three Types of Equation.** The directions defined by the covariant equation

$$T(dx, dy) = 0 \tag{35}$$

or, what is the same thing,

$$2\alpha_{11}dy = (\alpha_{12} + \alpha_{21} \pm \sqrt{I})dx \tag{35'}$$

are called the *characteristic directions*, and the solutions of the equation, the *characteristic curves*. Characteristic directions go over into characteristic directions, by any of the transformations considered. There are, then, three cases to consider with respect to any point of the region; if the characteristic directions are real and distinct at a point the equation (9) is said to be *hyperbolic* at the point; if they are real and coincident the equation is *parabolic*; if they are not real, the equation is *elliptic*. Equations (9) and (11) are of the same type, and the type is unchanged by any real transformation of the kinds considered.

The three types of equations can be reduced by real transformations of the independent and dependent variables to three normal forms respectively. We assume for convenience that in the region we are investigating we have $\alpha_{11} \neq 0$, and also that the first derivatives of the coefficients $\alpha_{ij}$, $\alpha_i$, are continuous as well as the coefficients themselves. This last restriction is not entirely necessary, but we are more interested in reducing the restrictions on the solutions than on the coefficients.

*The following equation is an identity:*

$$(36)\quad \int_C \left\{ \alpha_{12}\frac{\partial u}{\partial y}dy - \alpha_{21}\frac{\partial u}{\partial x}dx \right\}$$
$$= \int_C \left\{ \left( \frac{\alpha_{12}+\alpha_{21}}{2}\frac{\partial u}{\partial y} + \frac{\partial}{\partial y}\frac{-\alpha_{12}+\alpha_{21}}{2}u \right) dy \right.$$
$$\left. - \left( \frac{\alpha_{12}+\alpha_{21}}{2}\frac{\partial u}{\partial x} + \frac{\partial}{\partial x}\frac{\alpha_{12}-\alpha_{21}}{2}u \right) dx, \right.$$

and it may be proved in the same way as the extension of Green's theorem, already given.*

The normal forms are then obtained, as in the theory of linear partial differential equations, to be the following:

*Elliptic:*

$$(37)\quad \int_C \left\{ \frac{\partial u}{\partial x} + \alpha_1 u \right\} dy - \left\{ \frac{\partial u}{\partial y} + \alpha_2 u \right\} dx = \int\int (f - \alpha u) dx dy.$$

*Hyperbolic:*

$$(37')\quad \int_C \left\{ \frac{\partial u}{\partial y} + \alpha_1 u \right\} dy - \left\{ \frac{\partial u}{\partial x} + \alpha_2 u \right\} dx = \int\int (f - \alpha u) dx dy.$$

*Parabolic:*

$$(37'')\quad \int_C \alpha_1 u dy - \left\{ \frac{\partial u}{\partial y} + \alpha_2 u \right\} dx = \int\int (f - \alpha u) dx dy.$$

With the hypotheses just made, the new functions $\alpha_1$, $\alpha_2$ are continuous, but do not necessarily have continuous first partial derivatives. If we desire this last property, we must assume that the original coefficients $\alpha_{ij}$ possess continuous *second* partial derivatives. This assumption is necessary if we desire to use Green's theorem; without its use, however, we can still establish the existence, though perhaps not the uniqueness, of solutions of the equations, with reference to the usual boundary value problems.

The different types of equations do not arise in practise, however, by transformations of more general forms, determined by

* The most direct proof is that by approximating polynomials.

the values of $I$, as in the preceding paragraphs, but appear separately in conformity to certain types of physical problems, such as, for instance, those of potential, flow of heat, and vibration. Hence the transformations and the assumptions on which they are based are not so likely to present themselves in applications to physics. Here we have not space to give the detailed treatment of these three types, and therefore confine ourselves to the one which is perhaps least extensively studied, imposing merely the few conditions on the coefficients which are sufficient for the desired analysis of this type.

## § 3. The Parabolic Integro-Differential Equation of Bôcher Type

**54. Derivation of the Equation for the Flow of Heat.** Consider, for simplicity, a bar of length $l$, insulated except at the ends, and in particular the portion of it between $y = y_1$ and $y = y_2$ at times $x = x_1$ and $x = x_2$. The amount of heat that is contained in this portion of the bar at time $x_2$ is $\int_{y_1}^{y_2} cu(x_2, y)dy$, and the amount at time $x_1$ is $\int_{y_1}^{y_2} cu(x_1 y)dy$, where $c$ is the specific heat, and $u$ the temperature. On the other hand, by Newton's law, the amount that flows out through the end $y_2$ is $\int_{x_1}^{x_2} k\partial u(x, y_2)/\partial y dx$ and the amount that flows in through the end $y_1$ is $\int_{x_1}^{x_2} k\partial u(xy_1)/\partial y dx$, $k$ being the conductivity. Since the difference of the first two quantities must be equal to the difference of the second, *we have for any rectangle in the $x$, $y$ plane:*

$$\int cudy + k\frac{\partial u}{\partial y}dx = 0, \tag{38}$$

*if there are no interior sources of heat.*

If there are interior sources of heat which contribute an amount $\int_{y_1}^{y_2} dy \int_{x_1}^{x_2} f(xy)dx$ to the quantity of heat contained in the portion $y_1y_2$ of the bar, the equation becomes*

$$(39) \qquad \int cudy + k\frac{\partial u}{\partial y}dx = \int\int f(xy)dxdy.$$

If $c$ and $k$ are constants they can be absorbed by a change of variable, so that we shall have

$$(38') \qquad \int udy + \frac{\partial u}{\partial y}dx = 0,$$

$$(39') \qquad \int udy + \frac{\partial u}{\partial y}dx = \int\int f(xy)dxdy.$$

In three dimensions, corresponding to (38′) we have the equation

$$(40) \qquad \underset{t=t_2}{\int\int\int} udxdydz - \underset{t=t_1}{\int\int\int} udxdydz = \int_{t_1}^{t_2} dt \int\int \frac{\partial u}{\partial n}d\sigma,$$

which may be rewritten as an integral over a three-dimensional hyperspace, immersed in a 4-space.

**55. The Dirichlet Problem.** Instead of (39′), we consider the more general equation

$$(41) \qquad \int_C udy - \left(-\frac{\partial u}{\partial y} + \alpha_2 u\right)dx = \underset{\sigma}{\int\int}(f - \alpha u)dxdy,$$

where $C$ is any closed standard curve within the given region, and the functions $f$, $\alpha$, $\alpha_2$, $\partial\alpha_2/\partial y$ are continuous within and on the boundary of the given region.

The adjoint equation to (41) is

$$(41') \qquad \int_C - vdy - \left(-\frac{\partial v}{\partial y} + \beta_2 v\right)dx = \int\int_\sigma (g - \beta v)dxdy$$

in which

$$\beta_2 = -\alpha_2 \qquad \text{and} \qquad \beta = \alpha + \frac{\partial \alpha_2}{\partial y}.$$

* It would be more natural to represent the right-hand member of this equation by a two-dimensional Stieltjes integral (an additive and perhaps absolutely continuous functional of the rectangle $C$). We restrict ourselves to the case where $f$ itself exists, and is continuous. This same note applies of course to (5).

If $g$ is a continuous function the coefficients of (41′) satisfy the same conditions as the corresponding coefficients of (41).

We consider a region also slightly more general than in the corresponding physical problem. Denote by ${}_{x_0}R_{x_1}$ (following a notation used by W. A. Hurwitz) a region bounded on the left by the line $x = x_0$, on the right by the line $x = x_1$, above by the curve $y = \xi_2(x)$, and below by the curve $y = \xi_1(x)$. The functions $\xi_1$ and $\xi_2$ are to be continuous with their first derivatives, and are to have only a finite number of maxima and minima in the interval under consideration. Moreover, $\xi_1(x) > \xi_2(x)$, for $x \geqq x_0$.

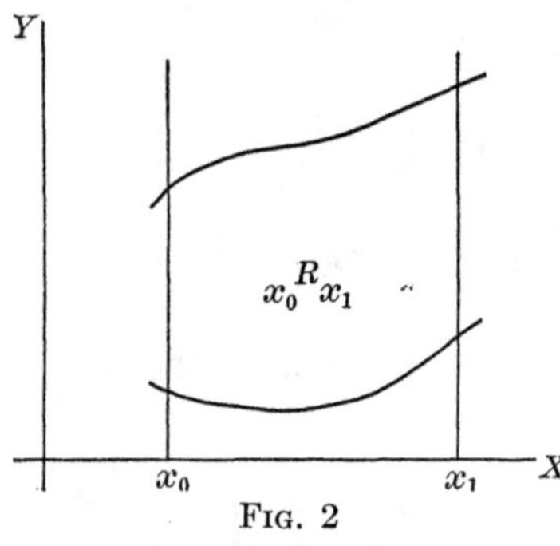


FIG. 2

We shall investigate solutions of (41) which are continuous with a continuous derivative in regard to $y$ within and on the boundary of ${}_{x_0}R_{x_1}$ (called *regular solutions*), and take on a continuous chain of boundary values along the open contour ${}_{x_0}r_{x_1}$, comprised by the parts $x = x_0$, $y = \xi_2(x)$ and $y = \xi_1(x)$ of the boundary of ${}_{x_0}R_{x_1}$. *There is one and only one such solution.*

Analogously, there is one and only one regular solution of the adjoint equation (41′) in the region ${}_{x_0}R_{x_1}$ which takes on given values along the contour comprised by $x = x_1$, $y = \xi_1(x)$ and $y = \xi_2(x)$. The proofs of the two existence theorems are similar, and it is therefore necessary to deal only with one.

**56. The Uniqueness of the Solution.** Define the function

$$h_{\alpha\beta}(xy\,|\,x'y') = \frac{(y'-y)^{\alpha}}{(x'-x)^{\beta}}\,e^{-\frac{(y'-y)^2}{4(x'-x)}}. \tag{42}$$

The function $h_{0\frac{1}{2}}$ as a function of $x$, $y$ is a solution of the adjoint of (38′), since it is seen by differentiation to be a solution of the equation

$$\frac{\partial^2 v}{\partial y^2} + \frac{\partial v}{\partial x} = 0.$$

As a function of $x'$, $y'$ it is a solution of (38′) itself. Its derivative in regard to $y'$ is

$$\frac{\partial h_{0\frac{1}{2}}}{\partial y'} = -\tfrac{1}{2}h_{1,\frac{3}{2}},$$

and both $h_{0\frac{1}{2}}$ and $h_{1\frac{3}{2}}$ are integrable over the region ${}_{x_0}R_{x'}$. Moreover,

$$\lim_{\bar{x}=x'-0} \frac{1}{2\sqrt{\pi}} \int_a^b \varphi(y) h_{0\frac{1}{2}}(\bar{x}y\,|\,x'y')dy = \varphi(y') \tag{43}$$

if $\xi_1(x') < y' < \xi_2(x')$, $y'$ being between $a$ and $b$, and $\varphi(y)$ is integrable, and continuous at $y = y'$.*

If we now define the Green's function $g(xy\,|\,x'y')$ for (41) by the formula

$$g(xy\,|\,x'y') = h_{0\frac{1}{2}}(xy\,|\,x'y') + g'(xy\,|\,x'y'), \tag{44}$$

where for a point $(x'y')$ inside ${}_{x_0}R_{x_1}$, $g(xy\,|\,x'y')$ is in $x$, $y$ a solution of the adjoint equation (41′), and $g'(xy\,|\,x'y')$ is a regular function which vanishes on the line $x = x'$ and on $y = \xi_1(x)$ and $y = \xi_2(x)$ takes on the negatives of the values of $h_{0\frac{1}{2}}$, then we have by a direct application of Green's theorem:

$$\begin{aligned} 2\sqrt{\pi}u(x'y') = &- \int_{x_0 r x'} \Big\{ u(xy)g(xy\,|\,x'y')dy \\ &- u(xy)\frac{\partial g(xy\,|\,x'y')}{\partial y}dx \Big\} + \iint f(xy)g(xy\,|\,x'y')dxdy, \end{aligned} \tag{45}$$

the term involving $\alpha_2$ dropping out, since $dx = 0$ when $g \neq 0$, on the boundary.

On account of the explicit formula (45), the solution must be unique, if regular solutions of (41) and (41′) taking on assigned boundary values exist.

**57. Existence of Solutions.** On account of the uniqueness of solutions of (41), there will be one and only one solution in the case when

$$\alpha_2 \equiv f \equiv \alpha \equiv 0,$$

* For a proof of these theorems see E. Levi, *Annali di Matematica*, vol. 14 (1908), p. 187, or W. A. Hurwitz, Randwertaufgaben der linearen partiellen Differentialgleichungen, Dissertation, Gottingen (1911).

namely, the known solution of the equation

$$\frac{\partial^2 u}{\partial y^2} - \frac{\partial u}{\partial x} = 0. \tag{46}$$

In particular, (46) will have a Green's function $G(xy|x'y')$.

The function

$$u(x'y') = \bar{u}(x'y') + \frac{1}{2\sqrt{\pi}} \iint\limits_{x_0 R_{x'}} G(xy|x'y') f(xy) dx dy,$$

where $\bar{u}(x'y')$ is the solution of (46) which takes on the given boundary values on ${}_{x_0}r_{x_1}$, will be the unique regular solution of

$$\int_C u dy - \left(-\frac{\partial u}{\partial y}\right) dx = \iint f dx dy,$$

which takes on the same boundary values. In fact, we may differentiate under the integral sign to find $\partial u/\partial x'$, and by substituting directly into the equation, and changing the order of integration, verify that the equation is satisfied. As is well known, the integral in the second member vanishes when $(x', y')$ is a point of the contour ${}_{x_0}r_{x_1}$.

Hence the unique regular solution of (41) must satisfy the equation:

$$u(x'y') = \bar{u}(x'y') + \frac{1}{2\sqrt{\pi}} \iint\limits_{x_0 R_{x'}} G(xy|x'y') \left\{ f - \alpha u - \frac{\partial}{\partial y}(\alpha_2 u) \right\}_{xy} dx dy, \tag{47}$$

since, with our assumptions, we have

$$\int_C \alpha_2 u dy = -\iint \frac{\partial}{\partial y}(\alpha_2 u) dx dy.$$

Hence, finally, if we write

$$\partial_{x'y'} u = -\alpha(x'y') u(x'y') - \frac{\partial}{\partial y'} [\alpha_2(x'y') u(x'y')],$$

$$\varphi(x'y') = \bar{u}(x'y') + \frac{1}{2\sqrt{\pi}} \iint G(xy|x'y') f(xy) dx dy,$$

the quantity $\partial_{x'y'}u$ must satisfy the integral equation

(48)
$$\partial_{x'y'}u(x'y') = \partial_{x'y'}\varphi(x'y') + \frac{1}{2\sqrt{\pi}}\iint\limits_{x_0R_{x'}} \partial_{x'y'}G(xy\,|\,x'y')\partial_{xy}u(xy)dxdy.$$

In this integral equation, the first term of the right-hand member is a continuous function.

On the other hand we know that there is a unique continuous solution of (48), which yields when applied to (47), since we can differentiate once with respect to $y$ under the integral sign, a regular solution of that equation, and therefore a regular solution of (41).

We can as a matter of fact go still further than this. There is a unique solution $k(xy\,|\,x'y')$ of the equations

(49)
$$\begin{aligned} k(xy\,|\,x'y') + \frac{1}{2\sqrt{\pi}}\partial_{x'y'}G(xy\,|\,x'y') &= \frac{1}{2\sqrt{\pi}}\iint\limits_{xR_{x'}} k(xy\,|\,\xi\eta)\partial_{x'y'}G(\xi\eta\,|\,x'y')d\xi d\eta \\ &= \frac{1}{2\sqrt{\pi}}\iint\limits_{xR_{x'}} \partial_{\xi\eta}G(xy\,|\,\xi\eta)k(\xi\eta\,|\,x'y')d\xi d\eta, \end{aligned}$$

which is called the resolvent kernel to $\partial_{x'y'}G(xy\,|\,x'y')/2\sqrt{\pi}$, and denoted by the symbol

$$\overline{\frac{1}{2\sqrt{\pi}}\partial_{x'y'}G(xy\,|\,x'y')}.$$

The solution of (48) may then be written in the form

$$\partial_{x'y'}u(x'y') = \partial_{x'y'}\varphi(x'y') - \iint\limits_{x_0R_{x'}} \overline{\left(\frac{1}{2\sqrt{\pi}}\partial_{x'y'}G(xy\,|\,x'y')\right)}\partial_{xy}\varphi(xy)dxdy.$$

The examination of the existence and continuity of $k(xy\,|\,x'y')$ demands consideration of the uniform convergence of the same improper integrals as in the case of (48).

**58. The Green's Function.** The Green's function for (41) is closely related to the function $k(xy|x'y')$. As a function of $(x'y')$ it is a solution of (41) itself, with $f \equiv 0$, and it may be deduced from this fact, and from (47), that the Green's function satisfies the equation

$$g(xy|x'y') = G(xy|x'y') + \frac{1}{2\sqrt{\pi}} \iint_{{}_xR_{x'}} G(\xi\eta|x'y')\partial_{\xi\eta}g(xy|\xi\eta)d\xi d\eta,$$

and hence the integral equation

$$\partial_{x'y'}g(xy|x'y') = \partial_{x'y'}G(xy|x'y') + \frac{1}{2\sqrt{\pi}} \iint_{{}_xR_{x'}} \partial_{x'y'}G(\xi\eta|x'y')\partial_{\xi\eta}g(xy|\xi\eta)d\xi d\eta.$$

Hence we have

$$\partial_{x'y'}g(xy|x'y') = -2\sqrt{\pi}\overline{\left(\frac{1}{2\sqrt{\pi}}\partial_{x'y'}G(xy|x'y')\right)}, \tag{50}$$

and

$$g(xy|x'y') = G(xy|x'y') - \iint_{{}_xR_{x'}} G(\xi\eta|x'y')\overline{\left(\frac{1}{2\sqrt{\pi}}\partial_{\xi\eta}G(xy|\xi\eta)\right)}d\xi d\eta. \tag{51}$$

## § 4. The Parabolic Integro-Differential Equation of the Usual Type

**59. The Generalized Green's Function.** For simplicity, let us add to the conditions on the boundary of the region, the requirements $\xi_2'(x) > 0$, $\xi_1'(x) < 0$, and deal with the equation

$$\frac{\partial u}{\partial x} - \frac{\partial^2 u}{\partial y^2} = \int_{x_y}^{x} A(x, \xi, y)u(\xi, y)d\xi,$$

or for still greater simplicity, with its generalization:

$$\int u dy - \left(-\frac{\partial u}{\partial y}\right) dx = \iint d\sigma \int_{x_y}^{x} A(x\xi y)u(xy)dx. \tag{52}$$

In these equations $(x_y, y)$ denotes the point on the boundary ${}_{x_0}r_x$ of which one co-ordinate is $y$.

If $u(xy)$ and $v(xy)$ are any two continuous functions, it may be proved by means of a change in the order of integration that the following identity holds:

$$(53)\quad \iint\limits_{x_0 R x_1} \left\{ v(xy) \int_{x_y}^{x} A(x\xi y) u(\xi y) d\xi - u(xy) \int_{x}^{x_1} A(\xi x y) v(\xi y) d\xi \right\} dx dy = 0.$$

If we define the generalized Green's function for (52) as the solution $S(xy \mid x'y')$ of the adjoint equation

$$\int - v dy - \left( - \frac{\partial v}{\partial y} \right) dx = \iint dx dy \int_{x_y}^{y} A(\xi x y) v(\xi y) d\xi,$$

which is equal to $h_{0\frac{1}{2}}$ plus a regular function which vanishes for $x = x'$, and takes on the values $- h_{0\frac{1}{2}}$ on the upper and lower boundaries, we can find a formula for it in the same way as in the case of (41). In this case, however, the fact that the quantity

$$(54)\quad u(x'y') = \frac{1}{2\sqrt{\pi}} \int_{x_0 r_{x'}} u(xy) \left\{ S(xy \mid x'y') dy - \frac{\partial}{\partial y} S(xy \mid x'y') dx \right\}$$

represents the solution of (52), which takes on the assigned boundary values depends essentially upon the identity (53). In other words, instead of Lagrange's identity we have as the basis of our extended Green's theorem an identity involving an iteration of integrals.

The case is again different from that of the integro-differential equations of so-called static type which will be treated in Lecture V, by a symbolic method, depending upon distributive and associative properties of the integral combinations involved. On the other hand, the function $S$ for the present case may be expressed in closed form, in terms of the Green's function for the parabolic differential equation

$$\frac{\partial^2 u}{\partial y^2} = \frac{\partial u}{\partial x}.$$

## § 5. The Differential Equation of Hyperbolic Type

**60. Functions of Zero Variation in Two Dimensions.** A treatment of the hyperbolic equation, analogous to that just given for the parabolic equation, may be developed. Since, however, the Riemann characteristic function for the hyperbolic equation is itself regular, the treatment does not depend upon the analysis of the properties of a discontinuous principal solution, and there is not the same interest in avoiding differentiation. The resulting integral equations are however interesting; they involve both simple and double integrals.*

The equation

$$(55)\quad \begin{aligned} u(x+t+t', y+t-t') - u(x+t, y+t) \\ - u(x+t', y-t') + u(x, y) = 0, \end{aligned}$$

where $t$ and $t'$ are arbitrary quantities, may be replaced by the equation

$$(56)\quad \frac{\partial^2 u}{\partial x^2} - \frac{\partial^2 u}{\partial y^2} = 0$$

* The equations satisfy the conditions specified in V. Volterra, *Rendiconti della R. Accademia dei Lincei*, vol. 5 (1896), 1° sem., p. 289.

if sufficient derivatives of the function $u$ exist. Otherwise, it is of interest to study the equation (55) directly. It may be stated geometrically in terms of an arbitrary rectangle with sides parallel to the lines $x \pm y = 0$; *the sum of the values of $u$ at the extremities of one diagonal is equal to the sum at the extremities of the other.*

The equation (55) has been used to plot solutions of the wave equation.* That it holds is a necessary and sufficient condition that $u(xy)$ be a function of zero variation in two dimensions;† such functions are obviously not restricted to constants, as they would be in one dimension.

To solve equation (55) we define a *stair* of points. Construct a broken line, with parts parallel to the lines $x \pm y = 0$, joining two end points $A$ and $B$, which do not lie on a line parallel to either of these two directions. Also, let no two parts of the broken line be collinear. The vertices of the broken line, including the end points, constitute the stair.

The *associated mesh* of a stair is the collection of intersections of all lines parallel to the directions $x \pm y = 0$, which contain a point of the stair. It may be established geometrically that *if a solution of* (55) *is assigned arbitrary values for the points of a stair it is determined uniquely at all the points of the associated mesh, and at no other points.*

The theorem just enunciated provides immediate proofs of existence theorems of (55), e. g., that a solution is determined uniquely by assigning arbitrary values along two lines, one parallel to $x + y = 0$ and the other parallel to $x - y = 0$; also that any solution may be written in the form

$$f(x + y) + \varphi(x - y)$$

wherever it exists. In fact, if we define two stairs as intersecting when their meshes have a point in common, we see that *we can assign arbitrary values to a solution of* (55) *at the points of any number of non-intersecting stairs.* If two stairs intersect, values of $u(xy)$ may be assigned on them independently, provided they are assigned so as to give the same values on the points of intersection.‡

* Professor Birkhoff calls my attention to the fact that this method is used in H. N. Davis, The Longitudinal Vibrations of a Stretched String, *Proceedings of the American Academy of Sciences*, vol. 41 (1906), pp. 693–727.

† De la Vallée-Poussin, *Transactions of the American Mathematical Society*, vol. 16 (1915), p. 493. A change of axes is involved.

‡ In the same way that (56) is related to (55), Laplace's equation is related to those in which the value of a function at a point is given as the mean of its values around the vertices of a polygon of $n$ sides of which the point is at the center. In the latter case there are properties of extension like the analytic extension of solutions of Laplace's equation. Hence in this case continuity at a point is a matter of "far-reaching" importance. See for the case of one dimension, Blumberg, *Bulletin of the American Mathematical Society*, vol. 23 (1917), p. 212; this reference considers also a generalization to two dimensions of more restricted character.

# LECTURE V

## DIRECT GENERALIZATIONS OF THE THEORY OF INTEGRAL EQUATIONS*

### § 1. Introduction: Some General Properties of the Stieltjes Integral

**61. The Stieltjes Integral Equation.** The resolution of implicit functional equations, and the form of the linear functional suggest the study of the equation

$$f(x) + \int_a^b \varphi(s) d_s \alpha(xs) = 0, \tag{1}$$

in which the subscript $s$ indicates that we are taking the variation in regard to $s$, or, more particularly,

$$\varphi(x) = f(x) + \lambda \int_a^b \varphi(s) d_s \alpha(xs), \tag{2}$$

which is a special case of that treated in Art. 35, and yet contains many forms of mixed linear equations as special cases of itself.

* This lecture is based on the following references:

E. H. Moore, On the foundations of a theory of linear integral equations, *Bulletin of the American Mathematical Society*, vol. 18 (1912), p. 335.

V. Volterra, Papers on integro-differential equations and permutable functions, *Rendiconti della R. Accademia dei Lincei*, ser. 5, vol. 18–20 (1909–11); *Lectures delivered at the celebration of the 20th anniversary of the foundation of Clark University* (1911);
Teoria delle potenze dei logaritmi e delle funzioni di composizione, *R. Accademia dei Lincei, Atti*, vol. 11 (1916), pp. 167–249. The results of the earlier papers are given in the *Leçons sur les fonctions de lignes*, Paris (1913) and in the *Vanuxem Lectures*, Princeton (1912).

G. C. Evans, Sopra L'algebra delle funzioni permutabili, *R. Accademia dei Lincei, Atti*, vol. 8 (1911);
L'algebra delle funzioni permutabili e non permutabili, *Rendiconti del Circolo Matematico di Palermo*, vol. 34 (1912);
The Cauchy problem for integro-differential equations, *Transactions of the American Mathematical Society*, vol. 15 (1914), pp. 215–226.

For the resolution of (2), we must first define the class $L$ of functions $\varphi(x)$.

Represent by $t_s(xs)$ the total variation function for $\alpha(xs)$, the variable $x$ being considered as a parameter. If for a set $E$ of values of $x$, or an interval $x_1x_2$ of values of $x$, the quantity $t_s(xs)$, which is of course $\leqq t_s(xb)$, remains finite, $\leqq T_\alpha$, the function $\alpha(xs)$ is said to be of *uniformly limited variation* in $s$ over the set $E$, or the interval $x_1x_2$, of values of $x$. In this case the approximation sum approaches its limit uniformly, and the measure of the approach of the sum to the integral is given by the quantity $\omega_\delta T_\alpha$, as follows from (16), Lecture III.

We may obtain also directly the inequality

$$\left|\int_a^b \varphi(s)d_s\alpha(xs)\right| \leqq MT_\alpha, \tag{3}$$

where $|\varphi(x)| \leqq M$.

Upon these inequalities is based the following theorem, about the continuity of Stieltjes integrals:

THEOREM. *If in the integral*

$$\psi(x) = \int_a^b \varphi(s)d_s\alpha(xs), \qquad \varphi(s) \text{ continuous, } a \leqq s \leqq b, \tag{4}$$

*$\alpha(xs)$ is of uniformly limited variation in $s$ for $x$ in the neighborhood of $x_0$, and if there is a set of values $F_{x_0}$ of $s$ which includes $a$ and $b$ and is dense in $ab$, such that $\alpha(xs)$ is continuous in $x$ at $x_0$, for $s$ in $F_{x_0}$, then $\psi(x)$ is continuous at $x_0$.**

It is evidently then desirable, for (2), to take as the class $L$ the class of all functions $\varphi(s)$, continuous $a \leqq s \leqq b$, in order to satisfy (*i*); the condition (*ii*) will also be satisfied if we take $|\lambda| < 1/T_\alpha$, as we see by (3). Accordingly, we have the theorem:

THEOREM. *If $\alpha(xs)$ is of uniformly limited variation in $s$ for $a \leqq x \leqq b$, and if for every value $x = x_0$ in this interval there is a set $F_{x_0}$ of values of $s$, including $a$ and $b$ and dense in $ab$, such that if $s$ is in $F_{x_0}$ the function $\alpha(xs)$ is continuous in $x$ at $x_0$, then equation (2) has one and only one solution $\varphi(x)$, continuous $a \leqq x \leqq b$, provided that $\lambda$ is small enough ($|\lambda| < 1/T_\alpha$).*

* This theorem, and the theorems of Art. 62 about the Stieltjes integral, are proved by H. C. Bray, *Annals of Mathematics*, vol. 19 (1918).

**62. Integrability of the Stieltjes Integral.** It may be verified that *if* $\alpha(xs)$ *is of uniformly limited variation in* $s$, *for* $x$ *in the interval* $x_1 \leqq x \leqq x_2$, *and if* $\gamma(x)$ *is of limited variation in that interval, then the integral*

$$\theta(s) = \int_{x_1}^{x_2} \alpha(xs) d\gamma(x) \tag{5}$$

*represents a function of limited variation.* In fact, we have the inequality

$$T_\theta \leqq T_\alpha T_\gamma. \tag{5'}$$

In the theorem given about equation (2), the finite jumps of $\alpha(xs)$ could themselves be functions of $x$ in position and magnitude. For closer study, *we restrict ourselves in the remainder of this article to functions* $\alpha(xs)$ *which are continuous in* $x$ *for all values of* $s$,—a restriction which demands that the finite jumps of $\alpha$ shall have locations independent of $x$. We restrict ourselves also of course to continuous functions $\varphi(x)$. With these assumptions understood, the following theorem about interchanging the order of integration may be deduced:

THEOREM. *If* $\alpha(xs)$ *is of uniformly limited variation in* $s$ *for* $x$ *in* $x_1x_2$, *and if* $\gamma(x)$ *is of limited variation, then we have*

$$\int_a^b \varphi(s) d_s \int_{x_1}^{x_2} \alpha(xs) d\gamma(x) = \int_{x_1}^{x_2} \left[ \int_a^b \varphi(s) d_s \alpha(xs) \right] d\gamma(x). \tag{6}$$

A corollary of this theorem, obtained by taking $\gamma(x) \equiv x$, is the formula

$$\int_{x_1}^{x_2} dx \int_a^b \varphi(s) d_s \alpha(xs) = \int_a^b \varphi(s) d_s \int_{x_1}^{x_2} \alpha(xs) dx. \tag{6'}$$

Upon the formula (6) may be constructed the Volterra theory of iterated kernels, and the Volterra relation. The latter takes the form

$$\begin{aligned} \alpha(xs) + A_\lambda(xs) &= \lambda \int_a^b \alpha(s's) d_{s'} A_\lambda(xs') \\ &= \lambda \int_a^b A_\lambda(s's) d_{s'} \alpha(xs'). \end{aligned} \tag{7}$$

Associated with (7) we have the equation

$$(8)\qquad \varphi(x) = f(x) - \lambda \int_a^b f(s) d_s A_\lambda(xs),$$

and the theorem:

THEOREM. *If $\alpha(xs)$ is continuous in $x$ for every value of $s$ and $x$, and is of uniformly limited variation in $s$ for $x$ in $ab$, and if $f(x)$ is continuous in $ab$, then* (2) *has one and only one continuous solution, and it may be written in the form* (8), *provided $\lambda$ is taken small enough* ($\leqq 1/T_\alpha$).

In fact, (8) follows from (2) by (7) in the same manner exactly, as in the corresponding theory of the ordinary integral equation;* and vice versa, (2) follows from (8). Hence our problem is reduced to finding a function $A_\lambda(xs)$, continuous in $x$ for every value of $s$, and of uniformly limited variation in $s$ for $x$ in $ab$, which satisfies both of the equations (7). This function is given by the formula

$$(9)\qquad A_\lambda(xs) = -\sum_0^\infty \lambda^i \alpha_i(xs),$$

where $\alpha_i$ is the $i$th iterated kernel:

$$\alpha_i(xs) = \int_a^b \alpha(s's) d_{s'} \alpha_{i-1}(xs'), \qquad i > 0,$$

$$\alpha_0(xs) = \alpha(xs).$$

These last formulæ may be rewritten for $i > 0$, in the form:

$$(9')\quad \alpha_i(xs) = \int_a^b \alpha_j(s's) d_{s'} \alpha_{i-j-1}(xs'), \qquad j = 0, 1, \cdots, i-1,$$

as we see by (6). As is verified by mathematical induction, all these functions are continuous in $x$ for every $s$; moreover they are all functions of uniformly limited variation in $s$. We have in fact from (5′) the inequality

$$T_{\alpha_i} \leqq (T_\alpha)^{i+1}.$$

* See for instance Bôcher, Introduction to the Study of Integral Equations, Cambridge (Eng.) (1909), pp. 21, 22.

Also, we have from (3) the inequality

$$|\alpha_i(xs)| \leq N|T_a|^i \qquad \text{where} \qquad |\alpha(xs)| \leq N.$$

Hence the series (9) is absolutely and uniformly convergent for $x$ and $s$ in $ab$, if $\lambda$ is taken small enough:

$$|\lambda| < \frac{1}{T_a}. \tag{10}$$

We know therefore that $A_\lambda(xs)$ is continuous in $x$ for every value of $s$.

It remains to point out that $A_\lambda(xs)$ is a function of uniformly limited variation in $s$. We know however that if a series of functions of limited variation, $\Sigma\varphi_i(x)$, has a limit $\varphi(x)$, and converges in such a way that the series of positive constants $\Sigma T_{\phi_i}$ also converges, then the convergence is uniform, and $\varphi(x)$ is a function of limited variation; moreover

$$T_\phi \leq \Sigma T_{\phi_i}.$$

We have then the inequality

$$T_A \leq \frac{T_a}{1 - \lambda T_a},$$

and the point is proved.

With the hypotheses given above, we cannot develop the Fredholm theory of the equation (2). It is not difficult to add the additional necessary postulate,* but rather than introduce artificiality into this treatment, which is so far closely related to its intuitional basis, let us turn to other points of view.

## § 2. The General Analysis of E. H. Moore

**63. Possible Points of View.** The theory of the linear integral equation

$$u(x) = \varphi(x) + \int_a^b K(x\xi)u(\xi)d\xi$$

* To enable us to deal with the function

$$\lim_{n=\infty} \sum_0^n \{\alpha(\xi_i s_i) - \alpha(\xi_i s_{i-1})\}.$$

admits of two types of direct generalization. On the one hand, by paying attention to the formal nature of the demonstrations involved in the theory, the variables, functions and linear operations involved may be generalized to the fullest extent that would enable them still to satisfy the same formal relations; on the other hand, by noticing the combinatorial properties of the operations which produce the iterated kernels, a calculus of these combinations may be created, and the theory extended far beyond the realms of linearity. The first of these methods has yielded, in the hands of Professor E. H. Moore, chapters of his *General Analysis*; the second has produced Volterra's theory of *Permutable Functions.*

In the original theory of integral equations the domain of the independent variable was the linear continuum. It was noticed immediately that the theory was independent of dimension, and could be generalized at once to $n$ dimensions and $n$-tple integrals, even to systems of such equations. Further than this, E. H. Moore has shown that considerations of order in general, in the domain of the independent variable, are immaterial. The method of successive approximation, the Fredholm method, and the Hilbert-Schmidt method involve no hypothesis whatever with respect to this domain. This fact itself gives an indication of the importance and basic nature of the theory of integral equations.

The essential nature of the theory may be obtained by noticing the analogies in theories that relate to diverse subjects, proceeding according to Professor Moore's dictum, "The existence of analogies between central features of various theories implies the existence of a general theory which underlies the particular theories and unifies them with respect to those central features," or we may merely make an abstraction of the formal nature of a single given development, and define the properties of abstract elements by postulates sufficient to produce the desired results. The latter is the method used by Russell in his "Principles of Mathematics." In fact, the General Analysis of E. H. Moore may be considered as an additional chapter in that treatment of mathematics.

The "General Analysis" constitutes a treatise on the abstract relations and classes of general variables, sufficient to afford in their properties, analogies with the usual analysis based on linear or multiply-dimensional continuous point sets.* In this lecture we consider merely the portion of that theory directly related to the theory of integral equations. We use of course the notation of Professor Moore.

**64. The Linear Equation and its Kernel.** The equation to be considered is the following:

$$(G) \qquad \xi = \eta - zJ\kappa\eta$$

or, more explicitly,

$$\xi(s) = \eta(s) - zJ_t\kappa(st)\eta(t),$$

in which $\kappa$ is called the kernel, and $\eta$ is the function to be determined; $J_t$ is a functional operation turning a product $\kappa\eta$ or $\kappa(st)\eta(t)$ into a function of the argument $s$, whose defining postulates will be given later; $\xi$ and $\eta$ are themselves functions of an argument $s$ or $t$, the argument having a range or domain $\mathfrak{P}$; and the equation $G$ holds for every $s$ of the range $\mathfrak{P}$.

The range $\mathfrak{P}$ is not necessarily a linear continuum, or multiply dimensional continuum, or point set,—although so far as I know, no applications have been given where the range is of necessity more general. The elements $p$ of $\mathfrak{P}$ may be numbers, functions, points, curves; moreover for part of the range the elements may be of one sort, and for part, of another. Thus, the equation $(G)$ contains as special cases, the equations

$$(\mathrm{I}) \qquad x = y - zky,$$

$$(\mathrm{II}_n) \qquad x_i = y_i - z\sum_1^n{}_j k_{ij}y_j, \qquad i = 1, 2, \cdots, n,$$

$$(\mathrm{III}) \qquad x_i = y_i - z\sum_1^\infty{}_j k_{ij}y_j, \qquad i = 1, 2, \cdots,$$

$$(\mathrm{IV}) \qquad \xi(s) = \eta(s) - z\int_a^b \kappa(st)\eta(t)dt, \qquad a \leq s \leq b,$$

* New Haven Mathematical Colloquium, New Haven (1910). See also the citation of Professor Moore on which this lecture is based, and summaries by G. D. Birkhoff, *Bulletin of the American Mathematical Society*, vol. 17 (1911), p. 414, and by O. Bolza, *Jahresbericht der deutschen Mathematiker-Vereinigung*, vol. 23 (1914), p. 248.

and the task of the analysis is to devise a system of postulates which will make the results in these cases merely specializations of the general results for equation ($G$). The methods used will be clear to anyone who is familiar with the usual analysis of equations (III) and (IV).

The connection established between (III) and (IV) is by means of *relatively uniform convergence.* A sequence of functions $\mu_n$, $n = 1, 2, \cdots$, on the range $\mathfrak{P}$ converges *uniformly* to a limit function $\theta$, *relatively* to a scale function $\sigma$,

$$\lim_{n=\infty} \mu_n = \theta, \qquad (\mathfrak{P}; \sigma),$$

provided that $n_0$ can be found, so that given $e$ the following inequality will be satisfied:

$$|\mu_n(p) - \theta(p)| \leq e|\sigma(p)|, \quad n \geq n_0.$$

It is also convenient to be able to speak of *relative uniformity as to a class* $\mathfrak{S}$ *of scale functions*:

$$\lim_{n=\infty} \mu_n = \theta, \qquad (\mathfrak{P}; \mathfrak{S}),$$

when any member of the class may be found which will serve as a scale function.

**65. Bases and Postulates for Equation** ($G$). In order to obtain a theory for the equation ($G$) we must arrange a *basis* of classes of functions related one to another with reference to the possibility of performing the operation $J$, and also certain limiting operations of successive approximation. Thus with reference to this equation we may postulate the basis

$$(11) \qquad \Sigma_4 = (\mathfrak{A}; \mathfrak{P}; \mathfrak{M}; \mathfrak{N} \equiv \mathfrak{M}_*{}^2; \mathfrak{R} \equiv (\mathfrak{M}\mathfrak{M})_*; J),$$

which we now proceed to explain.

In the scheme (11), which is merely a shorthand method of remembering what classes of functions we are dealing with, $\mathfrak{A}$ denotes the class of all real or all complex numbers, as we choose; $\mathfrak{P}$ denotes the domain of the variable in the general significance already mentioned; $\mathfrak{M}$ is the class of functions $\mu(p)$, of the variable $p$ in $\mathfrak{P}$, to which the functions $\eta$ and $\xi$ of equation $(G)$ belong; $\mathfrak{N}$ is the class of functions of $t$ on which the operation $J$ may be performed; and finally, $\mathfrak{K}$ denotes the class of functions to which the kernel function $\kappa(st)$ of $(G)$ must belong.

The significance of the equations

$$(12) \qquad \mathfrak{N} \equiv \mathfrak{M}_*{}^2$$

and

$$(13) \qquad \mathfrak{K} \equiv (\mathfrak{M}\mathfrak{M})_*$$

may now be made clear. The symbol $\mathfrak{M}^2$ denotes the class of product functions $\mu_1(p)\mu_2(p)$ of a single variable, of which the factors are functions of $\mathfrak{M}$. On the other hand, the symbol $(\mathfrak{M}\mathfrak{M})$ denotes the class of product functions $\mu_1(p_1)\mu_2(p_2)$ of two variables, of which the factors are functions of $\mathfrak{M}$; in this latter case, $p_1$ and $p_2$ are independent variables, each one ranging over $\mathfrak{P}$.

A symbol $\mathfrak{M}_*$ denotes the class of functions obtained by adding to $\mathfrak{M}$, first the functions

$$\bar{\mu} = a_1\mu_1 + a_2\mu_2 + \cdots + a_n\mu_n,$$

the functions $\mu_i$ being arbitrary functions of $\mathfrak{M}$, and the coefficients $a_i$ being arbitrary numbers from $\mathfrak{A}$ (i. e., arbitrary real or complex numbers as the case may be), thus forming the class designated as $\mathfrak{M}_L$, and second, the functions

$$(14) \qquad \mu_p = \lim_{i=\infty} \bar{\mu}_i,$$

where $\{\bar{\mu}_i\}$ is a sequence of functions $\bar{\mu}$ which converges uniformly to $\mu_p$ over $\mathfrak{P}$, relatively to a scale function which must be taken from $\mathfrak{M}_L$. It can easily be shown that if $\mathfrak{M}$ possesses the property $(D)$, given below, then $\mathfrak{M}_L$ and $\mathfrak{M}_*$ possess the same property, and uniform convergence relative to the class $\mathfrak{M}$ is the same as that relative to $\mathfrak{M}_L$ or $\mathfrak{M}_*$. Moreover $(\mathfrak{M}_*)_* = \mathfrak{M}_*$.

Hence the significance of (12) is that $\mathfrak{N}$ is the totality of functions $\nu(t)$ such that

$$(12') \qquad \nu(t) = \lim_{i=\infty} \nu_i(t), \qquad (\mathfrak{P}; \mathfrak{M}^2),$$

where $\{\nu_i(t)\}$ is a sequence of functions

$$\nu_i(t) = a_{i1}\bar{\mu}_{i1}(t)\mu_{i1}(t) + a_{i2}\bar{\mu}_{i2}(t)\mu_{i2}(t) + \cdots + a_{in}\bar{\mu}_{in}(t)\mu_{in}(t),$$

the functions $\bar{\mu}_{ij}$ and $\mu_{ij}$ being arbitrary functions from $\mathfrak{M}$, and the coefficients $a_{ij}$ arbitrary numbers from $\mathfrak{A}$. The convergence, as is indicated, is uniform over $\mathfrak{P}$, relatively to some scale function which is the product of two functions of $\mathfrak{M}$. Similarly, the significance of (13) is that $\mathfrak{N}$ is the totality of functions $\kappa(st)$ such that

$$(13') \qquad \kappa(st) = \lim_{i=\infty} \nu_i(st),$$

where $\{\nu_i(st)\}$ is a sequence of functions

$$\nu_i(st) = \sum_1^{n_i}{}_j a_{ij}\bar{\mu}_{ij}(s)\mu_{ij}(t).$$

The convergence is uniform over the range $(\mathfrak{P}\mathfrak{P})$ (i. e., the range of the composite variable $s$, $t$) relatively to some function $\bar{\mu}(s)\mu(t)$, as a scale function.

All of the description of the basis, just given, is implied by the array (11). In order to develop the complete analysis of the equation $(G)$ it is necessary merely to specify certain postulates which are to hold for the class of functions $\mathfrak{M}$, and the operation $J$.

As to the class of functions $\mathfrak{M}$, the postulates must be four, $(L)$, $(C)$, $(D_0)$ and $(D)$ as follows:

$(L)$ If $\mu_1, \cdots, \mu_n$ are functions of $\mathfrak{M}$, and $a_1, \cdots, a_n$ elements of $\mathfrak{A}$, then $a_1\mu_1 + \cdots + a_n\mu_n$ is a function of $\mathfrak{M}$.

$(C)$ If $\{\mu_n\}$ represents a sequence of functions of $\mathfrak{M}$, then the limit

$$\mu = \lim_{n=\infty} \mu_n, \qquad (\mathfrak{P}; \mathfrak{M})$$

is a function of $\mathfrak{M}$, provided that the convergence is uniform relatively to a scale function of $\mathfrak{M}$.

$(D_0)$ If $\mu$ is a function of $\mathfrak{M}$, there must be some real-valued nowhere-negative function $\mu_0$ (which may vary with $\mu$) of $\mathfrak{M}$, such that for every $p$ of $\mathfrak{P}$

$$|\mu(p)| \leqq \mu_0(p).$$

(*D*) If $\{\mu_n\}$ represents a sequence of functions of $\mathfrak{M}$, there must be a function $\mu$ of $\mathfrak{M}$, and a sequence of numbers $\{a_n\}$ of $\mathfrak{A}$ such that for every $p$ of $\mathfrak{P}$

$$|\mu_n(p)| \leqq |a_n \mu(p)|, \qquad n = 1, 2, \cdots.$$

The postulates (*L*) and (*C*) together may be stated by saying that

$$\mathfrak{M} \equiv \mathfrak{M}_*.$$

The operation $J$ must satisfy two postulates (*L*) and (*M*), as follows:

(*L*) If $J$ operates on a class of functions $\mathfrak{N}$, and $\nu$, $\nu_1$, $\nu_2$ are three functions of $\mathfrak{N}$ such that $\nu = a_1\nu_1 + a_2\nu_2$, then

$$J(\nu) = a_1 J(\nu_1) + a_2 J(\nu_2).$$

(*M*) There exists a functional operation $M$ (called a *modulus*) on real-valued nowhere-negative functions $\nu_0$ of $\mathfrak{N}$ such that $M(\nu_0)$ is a real non-negative number, for which a relation $|\nu(p)| \leqq \nu_0(p)$ holding for every $p$ of $\mathfrak{P}$ implies the relation $|J(\nu)| \leqq M(\nu_0)$.

These postulates suffice to prove the fundamental properties of the obvious generalizations of the Fredholm determinants and minors, familiar in the theory of the linear integral equation of the second kind. There exists a resolvent kernel $\lambda$ to $\kappa$ which is the ratio of two integral functions of the parameter $z$, the denominator depending on $z$ alone, and not on $s$, $t$, such that the relation (the Volterra relation)

$$\kappa(st) + \lambda(st) = z J_u \kappa(su)\lambda(ut) = z J_u \lambda(su)\kappa(ut) \tag{15}$$

is satisfied. Hence unless $z$ is a root of $\kappa$ (i. e., a value which makes vanish the denominator of $\lambda$) there is one and only one solution of (*G*); it has moreover the form:

$$\eta = \xi - z J\lambda\xi. \tag{16}$$

Rather than proceed into details which will be trivial to those familiar with the theory of integral equation, let us follow Professor Moore in some fundamental generalizations.

**66. The Equation** ($G^5$). The equation ($G$) with the significance

$$(G^5) \qquad \xi(s) = \eta(s) - z J_{tu}\kappa(st)\eta(u)$$

is suggested by the integral equation of the second kind, when the integral is iterated instead of simple. Thus in the above equation, we might have as a special case:

$$J_{tu}\kappa(st)\eta(u) \equiv \int_a^b dt\kappa(st) \int_a^b \omega(tu)\eta(u)du,$$

the $\omega$ being implicitly a part of the definition, in this case. What makes ($G^5$) important however is that it possesses a certain closure property (called by Moore *the closure property* $C_2$);* namely, if it is attempted to generalize ($G_5$) by the same sort of process by means of which ($G^5$) was itself suggested, nothing new is obtained. The operation

$$J_{tuvw}\kappa(stuv)\eta(w),$$

with its postulates, is reducible by a mere renaming of the general variables to the operation in equation ($G^5$) and its postulates. In this sense, *the equation* ($G^5$) *contains its own generalization.*

Since in ($G^5$) the $J$ is an operation on functions of two variables $t$, $u$ or $p_1$, $p_2$, the class $\mathfrak{N}$ must be related to $\mathfrak{M}$ in a different way than in $\Sigma_4$. In the basis which is called $\Sigma_5$ by Moore, the class $\mathfrak{N}$ becomes the class $(\mathfrak{M}\mathfrak{M})_* \equiv \mathfrak{N}$. Hence we may write the basis

$$(17) \qquad \Sigma_5 = (\mathfrak{A}; \mathfrak{P}; \mathfrak{M}; \mathfrak{N} \equiv (\mathfrak{M}\mathfrak{M})_*; J \text{ on } \mathfrak{N} \text{ to } \mathfrak{A}),$$

with the postulates ($L$), ($C$), ($D_0$), ($D$) for $\mathfrak{M}$ and the postulates ($L$), ($M$) for $J$; or the same situation may be stated by the basis

$$(\mathfrak{A}; \mathfrak{P}; \mathfrak{M} \equiv \mathfrak{M}_*; \mathfrak{N} \equiv (\mathfrak{M}\mathfrak{M})_*; J \text{ on } \mathfrak{N} \text{ to } \mathfrak{A}),$$

with the postulates ($D_0$), ($D$) for $\mathfrak{M}$, and the postulates ($L$), ($M$) for $J$. By putting $u = t$ the equation ($G^5$) reduces to the equation ($G$) with its earlier significance, and the basis $\Sigma_5$ to $\Sigma_4$.

* Moore interprets this closure property in terms of generalized scalar (inner) products, which form the "skeleton" of the class $\mathfrak{K}$.

It is to be noted that the equation ($G^5$), with the postulates imposed, encloses as special cases the equations (I), ($\text{II}_n$), (III), (IV) with the assumptions usually made for those theories.* This property is called *the closure property* $C_1$.

**67. The Closure Properties $C_3$ and $C_4$.** The equation in the significance ($G^5$) is its own generalization also from other points of view. Thus if we consider a set of $n$ simultaneous equations

$$(18) \qquad \xi_i(s) = \eta_i(s) - z \sum_1^n{}_j J_{tu} \kappa_{ij}(st)\eta_j(u)$$

all on the same basis $\Sigma_5$, or on different bases $\Sigma_5^i$, $i = 1, 2, \cdots, n$, they may be replaced by a single equation ($G^5$) on a new basis $\Sigma_5$, formed by compounding the old ones in the manner familiar in the theory of integral equations. The range $\mathfrak{P}$ of the new $\Sigma_5$ is the logical sum of the ranges $\mathfrak{P}_i$ of the $\Sigma_5^{(i)}$, and a function $\theta$ on this $\mathfrak{P}$ determines a function $\theta_i$ on each of the ranges $\mathfrak{P}_i$.† The range $\mathfrak{P}\mathfrak{P}$ becomes therefore the logical sum of the $n^2$ product ranges $\mathfrak{P}_i\mathfrak{P}_j$, etc.

The closure property specified in the preceding paragraph, indicated as $C_3$, is equivalent to the passage from (I) to ($\text{II}_n$). On account of the lack of necessity for postulates of order in the domain of the independent variable, this generalization when applied to ($G^5$) yields, as we have said, merely another equation ($G^5$). A further type of self-contained generalization, by what Moore calls **-composition,* constitutes *the closure property* $C_4$. This ingenious generalization is suggested by that from $\Sigma_4$ to $\Sigma_5$ or perhaps from a basis of (I) to $\Sigma_5$.

Given the system of bases $\Sigma^i$, with a common class $\mathfrak{A}$, the composite basis $\Sigma_{1\cdots n*}$ is determined as follows. The class $\mathfrak{A}$ of $\Sigma^*$ is the common $\mathfrak{A}$ for the $\Sigma^i$; the range $\mathfrak{P}$ for $\Sigma^*$ is the range in $n$ variables given as the product range of $\mathfrak{P}_1, \cdots, \mathfrak{P}_i$. The class $\mathfrak{M}$ on $\mathfrak{P}$ is the class of the functions of $n$ variables

$$\mathfrak{M} \equiv (\mathfrak{M}_1\mathfrak{M}_2\cdots\mathfrak{M}_n)_*,$$

* A detailed exposition of this closure property is given in the paper by O. Bolza already cited.

† The ranges $\mathfrak{P}_i$ need not of course be distinct. The range $\mathfrak{P}_1$, for instance, may consist merely of a subset of elements from the range $\mathfrak{P}_2$.

and the class $\mathfrak{K}$ on the range $\mathfrak{P}\mathfrak{P}$ is the class of functions of $2n$ variables

$$\mathfrak{K} = (\mathfrak{K}_1\mathfrak{K}_2\cdots\mathfrak{K}_n)_*.$$

As for the operation $J$, that is let become of the type of an iterated operation

$$J\kappa = J_1 J_2 \cdots J_n \kappa.$$

The postulates of Art. 66 holding for each of the bases $\Sigma^i$ imply the same postulates for the new basis $\Sigma_{1\ldots n*}$, and thus the new equation as developed is merely an instance of the original $(G^5)$.

Numerous instances suggest themselves. As a special case, $(G^5)$ contains the equation

$$(19)\quad \begin{aligned} \xi(s_1\cdots s_n) &= \eta(s_1\cdots s_n) \\ &\quad - zJ'_{t_1u_1}\cdots J^{(n)}_{t_nu_n}\kappa(s_1\cdots s_n,\, t_1\cdots t_n)\eta(u_1\cdots u_n). \end{aligned}$$

If the basis for $(II_n)$ is combined with the basis for $(G^5)$, the resulting equation is as follows:*

$$(20)\quad \xi(is) = \eta(is) - z\sum_1^n{}_j J_{tu}\kappa(isjt)\eta(ju), \qquad i = 1, 2, \cdots, n;$$

and if the basis for $(III)$ is combined with that for $(G^5)$ there results a theory of the infinite system of equations

$$\xi(is) = \eta(is) - z\sum_1^\infty{}_j J_{tu}\kappa(isjt)\eta(ju), \qquad i = 1, 2, 3, \cdots.$$

This obviously contains as a special case a theory for an infinite system of linear differential equations, in an infinite number of unknowns and one independent variable.

**68. Mixed Linear Equations.** A practical consequence of the closure property $C_3$ is that $(G^5)$ contains as a special case the mixed linear equation; in particular, the mixed linear *integral* equation, treated most significantly by W. A. Hurwitz.† This

* Equation (20) appears also under the closure property $C_3$.

† W. A. Hurwitz, *Transactions of the American Mathematical Society*, vol. 16 (1915), pp. 121–133.

equation may be studied in the form

$$(21) \qquad \xi = \eta - z \sum_{1}^{n}{}_j J_j \kappa_j \eta,$$

where the ranges $\mathfrak{P}_j$ may be taken as identical. In E. H. Moore's treatment this equation is taken as an example of a system of equations of the form (18), where the $n$ equations are identical. It is therefore a special case of the equation ($G^5$).

The *adjoint* of ($G^5$), which may be conveniently studied with it, is the equation

$$(22) \qquad \bar{\xi}(t) = \bar{\eta}(t) - z J_{rs} \kappa(st) \eta(r).$$

In the case of the equation (21) the adjoint is therefore a whole system of equations; it is moreover of the character specified by Hurwitz. In order however to obtain completely the form given by Hurwitz it would be necessary to generalize his theory of the *pseudo resolvent*.*

**69. Further Developments.** In the equation ($G^5$) the class $\mathfrak{R}$ of the functions $\kappa$ has been defined over the range $\mathfrak{P}\mathfrak{P}$. It is pointed out by Moore that there is no reason why $s$ and $t$ in $\kappa(st)$ should have the same range. In fact, if the range of the functions of $\mathfrak{M}$ is $\mathfrak{P}$, the range of the functions of $\mathfrak{R}$ may be $\mathfrak{P}\bar{\mathfrak{P}}$, where $\bar{\mathfrak{P}}$ is independent of $\mathfrak{P}$. This is the furthest point to which the generalization of the Fredholm theory, that is, the theory of the integral equation of the second kind, is carried.

This last form of generalization is impossible for the theory of the integral equation of the first kind (the Hilbert-Schmidt theory). Here the basis $\Sigma_5$ must be adhered to, and it is necessary to introduce the characteristic postulate of the symmetry of $\kappa(st)$ if $\kappa(st)$ is real, or, if $\kappa(st)$ is complex, that $\kappa(ts)$ shall be the conjugate complex quantity to $\kappa(st)$.

It is obvious that many theories may be amalgamated with the developments of this generalization. Thus some of the theory of linear and non-linear differential equations, and the theory of permutable functions may be so translated. Such generalizations are useful, but are apt to be somewhat facile.

* W. A. Hurwitz, *ibid.*, vol. 13 (1912), p. 408.

The consequence of specialization of the range of the general variable, say by the introduction of concepts like that of distance,* is however the subject of fruitful study.

**70. The Content of the Operation** $J$. So far the operation $J$ has been defined by postulates, and not explicitly. In order to get some idea of its generality for a given range of the general variable, let us choose the range as the most familiar one, namely, the one-dimensional continuum. Let us assume that the class $\mathfrak{M}$ contains (or can be extended by definition to contain) the totality of continuous functions over this range, which we may take to be the interval $ab$. *In this case, the operation is merely a Stieltjes integral*:

$$J_{tu}\kappa(st)\eta(u) = \int_a^b \eta(t)d_t\alpha(st). \tag{23}$$

In fact from the dominance property $(D_0)$ and the modular property $(M)$ it follows that if $s$ is given a constant value $s_0$, and $|\eta(t)| < 1$, then there is a constant $C_{s_0}$ such that

$$| J_{tu}\kappa(s_0t)\eta(u) | < C_{s_0}.$$

Hence for every $\eta$ it follows by the linearity property $(L)$ that the inequality

$$| J_{tu}\kappa(st)\eta(u) | < C_s \overset{b}{\underset{a}{\max}} |\eta| \tag{24}$$

is satisfied. This and the linearity property constitute the two Riesz conditions of Art. 40, and our statement is therefore proved.

We may express $\alpha(st)$ directly in terms of $\kappa(st)$. Either side of (23) is a linear functional of $\eta$, which we may denote by

$$\overset{b}{\underset{a}{T}}[\eta].$$

* Besides the references to Moore, see papers by Fréchét, and Pitcher, e. g., Pitcher, *American Journal of Mathematics*, vol. 36 (1914), pp. 261–266, where the literature is given. The fundamental memoir on this subject is Fréchet's Thesis, already cited.

If now, as in Lecture III, equation (23), we define

$$f_{u_1u_2} = 1, \qquad u_1 < u \leq u_2,$$
$$= 0, \qquad \text{otherwise, etc.,}$$

and also define the new symbol

$$(25) \qquad \overset{u_2}{\underset{u_1}{J}}{}_{tu}\kappa(st) = \overset{b}{\underset{a}{T}}[f_{u_1u_2}], \qquad \overset{u_2}{\underset{a}{J}}{}_{tu}\kappa(st) = \overset{b}{\underset{a}{T}}[f_{au_2}],$$

then we have

$$(26) \quad \alpha(su_2) - \alpha(su_1) = \overset{u_2}{\underset{u_1}{J}}{}_{tu}\kappa(st), \qquad \alpha(su_2) = \overset{u_2}{\underset{a}{J}}{}_{tu}\kappa(st),$$

which gives us $\alpha$ in terms of $\kappa$.

Let us now divide the interval $ab$ into sub-intervals by points $a = u_0, u_1, \cdots, u_n = b$, and let $s_i$ be a point in the region $u_{i-1} < s_i < u_i$. On account of the continuity of the linear functional, the following equation may be deduced:

$$(27) \qquad J_{tu}\kappa(ut) = \lim_{n=\infty} \sum_1^n{}_i(\alpha(s_iu_i) - \alpha(s_iu_{i-1})).$$

The left-hand member of (27) is one of the constituents of the Fredholm determinant, corresponding to $\int_a^b \kappa(tt)dt$ in the theory of integral equations.*

## § 3. The Theory of Permutable Functions, and Combinations of Integrals

**71. The Associative Combinations of the First and Second Kinds.** In this second form of generalization of the theory of integral equations, what is of primary importance is an associative combination of integrals. In fact, Volterra's theory rests upon the identity

$$(28) \quad \int_a^b ds_1 K_1(rs_1) \int_a^b K_2(s_1s_2)K_3(s_2s)ds_2 = \int_a^b \left[ \int_a^b K_1(rs_1)K_2(s_1s_2)ds_1 \right] K_3(s_2s)ds_2,$$

* See footnote at end of Art. 62.

and as a special case, putting $K_i(rs) = 0$ when $s > r$,

$$\int_s^r ds_1 K_1(rs_1) \int_s^{s_1} K_2(s_1s_2)K_3(s_2s)ds_2 = \int_s^r \left[ \int_{s_2}^r K_1(rs_1)K_2(s_1s_2)ds_1 \right] K_3(s_2s)ds_2. \tag{29}$$

This last equation is sometimes called *Dirichlet's formula,** and may of course be established directly. If we define

$$K_1K_2 = \int_a^b K_1(rs_1)K_2(s_1s)ds_1 \tag{30}$$

or

$$K_1K_2 = \int_s^r K_1(rs_1)K_2(s_1s)ds_1, \tag{31}$$

which are respectively the combinations of the second and first kinds, we shall have by (28) and (29) the equation

$$K_1(K_2K_3) = (K_1K_2)K_3, \tag{32}$$

which is the *associative law* for these symbolic products.†

The hypothesis of commutativity, if it is made,

$$K_1K_2 = K_2K_1, \tag{33}$$

is Volterra's *condition of permutability.*‡ *If two functions are permutable with a third, they are permutable with each other.*§

* U. Dini, Lezioni di analisi infinitesimale, Pisa, vol. 2, p. 925.

† In terms of Moore's General Analysis, if in $(G^5)$ we introduce a parameter $r$, we may regard $J_{tu}\kappa(st)\eta(ur)$ as a symbolic product of the functions $\kappa(sr)$ and $\eta(sr)$. If we restrict ourselves to the same operation $J$ and class $\mathfrak{M}$, and various kernels $\kappa$, $\omega$, $\eta$, etc., the succession of two applications of the operation turns out to be commutative (see the article by Moore on which this lecture is based, also Hildebrand, *Transactions of the American Mathematical Society*, vol. 18 (1917), pp. 73–96). Hence the triple product $\kappa\omega\eta$ is associative, and the theory of Volterra's generalization may be extended to the General Analysis.

‡ Volterra, *Rendiconti della R. Acc. dei Lincei*, vol. 19 (1910), 1st sem., pp. 169–180.

§ Vessiot, *Comptes Rendus*, vol. 154 (1912), pp. 682–684. A comprehensive study of permutable functions, with special reference to the case when the functions are analytic in $r$ and $s$ has been given by J. Pérès, Sur les fonctions permutables de première espèce de M. Vito Volterra, Thèse, no. d'ordre: 1567, Paris (1915).

**72. The Algebra of Permutable and Non-Permutable Functions.** In order to facilitate the inverse operation corresponding to division, we abandon slightly Volterra's notation and introduce complex quantities

$$\kappa = k + jK(rs),$$
$$\xi = u + jU(rs),$$

etc., where $k$ and $u$ are constants, and $K$ and $U$ are functions of $r$, $s$ as indicated. We say that $\kappa = \xi$ if $k = u$ and $K(rs) \equiv U(rs)$, and define the zero element and the addition and subtraction of elements in the usual way. In the quantity $\kappa$ we speak of $k$ as the *ordinary coefficient* and $K(rs)$ as the *functional coefficient*; and if the ordinary coefficient vanishes we speak of $\kappa$ as a *function of nullity*. Both $k$ and $K$ may contain extra parameters $x, y, \cdots$, which do not enter into the functional operation, now to be described.

We define the product

$$(34) \quad \kappa\xi = ku + j\{kU(rs) + uK(rs) + \int K(rs_1)U(s_1s)ds_1\},$$

where the integral sign denotes the combination of the first or second kind according to the algebra we are treating; if necessary to distinguish between these two products we may denote them by $[\kappa\xi]_1$ and $[\kappa\xi]_2$ respectively, or make use of the symbols $\int_1 KU$, $\int_2 KU$, $\int_1 U^n$, etc. Generally, we shall not need to impose a condition of permutability on the functions involved, and so we shall be using an algebra which does not contain the commutative property. The associative law for multiplication is however always satisfied, as well as the distributive.

We shall have both left-handed and right-handed division. In the algebra of the first kind, division by a function $\kappa$, not of nullity, is equivalent, by the definition of equality, to first an ordinary division (to satisfy the relation among the ordinary coefficients), and second, the resolution of an integral equation of the second kind of Volterra type. This resolution is always possible and unique, provided that the functions are finite

($|K(rs)| \leq M_K$), and continuous. In order to obtain the same unique result in the algebra of the second kind (which depends upon solving a Fredholm equation), we assume that every functional coefficient $K(rs)$ or $U(rs)$ contains a parameter, say $\lambda$, in such a way that the inequality

$$(35) \qquad |K(rs)| \leq \lambda M_K, \qquad M_K \text{ a constant,}$$

is satisfied; and we consider values of $\lambda$ in the neighborhood of $\lambda = 0$ ($|\lambda| < k/(b-a)M_K$).*

The idemfactor exists in both algebras, and has the value $1 + j0$. If we do not make the assumption of permutability, all the laws of algebra† are satisfied except the commutative law, with the proviso that division by a function of nullity corresponds to division by zero. *If we make the assumption of permutability, the results of the algebraic operations yield again permutable functions, and all the laws of elementary algebra are satisfied; in fact the symbolic algebra of the quantities* $\kappa, \xi, \cdots$ *is isomorphic with the algebra of their ordinary coefficients,* $k, u, \cdots$.

In particular, we can apply to these generalized integral equations the theory of Lagrange. The equations of degrees 1, 2, 3, 4 can be solved by making use of binomial equations as resolvents.‡

**73. The Volterra Relation and Reciprocal Functions.** The Volterra relation is that which holds between a given kernel and the kernel of the resolvent integral equation, and may be written in the form

$$(36) \qquad K(rs) + K'(rs) = \int KK'.$$

* Or values of $\lambda$ which are not special parameter values for the functions concerned. See C. E. Seely, Certain Non-Linear Integral Equations, Dissertation, Lancaster (1914).

† See for instance Huntington, *Annals of Mathematics*, 2d series, vol. 8 (1906). It must be remembered that in a non-commutative algebra

$$\frac{1}{ab} = \left(\frac{1}{b}\right)\left(\frac{1}{a}\right).$$

‡ The solution of binomial equations depends upon expansion in series; see Art. 75, below.

The functions $K$ and $K'$ we shall speak of as *reciprocal*; they will be permutable. If now, we write

$$\kappa = 1 - jK(rs), \qquad \kappa' = 1 - jK'(rs), \tag{37}$$

equation (36) takes on the special form

$$\kappa\kappa' = 1. \tag{37'}$$

On account of the permutability of $K$ and $K'$ we have also

$$\kappa'\kappa = 1.$$

Let us, by putting a bar over a function, denote the function reciprocal to it. The formula for division in general may be expressed simply, in terms of this notation. In fact, we have

$$\begin{aligned}\frac{1}{u + jU(rs)} &= \frac{1}{u}\left(\frac{1}{1 - j\left\{-\frac{1}{u}U(rs)\right\}}\right)\\ &= \frac{1}{u} - j\frac{1}{u}\overline{\left(-\frac{1}{u}U(rs)\right)}.\end{aligned} \tag{38}$$

Moreover by writing (36) in the form

$$jK(rs) + j\overline{K}(rs) = jK(rs)j\overline{K}(rs)$$

we get the formula

$$j\overline{K}(rs) = \frac{-jK(rs)}{1 - jK(rs)}. \tag{38'}$$

Let $U_1 \cdots U_m$ be continuous functions of $r$, $s$, permutable among themselves or not, and let $\overline{U}_1, \cdots, \overline{U}_m$ be the reciprocal functions. Then the functions $U$ and $V$, defined by the equations

$$\begin{aligned} jU &= 1 - (1 - jU_1)^{p_1}(1 - j\overline{U}_1)^{q_1}\cdots(1 - jU_m)^{p_m}(1 - j\overline{U}_m)^{q_m},\\ jV &= 1 - (1 - jU_m)^{q_m}(1 - j\overline{U}_m)^{p_m}\cdots(1 - jU_1)^{q_1}(1 - j\overline{U}_1)^{p_1},\end{aligned} \tag{39}$$

where the $p_i$, $q_i$ are arbitrary integers, positive or negative, are reciprocal functions. In fact it may be at once verified that we have

$$(1 - jU)(1 - jV) = (1 - jV)(1 - jU) = 1.$$

In particular, *if* $K_1(rs)$ *and* $K_2(rs)$ *are two continuous functions, and* $\overline{K}_1$ *and* $\overline{K}_2$ *are their reciprocal functions, then the functions*

$$(40)\qquad \begin{aligned} K(rs) &= K_1(rs) + K_2(rs) - \int K_1(rs_1)K_2(s_1s)ds_1, \\ \overline{K}(rs) &= \overline{K}_1(rs) + \overline{K}_2(rs) - \int \overline{K}_2(rs_1)\overline{K}_1(s_1s)ds_1 \end{aligned}$$

*are reciprocal.**

This theorem has some interesting special cases. If we take $K_1 = U$ and $K_2 = -U$, we get from (40):

$$K(rs) = \int U(rs_1)U(s_1s)ds_1,$$

$$\overline{K}(rs) = \overline{U}(rs) + \overline{(-U(rs))} - \int \overline{U}(rs_1)\overline{(-U(s_1s))}ds_1.$$

But if we form $j\overline{U}j\overline{(-U)}$ by (38′), we have

$$\int \overline{U}(rs_1)\overline{(-U(s_1s))}ds_1 = \overline{\left(\int U(rs_1)U(s_1s)ds_1\right)} = \overline{K}(rs),$$

and combining this with the previous result, we find that *the reciprocal function to* $\int U(rs_1)U(s_1s)ds_1$ *is* $\frac{1}{2}\{\overline{U}(rs) + \overline{(-U(rs))}\}$.

If $K_1$ and $K_2$ are orthogonal, i. e., if $\int K_1K_2 = 0$, equation (38′) tells us that $\overline{K}_1$ and $\overline{K}_2$ are orthogonal. Hence from (40), if $K_1$ and $K_2$ are orthogonal functions, the reciprocal function to $K_1 + K_2$ is $\overline{K}_1 + \overline{K}_2$:†

$$\overline{(K_1 + K_2)} = \overline{K}_1 + \overline{K}_2.$$

If $\lambda$ is not a root (characteristic value) of $K_1$ or $K_2$ (that is, a value for which $\overline{K}_1$ or $\overline{K}_2$ fails to exist) then it is not a root of the function $K_1 + K_2 - \int K_1K_2$.

**74. Fredholm's Theorem of Multiplication.** In this article let us disregard temporarily the parameter $\lambda$ and the condition (35).

* This theorem is implied by a remark of Fredholm that the transformations of the form $S_f(\varphi) = \varphi(x) - \int^b f(xs)\varphi(s)ds$ form a group, the product transformation $S_F = S_gS_f$ being given by $F = f + g + \int gf$; see the fundamental memoir, *Acta Mathematica*, vol. 27, p. 372.

† Lalesco, Théorie des équations intégrales, Paris (1912), p. 41.

The functions $D(rs)$ and $D$ defined by Fredholm,

$$
\begin{aligned}
D(rs) &= K(rs) - \int_a^b K\begin{pmatrix} rs_1 \\ ss_1 \end{pmatrix} ds_1 \\
&\qquad + \frac{1}{2!}\int_a^b \int_a^b K\begin{pmatrix} rs_1s_2 \\ ss_1s_2 \end{pmatrix} ds_1ds_2 - \cdots, \qquad (41)\\
D &= 1 - \int_a^b K(s_1s_1)ds_1 + \frac{1}{2!}\int_a^b \int_a^b K\begin{pmatrix} s_1s_2 \\ s_1s_2 \end{pmatrix} ds_1ds_2 - \cdots,
\end{aligned}
$$

serve to express the resolvent kernel in the form

$$\overline{K}(rs) = -\frac{D(rs)}{D}; \tag{42}$$

moreover, if we form the variation $\delta K$ of $K$ (e. g., $(\partial K/\partial \lambda)d\lambda$), we have the formula*

$$\delta \log D = \int_a^b ds\{\delta K(ss) - \int_a^b \overline{K}(ss_1)\delta K(s_1s)ds_1. \tag{43}$$

This may be written in the form

$$\delta \log D = \int_a^b \{(1 - j\overline{K})j\delta K\}_{r=s}ds. \tag{43'}$$

If we have any two functions $\varphi(rs)$ and $\psi(rs)$, we may verify directly the formula

$$\int_a^b \{j\varphi j\psi\}_{r=s}ds = \int_a^b \{j\psi j\varphi\}_{r=s}ds. \tag{44}$$

Hence (43) may also be written in the form

$$\delta \log D = \int_a^b \{j\delta K(1 - j\overline{K})\}_{r=s}ds. \tag{43''}$$

Consider now the expression (43′) when $K = K_1 + K_2 - \int K_1K_2$. We have by direct differentiation:

$$\delta K = (1 - jK_1)j\delta K_2 + j\delta K_1(1 - jK_2);$$

* Fredholm, loc. cit., p. 380.

hence (43′) becomes

$$\delta \log D = \int_a^b \{(1 - j\bar{K})(1 - jK_1)j\delta K_2 \\ + (1 - j\bar{K})j\delta K_1(1 - jK_2)\}_{r=s} ds,$$

the last term of which, by (44), may be written

$$\int_a^b \{j\delta K_1(1 - jK_2)(1 - j\bar{K})\}_{r=s} ds.$$

But, by (40), we have

$$1 - j\bar{K} = (1 - j\bar{K}_2)(1 - j\bar{K}_1),$$

and therefore, making this substitution,

$$\delta \log D = \int_a^b \{(1 - j\bar{K}_2)j\delta K_2\}_{r=s} ds + \int_a^b \{j\delta K_1(1 - j\bar{K}_1)\}_{r=s} ds,$$

or, by (43′) and (43″),

$$\delta \log D = \delta \log D_1 + \delta \log D_2.$$

Hence

$$\log D - \log D_1 D_2 = \text{const.}$$

If we replace $K_1$ by $\mu K_1$ and $K_2$ by $\mu K_2$, and write this equation for $\mu = 0$, we find $D = D_1 = D_2 = 1$, and this constant is zero; therefore for $\mu = 1$ we have

(45) $$D = D_1 D_2,$$

which is Fredholm's *theorem of multiplication*.

If $K(rs)$ is an integral analytic function of a parameter $\lambda$, then $D(\lambda)$ and $D(rs\lambda)$ will be integral analytic functions of $\lambda$, without regard to (35). The equation (43′) will then take the form

$$\frac{d}{d\lambda} \log D(\lambda) = \int_a^b \left\{ (1 - j\bar{K})j \frac{\partial K}{\partial \lambda} \right\}_{r=s} ds.$$

Hence *if* $K_1$ *and* $K_2$ *are integral analytic functions of a parameter* $\lambda$, *and* $K = K_1 + K_2 - \int K_1 K_2$, *then*

(45′) $$D(\lambda) = D_1(\lambda) D_2(\lambda),$$

*and*

$$D(rs\lambda) = D_2(\lambda)D_1(rs\lambda) + D_1(\lambda)D_2(rs\lambda) + \int_a^b D_2(rs_1\lambda)D_1(s_1s\lambda)ds_1. \tag{45''}$$

**75. Developments in Series.** Volterra's fundamental theorem upon the convergence of series of symbolic powers, the combination being of the first or second kind, is that *if the series*

$$a_0 + a_1z + a_2z^2 + \cdots \tag{46}$$

*is convergent for some value of* $z \neq 0$, *then the series*

$$a_0 + a_1zf(rs) + a_2z^2 \int f(rs_1)f(s_1s)ds_1 + a_3z^3 \int\int f(rs_1)f(s_1s_2)f(s_2s)ds_1ds_2 + \cdots, \tag{46'}$$

*where* $f(rs)$ *is any finite continuous function, is convergent for all values of* $z$, *if the integral combination is of the first kind (variable limits), and for sufficiently small values of* $z$ *if the combination is of the second kind (constant limits).* By means of this theorem, new transcendental functions, with special applications to integro-differential equations, may be defined and treated.

The corresponding theorem for symbolic power series in functions $\xi = u + jU(rs)$ contains this theorem as a special case. For the combination of the second kind, we assume the condition (35).

THEOREM. *Given the power series in* $u$,

$$a_0 + a_1u + a_2u^2 + \cdots, \tag{47}$$

*convergent for* $|u| \leq \rho$, *the symbolic power series*

$$a_0 + a_1\xi + a_2\xi^2 + \cdots \tag{47'}$$

*in which* $\xi = u + jU(rs)$ *will be convergent for* $|u| \leq \rho'$, *however large* $M_U$ *may be, provided that* $\rho' < \rho$.

The theorem can be verified at once for combinations of the second kind. In fact, if we choose a positive quantity $x$ so that at the same time, $x > 1$ and $x > |b - a|$, we shall have

$$U(rs) \leq \lambda x M, \qquad M = M_U,$$
$$|\xi^k| \leq (\rho' + \lambda x M)^k,$$

and so if $|\lambda| \leq (\rho - \rho')/xM$, we shall have $|\xi^k| \leq \rho^k$, and the series will be absolutely convergent (and uniformly with respect to the variables $xy$).

On the other hand, if the equation is of the first kind, we have

$$|U(rs)| \leq M, \qquad M = M_U,$$

whence

$$|\xi^k| \leq P_k,$$

where

$$P_k = \rho'^k + k\rho'^{k-1}M + \cdots + \frac{k!\,\rho'^{k-1}M^i x^{i-1}}{i!\,(i-1)!\,(k-i)!} + \cdots + \frac{M^k x^{k-1}}{(k-1)!},$$

$x$ being greater than $|b - a|$ (the variables $r$ and $s$ are contained between limits $a$ and $b$). If we choose a $\rho''$ so that $\rho' < \rho'' < \rho$, the original series will be dominated by the series

$$S = P\sum_{k=1}^{\infty}\frac{P_k}{\rho''^k},$$

where $P$ is some constant.

If we split the expression for $P_{k+1}$ after the $i + 1$st term, we shall have

$$P_{k+1} < \rho'\frac{k+1}{k+1-i}P_k + \frac{Mx(k+1)}{i(i+1)}P_k,$$

as is easily verified. Hence

$$\frac{P_{k+1}}{\rho''P_k} < \frac{\rho'}{\rho''} + \frac{i}{k+1-i} + \frac{Mx}{\rho''}\frac{k+1}{i^2}.$$

But we can choose $i$ as a function of $k$ so that each of the last two terms vanishes as $k$ becomes infinite,* and therefore

$$\lim_{k=\infty}\frac{P_{k+1}}{\rho''P_k} < 1,$$

* For example, take $i$ as the nearest integer to $k^{2/3}$.

and the dominating series is convergent. Thus the theorem is proved.

The theorem can now be extended to the case where the coefficients $a_k$ are no longer constants, but may be of the form $a_k + jA_k(rs)$.

THEOREM. *The two series*

$$\alpha_0 + \alpha_1 \xi + \alpha_2 \xi^2 + \cdots,$$
$$\alpha_0 + \xi \alpha_1 + \xi^2 \alpha_2 + \cdots,$$

*in which* $\alpha_i = a_i + jA_i(rs)$, $\xi = u + jU(rs)$, *are convergent for* $|u| \leq \rho'$ *(uniformly in rs), however large* $M_U$ *may be, provided that the series*

$$\alpha_0 + \alpha_1 u + \alpha_2 u^2 + \cdots$$

*is convergent for* $u = \rho$, *with* $\rho' < \rho$, *and remains finite* $\leq P$ *for* $u = \rho$ *and r, s arbitrary within ab.*

**76. Extension of Analytic Functions.** The convergence theorems just obtained enable us to generalize without further proof every analytic function, *together with whatever properties may be established by a comparison of power series.* Thus the relations between sin $u$, cos $u$, $e^u$ may be generalized; the addition theorems, the moduli of periodicity, certain integro-differential equations which the functions satisfy may also be written immediately for such functions and for the $\Theta$ functions.

We define

$$e^{\xi} = 1 + \xi + \frac{\xi^2}{2!} + \cdots. \tag{48}$$

This series in the theory of functions of a complex variable is convergent for all values of the variable; hence in the present case, the series (48) is convergent for all values of $\lambda$, $u$, $M_U$. We have

$$e^{\xi+\eta} = e^{\xi} e^{\eta}. \tag{49}$$

$$e^{\xi + 2m\pi i} = e^{\xi}, \qquad m = \pm 1, \pm 2, \cdots. \tag{50}$$

From (49) it follows that $e^{\xi}$ cannot vanish (identically, of course, in $r$, $s$) for any limited function $\xi_0 = u_0 + jU(rs)$. For

$e^{1+j0} \neq 0$, and if we should have $e^{\xi_0} = 0$, then

$$e^{\xi} = e^{\xi - \xi_0} e^{\xi_0} = 0.$$

From the addition theorem (49) we have

$$e^{u + jU(rs)} = e^u e^{jU(rs)}.$$

Hence if we denote the functional coefficient of $e^{\xi}$ by $E(u, U)$, we shall have by (49),

$$E(u, U) = e^u E(0, U),$$

where

$$\begin{aligned} E(0, U) &= U(rs) + \frac{1}{2!}\int U(rs_1)U(s_1 r)ds_1 \\ &\quad + \frac{1}{3!}\int\int U(rs_1)U(s_1 s_2)U(s_2 s)ds_1 ds_2 + \cdots. \end{aligned} \tag{51}$$

We may write

$$e^{\xi} = e^u(1 + jE(0, U)). \tag{51'}$$

It can be shown that the only modulus of periodicity possessed by $e^{\xi}$ is the one already given, namely $U_0 = 0$, $u_0 = 2\pi i$. Hence the function $E(0, U)$, considered as a functional of $U$, has no period. It cannot vanish unless $U = 0$.

If we substitute (51′) into the addition theorem (49) we obtain the addition theorem for $E(0, U)$,

$$\begin{aligned} E(0, U + V) &= E(0, U) + E(0, V) \\ &\quad + \int E(0, U(rs_1))E(0, V(s_1 s))ds_1. \end{aligned} \tag{52}$$

The function $E(0, zU)$, in accordance with (51), was defined by Volterra and considered as a transcendental function of $z$, with the addition theorem corresponding to (52). It has no period in $z$ and cannot vanish unless $z = 0$. This function sometimes is called the *Volterra transcendental.*

The addition theorem for $E(0, U)$ reduces to the Volterra relation if $V$ is put equal to $-U$. Hence, *given the function $U$, the two quantities $-E(0, U)$, $-E(0, -U)$ are reciprocal functions.*

The theory of the extended $\Theta$ functions depends directly on the theory of the function $E(0, U)$. In fact, we define

$$\vartheta(\xi, \beta) = \sum_{-\infty}^{\infty}{}_n e^{n^2\beta + 2n\xi}$$

with $\xi = u + jU(rs)$, $\beta = b + jB(rs)$, and assume the real part of $b$ to be negative.

**77. Integro-Differential Equations of Static Type, and Green's Theorem.** If we let our functions $\xi$, etc., contain parameters $x, y, \cdots$, distinct from the variables $r, s$, and introduce differential operators with regard to these variables, we have the formula

$$\frac{\partial}{\partial x}(\xi_1\xi_2) = \xi_1\frac{\partial \xi_2}{\partial x} + \frac{\partial \xi_1}{\partial x}\xi_2,$$

with or without a hypothesis of permutability. The equations which involve symbolic differentiation formulæ of this sort yield a class of integro-differential equations with the variables of integration distinct from those of differentiation. They may be called of *static type*, since they were first applied to the problem of *static hysteresis*, and the analysis of slow motion.

We may treat the general linear differential expression of this sort. Thus, if we have the expression of the second order

$$(53)\qquad \begin{aligned} L(\xi) = \alpha_{11}\frac{\partial^2\xi}{\partial x^2} + 2\alpha_{12}\frac{\partial^2\xi}{\partial x\partial y} + \alpha_{22}\frac{\partial^2\xi}{\partial y^2} \\ + \alpha_1\frac{\partial\xi}{\partial x} + \alpha_2\frac{\partial\xi}{\partial y} + \alpha\xi, \end{aligned}$$

with

$$\xi = u(xy) + jU(xy\,|\,rs),$$
$$\alpha_{ik} = a_{ik}(xy) + jA_{ik}(xy\,|\,rs), \qquad \text{etc.,}$$

we define the adjoint expression

$$(54)\qquad \begin{aligned} M(\eta) = \frac{\partial^2\eta}{\partial x^2}\beta_{11} + 2\frac{\partial^2\eta}{\partial x\partial y}\beta_{12} + \frac{\partial^2\eta}{\partial y^2}\beta_{22} \\ + \frac{\partial\eta}{\partial x}\beta_1 + \frac{\partial\eta}{\partial y}\beta_2 + \eta\beta, \end{aligned}$$

with

$$\beta_{ij} = \alpha_{ij},$$

$$(55)\quad \beta_1 = 2\frac{\partial \alpha_{11}}{\partial x} + 2\frac{\partial \alpha_{12}}{\partial y} - \alpha_1, \qquad \beta_2 = 2\frac{\partial \alpha_{12}}{\partial x} + 2\frac{\partial \alpha_{22}}{\partial y} - \alpha_2,$$

$$\beta = \frac{\partial^2 \alpha_{11}}{\partial x^2} + 2\frac{\partial^2 \alpha_{12}}{\partial x \partial y} + \frac{\partial^2 \alpha_{22}}{\partial y^2} - \frac{\partial \alpha_1}{\partial x} - \frac{\partial \alpha_2}{\partial y} + \alpha.$$

The formulæ for $M(\eta)$ and its coefficients are the well-known ones for differential equations, except that attention is paid to the order of the factors, to avoid the necessity of a hypothesis of permutability.

If we write

$$S_1 \equiv \eta\left(\alpha_{11}\frac{\partial \xi}{\partial x} + \alpha_{12}\frac{\partial \xi}{\partial y}\right) - \left(\frac{\partial \eta}{\partial x}\alpha_{11} + \frac{\partial \eta}{\partial y}\alpha_{12}\right)\xi$$

$$+ \eta\left(\alpha_1 - \frac{\partial \alpha_{11}}{\partial x} - \frac{\partial \alpha_{12}}{\partial y}\right)\xi,$$

(56)

$$S_2 = \eta\left(\alpha_{12}\frac{\partial \xi}{\partial x} + \alpha_{22}\frac{\partial \xi}{\partial y}\right) - \left(\frac{\partial \eta}{\partial x}\alpha_{12} + \frac{\partial \eta}{\partial y}\alpha_{22}\right)\xi$$

$$+ \eta\left(\alpha_2 - \frac{\partial \alpha_{12}}{\partial x} - \frac{\partial \alpha_{22}}{\partial y}\right)\xi,$$

we have Lagrange's identity:

$$(57)\qquad \eta L(\xi) - M(\eta)\xi = \frac{\partial S_1}{\partial x} + \frac{\partial S_2}{\partial y},$$

and Green's theorem:

$$(58)\quad \int\!\!\int [\eta L(\xi) - M(\eta)\xi] dx dy = \int_C [S_1 \cos x, n + S_2 \cos y, n] ds.$$

The equivalent of this theorem was given first by Volterra for the integro-differential equation appearing as a generalization of Laplace's equation in three dimensions. In two dimensions, the equation is obtained by writing

$$(59)\quad \alpha_{11} = 1 + jA_{11}(rs), \qquad \alpha_{22} = 1 + jA_{22}(rs),$$

$$\alpha_{12} = \alpha_1 = \alpha_2 = \alpha = 0.$$

The use of a function analogous to the Green's function was also pointed out, based on a particular solution analogous to *log* $r$*.

**78. The Method of Particular Solutions.** The method of particular solutions may be generalized not only to the integro-differential equations we are now discussing, but also to those where the same variable appears in both differentiation and integration.† Consider however, as an example, the generalization of Laplace's equation which we have already mentioned:

$$(59') \qquad \alpha_{11}\frac{\partial^2 \xi}{\partial x^2} + \alpha_{22}\frac{\partial^2 \xi}{\partial y^2} = 0,$$

which may for combinations of the second kind be written explicitly in the form

$$(59'') \quad \frac{\partial^2 U}{\partial x^2} + \frac{\partial^2 U}{\partial y^2} + \int_a^b \left\{ A_{11}(rt)\frac{\partial^2 U(xy \mid ts)}{\partial x^2} + A_{22}(rt)\frac{\partial^2 U(xy \mid ts)}{\partial y^2} \right\} dt = 0.$$

We proceed to obtain the solution of this equation, of form $jU(xy \mid rs)$, which vanishes when $x = 0$, when $x = c$, and when $y = d$, and takes on the values

$$U(x0 \mid rs) = f(xrs)$$

when $y = 0$.

If we write $\beta_1{}^2 = \alpha_{11}$, $\beta_2{}^2 = \alpha_{22}$ where $\beta_1 = 1 + jB_1(rs)$, $\beta_2 = 1 + jB_2(rs)$, the function

$$\xi_m = \frac{e^{\frac{m\pi(d-y)}{c}\beta} - e^{\frac{-m\pi(d-y)}{c}\beta}}{e^{\frac{m\pi d}{c}\beta} - e^{\frac{-m\pi d}{c}\beta}} \sin\frac{m\pi x}{c},$$

in which

$$\beta = \frac{1}{\beta_2}\beta_1 = 1 + B(rs),$$

will be a particular solution of (59′) which vanishes for $x = 0$, $x = c$, $y = d$ and takes on the value $\sin m\pi x/c$ for $y = 0$. The function

$$\xi = \sum_1^\infty {}_m \xi_m \tilde{\omega}_m,$$

with

$$\tilde{\omega}_m = \frac{2}{c}\int_0^c \xi_{y=0} \sin\frac{m\pi x}{c}\,dx,$$

will be the solution which takes on given values for $y = 0$, assuming the necessary conditions for convergence. Our problem is solved if we let

$$\xi_{y=0} = jf(x, r, s).$$

* The special case in which I describe this function as reducing to the ordinary Green's function is invalid (*Rendiconti del Circolo Matematico di Palermo*, vol. 34, p. 25).

† Volterra, *Rendiconti della R. Accademia dei Lincei*, vol. 21, 2d semester, p. 1; Evans, ibid., p. 25.

In case the length $d$ is allowed to become infinite, the solution takes the form

$$(60)\quad U(xy \mid rs) = \sum_1^\infty {}_m e^{\frac{-m\pi y}{c}} \left\{ P_m(rs) + \int_a^b E\left(0, \frac{-m\pi y}{c} B(rt)\right) P_m(ts)dt \right\} \sin \frac{m\pi x}{c},$$

with

$$P_m(rs) = \frac{2}{c} \int_0^c f(xrs) \sin \frac{m\pi x}{c} dx.$$

Instead of constant limits $ab$ in (59″) and (60) we may of course use variable limits $sr$. It is noticeable that the variable $s$ takes merely the role of a parameter in both (59″) and (60), and so the solution may be regarded merely as a function of the three variables $x$, $y$, $r$, the $s$ being omitted.

**79. The Cauchy Problem for Integro-Differential Equations.** Consider the system of partial equations

$$(61)\quad \frac{\partial \xi_i}{\partial x} = F_i\left(\frac{\partial \xi_1}{\partial x}, \cdots, \frac{\partial \xi_n}{\partial x};\ \xi_1, \cdots, \xi_n;\ x, y \mid rs\right),$$

where the $F_i$ are analytic functions of their first $2n + 2$ arguments, in a certain $(2n + 2)$-dimensional neighborhood, with coefficients which are continuous functions of $r$ and $s$ $(a \leqq r \leqq b,\ a \leqq s \leqq b)$. The $(2n + 2)$-dimensional neighborhood is to include the values determined by the ordinary coefficients of certain given functions $\xi_1{}^0(x \mid rs), \cdots, \xi_n{}^0(x \mid rs)$, which are analytic in $x$ in the neighborhood of $x = 0$. These functions are assumed to contain a parameter $\lambda$ in accordance with (35).

THEOREM. *There is one and only one system of solutions $\xi_1, \cdots, \xi_n$ of* (61) *which are analytic at the origin in $x$ and $y$, and which, for $y = 0$, take on the given values $\xi_1{}^0, \cdots, \xi_n{}^0$.*

The proof of this theorem is based on the convergence theorem already given. It serves as a generalization of some of Volterra's theorems which establish the existence of what corresponds to general and complete integrals of integro-differential equations of this type. The unique determination of these solutions by initial conditions depends however on the theory of division developed in terms of the complex algebra.

If the coefficients (as functions of $r$, $s$) of the $F_i$ are permutable among themselves and with the functions $\xi_1{}^0, \cdots, \xi_n{}^0$, the solutions will be permutable with those coefficients and with each other.

Any integro-differential equation of static type, if it can be solved for the highest derivative with respect to $y$, can be rewritten in the form (61). In particular, the equation described in (59), (59′), or (59″) may be reduced to that form unless $A_{22}(rs)$ fails to have a resolvent kernel. Hence if $D_{A_{22}} \neq 0$, (59″) has a unique analytic solution which with its first derivative in regard to $y$ is arbitrarily assigned (analytically in $x$) on the $x$-axis.

In general, to reduce an integro-differential equation to symbolic form involves substituting the quantity $\xi = jU$ for the unknown $U(xy \mid rs)$. In the symbolic form, we are interested, therefore, mainly in solutions of nullity.

This remark has bearing in connection with the theory of *characteristics*. Consider the equation of the second order, linear in the derivatives of highest order:

$$\alpha_{11}\frac{\partial^2\xi}{\partial x^2} + 2\alpha_{12}\frac{\partial^2\xi}{\partial x\partial y} + \alpha_{22}\frac{\partial^2\xi}{\partial y^2} + \lambda = 0, \tag{62}$$

the quantities $\alpha_{11}$, $\alpha_{12}$, $\alpha_{22}$, $\lambda$ being functions of $\xi$, $\partial\xi/\partial x$, $\partial\xi/\partial y$, $x$, $y$, $r$, $s$ of the type previously specified, with the region of analyticity as the neighborhood of the analytic curve $y = \varphi(x)$. We assume that along this curve we are given $\xi$ and $\partial\xi/\partial y$, or what amounts to the same thing, $\xi$, $\partial\xi/\partial x$, $\partial\xi/\partial y$ as analytic functions of $x$.

Precisely as in the theory of differential equations,* by expressing $\partial^2\xi/\partial x^2$ and $\partial^2\xi/\partial x\,\partial y$ for points on $y = \varphi(x)$ in terms of $\partial\xi \mid \partial y$ and $\partial^2\xi/\partial y^2$, we have from (62), as the equation for the determination of $\partial^2\xi/\partial y^2$, the following:

$$\Gamma\xi_{22} + \Pi = 0, \tag{63}$$

in which

$$\begin{aligned}\Gamma &= \alpha_{11}\left(\frac{dy}{dx}\right)^2 - 2\alpha_{12}\frac{dy}{dx} + \alpha_{22},\\ \Pi &= \alpha_{11}\left(\frac{d\xi_1}{dx} - \frac{dy}{dx}\frac{d\xi_2}{dx}\right) + 2\alpha_{12}\frac{d\xi_2}{dx} + \lambda,\end{aligned} \tag{64}$$

where $d/dx$ refers to differentiation along the curve, and $\xi_1$ and $\xi_2$ denote $\partial\xi/\partial x$ and $\partial\xi/\partial y$ respectively. In these equations it is important to preserve the order of all quantities that involve the $j$, so as not to necessitate the introduction of a hypothesis of permutability.

The equation (63) enables us to determine $\xi_{22}$ unless $\Gamma = g + jG$ is a function of nullity at some point of the curve $y = \varphi(x)$; i. e., unless

$$g = 0. \tag{65}$$

The curves defined by (65) may be called the *ordinary characteristics* of the integro-differential equation. On account of the way the symbolic equation is formed from the integro-differential equation, equation (65), which involves no functional coefficients, is a pure differential equation, and is independent of the solution $\xi = jU$. *The ordinary characteristics are independent of the solution of the integro-differential equation, and depend merely on its coefficients.*

If we make an analytic transformation of the independent variables $x$, $y$ which reduces the curve $y = \varphi(x)$ to the $x$-axis, it is immediately verifiable that a sufficient condition that the transformed equation be solvable for $\partial^2\xi/\partial y^2$ is that the curve $y = \varphi(x)$ be nowhere tangent to an ordinary characteristic. *If $y = \varphi(x)$ is nowhere tangent to an ordinary characteristic, the given values of $U$ and $\partial U/\partial y$ uniquely determine a solution of the integro-differential equation.*

On the other hand, this condition is not necessary, since it is sometimes possible to divide by a function of nullity. It may happen that every curve in the plane is an ordinary characteristic, and yet that given values of $U$ and

* Hadamard, Leçons sur la propogation des ondes, Paris (1913), chap. 7.

$\partial U/\partial y$ uniquely determine a solution in the neighborhood of $y = \varphi(x)$. For the equation, by differentiation or perhaps in other ways, may be transformed into one with definite ordinary characteristics to which $y = \varphi(x)$ is nowhere tangent.

If, however, along an ordinary characteristic we are able to determine $\xi$ so that the functional coefficient of $\Gamma$ shall vanish:

$$G = 0, \tag{66}$$

the solution and its derivatives will be defined all along the characteristic, provided they are defined at a single point of it.

**80. Functions of Nullity.** In general, as in the preceding paragraphs, the region between necessary and sufficient conditions is filled by the theory of functions of nullity. The difficulty of this theory is commensurate with that of the integral equation of the first kind, on which it is based.

Volterra has given a comprehensive treatment of this subject, for the combination of the first kind, of wider import than its sub-title in these lectures suggests. Consider then, without regard to the complex units, the combination

$$\psi = \overset{*}{g}\overset{*}{\varphi} = \int_s^r g(rs_1)\varphi(s_1s)ds_1, \tag{67}$$

according to the notation of Volterra. The $m$th power of $f$ is thus obviously defined.

If $m$ is such that

$$\psi(rs) = (r - s)^m f(rs), \tag{68}$$

with $f(rs)$ continuous and $f(ss) \neq 0$, $\psi$ is said to be a *function of order* $m + 1$. In (68), $f(rs)$ is called the *characteristic* of $\psi(rs)$, and $f(rr)$ is called its *diagonal.*

*The product in the above sense of a function of order $m$ and a function of order $n$ is of order $m + n$, and the $m$th power of a function of order $n$ is of order $mn$.*

The solution of the equation

$$\overset{*}{\psi}\overset{*}{\psi} = f$$

allows us to define $\overset{*}{f}{}^{1/2}$. In fact if $f$ is of order 1, $\overset{*}{f}{}^{1/2}$ is of order $\frac{1}{2}$,

i. e., becomes infinite to the order $\frac{1}{2}$ as $r$ approaches $s$. Similarly $\overset{*}{f}{}^{1/n}$ may be defined, and turns out to be of order $1/n$, i. e., to become infinite like $(s-r)^{n-1/n}$. There will be $n$ quantities $\overset{*}{f}{}^{1/n}$, obtained by multiplying one of them by the $n$th roots of unity.

These functions, $\overset{*}{f}{}^{m}$, $\overset{*}{f}{}^{1/n}$, and also $\overset{*}{f}{}^{m/n} = (\overset{*}{f}{}^{1/n})^m$, turn out to be permutable with $f$ itself. Since two functions permutable with a third are permutable with each other, the functions permutable with a given function form what may be called a group of *permutable functions. Given a function of order* 1 *we have therefore seen how to find a function of any assigned rational order which belongs to its group.*

If $f$ is a function of a certain order $\alpha$, whose diagonal is positive, then we have

$$\overset{*}{f}{}^{m/n} = (r-s)^{m\alpha/n-1} L\left(rs\,\middle|\,\frac{m}{n}\right),$$

where the function $L$ is the characteristic, taken with a positive diagonal. Suppose that as $m/n$ approaches $z$, $L(rs|m/n)$ approaches some function $L(rs|z)$ uniformly; then if $z$ is irrational, we define

$$\overset{*}{f}{}^{z} = \lim_{m/n=z} \overset{*}{f}{}^{m/n}.$$

On this basis it can be shown that all the algebraic calculus of positive exponents becomes extensible to the theory of powers of composition, and we have

$$\text{(69)}\qquad \begin{aligned} \overset{*}{f}{}^{z}\overset{*}{f}{}^{z_1} &= \overset{*}{f}{}^{z+z_1}, \\ (\overset{*}{f}{}^{z})^{z_1} &= \overset{*}{f}{}^{zz_1}, \end{aligned}$$

Further elements $\overset{*}{f}/\overset{*}{\psi}$, $\overset{*}{f}{}^{-1}$, $\overset{*}{f}_0$ can be defined so as to be included in a group of permutable functions; they no longer all denote functions in the ordinary sense, but serve as abstract elements which may be used in calculation according to the commutative, distributive and associative laws, and serve to lead from functions which have a real meaning in the ordinary sense to others which have also a real meaning by means of these formal processes.

Thus the function

$$F[f] = \overset{*}{f}{}^{0} + f + \frac{1}{2!}\overset{*}{f}{}^{2} + \frac{1}{3!}\overset{*}{f}{}^{3} + \cdots$$

may be defined; for which, as in Art. 76, there is the formal addition theorem

$$F[\overset{*}{f} + \overset{*}{\varphi}] = F[\overset{*}{f}]F[\overset{*}{\varphi}],$$

$f$ and $\varphi$ being two functions of the same group, and the periodicity property

$$F[\overset{*}{f} + 2\pi i f_0] = F[\overset{*}{f}],$$

formal properties which however become actual upon combination with other functions of the same group.

Given a function $\varphi$ of definite positive order, we have the series

$$\cdots\ \overset{*}{\varphi}{}^{-3},\ \overset{*}{\varphi}{}^{-2},\ \overset{*}{\varphi}{}^{-1},\ \overset{*}{\varphi}{}^{0},\ \varphi,\ \overset{*}{\varphi}{}^{2},\ \overset{*}{\varphi}{}^{3},\ \cdots$$

which may be called a *progression of composition,* with *ratio* or *base* $\varphi$. The exponents are called the *logarithms of composition.* The study of these logarithms leads to a new category of integral equations and to the solution of these equations.

Foot-note to p. 73:

In the first rank should be a reference to C. W. Oseen, with whose work the author was unfamiliar until the above lectures were in proof. See C. W. Oseen, Über die Bedeutung der Integralgleichungen in der Theorie der Bewegung einer reibenden, unzusammendrückbaren Flüssigkeit, *Arkiv för Matematik, Astronomi och Fysik,* Band 6 (1911), No. 23. Here an extension of the corresponding Green's theorem is given.

AMERICAN MATHEMATICAL SOCIETY
COLLOQUIUM LECTURES, VOLUME V

# THE CAMBRIDGE COLLOQUIUM
1916

PART II

## ANALYSIS SITUS

BY

OSWALD VEBLEN

NEW YORK
PUBLISHED BY THE
AMERICAN MATHEMATICAL SOCIETY
501 WEST 116TH STREET
1922

PRESS OF
THE NEW ERA PRINTING COMPANY
LANCASTER, PA.

## AUTHOR'S PREFACE

The Cambridge Colloquium lectures on Analysis Situs were intended as an introduction to the problem of discovering the $n$-dimensional manifolds and characterizing them by means of invariants. For the present publication the material of the lectures has been thoroughly revised and is presented in a more formal way. It thus constitutes something like a systematic treatise on the elements of Analysis Situs. The author does not, however, imagine that it is in any sense a definitive treatment. For the subject is still in such a state that the best welcome which can be offered to any comprehensive treatment is to wish it a speedy obsolescence.

The definition of a manifold which has been used is that which proceeds from the consideration of a generalized polyhedron consisting of $n$-dimensional cells. The relations among the cells are described by means of matrices of integers and the properties of the manifolds are obtained by operations with the matrices. The most important of these matrices were introduced by H. Poincaré to whom we owe most of our knowledge of $n$-dimensional manifolds* for the cases in which $n > 2$. But it is also found convenient to employ certain more elementary matrices of incidence whose elements are reduced modulo 2, and from which the Poincaré matrices can be derived.

The operations on the matrices lead to combinatorial results which are independent of the particular way in which a manifold is divided into cells and therefore lead to theorems of Analysis Situs. The proof that this is so is based on an article by J. W. Alexander in the Transactions of the American Math-

* Poincaré's work is contained in the following four memoirs: Analysis Situs, Journal de l'École Polytechnique, 2d Ser., Vol. 1 (1895); Complément a l'Analysis Situs, Rendiconti del Circolo Matematico di Palermo, Vol. 13 (1899); Second Complément, Proceedings of the London Mathematical Society, Vol. 32 (1900); Cinquième Complément, Rendiconti, Vol. 18 (1904). The third and fourth Complements deal with applications to Algebraic Geometry, into which we do not go.

ematical Society, Vol. 16 (1915), p. 148. The continuous transformations and the singularities (in the way of overlapping, etc.) which are allowed in this proof are completely general, so that we are able to avoid the difficulties, foreign to Analysis Situs, which beset those treatments of the subject which restrict attention to analytic transformations or singularities.

It will be seen that, aside from this one question which has to be dealt with in order to give significance to the combinatorial treatment, we leave out of consideration all the work that has been done on the point-set problems of Analysis Situs and on its foundation in terms of axioms or definitions other than those actually used in the text. We have also been obliged by lack of space to leave out all reference to the applications. We have not even given a definition of an $n$-cell by means of a set of equations and inequalities, or the discussion of orientation by means of the signs of determinants. These are to be found in very readable form in Poincaré's first paper, where they are given as the basis of his work. They belong properly, however, to the applications of the subject. For in nearly all cases when Poincaré (or anyone else) has proved a theorem of Analysis Situs, he has been obliged to set up a machinery which is equivalent to a set of matrices.

No attempt has been made to give a complete account of the history and literature of the subject. These are covered for the period up to 1907 by the article on Analysis Situs by Dehn and Heegaard in the Encyklopädie (Vol. $\text{III}_1$, p. 153); and the more important works subsequent to that date which bear on our part of the subject are referred to in Chap. V. I take pleasure in acknowledging my indebtedness to Professor J. W. Alexander who has read the manuscript and made many valuable suggestions, and also to Dr. Philip Franklin who has helped with the manuscript, the drawings, and the proof-sheets.

PRINCETON, May, 1921.

# CONTENTS

## CHAPTER I

### Linear Graphs



## CHAPTER II

### Two-dimensional Complexes and Manifolds

## CHAPTER III

### Complexes and Manifolds of $N$ Dimensions



## CHAPTER IV

### Orientable Manifolds

## CHAPTER V

### The Fundamental Group and Certain Unsolved Problems

# CHAPTER I

## LINEAR GRAPHS

### Fundamental Definitions

1. We shall presuppose a knowledge of some of the elementary properties of the real Euclidean space of $n$ dimensions ($n \leqq 3$ for the first two chapters). In such a space, the points collinear with and between two distinct points constitute a *segment* or *one-dimensional simplex* whose *ends* or *vertices* are the given points. The ends are not regarded as points of the segment. For obvious reasons of symmetry, a single point will be referred to as a 0-*dimensional simplex.*

2. Consider any set of objects in (1–1) correspondence* with the points of a segment and its two ends. The objects corresponding to the points of the segment constitute a *one-dimensional cell* or 1-*cell* and those corresponding to the ends constitute the *ends* or *boundary* of the 1-cell. In like manner a single object may be referred to as a 0-*cell.*

In the cases which are usually considered the objects which constitute a cell and its boundary are points of a $k$-space and the correspondence which defines the cell is continuous. Consequently a 1-cell is an arc of curve joining two distinct points. In the general case, however, it would be meaningless to say that the correspondence was continuous because continuity implies previously determined order relations, and here the order relations of a cell are determined by means of the defining correspondence.

The objects which constitute a cell and its boundary will always be referred to as "points" in the following pages. The

* By (1–1) correspondence we mean a correspondence which is one-to-one reciprocal; i.e., a (1–1) correspondence between two sets $[A]$ and $[B]$ is such that each $A$ corresponds to one and only one $B$ and each $B$ is the correspondent of one and only one $A$.

order relations among any set of points on the cell or its boundary are by definition identical with those of the corresponding points of the segment and its boundary. Hence, in particular, a point $P$ is a *limit point* of a set of points $[X]$ of a cell and its boundary if and only if the corresponding point $P$ of the segment is a limit point of the corresponding set of points $[X]$ of the segment and its boundary.

A *continuous transformation* of a cell and its boundary into itself or into another cell and its boundary is now defined as a transformation of the cell and its boundary which if it carries a set $[X]$ to a set $[X']$ carries every limit point of $[X]$ to a limit point of $[X']$.

3. A *zero-dimensional complex* is a set of distinct 0-cells, finite in number. A *one-dimensional complex* or a *linear graph* is a zero-dimensional complex together with a finite number of 1-cells bounded by pairs of its 0-cells, such that no two of the 1-cells

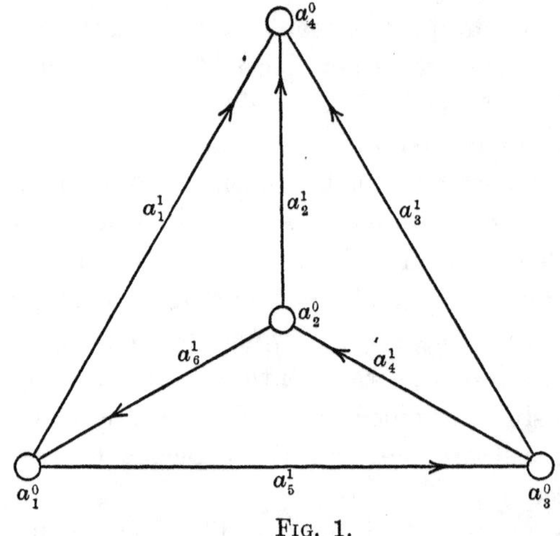


FIG. 1.

have a point in common and each 0-cell is an end of at least one 1-cell. Let us denote the number of 0-cells by $\alpha_0$ and the number of 1-cells by $\alpha_1$. The 0-cells are sometimes called *vertices* and the 1-cells *edges*.

For example, the vertices and edges of a tetrahedron (fig. 1) constitute a linear graph for which $\alpha_0 = 4$ and $\alpha_1 = 6$. A linear graph is not necessarily assumed to lie in any space, being defined in a purely abstract way. It is obvious, however, that if $\alpha_0$ points be chosen arbitrarily in a Euclidean three-space they can be joined by pairs in any manner whatever by $\alpha_1$ non-intersecting simple arcs. Therefore, any linear graph may be thought of as situated in a Euclidean three-space.

For some purposes it is desirable to use the term one-dimensional complex to denote a more general set of 1-cells and 0-cells than that described above. For example, a 1-cell and its two ends form a one-dimensional complex according to the definition above, but a 1-cell by itself or a 1-cell and one of its ends do not. In the following pages we shall occasionally refer to an arbitrary subset of the 1-cells and 0-cells of a linear graph as a *generalized one-dimensional complex*.

4. A transformation $F$ of a set of points $[X]$ of a complex $C_1$ into a set of points $[X']$ of the same or another complex is said to be *continuous* if and only if it is continuous in the sense of § 2 on each complex composed of a 1-cell of $C_1$ and its ends (i.e., if the transformation effected by $F$ on those $X$s which are on such a 1-cell and its ends is continuous). A (1–1) continuous transformation of a complex into itself or another complex is called, following Poincaré, a *homeomorphism*. Two complexes related by a homeomorphism are said to be *homeomorphic*.

The set of all homeomorphisms by which a linear graph is carried into itself obviously forms a group. Any theorem about a linear graph which states a property which is left invariant by all transformations of this group is a theorem of *one-dimensional Analysis Situs*. The group of homeomorphisms of a linear graph is its *Analysis Situs group*.

## Order Relations on Curves

5. By an *open curve* is meant the set of all points of a complex composed of a 1-cell and its two ends. By a *closed curve* is meant the set of all points of a complex $C_1$ consisting of two distinct 0-cells $a_1^0$, $a_2^0$ and two 1-cells $a_1^1$, $a_2^1$, each of which has $a_1^0$

and $a_2^0$ as ends but which have no common points (fig. 2). The most elementary theorems about curves are those which codify the order relations. They may be stated (without proof) as follows:

Let us denote a 1-cell and its ends by $a^1$, $a_1^0$ and $a_2^0$. If $a_3^0$ is any point of $a^1$, there are two 1-cells $a_1^1$ and $a_2^1$ such that $a_1^1$ has $a_1^0$ and $a_3^0$ as it ends, $a_2^1$ has $a_3^0$ and $a_2^0$ as its ends, and every point of $a^1$ is either on $a_1^1$ or $a_2^1$ or identical with $a_3^0$. The 1-cell $a^1$ is said to be *separated* into the 1-cells $a_1^1$ and $a_2^1$ by the 0-cell $a_3^0$.

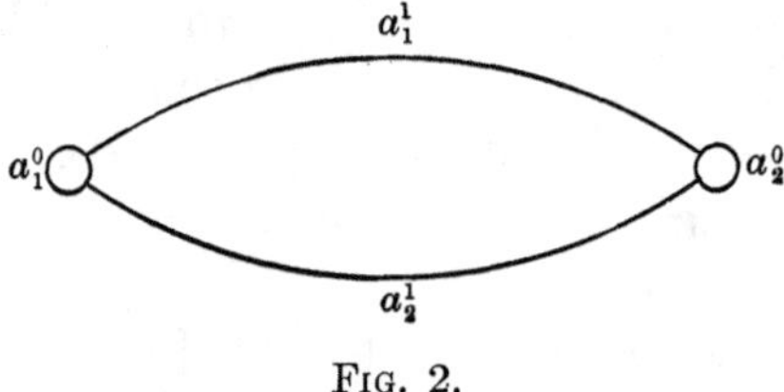


FIG. 2.

A 0-cell is said to be *incident* with a 1-cell if and only if it is an end of the 1-cell; and under the same conditions the 1-cell is said to be incident with the 0-cell. It follows directly from the theorem on separation in the paragraph above that $n$ distinct points of the 1-cell $a^1$ determine $n + 1$ 1-cells such that the $n$ points (or 0-cells) may be denoted by $b_1^0, b_2^0, \cdots, b_n^0$ and the $n + 1$ 1-cells by $b_1^1, b_2^1, \cdots, b_{n+1}^1$ in such a way that each cell is incident with the cell which directly precedes or directly follows it in the sequence $a_1^0, b_1^1, b_1^0, b_2^1, \cdots, b_n^0, b_{n+1}^1 a_2^0$.

If $b_1^0, b_2^0, \cdots, b_n^0$ are $n$ distinct points of a closed curve the remaining points of the curve constitute $n$ 1-cells $b_i^1$ $(i = 1, 2, \cdots, n)$, no two of which have a point in common, such that each $b_i^0$ is incident with just two of them.

6. A little reflection will convince the reader that many of the theorems about functions of one real variable and about linear sets of points belong to one-dimensional Analysis Situs. As an example we may cite the theorem that any nowhere dense perfect set of points on a closed curve can be transformed into any other such set by a (1–1) continuous

transformation of the curve. The Heine-Borel theorem is another case in point.

The theorems of Analysis Situs may be divided somewhat roughly into two classes, those dealing essentially with continuity considerations (of which the theorem on perfect sets of points cited above may serve as an illustration), and those having an essentially combinatorial character. It is the theorems of the latter class which will occupy most of our attention in the following pages, though we shall continually make use of theorems of the former class without proving them.

### Singular Complexes

7. Let $F$ be a correspondence between a 0-dimensional complex $C_0$ and a set of points $[P]$ of any complex $C$ (for the present, $C$ is 0- or 1-dimensional) in which each point of $C_0$ corresponds to a single $P$ and each $P$ is the correspondent of one or more points of $C_0$. The object obtained by associating any point $X$ of $C_0$ with the point $P$ which is its image under $F$ will be denoted by $F(X)$ and called a point *on* $C$; it is said to *coincide* with $P$ and $P$ to coincide with it. The set of all points $F(X)$ on $C$ is called a 0-dimensional complex *on* $C$. If any $P$ is the correspondent of more than one point $X$ of $C_0$, $F(X)$ is called a *singular point* and the complex on $C$ is said to be *singular*.

8. Let $C_1$ be a generalized one-dimensional complex and let $F$ be a continuous correspondence between $C_1$ and a set of points $[P]$ of a complex $C$, in which each point of $C_1$ corresponds to a single $P$ and each $P$ is the correspondent of at least one point of $C_1$. The object obtained by associating any point $X$ of $C_1$ with the point $P$ which is its image under this correspondence will be called a *point on* $C$ and is uniquely denoted by the functional notation $F(X)$; it is said to *coincide* with $P$ and $P$ is said to *coincide* with it. The set of all points $F(X)$ on $C$ is in a (1–1) continuous correspondence with the points of $C_1$ and thus constitutes a one-dimensional complex $C_1'$ identical in structure with $C_1$. The one-dimensional complex $C_1'$ is said to be *on* $C$. If any of the points $P$ is the correspondent under $F$ of more than one

point of $C_1$, $C_1'$ is called a *singular complex on* $C$ and the point $P$ in question a *singular point.* If the correspondence $F$ is (1–1), $C_1'$ is said to be *non-singular.*

It is to be emphasized that in the definitions above $F$ is a perfectly general continuous function. Thus, for example, all the points of a 1-cell of $C_1'$ may be imaged on a single point of $C$. In the rest of this chapter we shall be referring to nonsingular complexes more often than to singular ones. We shall therefore understand that a complex is nonsingular unless the opposite is stated.

9. Let $P$ be any point of a generalized one-dimensional complex $C_1$. If $P$ is a point of a 1-cell of $C_1$ let $Q_1$ and $Q_2$ be two points of this 1-cell such that $P$ is between them. If $P$ is a vertex, let $Q_1, Q_2, \cdots, Q_j$ be a set of points, one on each 1-cell of which $P$ is an end. The set of points composed of $P$ and of all points between $P$ and the points $Q_1, Q_2, \cdots, Q_j$ is called a *neighborhood* of $P$.

A generalized one-dimensional complex $C_1'$ which is on $C_1$ is said to *cover* $C_1$ in case there is at least one point of $C_1'$ on each point of $C_1$ and there exists for every point of $C_1'$ a neighborhood which is a non-singular complex on $C_1$. In case the number of points of $C_1'$ which coincide with a given point of $C_1$ is finite and equal to $n$ for every point of $C_1$, $C_1'$ is said to *cover* $C_1$ *n times.*

The only connected complex which can cover a 1-cell is a 1-cell, and it can cover it only once. *A closed curve,* on the other hand, *can be covered any number of times by another closed curve.*

The truth of the latter statement may be seen very simply as follows. Let $C_1$ and $C_1'$ be two circles in a Euclidean plane. Denote any point on $C_1$ by a coordinate $\theta(0 < \theta \leqq 2\pi)$, and any point on $C_1'$ by $\theta'$ $(0 < \theta' \leq 2\pi)$. Let each point, $\theta$, of $C_1$ correspond to the $n$ points

$$\theta' = \frac{\theta}{n}, \qquad \theta' = \frac{2\theta}{n}, \qquad \cdots, \qquad \theta' = \frac{(n-1)\theta}{n}, \qquad \theta' = \theta,$$

of $C_1'$. In case $n = 2$, for example, a pair of opposite points of $C_1'$ corresponds to a single point of $C_1$.

## The Simplest Invariants

10. One of the first objects of Analysis Situs is to find the numerical invariants of complexes under the group of homeomorphisms. By an invariant under this group we mean a number $I(C)$ determined by a complex $C$ in such a way that if $C'$ be any complex homeomorphic with $C$, the number $I(C')$ determined in the same way for $C'$ is the same as $I(C)$.

11. Starting with any point $O$ of a complex $C_1$ consider all points of $C_1$ which can be joined to this one by open curves, singular or not,* on $C_1$. This set of points will contain all points of a certain set of 0-cells and 1-cells of $C_1$ (a sub-complex of $C_1$) which we may call $C_1'$. Since any two points of $C_1'$ can be joined to $O$ by open curves, they can be joined to each other by an open curve. Hence the same set of points is determined if any other point of $C_1'$ replace $O$ in the definition of $C_1'$.

Since $C_1$ is composed of a finite number of 0-cells and 1-cells altogether, it is composed of a finite number of sub-complexes defined in the same way that $C_1'$ is defined in the paragraph above. The number of these sub-complexes contained in $C_1$ is obviously an invariant in the sense defined in § 10, for if two complexes $C_1$ and $C_1'$ are homeomorphic, any curve on $C_1$ corresponds to a curve on $C_1'$. *This number shall be denoted by* $R_0$. If $R_0 = 1$, $C_1$ is said to be *connected.*

12. Let us denote the number of 0-cells in a complex $C_1$ by $\alpha_0$ and the number of 1-cells by $\alpha_1$. *The number* $\alpha_0 - \alpha_1$ *is an invariant.*

To prove this, let us first observe that if $C_1$ be modified by introducing any point of one of its 1-cells as a 0-cell and thereby separating the 1-cell into two 1-cells, the number $\alpha_0 - \alpha_1$ is unchanged. For $\alpha_0$ is changed to $\alpha_0 + 1$ and $\alpha_1$ is changed to $\alpha_1 + 1$.

Now consider two linear graphs $C_1$ and $C_1'$ between which there is a (1–1) continuous correspondence $F$. Suppose that

* No generality is gained by allowing the curves to be singular, but the argument is slightly easier, and more in the spirit of its generalizations to $n$ dimensions.

$C_1$ has $\alpha_0$ 0-cells and $\alpha_1$ 1-cells and $C_1'$ has $\alpha_0'$ 0-cells and $\alpha_1'$ 1-cells. Each 0-cell of $C_1$ which is an end of only one 1-cell will correspond under $F$ to a 0-cell of $C_1'$ having the same property; otherwise $F$ could not be continuous. In like manner, each 0-cell of $C_1$ which is an end of more than two 1-cells will correspond to a 0-cell of $C_1'$ which is an end of an equal number of 1-cells. For the same reasons, a 0-cell of $C_1'$ which is an end of only one, or of more than two, 1-cells is the correspondent of a like 0-cell of $C_1$.

A certain number of 0-cells of $C_1$ which are ends of two 1-cells each may correspond to points of $C_1'$ which are not vertices. Suppose there are $k$ such 0-cells of $C_1$ and therefore $k$ corresponding points of $C_1'$. As explained above, any one of these points of $C_1'$ may be introduced as a vertex, thereby changing $C_1'$ into a complex with one more 0-cell and one more 1-cell. Repeating this step $k$ times $C_1'$ is changed into a complex $C_1''$ having $\alpha_0' + k$ 0-cells and $\alpha_1' + k$ 1-cells. The correspondence $F$ will carry every vertex of $C_1$ into a vertex of $C_1''$.

Certain of the vertices of $C_1''$, however, may not be the correspondents under $F$ of vertices of $C_1$. Suppose there are $n$ such vertices of $C_1''$. By precisely the reasoning used in the last paragraph the points of $C_1$ which correspond to these $n$ vertices of $C_1''$ may be introduced as vertices of $C_1$, converting $C_1$ into a complex $\overline{C}_1$ having $\alpha_0 + n$ 0-cells and $\alpha_1 + n$ 1-cells.

The complexes $C_1''$ and $\overline{C}_1$ have been defined so that under the (1–1) correspondence $F$ each vertex of $\overline{C}_1$ corresponds to a vertex of $C_1''$ and each 1-cell of $\overline{C}_1$ to a 1-cell of $C_1''$. Hence

$$\alpha_0 + n = \alpha_0' + k \qquad \text{and} \qquad \alpha_1 + n = \alpha_1' + k,$$

from which it follows that

$$\alpha_0 - \alpha_1 = \alpha_0' - \alpha_1'.$$

13. The invariant number $\alpha_0 - \alpha_1$ is called the *characteristic** of the linear graph. The number $\alpha_1 - \alpha_0 + R_0$ is called the

* Cf. W. Dyck, *Math. Ann.*, Vol. 32, p. 457.

*cyclomatic number** and denoted by $\mu$. In the case of a connected complex

$$\mu = \alpha_1 - \alpha_0 + 1.$$

The two invariants, $R_0$ and $\alpha_0 - \alpha_1$ are evidently not sufficient to characterize a linear graph completely. There is a rather elaborate theory of linear graphs† in existence which we shall not attempt to cover. Instead we shall go into detail on questions which cluster around the two invariants already found, because this part of the theory is the basis of important generalizations to $n$ dimensions.

**Symbols for Sets of Cells**

14. Let us denote the 0-cells of a one-dimensional complex $C_1$ by $a_1^0, a_2^0, \cdots, a_{\alpha_0}^0$ and the 1-cells by $a_1^1, a_2^1, \cdots, a_{\alpha_1}^1$.

Any set of 0-cells of $C_1$ may be denoted by a symbol $(x_1, x_2, \cdots, x_{\alpha_0})$ in which $x_i = 1$ if $a_i^0$ is in the set and $x_i = 0$ if $a_i^0$ is not in the set. Thus, for example, the pair of points $a_1^0$, $a_4^0$ in fig. 1 is denoted by (1, 0, 0, 1). The total number of symbols $(x_1, x_2, \cdots, x_{\alpha_0})$ is $2^{\alpha_0}$. Hence the total number of sets of 0-cells, barring the null-set, is $2^{\alpha_0} - 1$. The symbol for a null-set, $(0, 0, \cdots, 0)$ will be referred to as *zero* and denoted by 0.

The marks 0 and 1 which appear in the symbols just defined, may profitably be regarded as residues, modulo 2, i.e., as symbols which may be combined algebraically according to the rules

$$0+0=1+1=0,\ 0+1=1+0=1,\ 0\times0=0\times1=1\times0=0,\ 1\times1=1.$$

Under this convention the *sum* (mod 2) of two symbols, or of the two sets of points which correspond to the symbols $(x_1, x_2, \cdots, x_{\alpha_0}) = X$ and $(y_1, y_2, \cdots, y_{\alpha_0}) = Y$, may be defined as $(x_1 + y_1,\ x_2 + y_2,\ \cdots,\ x_{\alpha_0} + y_{\alpha_0}) = X + Y$. Geometrically, $X + Y$ is the set of all points which are in $X$ or in $Y$ but not in both.‡

* The term is due to J. B. Listing, Census räumliche Komplexe, Göttingen, 1862. But the significance of this constant had been clearly brought out by G. Kirchhoff in the paper referred to in § 36 below.

† Cf. Dehn-Heegaard, Encyklopädie, III, AB, 3, pp. 172–178.

‡ In other words, $X + Y$ is the difference between the logical sum and the logical product of the two sets of points. In terms of the logical operations, if $S$ and $S'$ are the given sets, this one is $S + S' - SS'$.

For example, if $X = (1, 0, 0, 1)$ and $Y = (0, 1, 0, 1)$ $X + Y = (1, 1, 0, 0)$; i.e., $X$ represents $a_1^0$ and $a_4^0$, $Y$ represents $a_2^0$ and $a_4^0$, and $X + Y$ represents $a_1^0$ and $a_2^0$. Since $a_4^0$ appears in both $X$ and $Y$, it is suppressed in forming the sum, modulo 2.

This type of addition has the obvious property that if two sets contain each an even number of 0-cells, the sum (mod. 2) contains an even number of 0-cells.

15. Any set, $S$, of 1-cells in $C_1$ may be denoted by a symbol $(x_1, x_2, \cdots, x_{\alpha_1})$ in which $x_i = 1$ if $a_i^1$ is in the set and $x_i = 0$ if $a_i^1$ is not in the set. The 1-cells in the set may be thought of as labelled with 1's and those not in the set as labelled with 0's. The symbol is also regarded as representing the one-dimensional complex composed of the 1-cells of $S$ and the 0-cells which bound them. Thus, for example, in fig. 1 the boundaries of two of the faces are $(1, 0, 1, 0, 1, 0)$ and $(1, 1, 0, 0, 0, 1)$.

The sum (mod. 2) of two symbols $(x_1, x_2, \cdots, x_{\alpha_1})$ is defined in the same way as for the case of symbols representing 0-cells. Correspondingly if $C_1'$ and $C_1''$ are one-dimensional complexes which have a certain number (which may be zero) of 1-cells in common and have no other common points except the ends of these 1-cells, the *sum*

$$C_1' + C_1'' \quad (\text{mod. } 2)$$

is defined as the one-dimensional complex obtained by suppressing all 1-cells common to $C_1'$ and $C_1''$ and retaining all 1-cells which appear only in $C_1'$ or in $C_1''$. For example, in fig. 1, the sum of the two curves represented by $(1, 0, 1, 0, 1, 0)$ and $(1, 1, 0, 0, 0, 1)$ is $(0, 1, 1, 0, 1, 1)$ which represents the curve composed of $a_2^1$, $a_3^1$, $a_5^1$, $a_6^1$ and their ends.

### The Matrices $H_0$ and $H_1$

16. It has been seen in § 11 that any one-dimensional complex falls into $R_0$ sub-complexes each of which is connected. Let us denote these sub-complexes by $C_1^1, C_1^2, \cdots, C_1^{R_0}$, and let the notation be assigned in such a way that $a_i^0$ $(i = 1, 2, \cdots, m_1)$ are the 0-cells of $C_1^1$, $a_i^0$ $(i = m_1 + 1, \cdots, m_2)$ those of $C_1^2$, and so on.

With this choice of notation, the sets of vertices of $C_1^1$, $C_1^2$, $\cdots$, $C_1^{R_0}$, respectively, are represented by the symbols $(x_1, x_2, \cdots, x_{\alpha_0})$ which constitute the rows of the following matrix.

$$\mathrm{H}_0 = \left\| \begin{array}{cccc} \overbrace{1\ 1\ \cdots\ 1}^{m_1} & \overbrace{0\ 0\ \cdots\ 0}^{m_2 - m_1} & \cdots & \overbrace{0\ 0\ \cdots\ 0}^{\alpha_0 - m_{R_0-1}} \\ 0\ 0\ \cdots\ 0 & 1\ 1\ \cdots\ 1 & \cdots & 0\ 0\ \cdots\ 0 \\ \cdot & & & \cdot \\ \cdot & & & \cdot \\ \cdot & & & \cdot \\ \cdot & & & \cdot \\ 0\ 0\ \cdots\ 0 & 0\ 0\ \cdots\ 0 & \cdots & 1\ 1\ \cdots\ 1 \end{array} \right\| = \| \eta_{ij}^0 \|.$$

For most purposes it is sufficient to limit attention to connected complexes. In such cases $R_0 = 1$, and $\mathrm{H}_0$ consists of one row all of whose elements are 1.

17. By the definition in § 5 a 0-cell is *incident* with a 1-cell if it is one of the ends of the 1-cell, and under the same conditions the 1-cell is incident with the 0-cell. The incidence relations between the 0-cells and 1-cells may be represented in a table or matrix of $\alpha_0$ rows and $\alpha_1$ columns as follows: The 0-cells of $C_1$ having been denoted by $a_i^0$, $(i = 1, 2, \cdots, \alpha_0)$ and the 1-cells by $a_j^1$, $(j = 1, 2, \cdots, \alpha_1)$, let the element of the $i$th row and the $j$th column of the matrix be 1 if $a_i^0$ is incident with $a_j^1$ and let it be 0 if $a_i^0$ is not incident with $a_j^1$.

For example, the table for the linear graph of fig. 1 formed by the vertices and edges of a tetrahedron is as follows:

| | $a_1^1$ | $a_2^1$ | $a_3^1$ | $a_4^1$ | $a_5^1$ | $a_6^1$ |
|---|---|---|---|---|---|---|
| $a_1^0$ | 1 | 0 | 0 | 0 | 1 | 1 |
| $a_2^0$ | 0 | 1 | 0 | 1 | 0 | 1 |
| $a_3^0$ | 0 | 0 | 1 | 1 | 1 | 0 |
| $a_4^0$ | 1 | 1 | 1 | 0 | 0 | 0 |

In the case of the complex used in § 5 to define a simple closed curve the incidence matrix is

$$\left\| \begin{array}{cc} 1 & 1 \\ 1 & 1 \end{array} \right\|.$$

We shall denote the element of the $i$th row and $j$th column of the matrix of incidence relations between the 0-cells and 1-cells by $\eta_{ij}^1$ and the matrix itself by

$$\| \eta_{ij}^1 \| = \text{H}_1.$$

The $i$th row of $\text{H}_1$ is the symbol for the set of all 1-cells incident with $a_i^0$ and the $j$th column is the symbol for the set of two 0-cells incident with $a_j^1$.

The condition which we have imposed on the graph, that both ends of every 1-cell shall be among the $\alpha_0$ 0-cells, implies that every column of the matrix contains exactly two 1's. Conversely, any matrix whose elements are 0's and 1's and which is such that each column contains exactly two 1's can be regarded as the incidence matrix of a linear graph. For to obtain such a graph it is only necessary to take $\alpha_0$ points in a 3-space, denote them arbitrarily by $a_1^0, a_2^0, \cdots, a_{\alpha_0}^0$, and join the pairs which correspond to 1's in the same column successively by arcs not meeting the arcs previously constructed.

This construction also makes it evident that there is a (1–1) continuous correspondence between any two graphs corresponding to the same matrix $\text{H}_1$.

## Zero-dimensional Circuits

18. A pair of 0-cells is called a 0-*dimensional circuit* or a 0-*circuit* or a 0-*dimensional manifold.* When we refer to sets of 0-circuits we shall always mean sets of 0-circuits no two of which have a point in common. With this understanding, any even number of 0-cells is a set of 0-circuits and the sum (mod. 2) of any number of 0-circuits is a set of 0-circuits.

If two 0-cells are the ends of an open curve on $C_1$ (cf. § 5) they are said to *bound* the open curve and *to be connected* by it. Such a pair of 0-cells is called a *bounding* 0-*circuit.* For example, in fig. 1, $a_1^0$ and $a_3^0$ bound the curve $a_5^1$ and also bound the curve $a_1^1 a_4^0 a_3^1$.

19. In the symbol $(x_1, x_2, \cdots, x_{\alpha_0})$ for a bounding 0-circuit all the $x$'s are 0 except two which correspond to a pair of vertices belonging to one of the connected complexes into which $C_1$ falls according to § 11. This symbol must therefore satisfy the following equations,

$$(\mathrm{H}_0) \qquad \begin{array}{llll} x_1 & + x_2 + & \cdots + x_{m_1} & = 0, \\ x_{m_1+1} & + & \cdots + x_{m_2} & = 0, \\ \cdot & & \cdot & \\ \cdot & & \cdot & \\ \cdot & & \cdot & \\ x_{m_{R_0-1}+1} & + & \cdots + x_{\alpha_0} & = 0, \end{array}$$

in which the variables are reduced modulo 2, as explained in § 14. The matrix of these equations is $\mathrm{H}_0$.

Since the symbol for any set of bounding 0-circuits is the sum (mod. 2) of the symbols for the 0-circuits of the set, it follows that any such symbol satisfies the equations $(\mathrm{H}_0)$. This is also evident because in the symbol for any set of bounding 0-circuits an even number of the $x$'s in each of these equations must be 1. Hence any such symbol satisfies $(\mathrm{H}_0)$. On the other hand, the symbol for a non-bounding 0-circuit will not satisfy the equations $(\mathrm{H}_0)$ because the two $x$'s which are not zero in this symbol appear in different equations; and, in general, any symbol for a set of vertices of which an odd number are in some connected sub-complex of $C_1$ will fail to satisfy these equations. *Hence the set of all solutions of* $(\mathrm{H}_0)$ *is the set of all symbols for sets of bounding 0-circuits.*

Since no two of these equations have a variable in common, they are linearly independent. Hence *all solutions of* $(\mathrm{H}_0)$ *are linearly dependent (mod. 2) on a set of* $\alpha_0 - R_0$ *linearly independent solutions.*

20. Denoting the connected sub-complexes of $C_1$ by $C_1^1$, $C_1^2$, $\cdots$, $C_1^{R_0}$ as in § 16 let the notation be so assigned that $a_1^1$, $\cdots$, $a_{m_1}^1$ are the 1-cells in $C_1^1$; $a_{m_1+1}^1$, $\cdots$, $a_{m_2}^1$ the 1-cells in $C_1^2$; and so on. The matrix $\mathrm{H}_1$ then must take the form

| I | 0 | 0 | 0 | |
|---|---|---|---|---|
| 0 | II | 0 | 0 | |
| 0 | 0 | III | | |
| | | | | |

where all the non-zero elements are to be found in the matrices I, II, III, etc., and I is the matrix of $C_1^1$, II of $C_1^2$, etc. This is evident because no element of one of the complexes $C_1^1$ is incident with any element of any of the others.

There are two non-zero elements in each column of $H_1$. Hence if we add the rows corresponding to any of the blocks I, II, etc. the sum is zero (mod. 2) in every column. Hence the rows of $H_1$ are connected by $R_0$ linear relations.

Any linear combination (mod. 2) of the rows of $H_1$ corresponds to adding a certain number of them together. If this gave zeros in all the columns it would mean that there were two or no 1's in each column of the matrix formed by the given rows, and this would mean that any 1-cell incident with one of the 0-cells corresponding to these rows would also be incident with another such 0-cell. These 0-cells and the 1-cells incident with them would therefore form a sub-complex of $C_1$ which was not connected with any of the remaining 0-cells and 1-cells of $C_1$. Hence it would consist of one or more of the complexes $C_1^i$ ($i = 1, 2, \cdots, R_0$) and the linear relations with which we started would be dependent on the $R_0$ relations already found. Hence there are exactly $R_0$ linearly independent linear relations among the rows of $H_1$, so that if $\rho_1$ is the rank of $H_1$,

$$\rho_1 = \alpha_0 - R_0.$$

It follows that there is a set of $\alpha_0 - R_0$ columns of $H_1$ upon which all columns are linearly dependent. Since every column of $H_1$ is a solution of $(H_0)$ and since all solutions of $(H_0)$ are linearly dependent on $\alpha_0 - R_0$ such solutions, all solutions of $(H_0)$ are linearly dependent on columns of $H_1$. In other words *any bounding* 0-*circuit is the sum of some of the* 0-*circuits which bound the* 1-*cells* $a_1^1, \cdots, a_{\alpha_1}^1$.

A linearly independent set of solutions of a set of linear equations upon which all other solutions are linearly dependent is called a *complete set* of solutions. Thus a set of $\rho_1$ linearly independent columns of $H_1$ form a complete set of solutions of $(H_0)$. The corresponding set of 0-circuits is also called a *complete set.*

21. If $R_0 = 1$ the complex $C_1$ is connected and all its 0-circuits are bounding and expressible linearly (mod. 2) in terms of $\alpha_0 - 1$ of the 0-circuits which bound 1-cells.

In case $R_0 > 1$, a 0-circuit obtained by taking two points, one from each of a pair of the sub-complexes $C_1^i$ $(i = 1, 2, \cdots, R_0)$ is a non-bounding 0-circuit, while one obtained by taking two points from the same complex $C_1^i$ is bounding.

If $R_0 = 2$ any two 0-cells are both in $C_1^1$, or both in $C_1^2$, or one in $C_1$ and the other in $C_1^2$. A pair of the last type forms a non-bounding 0-circuit and all non-bounding 0-circuits are of this type. If $a_i^0 a_k^0$ is a 0-circuit of the last type any other non-bounding 0-circuit $a_l^0 a_m^0$ is such that one of its points, say $a_l^0$, is in the same connected complex with $a_i^0$ and the other with $a_k^0$. Hence $a_l^0 a_m^0$ is the sum (mod. 2) of $a_i^0 a_k^0$ and the two bounding 0-circuits $a_i^0 a_l^0$ and $a_k^0 a_m^0$. Hence any non-bounding 0-circuit is obtainable by adding bounding 0-circuits to a fixed non-bounding 0-circuit.

By a repetition of this reasoning one finds in the general case that $R_0 - 1$ is *the number of non-bounding* 0-*circuits which must be adjoined to the bounding ones in order to have a set in terms of which all the* 0-*circuits are linearly expressible* (*mod.* 2). These $R_0 - 1$ non-bounding 0-circuits can obviously be chosen to consist of the pairs of 0-cells, $a_1^0$, $a_i^0$ $(i = m_1 + 1, m_2 + 1, \cdots, m_{R_0-1} + 1)$.

## One-dimensional Circuits.

22. A connected linear graph each vertex of which is an end of two and only two 1-cells is called a *one-dimensional circuit* or a 1-*circuit*. By the theorems of § 5 any closed curve is decomposed

by any finite set of points on it into a 1-circuit. Conversely, it is easy to see that the set of all points on a 1-circuit is a simple closed curve. It is obvious, further, that any linear graph such that each vertex is an end of two and only two 1-cells is either a 1-circuit or a set of 1-circuits no two of which have a point in common.

Consider a linear graph $C_1$ such that each vertex is an end of an even number of edges. Let us denote by $2n_i$ the number of edges incident with each vertex $a_i^0$. The edges incident with each vertex $a_i^0$ may be grouped arbitrarily in $n_i$ pairs no two of which have an edge in common; let these pairs of edges be called the pairs associated with the vertex $a_i^0$. Let $C_1'$ be a graph coincident with $C_1$ in such a way that (1) there is one and only one point of $C_1'$ on each point of $C_1$ which is not a vertex and (2) there are $n_i$ vertices of $C_1'$ on each vertex $a_i^0$ of $C_1$ each of these vertices of $C_1'$ being incident only with the two edges of $C_1'$ which coincide with a pair associated with $a_i^0$.

The linear graph $C_1'$ has just two edges incident with each of its vertices and therefore consists of a number of 1-circuits. Each of these 1-circuits is coincident with a 1-circuit of $C_1$, and no two of the 1-circuits of $C_1$ thus determined have a 1-cell in common. Hence $C_1$ consists of a number of 1-circuits which have only a finite number of 0-cells in common.

It is obvious that a linear graph composed of a number of closed curves having only a finite number of points in common has an even number of 1-cells incident with each vertex. Hence *a necessary and sufficient condition that $C_1$ consist of a number of 1-circuits having only 0-cells in common is that each 0-cell of $C_1$ be incident with an even number of 1-cells.* A set of 1-circuits having only 0-cells in common will be referred to briefly as a set of 1-circuits.

23. The sum of the symbols $(x_1, x_2, \cdots, x_{\alpha_0})$ for the 0-circuits which bound the 1-cells of a 1-circuit is $(0, 0, \cdots, 0)$ because each 0-cell appears in two and only two of these 0-circuits. Hence *any 1-circuit or set of 1-circuits determines a linear relation, modulo 2, among the bounding 0-circuits.*

Conversely, *any linear relation among the* 0-*circuits which bound* 1-*cells of a complex determines a* 1-*circuit or set of* 1-*circuits.* For if the sum of a set of 0-circuits reduces to $(0, 0, \cdots, 0)$ each 0-cell must enter in an even number of 0-circuits, i.e., as an end of an even number of 1-cells.

24. Let us now inquire under what circumstances a symbol $(x_1, x_2, \cdots, x_{\alpha_1})$ for a one-dimensional complex contained in $C_1$ will represent a 1-circuit or a system of 1-circuits.

Consider the sum

$$\eta_{i1}{}^1 x_1 + \eta_{i2}{}^1 x_2 + \cdots + \eta_{i\alpha_1}{}^1 x_{\alpha_1}$$

where the coefficients $\eta_{ij}{}^1$ are the elements of the ith row of $H_1$. Each term $\eta_{ij}{}^1 x_j$ of this sum is 0 if $a_j{}^1$ is not in the set of 1-cells represented by $(x_1, x_2, \cdots, x_{\alpha_1})$ because in this case $x_j = 0$; it is also zero if $a_j{}^1$ is not incident with $a_i{}^0$ because $\eta_{ij}{}^1 = 0$ in this case. The term $\eta_{ij}{}^1 x_j = 1$ if $a_j{}^1$ is incident with $a_i{}^0$ and in the set represented by $(x_1, x_2, \cdots, x_{\alpha_1})$ because in this case $\eta_{ij}{}^1 = 1$ and $x_j = 1$. Hence there are as many non-zero terms in the sum as there are 1-cells represented by $(x_1, x_2, \cdots, x_{\alpha_1})$ which are incident with $a_i{}^0$. Hence by § 22 the required condition is that the number of non-zero terms in the sum must be even. In other words if the $x$'s and $\eta_{ij}{}^1$'s are reduced modulo 2 as explained in § 14 we must have

$$(\mathrm{H}_1) \qquad \sum_{j=1}^{\alpha_1} \eta_{ij}{}^1 x_j = 0 \qquad (i = 1, 2, \cdots, \alpha_0)$$

if and only if $(x_1, x_2, \cdots, x_{\alpha_1})$ represents a 1-circuit or set of 1-circuits. The matrix of this set of equations (or congruences, mod. 2) is $\mathrm{H}_1$.

25. If the rank of the matrix $\mathrm{H}_1$ of the equations $(\mathrm{H}_1)$ be $\rho_1$ the theory of linear homogeneous equations (congruences, mod. 2) tells us that there is a set of $\alpha_1 - \rho_1$ linearly independent solutions of $(\mathrm{H}_1)$ upon which all other solutions are linearly dependent. This means geometrically that *there exists a set of* $\alpha_1 - \rho_1$ 1-*circuits or systems of* 1-*circuits from which all others can be obtained by repeated applications of the operation of adding*

*(mod. 2) described in* § 14. We shall call this a *complete set* of 1-circuits or systems of 1-circuits.

Since $\rho_1 = \alpha_0 - R_0$ (§ 20), the number of solutions of ($H_1$) in a complete set is

$$\mu = \alpha_1 - \alpha_0 + R_0,$$

where $\mu$ is the cyclomatic number defined in § 13. For the sake of uniformity with a notation used later on we shall also denote $\mu$ by $R_1 - 1$. Thus we have

$$\alpha_0 - \alpha_1 = 1 + R_0 - R_1.$$

### Trees.

26. A connected linear graph which contains no 1-circuits is called a *tree*. As a corollary of the last section it follows that *a linear graph is a set of $R_0$ trees if and only if* $\mu = 0$.

Any connected linear graph $C_1$ can be reduced to a tree by removing $\mu$ properly chosen 1-cells. For let $a_p^1$ $(p = i_1, i_2, \cdots, i_{\rho_1})$ be a set of 1-cells whose boundaries form a complete set of 0-circuits (§ 20). The remaining 1-cells of $C_1$ are $\mu$ in number and will be denoted by $a_p^1$ $(p = j_1, j_2, \cdots, j_\mu)$. If these $\mu$ 1-cells are removed from $C_1$ the linear graph $T_1$ which remains is connected because every bounding 0-circuit of $C_1$ is linearly expressible in terms of the boundaries of the 1-cells $a_p^1$ $(p = i_1, i_2, \cdots, i_{\rho_1})$ of $T_1$ and hence any two 0-cells of $C_1$ are joined by a curve composed of 1-cells of $T_1$. But since the cyclomatic number of $C_1$ is $\mu = \alpha_1 - \alpha_0 + 1$, the removal of $\mu$ 1-cells reduces it to 0 and hence reduces $C_1$ to a tree. In like manner, if $C_1$ is a linear graph for which $R_0 > 1$, it can be reduced to $R_0$ trees by removing $\mu = \alpha_1 - \alpha_0 + R_0$ properly chosen 1-cells.

27. There is at least one 1-circuit of $C_1$ which contains the 1-cell $a_{j_1}^1$, for otherwise $C_1$ would be separated into two complexes by removing this 1-cell. Call such a 1-circuit $C_1^1$. In the complex obtained by removing $a_{j_1}^1$ from $C_1$ there is, for the same reason, a 1-circuit $C_1^2$ which contains $a_{j_2}^1$, and so on. Thus there is a set of 1-circuits $C_1^1, C_1^2, \cdots, C_1^\mu$ such that $C_1^p$ $(p = 1, 2, \cdots, \mu)$ contains $a_{j_p}^1$. These 1-circuits are linearly independent

because $C_1^{k-1}$ contains a 1-cell, $a_{j_{k-1}}^1$, which does not appear in any of the circuits $C_1^{\mu}$, $C_1^{\mu-1}$, $\cdots$, $C_1^k$ and therefore cannot be linearly dependent on them. Hence $C_1^1$, $C_1^2$, $\cdots$, $C_1^{\mu}$ constitute a complete set of 1-circuits. This sharpens the theorem of § 25 a little in that it establishes that there is a complete set of solutions of ($H_1$) each of which represents a single 1-circuit.

## Geometric Interpretation of Matrix Products.

28. According to the definition of multiplication of matrices,

$$||a_{ij}||\cdot||b_{jk}|| = ||c_{ik}||$$

if and only if

$$\sum_{j=1}^{\beta} a_{ij}b_{jk} = c_{ik},$$

$\beta$ being the number of columns in $||a_{ij}||$ and the number of rows in $||b_{jk}||$.

Hence the equations ($H_0$) of § 19 are equivalent to the matrix equation,

$$H_0 \cdot \left\| \begin{matrix} x_1 \\ x_2 \\ \cdot \\ \cdot \\ \cdot \\ x_{\alpha_0} \end{matrix} \right\| = \left\| \begin{matrix} 0 \\ 0 \\ \cdot \\ \cdot \\ \cdot \\ 0 \end{matrix} \right\|,$$

in which the matrix on the right has one column containing $R_0$ zeros.

Since each column of the matrix $H_1$ is the symbol (as defined in § 14) for a bounding 0-circuit, (i.e., the $j$th column is the symbol for the 0-circuit which bounds $a_j^1$) any column of $H_1$ is a solution $(x_1, x_2, \cdots, x_{\alpha_0})$ of the set of equations ($H_0$). By the remark above we may express this result in the form,

$$H_0 \cdot H_1 = 0,$$

where 0 is the symbol for a matrix all of whose elements are zero.

29. By the *boundary* of a one-dimensional complex is meant the set of 0-cells each of which is incident with an odd number of 1-cells of the complex. So, for example, a 1-circuit is a linear graph which has no boundary.

From the definition (§ 14) of addition (mod. 2) of sets of points it is clear that the sum of the boundaries of two 1-cells is the boundary of the complex consisting of the two 1-cells and their ends. By repeated application of this reasoning we prove that the boundary of any one-dimensional complex is an even number of 0-cells, i.e., a number of 0-circuits.

Now consider a one-dimensional complex $C_1'$ represented by the symbol $(x_1, x_2, \cdots, x_{\alpha_1})$ for its 1-cells. According to the reasoning in § 24 each term of

$$\eta_{i1}{}^1 x_1 + \eta_{i2}{}^1 x_2 + \cdots + \eta_{i\alpha_1}{}^1 x_{\alpha_1}$$

is 1 or 0 according as the corresponding 1-cell is or is not both in $C_1'$ and incident with $a_i^0$. Hence this expression is 1 or 0 (mod. 2) according as $a_i^0$ is or is not a boundary point of $C_1'$. Hence if we set

$$\eta_{i1}{}^1 x_1 + \eta_{i2}{}^1 x_2 + \cdots + \eta_{i\alpha_1}{}^1 x_{\alpha_1} = y_i \quad (i = 1, 2, \cdots, \alpha_0)$$

the symbol $(y_1, y_2, \cdots, y_{\alpha_0})$ thus determined represents the set of points which bounds $C_1'$.

Recalling the rule for multiplying matrices, we see that this result may be stated as follows:

$$\mathrm{H}_1 \cdot \left\| \begin{matrix} x_1 \\ x_2 \\ \cdot \\ \cdot \\ \cdot \\ x_{\alpha_1} \end{matrix} \right\| = \left\| \begin{matrix} y_1 \\ y_2 \\ \cdot \\ \cdot \\ \cdot \\ y_{\alpha_0} \end{matrix} \right\|$$

if and only if $(y_1, y_2, \cdots, y_{\alpha_0})$ denotes the set of points which bounds the complex denoted by $(x_1, x_2, \cdots, x_{\alpha_1})$.

### Reduction of $H_0$ and $H_1$ to Normal Form.

30. Let us define two matrices $B_0$ and $B_1$ as follows:

$B_0$ is a matrix of $\alpha_0$ rows and $\alpha_0$ columns of which the first column is the symbol for $a_1^0$, the next $R_0 - 1$ columns are the symbols for the non-bounding 0-circuits enumerated at the end of § 21, and the last $\alpha_0 - R_0$ columns are the symbols for the boundaries of the 1-cells $a_j^1$ $(j = i_1, i_2, \cdots, i_{\rho_1})$ of the trees of § 26.

$B_1$ is a matrix of $\alpha_1$ rows and $\alpha_1$ columns of which the first $\rho_1$ columns are the symbols for $a_j^1$ $(j = i_1, i_2, \cdots, i_{\rho_1})$, and the last $\alpha_1 - \rho_1$ columns are the symbols for the 1-circuits $C_1^1$, $C_1^2$, $\cdots$, $C_1^\mu$.

The determinants of these two matrices are evidently 1 because the columns of $B_0$ represent a linearly independent set of 0-dimensional complexes and the columns of $B_1$ a linearly independent set of 1-dimensional complexes.

The matrix $B_0$ has the properties: (1) all bounding 0-circuits are linearly dependent (mod. 2) upon the 0-circuits represented by its last $\rho_1$ columns; (2) all non-bounding 0-circuits are linearly dependent on its last $\alpha_0 - 1$ columns; (3) all sets of 0-cells are linearly dependent on all its columns.

The matrix $B_1$ has the properties: (1) all 1-circuits are linearly dependent upon the 1-circuits represented by its last $\mu$ columns and (2) all sets of 1-cells are linearly dependent on all its columns.

31. From § 29 and the definition of $B_1$ it is clear that the first $\rho_1$ columns of the product $\mathrm{H}_1 \cdot B_1$ must be the symbols for the boundaries of the 1-cells represented by the first $\rho_1$ columns of $B_1$. Hence the first $\rho_1$ columns of the product $\mathrm{H}_1 \cdot B_1$ are the same as the last $\rho_1$ columns of $B_0$. The remaining columns of $\mathrm{H}_1 \cdot B_1$ must be composed entirely of zeros since the remaining columns of $B_1$ represent 1-circuits. Hence

$$(1) \qquad \mathrm{H}_1 \cdot B_1 = A_0 \cdot \mathrm{H}_1^*,$$

where

$$\mathrm{H}_1^* = \left\| \begin{matrix} 1 & 0 & \cdots & 0 & 0 & \cdots & 0 \\ 0 & 1 & \cdots & 0 & 0 & \cdots & 0 \\ \cdot & \cdot & & \cdot & \cdot & & \cdot \\ \cdot & \cdot & & \cdot & \cdot & & \cdot \\ \cdot & \cdot & & \cdot & \cdot & & \cdot \\ 0 & 0 & \cdots & 1 & 0 & \cdots & 0 \\ \cdot & \cdot & & \cdot & \cdot & & \cdot \\ \cdot & \cdot & & \cdot & \cdot & & \cdot \\ \cdot & \cdot & & \cdot & \cdot & & \cdot \\ 0 & 0 & \cdots & 0 & 0 & \cdots & 0 \end{matrix} \right\|$$

is a matrix of $\alpha_0$ rows and $\alpha_1$ columns of which all elements are

0's except the first $\rho_1$ elements of the main diagonal, and $A_0$ is a matrix of $\alpha_0$ rows and $\alpha_0$ columns whose first $\rho_1 = \alpha_0 - R_0$ columns are identical with the last $\rho_1$ columns of $B_0$ and whose last $R_0$ columns are identical with the first $R_0$ columns of $B_0$. Since the determinant of $B_0$ is 1, the determinant of $A_0$ is 1. Hence (1) may be written

$$(2) \qquad A_0^{-1} \cdot \mathrm{H}_1 \cdot B_1 = \mathrm{H}_1^*.$$

From the point of view of the algebra of matrices (mod. 2) the determination of the two matrices $A_0^{-1}$ and $B_1$ is the solution of the problem of reducing $\mathrm{H}_1$ to its normal or unitary form, $\mathrm{H}_1^*$. Geometrically (cf. § 30) these matrices may be regarded as summarizing the theory of circuits in a linear graph. It will be found that this geometrical significance of the reduction of $\mathrm{H}_1$ to its normal form generalizes to $n$ dimensions. For the sake of completeness we shall also carry out the analogous reduction of $\mathrm{H}_0$.

32. From § 28 and the definition of $B_0$ it is clear that

$$(1) \qquad \mathrm{H}_0 \cdot B_0 = \left\| \begin{array}{cccccccc} 1 & 1 & 1 & \cdots & 1 & 0 & \cdots & 0 \\ 0 & 1 & 0 & \cdots & 0 & 0 & \cdots & 0 \\ 0 & 0 & 1 & \cdots & 0 & 0 & \cdots & 0 \\ \cdot & \cdot & \cdot & & \cdot & \cdot & & \cdot \\ \cdot & \cdot & \cdot & & \cdot & \cdot & & \cdot \\ \cdot & \cdot & \cdot & & \cdot & \cdot & & \cdot \\ 0 & 0 & 0 & \cdots & 1 & 0 & \cdots & 0 \end{array} \right\|$$

the right-hand member of this equation being a matrix of $R_0$ rows and $\alpha_0$ columns. Each of the first $R_0$ columns of this matrix contains a 1 for each of the complexes $C_1^i$ $(i = 1, 2, \cdots, R_0)$ which contains a 0-cell of the set represented by the corresponding columns of $B_0$. The last $\alpha_0 - R_0$ columns contain nothing but 0's because the last $\alpha_0 - R_0$ columns of $B_0$ represent bounding 0-circuits. This equation may also be written in the form

$$(2) \qquad \mathrm{H}_0 \cdot B_0 = A \cdot \mathrm{H}_0^*$$

in which $A$ is a square matrix of $R_0$ columns identical with the first $R_0$ columns of $\mathrm{H}_0 \cdot B_0$ and $\mathrm{H}_0^*$ is a matrix of $R_0$ rows and $\alpha_0$ columns all elements of which are 0 except the $R_0$ elements of the main diagonal, which are all 1.

The determinant of the matrix $A$ is unity and $A$ therefore has a unique inverse $A^{-1}$. Hence (2) becomes

$$A^{-1}\cdot \mathrm{H}_0 \cdot B_0 = \mathrm{H}_0^*. \tag{3}$$

Thus $A^{-1}$ and $B_0$ are a pair of matrices by means of which $\mathrm{H}_0$ is transformed to the normal form $\mathrm{H}_0^*$.

## Oriented Cells.

33. We turn now to the notion of "orientation" or "sense of description" of a complex. The definitions adopted will doubtless seem very artificial, but this is bound to be the case in defining any idea so intuitionally elemental as that of "sense."

A 0-cell associated with the number $+1$ or $-1$ shall be called an *oriented* 0-*cell* or *oriented point*.* In the first case the oriented 0-cell is said to be *positively oriented* and in the second case it is said to be *negatively oriented*; the two oriented points are called *negatives* of each other. A set of oriented 0-cells is called an *oriented* 0-*dimensional complex*.

A pair of oriented 0-cells, formed by associating one point of a 0-circuit with $+1$ and the other with $-1$ shall be called an *oriented* 0-*circuit* or an *oriented* 0-*dimensional manifold*. If a 0-circuit is bounding, any oriented 0-circuit formed from it is also said to be *bounding*.

34. The ends $a_1^0$, $a_2^0$ of a 1-cell $a^1$ when associated each with $+1$ determine two oriented 0-cells which may be called $\sigma_1^0$ and $\sigma_2^0$ respectively. Therefore the ends of $a^1$ determine two oriented 0-circuits, namely $\sigma_1^0, -\sigma_2^0$ and $-\sigma_1^0, \sigma_2^0$. The object formed by associating $a^1$ with either of these 0-circuits is called an *oriented* 1-*cell*.

The oriented 1-cell $\sigma^1$ formed by associating $a^1$ with $\sigma_1^0, -\sigma_2^0$ is said to be *positively related* to $\sigma_1^0$ and $-\sigma_2^0$ and *negatively related* to $-\sigma_1^0$ and $\sigma_2^0$. An oriented 0-cell is said to be positively or negatively related to an oriented 1-cell according as the 1-cell is positively or negatively related to it.

The point $a_1^0$ is called the *terminal point* and $a_2^0$ the *initial*

* In analytic applications the number $\pm 1$ associated with a point is usually determined by the sign of a functional determinant.

*point* of the oriented 1-cell $\sigma^1$ formed by associating $a^1$ with $\sigma_1^0$, $-\sigma_2^0$. In diagrams it is convenient to denote an oriented 1-cell by marking it with an arrow pointing from the initial point to the terminal point.

In the following sections we shall denote the oriented 0-cells obtained by associating each of the 0-cells $a_1^0, a_2^0, \cdots, a_{\alpha_0}^0$ of a complex $C_1$ with $+1$, by $\sigma_1^0, \sigma_2^0, \cdots, \sigma_{\alpha_0}^0$ respectively. We shall also denote an arbitrary one of the two oriented 1-cells which can be formed from $a_i^1$ ($i = 1, 2, \cdots, \alpha_1$) by $\sigma_i^1$. Any set of oriented 1-cells will be called an *oriented one-dimensional complex.* Thus any linear graph can be converted into an oriented complex in $2^{\alpha_1}$ ways.

35. The cells of a 1-circuit, when oriented by the process described above give rise to a sequence of oriented 0-cells and 1-cells,

(1) $$\sigma_1^0, \sigma_1^1, \sigma_2^0, \sigma_2^1, \cdots \sigma_{\alpha_0}^0, \sigma_{\alpha_0}^1, \sigma_1^0,$$

in which each oriented cell is either positively or negatively related to the one which follows it. According to the convention that $\sigma_i^0$ is formed from $a_i^0$ by associating it with $+1$, each $\sigma_i^1$ is negatively related to the oriented 0-cell which follows it if it is positively related to the one which precedes it, and *vice versa.* Hence by assigning the notation so that $\sigma_j^1$ is in every case positively related to the oriented 0-cell which precedes it in the sequence (1) we can arrange that $\sigma_1^1, \sigma_2^1, \cdots, \sigma_{\alpha_1}^1$, represent a set of oriented 1-cells such that each oriented 0-cell positively related to one oriented 1-cell of the set is negatively related to another. Such an oriented complex formed from the 1-cells of a 1-circuit is called an *oriented* 1-*circuit.*

It is obvious that the only other oriented 1-circuit which can be formed from the given 1-circuit is that composed of $-\sigma_1^1$, $-\sigma_2^1, \cdots, -\sigma_{\alpha_0}^1$. For if one of the oriented 1-cells in an oriented 1-circuit be replaced by its negative each of the other 1-cells must be replaced by its negative. The other oriented complexes which can be formed from the 1-circuit are not oriented 1-circuits.

Intuitionally this discussion means that if the oriented 1-cells of an oriented 1-circuit are marked by arrows as in § 34, the arrows must all be pointed in the same direction.

**Matrices of Orientation.**

36. The relations between the oriented 0-cells and oriented 1-cells which can be formed from the cells of a complex $C_1$ may be studied by means of two matrices which are closely analogous to $H_0$ and $H_1$. The new matrices will be called *matrices of orientation,* and denoted by $E_0$ and $E_1$. In our treatment they are derived from $H_0$ and $H_1$ and their theory is entirely parallel to that of $H_0$ and $H_1$. They are, however, the one- and two-dimensional instances of the matrices $E_i$ which form the central element in Poincare's work on Analysis Situs. The matrix $E_1$ may be said to date back to the article by G. Kirchoff in Poggendorf's Annalen der Physik, Vol. 72 (1847), p. 497, on the flow of electricity through a network of wires, in which Kirchoff made use of a system of linear equations having $E_1$ as its matrix. This paper is doubtless the first important contribution to the theory of linear graphs.

37. Any set of oriented 0-cells may be denoted by a symbol $(x_1, x_2, \cdots, x_{\alpha_0})$ in which $x_i$ is $+1$ if $\sigma_i^0$ is in the set, $-1$ if $-\sigma_i^0$ is in the set, and 0 if neither $\sigma_i^0$ nor $-\sigma_i^0$ is in the set. The symbols for the bounding oriented 0-circuits of a complex $C_1$ satisfy a set of equations, $(E_0)$, identical with the equations $(H_0)$ of § 19 except that the variables are taken to be integers instead of being reduced modulo 2. The corresponding matrix will be denoted by

$$E_0 = ||\epsilon_{ij}^0|| \quad (i = 1, 2, \cdots, R_0;\ j = 1, 2, \cdots, \alpha_0).$$

If the complex is connected, $R_0 = 1$ and this matrix reduces to a one-rowed matrix

$$||1, 1, \cdots, 1||$$

all of whose $\alpha_0$ elements are unity. The equations $(E_0)$ have $\alpha_0 - R_0$ linearly independent solutions, and if $r_0$ is the rank of $E_0$

$$r_0 = \rho_0 = R_0.$$

38. The relations between the oriented 0-cells $\sigma_i^0$ and oriented 1-cells $\sigma_j^1$ of an oriented complex $C_1$ may be denoted by a matrix

$$E_1 = ||\epsilon_{ij}^1|| \quad (i = 1, 2, \cdots, \alpha_0;\ j = 1, 2, \cdots, \alpha_1)$$

in which $\epsilon_{ij}^1$ is $+1$ if $\sigma_i^0$ is positively related to $\sigma_j^1$, is $-1$ if $\sigma_i^0$ is negatively related to $\sigma_j^1$, and is 0 if $a_i^0$ is not an end of $a_j^1$.

This matrix can be formed from $H_1$ by changing a 1 in each column to $-1$, for each $\sigma_i^1$ is positively related to one of the $\sigma^0$s formed from the ends of $a_i^1$ and negatively related to the other. The choice of the $-1$ is determined by the arbitrary choice in the definition of $\sigma_i^1$.

For example, the vertices and edges of the tetrahedron in fig. 1 when oriented as indicated by the arrows constitute an oriented complex represented by the following matrix:

$$E_1 = \begin{Vmatrix} -1 & 0 & 0 & 0 & -1 & 1 \\ 0 & -1 & 0 & 1 & 0 & -1 \\ 0 & 0 & -1 & -1 & 1 & 0 \\ 1 & 1 & 1 & 0 & 0 & 0 \end{Vmatrix}$$

39. Each column of the matrix $E_1$ is the symbol (§ 37) for a bounding oriented 0-circuit and hence is a solution of the set of equations $(E_0)$. In the notation of matrices, this means

$$(1) \qquad E_0 \cdot E_1 = 0.$$

The matrix $E_1$ falls into a set of matrices I, II, III, etc. corresponding to those into which $H_1$ is decomposed in §20. The sum of the rows of any one of these matrices I, II, III is zero because each column has one $+1$ and one $-1$. On the other hand the rows of such a matrix, say I, cannot be subject to any other linear relation because one of the variables could be eliminated between this relation and the one which states that the sum of the rows is zero, and the resulting relation on being reduced modulo 2 would give a linear relation among the rows of $H_1$ of a type which has been shown in § 20 to be non-existent. Hence the rows of $E_1$ are subject to $R_0$ linearly independent linear relations. Hence if $r_1$ denote the rank of $E_1$,

$$r_1 = \rho_1 = \alpha_0 - R_0.$$

40. The form of the matrices $E_0$ and $E_1$ has been limited somewhat by the convention that $\sigma_1^0, \sigma_2^0, \cdots, \sigma_{\alpha_0}^0$ denote 0-cells each associated with $+1$. If we interchange the significance of $\sigma_i^0$ and $-\sigma_i^0$, so that $\sigma_i^0$ represents $a_i^0$ associated with $-1$, it is necessary to change the 1 in the $i$th column of $E_0$ to $-1$ and to make corresponding changes in the columns of $E_1$ so that these columns of $E_1$ shall be solutions of $(E_0)$.

Thus, to interchange the meanings of $\sigma_i^0$ and $-\sigma_i^0$ for arbitrary values of $i$ amounts merely to changing an arbitrary set of 1's in $E_0$ to $-1$'s, and to determining the signs in $E_1$ so that $E_0 \cdot E_1 = 0$. The rest of the discussion on this slightly more general foundation does not differ in essentials from that already given.

## Oriented 1-circuits.

41. Every oriented 1-circuit corresponds to a linear relation among the oriented 0-circuits which bound the oriented 1-cells of which it is composed, for if a given oriented 0-cell is positively related to one such oriented 1-cell, its negative is, by the terms of the definition, positively related to another oriented 1-cell of the oriented 1-circuit. Conversely any linear relation among the bounding 0-circuits determines an oriented 1-circuit or set of oriented 1-circuits. All this is analogous to § 23. Taken with § 39 it establishes that the number of linearly independent linear relations among oriented 0-circuits is the same as among 0-circuits when reduced modulo 2.

42. Any set of oriented 1-cells of a complex $C_1$ may be denoted by $(x_1, x_2, \cdots, x_{\alpha_1})$ where $x_i = 1$ if $\sigma_i^1$ is in the set, $x_i = -1$ if $-\sigma_i^1$ is in the set, and $x_i = 0$ if neither $\sigma_i^1$ nor $-\sigma_i^1$ is in it. The necessary and sufficient condition that such a symbol represent an oriented 1-circuit is that it satisfy the system of equations,

$$(E_1) \qquad \sum_{j=1}^{\alpha_1} \epsilon_{ij}^1 x_j = 0 \qquad (i = 1, 2, \cdots, \alpha_0),$$

the matrix of which is $E_1$. For in this set, the equation,

$$(1) \qquad \epsilon_{i1}^1 x_1 + \epsilon_{i2}^1 x_2 + \cdots + \epsilon_{i\alpha_1}^1 x_{\alpha_1} = 0$$

corresponds to the oriented 0-cell $\sigma_i^0$. A term $\epsilon_{ij}^1 x_j$ of the left member is zero if $\epsilon_{ij}^1 = 0$ or if $x_j = 0$, that is, if $\sigma_i^1$ is not an end of $\sigma_j^1$ or if the set of oriented 1-cells does not contain $\pm \sigma_j^1$. The term $\epsilon_{ij}^1 x_j$ is $+1$ if $\epsilon_{ij}^1$ and $x_j$ are of the same sign, that is if the set of oriented 1-cells contains $\sigma_j^1$ and the latter is positively related to $\sigma_i^0$ or if it contains $-\sigma_j^1$ and $-\sigma_j^1$ is positively related to $\sigma_i^0$; hence there are as many $+1$ terms in the left member of (1) as there are oriented 1-cells in the set $(x_1, x_2, \cdots, x_{\alpha_1})$ which are positively related to $\sigma_i^0$. In like manner there are as many $-1$ terms as there are oriented 1-cells in the set which are negatively related to $\sigma_i^0$. Hence *the left-hand member of* (1) *is the difference between the number of oriented* 1-*cells in the set which are positively related to* $\sigma_i^0$ *and the number which are negatively related to* $\sigma_i^0$. Hence an oriented 1-circuit satisfies the equations ($\mathrm{E}_1$).

Since the number of variables $x_j$ in the equations ($\mathrm{E}_1$) is $\alpha_1$ and the rank of the equations is $\alpha_0 - R_0$ (cf. § 39) the number of solutions in a complete set is $\mu$ where

$$\mu = \alpha_1 - \alpha_0 + R_0.$$

Such a complete set is obviously obtained by converting the $\mu$ 1-circuits of § 26 into oriented 1-circuits. The symbols $(x_1, x_2, \cdots, x_{\alpha_1})$ for these 1-circuits are linearly independent solutions of ($\mathrm{E}_1$) in which the $x$'s are 0 or $\pm 1$.

It is obvious that the equations ($\mathrm{E}_1$) have solutions in which the $x$'s are integers different from 0 and $\pm 1$. In order to interpret these solutions we shall return to the notion of a singular complex on $C_1$ (§ 8).

## Symbols for Oriented Complexes.

43. If a 0-cell $\bar{a}^0$ on $C_1$ (in the sense of § 7) is associated with $+1$ or $-1$ the resulting oriented 0-cell $\bar{\sigma}^0$ is said to be *on* $C_1$, and if $\bar{a}^0$ coincides with a 0-cell $a_i^0$ of $C_1$, $\bar{\sigma}^0$ is said to *coincide* with $\sigma_i^0$ or $-\sigma_i^0$ according as $\bar{\sigma}^0$ is positively or negatively oriented.

Let $C_1'$ be any linear graph on $C_1$ such that each 1-cell of $C_1'$

covers a 1-cell of $C_1$ just once (cf. § 9). If the cells of both complexes are oriented, an oriented 1-cell $\sigma_p^1$ of $C_1'$ will be said to *coincide* with an oriented 1-cell $\sigma_q^1$ of $C_1$ if and only if (1) each point of $\sigma_p^1$ coincides with a point of $\sigma_q^1$ and (2) each oriented 0-cell of $C_1'$ is positively or negatively related to $\sigma_p^1$ according as it coincides with an oriented 0-cell of $C_1$ which is positively or negatively related to $\sigma_q^1$.

44. A symbol $(x_1, x_2, \cdots, x_{\alpha_i})$ in which the $x$'s are positive or negative integers or 0 will be taken to represent a set of oriented $i$-cells ($i = 0$ or 1) on $C_1$ in which (1) if $x_j$ ($j = 1, 2, \cdots, \alpha_i$) is positive there are $x_j$ oriented $i$-cells coinciding with $\sigma_j^i$, (2) if $x_j$ is negative there are $-x_j$ oriented $i$-cells coinciding with $-\sigma_j^i$, and (3) if $x_j = 0$ there are no oriented $i$-cells coinciding with $\sigma_j^i$ or $-\sigma_j^i$.

In case the numbers $x_j$ ($j = 1, 2, \cdots, \alpha_i$; $i = 0, 1$), have a common factor different from unity, i.e., in case

$$(x_1, x_2, \cdots, x_{\alpha_i}) = (z_1 d, z_2 d, \cdots, z_{\alpha_i} d)$$

this symbol represents a set of $d$ complexes each of which may be represented by $(z_1, z_2, \cdots, z_{\alpha_i})$. The oriented complex $(x_1, x_2, \cdots, x_{\alpha_i})$ is said to *cover* the oriented complex $(z_1, z_2, \cdots, z_{\alpha_i})$ *d times*. This use of the term 'cover' is in agreement with the usage of § 9, for the complex from which $(z_1 d, z_2 d, \cdots, z_{\alpha_1} d)$ is obtained by orientation covers the one from which $(z_1, z_2, \cdots, z_{\alpha_1})$ is obtained $d$ times according to the definition in § 9.

45. If $(x_1, x_2, \cdots, x_{\alpha_i})$ and $(y_1, y_2, \cdots, y_{\alpha_i})$ are symbols for two sets of oriented $i$-cells ($i = 0, 1$), the symbol $(x_1 + y_1, x_2 + y_2, \cdots, x_{\alpha_i} + y_{\alpha_i})$ is called the *sum* of the two symbols and the set of oriented $i$-cells which it represents is called the *sum* of the two sets of oriented $i$-cells.

For example, in fig. 1 the oriented 1-circuit composed of $\sigma_4^1, \sigma_5^1, \sigma_6^1$ may be denoted by (0, 0, 0, 1, 1, 1) and the oriented 1-circuit composed of $\sigma_2^1, \sigma_4^1, -\sigma_3^1$ may be denoted by (0, 1, $-$ 1, 1, 0, 0). Their sum is (0, 1, $-$ 1, 2, 1, 1). If each of $\sigma_2^1, \sigma_4^1$ and $-\sigma_3^1$ be replaced by its negative the sum becomes

(0, − 1, 1, 0, 1, 1). In the first case the sum is a pair of oriented 1-circuits, $\sigma_4^1$ appearing once in each; in the second case the sum is a single oriented 1-circuit.

It can be proved by an argument analogous to that used in § 22 that the sum of any set of oriented 1-circuits can be regarded as a set of oriented 1-circuits. Hence any solution of the equations ($E_1$) represents a set of oriented 1-circuits.

46. By the *boundary* of an oriented 1-cell is meant the pair of oriented points which are positively related to it. By the *boundary* of any oriented one-dimensional complex is meant the sum of the boundaries of the oriented 1-cells composing it.

From this definition it follows directly that an oriented 1-circuit has no boundary and that any set of oriented 1-cells without a boundary may be regarded as a set of 1-circuits.

If $(x_1, x_2, \cdots, x_{a_1})$ is the symbol for a single oriented 1-cell, it is obvious from the reasoning used in § 42 that $(y_1, y_2, \cdots, y_{a_0})$ is the symbol for its boundary if and only if

$$(1) \qquad E_1 \cdot \left\| \begin{matrix} x_1 \\ x_2 \\ \cdot \\ \cdot \\ \cdot \\ x_{a_1} \end{matrix} \right\| = \left\| \begin{matrix} y_1 \\ y_2 \\ \cdot \\ \cdot \\ \cdot \\ y_{a_0} \end{matrix} \right\| .$$

But the most general symbol $(x_1, x_2, \cdots, x_{a_1})$ in which the $x$'s are integers or zero can be expressed as a sum of symbols for oriented 1-cells, and by the algebraic properties of matrices,

$$(2) \qquad E_1 \cdot \left\| \begin{matrix} x_1 + x_1' \\ x_2 + x_2' \\ \cdot \\ \cdot \\ \cdot \\ x_{a_1} + x_{a_1}' \end{matrix} \right\| = E_1 \cdot \left\| \begin{matrix} x_1 \\ x_2 \\ \cdot \\ \cdot \\ \cdot \\ x_{a_1} \end{matrix} \right\| + E_1 \cdot \left\| \begin{matrix} x_1' \\ x_2' \\ \cdot \\ \cdot \\ \cdot \\ x_{a_1}' \end{matrix} \right\| .$$

Hence in the general case, $(y_1, y_2, \cdots, y_{a_0})$ is the symbol for the boundary of $(x_1, x_2, \cdots, x_{a_1})$ if and only if (1) is satisfied.

### Normal Forms for $\mathrm{E}_0$ and $\mathrm{E}_1$.

47. All columns, except the first one, of the matrix $B_0$ which appeared (§ 32) in the reduction of $\mathrm{H}_0$ to normal form are symbols for 0-circuits. Hence by changing one of the 1's in each column after the first column to $-1$, $B_0$ is converted into a matrix, $D_0$, of which the first column represents the oriented 0-cell $\sigma_1^0$, the next $R_0 - 1$ columns represent linearly independent non-bounding oriented 0-circuits, and the last $\alpha_0 - R_0$ columns represent linearly independent bounding oriented 0-circuits. The product $E_0 \cdot D_0$ is clearly obtained from $\mathrm{H}_0 \cdot B_0$ by changing one 1 to $-1$ in each column from the second to the $R_0$th. Hence

(1) $$\mathrm{E}_0 \cdot D_0 = C \cdot \mathrm{E}_0^*,$$

where $\mathrm{E}_0^*$ is the same as $\mathrm{H}_0^*$ and $C$ is obtained from $A$ by changing one 1 into $-1$ in each column except the first. The determinant of $C$ is $\pm 1$. Hence there exists a matrix $C^{-1}$ whose elements are integers and (1) can be written in the form

(2) $$C^{-1} \cdot \mathrm{E}_0 \cdot D_0 = \mathrm{E}_0^*.$$

The reduction of $\mathrm{E}_0$ to normal form, therefore, is completely parallel to the corresponding reduction of $\mathrm{H}_0$.

48. Let $D_1$ be a square matrix of $\alpha_1$ rows formed from $B_1$ (§ 30) by changing 1's into $-1$'s in such a way that the first $\rho_1$ columns become the symbols for $\alpha_0 - R_0$ oriented 1-cells whose boundaries are represented by the last $\alpha_0 - R_0$ columns of $D_0$, and the remaining $\alpha_1 - \alpha_0 + R_0$ columns become the symbols for a complete set of oriented 1-circuits. The product $\mathrm{E}_1 \cdot D_1$ is a matrix of $\alpha_0$ rows and $\alpha_1$ columns of which the first $\alpha_0 - R_0$ columns represent the oriented 0-circuits bounding the corresponding 1-cells and the remaining columns are composed only of zeros. Hence

(1) $$\mathrm{E}_1 \cdot D_1 = C_0 \cdot \mathrm{E}_1^*,$$

in which $\mathrm{E}_1^*$ is the matrix of $\alpha_0$ rows and $\alpha_1$ columns having 1's in the first $\rho_1$ places of the main diagonal and 0's in all other places, and $C_0$ is obtained from $A_0$ (cf. § 31) by converting the columns of the latter into symbols for oriented cells and circuits. Thus $C_0$ is also obtainable from $D_0$ by a permutation of columns.

The determinant of $D_0$ is easily seen to be $\pm 1$. Hence the equation (1) can be put in the form

$$C_0^{-1} \cdot \mathrm{E}_1 \cdot D_1 = \mathrm{E}_1^*, \tag{2}$$

which shows that $\mathrm{E}_1^*$ can be regarded as a normal form for the matrix $\mathrm{E}_1$.

## Matrices of Integers.

49. The equation (2) of § 48 can be obtained directly from the general theory of matrices whose elements are integers.* The fundamental theorem of this theory is that for any matrix E of $\alpha_1$ rows and $\alpha_2$ columns whose elements are integers there exist two square matrices $C$ and $D$ of $\alpha_1$ rows and $\alpha_2$ rows respectively, each of determinant $\pm 1$, such that

$$C \cdot \mathrm{E} \cdot D = \mathrm{E}^* \tag{1}$$

where E* is a matrix of $\alpha_1$ rows and $\alpha_2$ columns

$$\mathrm{E}^* = \left\| \begin{array}{cccccc} d_1 & 0 & \cdots & 0 & \cdots & 0 \\ 0 & d_2 & \cdots & 0 & \cdots & 0 \\ \cdot & \cdot & & \cdot & & \cdot \\ \cdot & \cdot & & \cdot & & \cdot \\ \cdot & \cdot & & \cdot & & \cdot \\ 0 & 0 & \cdots & d_r & \cdots & 0 \\ \cdot & \cdot & & \cdot & & \cdot \\ \cdot & \cdot & & \cdot & & \cdot \\ \cdot & \cdot & & \cdot & & \cdot \\ 0 & 0 & \cdots & 0 & \cdots & 0 \end{array} \right\|$$

in which $d_1$ is the highest common factor of all the elements of $\mathrm{E}_2$, $d_1 d_2$ the H.C.F. of all the two-rowed determinants which can be found by removing rows and columns from E, and finally, $d_1 d_2 \cdots d_r$ the H.C.F. of all the $r$-rowed determinants which can be formed from E. The number $d_1$ is the H.C.F. of all the numbers $d_1\ d_2\ d_3 \cdots d_r$, $d_2$ is the H.C.F. of $d_2, d_3, \cdots, d_r$, etc.

* The part of this theory which is needed for our purposes is the subject of an expository article by P. Franklin and the author which is to be published in Vol. 23 of the Annals of Mathematics.

The numbers $d_1, d_2, \cdots, d_r$ are called the *invariant factors*, or the *elementary divisors* of the matrix E. They are invariants in the sense that if E is multiplied on the left by a square matrix of $\alpha_1$ rows and determinant unity and on the right by any square matrix of $\alpha_2$ rows and determinant unity, the resulting matrix will be such that the H.C.F. of all the $k$-rowed determinants which can be formed from it is $d_1 \cdot d_2 \cdot \cdots, d_k$ $(k = 1, 2, \cdots, r_2)$.

If all elements be reduced modulo 2, E reduces to a matrix H all of whose elements are 0 or 1. The equation (1) reduces to an equation like (2) of § 31. The rank of E differs from the rank of H by the number of $d$'s which contain 2 as a factor.

50. In view of the general theory it is seen that the matrix $E_1$ for a linear graph is characterized by the fact that *its invariant factors are all* $\pm 1$. On this account the theory of the matrix $E_1$ is essentially the same as that of $H_1$. When we come to the generalizations to two and more dimensions, the invariant factors of the matrix will no longer have this simple property and the invariant factors will turn out to be important Analysis Situs invariants.

# CHAPTER II

## TWO-DIMENSIONAL COMPLEXES AND MANIFOLDS

### Fundamental Definitions

1. In a Euclidean space three non-collinear points and the segments which join them by pairs constitute the boundary of a finite region in the plane of the three points. This region is called a *triangular region* or *two-dimensional simplex* and the three given points are called its *vertices*. The points of the boundary are not regarded as points of the region.

Consider any set of objects in $(1 - 1)$ correspondence with the points of a two-dimensional simplex and its boundary. The objects corresponding to the points of the simplex constitute what is called a *two-dimensional cell* or *2-cell*, and those corresponding to the boundary of the simplex what is called the *boundary of the 2-cell.*

The objects which constitute a cell and its boundary will hereafter be referred to as " points," and the remarks in § 2, Chap. I, with regard to order relations are carried over without change to the two-dimensional case. The boundary of a 2-cell obviously satisfies the definition given in Chap. I of a curve.

2. A *two-dimensional complex* may be defined as a one-dimensional complex $C_1$ together with a number, $\alpha_2$, of 2-cells whose boundaries are 1-circuits of the one-dimensional complex, such that each 1-cell is on the boundary of at least one 2-cell and no 2-cell has a point in common with another 2-cell or with $C_1$. The order relations of the points of the boundary of each 2-cell must coincide with the order relations determined among these points as points of the 1-circuit of the one-dimensional complex which coincides with the boundary. (Compare the footnote to § 2, Chap. III.)

The surface of a tetrahedron (cf. fig. 1) is a simple example of a two-dimensional complex. Any polyhedron or combination of polyhedra in a Euclidean space will furnish a more complicated example.

An arbitrary subset of the 0-cells, 1-cells, and 2-cells of a two-dimensional complex will be occasionally referred to as a *generalized two-dimensional complex.*

3. The definitions of limit point and continuous transformation given in Chap. I may be generalized directly to two-dimensional complexes and we take them for granted without further discussion. As in § 4, Chap. I, two complexes are said to be *homeomorphic* if there exists a $(1 - 1)$ continuous correspondence between them; and any such correspondence is called a *homeomorphism.* The two complexes will in general be defined in quite different ways so that the numbers $\alpha_0$, $\alpha_1$, $\alpha_2$ are different; but if the two complexes are homeomorphic there is a $(1 - 1)$ continuous correspondence between them as sets of points.

Any proposition about a complex or set of complexes which is unaltered under the group of all homeomorphisms of these complexes is called a proposition of *two-dimensional Analysis Situs.*

## Matrices of Incidence

4. The 0-cells and 1-cells on the boundary of a 2-cell are said to be *incident* with the 2-cell and the 2-cell to be *incident* with the 0-cells and 1-cells of its boundary. The incidence relations between the 1-cells and 2-cells of a two-dimensional complex $C_2$ may be indicated by a table or matrix analogous to that described in § 17, Chap. I. The 2-cells, $\alpha_2$ in number, shall be denoted by $a_1^2, a_2^2, \cdots, a_{\alpha_2}^2$. The matrix $\text{H}_2 = \| \eta_{ij}^2 \|$ which describes the incidence relations between the 1-cells and 2-cells is such that $\eta_{ij}^2 = 0$ if $a_i^1$ is not incident with $a_j^2$ and $\eta_{ij}^2 = 1$ if $a_i^1$ is incident with $a_j^2$.

In the case of the tetrahedron in fig. 1, let us denote the 2-cells opposite the vertices $a_1^0, a_2^0, a_3^0, a_4^0$ by $a_1^2, a_2^2, a_3^2, a_4^2$ respectively. The table of incidence relations becomes

| | $a_1^2$ | $a_2^2$ | $a_3^2$ | $a_4^2$ |
|---|---|---|---|---|
| $a_1^1$ | 0 | 1 | 1 | 0 |
| $a_2^1$ | 1 | 0 | 1 | 0 |
| $a_3^1$ | 1 | 1 | 0 | 0 |
| $a_4^1$ | 1 | 0 | 0 | 1 |
| $a_5^1$ | 0 | 1 | 0 | 1 |
| $a_6^1$ | 0 | 0 | 1 | 1 |

5. Since each column of $H_2$ contains $\alpha_1$ elements it may be regarded as a symbol $(x_1, x_2, \cdots, x_{\alpha_1})$ in the sense of § 15, Chap. I for a set of 1-cells. The $j$th column of $H_2$ is, in fact the symbol for the 1-cells on the boundary of the 2-cell $a_j^2$. It is therefore the symbol for a 1-circuit. Hence the *columns of* $H_2$ *are solutions of the equations* $(H_1)$. That is to say

$$\sum_{j=1}^{\alpha_1} \eta_{ij}^1 \eta_{jk}^2 = 0 \qquad (i = 1, \cdots, \alpha_0, k = 1, \cdots, \alpha_2)$$

or, in terms of the multiplication of matrices,

$$H_1 \cdot H_2 = 0, \tag{1}$$

where 0 stands for the matrix all of whose elements are zero.

It should be recalled here that we have already proved in § 28, Chap. 1 that

$$H_0 \cdot H_1 = 0.$$

The ranks of the matrices $H_0$, $H_1$, $H_2$, computed modulo 2, will be denoted by $\rho_0$, $\rho_1$, $\rho_2$ respectively.

6. From the point of view of Analysis Situs a two-dimensional complex is fully described by the three matrices $H_0$, $H_1$, $H_2$ for there is no difficulty in proving that if two two-dimensional complexes have the same matrices there is a $(1 - 1)$ continuous correspondence between them. Our definitions are such that the boundary of every 1-cell is a pair of distinct points and the boundary of every 2-cell a non-singular curve. Hence a figure composed of a 1-cell incident with a 0-cell or a 2-cell is in $(1 - 1)$ continuous correspondence with any other such figure.

If two complexes $C_2$ and $\bar{C}_2$ have the same matrices their 0-cells, 1-cells and 2-cells may be denoted by $a_i^0$, $a_j^1$, $a_k^2$ and

$b_i^0$, $b_j^1$, $b_k^2$ in such a way that whenever $a_j^1$ for any value of $i$, $j$, $k$ is incident with $a_i^0$ or $a_k^2$, the $b_j^1$ for the same values of $j$ is incident with the $b_i^0$ or $b_k^2$ with the same value of $i$ or $k$. A $(1 - 1)$ continuous correspondence is then set up between $C_2$ and $\bar{C}_2$ by requiring: (1) that $a_i^0$ correspond to $b_i^0$ for each value of $i$, (2) that $a_j^1$ and its ends correspond to $b_j^1$ and its ends for each value of $j$ in a $(1 - 1)$ continuous correspondence such that the correspondence between the ends is that set up under (1), and (3) that $a_k^2$ and its boundary correspond to $b_k^2$ and its boundary in a $(1 - 1)$ continuous correspondence by which the boundaries correspond in the correspondence set up under (2).

## Subdivision of 2-Cells

7. The properties of a two-dimensional complex will be obtained by studying the combinatorial relations codified in the matrices $H_0$, $H_1$, $H_2$ in connection with the continuity properties of the 2-cell. The latter properties, according to the definition in § 1, depend on the order relations in a Euclidean plane and, in particular, on the theory of planar polygons. The theory of polygons can be built up in terms of the incidence matrices. For consider a set of $n$ straight lines in a Euclidean plane. They separate it into a number $\alpha_2$ of planar convex regions and intersect in a number $\alpha_0$ of points which divide the lines into a number $\alpha_1$ of linear convex regions. The $\alpha_0$ points can be treated as 0-cells, the $\alpha_1$ linear convex regions as 1-cells and the $\alpha_2$ planar convex regions as 2-cells. Any polygon is a 1-circuit, and the theory of linear dependence as developed in our first chapter can be applied to the proof of the fundamental theorems on polygons. For the details of this theory, which belongs to affine geometry rather than to Analysis Situs, the reader is referred to Chapters II and IX of the second volume of Veblen and Young's Projective Geometry.

8. The $(1 - 1)$ correspondence with the interior and boundary of a triangle which defines a 2-cell and its boundary determines a system of 1-cells in the 2-cell which are the correspondents of the straight 1-cells in the interior of the triangle. By regarding this

system of 1-cells as the *straight 1-cells* and defining the *distance* between any two points of the 2-cell and its boundary as the distance between the corresponding two points of the interior of the triangle, we can carry over all the theorems of the elementary geometry of a triangle to the 2-cell. The notions of distance and straightness so developed, however, are not invariant under the group of homeomorphisms, and the corresponding theorems are not theorems of Analysis Situs. For purposes of Analysis Situs the theorem of interest here is simply that there exists a system of 1-cells which are in $(1-1)$ continuous correspondence with the straight 1-cells of the interior of a triangle of the Euclidean plane.

There is no great difficulty in making the definition of straightness and distance for all the cells of a complex $C_2$ in such a way that the distance between any two points of a 1-cell is the same with respect to every 2-cell incident with the 1-cell. We shall not need to do this and therefore shall not give the construction in detail.

9. The following theorems follow immediately from the homeomorphism between a 2-cell and the triangle used in defining it:

If two points $A$ and $B$ of the boundary of a 2-cell $a^2$ are joined by a straight 1-cell $a^1$ consisting of points of $a^2$, the remaining points of $a^2$ constitute two 2-cells each of which is bounded by $a^1$, $A$, $B$ and one of the two 1-cells into which the boundary of $a^2$ is divided by $A$ and $B$.

If the boundaries of two 2-cells $a_1^2$ and $a_2^2$ have a 1-cell $a^1$ and its ends in common, and the 2-cells and their boundaries have no other common points, then $a^1$, $a_1^2$ and $a_2^2$ constitute a 2-cell.

If there is a $(1-1)$ continuous correspondence $F'$ between the boundaries of two 2-cells $a_1^2$ and $a_2^2$, there exists a $(1-1)$ continuous correspondence $F$ between the interior and boundary of $a_1^2$ and the interior and boundary of $a_2^2$ which effects the correspondence $F'$ between the boundaries.

A point of a 2-cell can be joined to a set of points $A_1, A_2, \cdots, A_n$ of its boundary by a set of 1-cells $a_1^1, a_2^1, \cdots, a_n^1$ which are in the 2-cell and have no points in common. The 2-cell is thus decomposed into $n$ 2-cells $a_1^2, a_2^2, \cdots, a_n^2$ such that the sum of their boundaries (mod. 2) is the boundary of $a^2$ and such that the incidence relations between them and $a_1^1, a_2^1, \cdots, a_n^1$ are the same as the incidence relations between the 0-cells and 1-cells of a 1-circuit.

Conversely, if $a_1^1, a_2^1, \cdots, a_n^1$ and $a_1^2, a_2^2, \cdots, a_n^2$ are 1-cells and 2-cells all incident with the same point $a^0$ and also incident with one another in such a way that the incidence relations between the 1-cells and 2-cells are the same as those between the 0-cells and 1-cells of a 1-circuit, then the point $a^0$ and the points of $a_1^1, a_2^1, \cdots, a_n^1$ and $a_1^2, a_2^2, \cdots, a_n^2$ constitute a 2-cell $a^2$ which is bounded by the sum (mod. 2) of the boundaries of the 2-cells $a_1^2, a_2^2, \cdots, a_n^2$.

10. The first of the theorems in the last section is a special case of the theorem that any 1-cell which is in a 2-cell and joins two points of its boundary decomposes the 2-cell into two 2-cells. This more general theorem depends on the theorem of Jordan, that any simple closed curve in a Euclidean plane separates the plane into two regions, the interior and the exterior; and also on the theorem of Schoenflies that the interior of a simple closed curve is a 2-cell of which the curve is the boundary.

We shall not need to use these more general forms of the separation theorems because we need, in general, merely the existence of curves which separate cells, and this is provided for in the theorems of the last section. In connection with the Jordan theorem, reference may be made to the proof by J. W. Alexander, Annals of Math., Vol. 21 (1920), p. 180.

## Maps

11. With the aid of the theorems on separation a 2-cell $a^2$ may be subdivided into further 2-cells as follows: Let any two points $a_1^0$ and $a_2^0$ of the boundary of the 2-cell be joined by a straight 1-cell $a_1^1$ consisting entirely of points of the 2-cell. The 2-cell is thus separated into two 2-cells $a_1^2$ and $a_2^2$. The boundary of $a^2$ is likewise separated into two 1-cells $a_1^1$ and $a_2^1$ which have $a_1^0$ and $a_2^0$ as ends. The 0-cells, 1-cells and 2-cells into which $a^2$ is

thus subdivided constitute a 2-dimensional complex $C_2$ whose matrices are

$$\mathrm{H}_0 = \left\| 1 \quad 1 \right\|, \qquad \mathrm{H}_1 = \left\| \begin{matrix} 1 & 1 & 1 \\ 1 & 1 & 1 \end{matrix} \right\|, \qquad \mathrm{H}_2 = \left\| \begin{matrix} 1 & 1 \\ 1 & 0 \\ 0 & 1 \end{matrix} \right\|.$$

The numbers $\alpha_0$, $\alpha_1$, $\alpha_2$ for $C_2$ are respectively 2, 3, 2, so that

$$\alpha_0 - \alpha_1 + \alpha_2 = 1.$$

This subdivision of $a^2$ may be continued by two processes: (1) introducing a point of a 1-cell as a new 0-cell and (2) joining two 0-cells of the boundary of a 2-cell by a 1-cell composed entirely of points of the 2-cell. The first process increases the number of 0-cells and 1-cells each by 1. The second process increases the number of 1-cells and 2-cells each by 1. Hence any number of repetitions of the two processes leave the number $\alpha_0 - \alpha_1 + \alpha_2$ invariant.

Any two-dimensional complex obtainable from a 2-cell by subdivision of the kind described above is called a *simply connected map*; and it can easily be proved that any two-dimensional complex which is homeomorphic with the interior and boundary of a 2-cell is a simply connected map.

The number $\alpha_0 - \alpha_1 + \alpha_2$ determined by any complex $C_2$ having $\alpha_0$ 0-cells, $\alpha_1$ 1-cells and $\alpha_2$ 2-cells is called the *characteristic* of $C_2$. Thus we have proved that *the characteristic of a simply connected map is 1.*

12. There are a number of interesting theorems about simply connected maps which must be omitted here because they are of too special a nature. Many of them are related to the *four-color problem*: is it possible to color the cells of a simply connected map with four colors in such a way that no two 2-cells which are incident with the same 1-cell are colored alike? This problem is still unsolved, in spite of numerous attempts. In addition to the references in the Encyclopädie, Vol. III$_1$, p. 177, the following references may be cited: Birkhoff, The reducibility of maps, American Journal of Mathematics, Vol. 35, p. 115; Veblen, Annals of Mathematics, Vol. 14 (1912), p. 86; and a forthcoming article by P. Franklin in the American Journal.

## Regular Subdivision

13. It will often be found convenient to work with complexes whose 2-cells are each incident with three 0-cells and three 1-cells. Such 2-cells will be called *triangles* and a complex subdivided into triangles will be said to be *triangulated.* Any complex $C_2$ may be triangulated by the following process which is called a *regular subdivision.*

Let $P_k^2$ $(k = 1, 2, \cdots, \alpha_2)$ be an arbitrary point of the 2-cell $a_k^2$, $P_j^1$ $(j = 1, 2, \cdots, \alpha_1)$ an arbitrary point of the 1-cell $a_j^1$ and $P_i^0$ $(i = 1, 2, \cdots, \alpha_0)$ another name for the 0-cell $a_i^0$. The points $P_j^i$ $(i = 0, 1, 2; j = 1, 2, \cdots, \alpha_i)$ are to be the vertices of the complex $\overline{C}_2$.

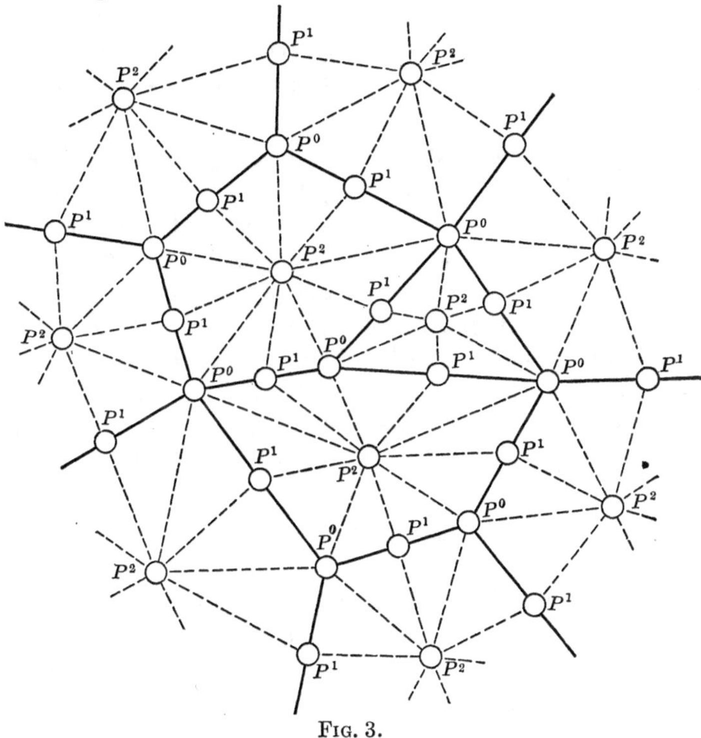


Fig. 3.

Each $P_j^1$ separates the $a_j^1$ on which it lies into two 1-cells. The 1-cells so defined are to be among the 1-cells of $\overline{C}_2$. The remaining 1-cells of $\overline{C}_2$ are obtained by joining each $P_k^2$ to each of the points $P_i^0$ and $P_j^1$ of the boundary of $a_k^2$ by a 1-cell in $a_k^2$ in such a way that no two of these 1-cells have a point in common (§ 9). Each 2-cell $a_k^2$ is thus decomposed into a set of 2-cells each of which is bounded by three of the 1-cells of $\overline{C}_2$, one on the boundary of $a_k^2$ and two interior to $a_k^2$. The 2-cells thus obtained are the 2-cells of $\overline{C}_2$.

The complex $\overline{C}_2$ is called a *regular subdivision* of $C_2$ and is also called a *regular complex*. No two 0-cells of $\overline{C}_2$ are joined by more than one 1-cell of $\overline{C}_2$. Moreover no 1-cell of $\overline{C}_2$ joins two points $P_k^i$, $P_l^j$ which have equal superscripts. Hence any 1-cell of $\overline{C}_2$ may be denoted by $P_k^iP_l^j$ with $i < j$. No three 0-cells of $\overline{C}_2$ are vertices of more than one 2-cell of $\overline{C}_2$, and furthermore one of the three vertices incident with any 2-cell is a $P_i^0$, one is a $P_j^1$, and one is a $P_k^2$. Hence any 2-cell of $\overline{C}_2$ may be denoted by $P_i^0P_j^1P_k^2$.

14. Any vertex of $\overline{C}_2$ together with the 1-cells and 2-cells which are incident with it is called a *triangle star*, and the vertex is called the *center* of the triangle star. Any point $P$ of $C_2$ may be taken as the center of a triangle star of $\overline{C}_2$. For if $P$ is on a 1-cell $a_i^1$ of $C_2$ it can be chosen as the corresponding $P_i^1$ and if it is on a 2-cell $a_i^2$ it can be chosen as the corresponding $P_i^2$. The set of all triangle stars of a given regular complex is such that each point of the complex is in at least one of them.

If $C_2$ is itself regular any two vertices of $C_2$ which are within or on the boundary of a triangle star of $\overline{C}_2$ are joined by a 1-cell of $C_2$.

15. The method of regular subdivision is useful in continuity arguments where it is desirable to subdivide a given complex into "arbitrarily small" cells. Let a complex $C_2$ in which a definition of straight lines and of distance has been introduced as described in § 8, be subjected to a regular subdivision into a complex $C_2^1$ and let $C_2^1$ be regularly subdivided into $C_2^2$, and so on, thus determining a sequence of complexes $C_2$, $C_2^1$, $\cdots$, $C_2^n$, $\cdots$, each of which is a regular subdivision of the one preceding it. Let us require also that each new 0-cell introduced in a 1-cell in the

process of subdivision shall be the mid-point of the 1-cell, that each point interior to a triangular 2-cell (the point $P_k^2$ of § 13) shall be the center of gravity (intersection point of the medians) of the triangle, and that the 1-cells introduced shall be straight. With these conventions, it is evident that for every number $\delta > 0$ there exists a number $N_\delta$ such that if $n > N_\delta$ every 1-cell in $C_2^n$ is of length less than $\delta$.

16. The relationship between $C_2$ and $\overline{C}_2$ may be stated as follows: (1) each 2-cell $a_k^2$ of $C_2$ is the sum (mod. 2) of all 2-cells $P_i^0P_j^1P_k^2$ of $\overline{C}_2$ incident with $P_k^2$; (2) each 1-cell $a_j^1$ of $C_2$ is the sum of the two 1-cells $P_i^0P_j^1$ of $\overline{C}_2$ incident with $P_j^1$; and (3) each 0-cell $a_i^0$ of $C_2$ is the vertex $P_i^0$ of $\overline{C}_2$.

Hence the complex $\overline{C}_2$ may be converted into $C_2$ by a series of steps of two sorts; (1) combine two 2-cells whose boundaries have one and only one 1-cell in common into a new 2-cell, suppressing the common 1-cell and (2) combine two 1-cells both incident with a 0-cell which is not incident with any other 1-cell into a new 1-cell, suppressing the common 0-cell.

The first type of step requires that the matrix $\mathrm{H}_2$ of $\overline{C}_2$ be modified by adding the column representing one of the two 2-cells to the one representing the other, removing the column representing the first of the two 2-cells, and also removing the row corresponding to the 1-cell which is suppressed. The row which is removed contained only two 1's before the two columns were added, because the 1-cell to which it corresponds is incident with only two 2-cells. After the one column is added to the other this row contains only one 1 and this 1 is common to the row and column removed. Hence the first type of step has the effect of reducing the rank of $\mathrm{H}_2$ by 1.

It also has the effect of removing the column of $\mathrm{H}_1$ corresponding to the 1-cell suppressed. This 1-cell is on the boundary of a 2-cell. Hence the 0-circuit represented by the column removed is linearly dependent on the columns corresponding to the other 1-cells of the boundary of this 2-cell. Hence the removal of this column leaves the rank of $\mathrm{H}_1$ unaltered.

The first type of step thus changes $\rho_2$ and $\rho_1$ into $\rho_2 - 1$ and

$\rho_1$ respectively. It obviously changes $\alpha_0$, $\alpha_1$, and $\alpha_2$ into $\alpha_0$, $\alpha_1 - 1$ and $\alpha_2 - 1$ respectively. A similar argument shows that the second type of step changes $\rho_2$ and $\rho_1$ into $\rho_2$ and $\rho_1 - 1$ respectively and also changes $\alpha_0$, $\alpha_1$, $\alpha_2$ into $\alpha_0 - 1$, $\alpha_1 - 1$, and $\alpha_2$ respectively. Hence the numbers

$$\alpha_0 - \alpha_1 + \alpha_2$$

$$\alpha_1 - \rho_1 - \rho_2$$

$$\alpha_2 - \rho_2$$

are the same for $\bar{C}_2$ as for $C_2$. This is a special case of the more general theorem, to be proved later, that these numbers are invariants of $C_2$ under the group of all homeomorphisms.

### Manifolds and 2-Circuits

17. By the *boundary* of a 2-dimensional complex $C_2$ is meant the one-dimensional complex containing each 1-cell of $C_2$ which is incident with an odd number of 2-cells of $C_2$.

By a *2-dimensional circuit* or a *2-circuit* is meant a 2-dimensional complex $C_2$ without a boundary such that any 2-dimensional complex whose 2-cells are a subset of the 2-cells of $C_2$ has a boundary. Thus any 2-dimensional complex in which each 1-cell is incident with an even number of 2-cells is evidently a 2-circuit or a set of 2-circuits having only 0-cells and 1-cells in common.

A 2-dimensional complex containing no 2-circuits is called a 2-dimensional *tree*.

18. By a *neighborhood* of a point $P$ of a complex $C_2$ is meant any set $S$ of 0-cells, 1-cells and 2-cells composed of points of $C_2$ and such that any set of points of $C_2$ having $P$ as a limit point contains points on the cells of $S$. Thus any triangle star of a regular complex is a neighborhood of its center. Since (cf. § 14) any point of a complex $C_2$ can be made a vertex of a regular subdivision of $C_2$, the process of regular subdivision gives an explicit method of finding a neighborhood of any point of $C_2$.

19. If $C_2$ is a 2-circuit of which every point has a neighborhood which is a 2-cell, then the set of all points on $C_2$ is called a *closed*

*two-dimensional manifold.** If $\overline{C}_2$ is a regular subdivision of a 2-circuit $C_2$ then it is evident that $C_2$ defines a manifold if and only if it is true that for each vertex $P$ of $\overline{C}_2$ the incidence relations between the 1-cells and 2-cells of $\overline{C}_2$ which are incident with $P$ are the same as those between the 0-cells and 1-cells of a 1-circuit.

A set of points obtainable from a closed two-dimensional manifold by removing a finite number of 2-cells no two of which have an interior or boundary point in common is called an *open two-dimensional manifold.* In the rest of this chapter the term manifold will mean "closed manifold" unless the opposite is specified.

20. The simplest example of a two-dimensional manifold is one determined by a complex consisting of two 0-cells, two 1-cells and two 2-cells, each 0-cell being incident with both 1-cells and each 1-cell with both 2-cells. Thus the matrices defining the manifold are

$$H_0 = \begin{Vmatrix} 1 & 1 \end{Vmatrix}, \qquad H_1 = H_2 = \begin{Vmatrix} 1 & 1 \\ 1 & 1 \end{Vmatrix}.$$

Such a manifold is called a *two-dimensional sphere.* It is easily seen to be homeomorphic with the surface of a tetrahedron.

21. A simple example of an open manifold, $M_2$, is obtained from a rectangle $ABCD$ (fig. 4) by setting up a $1-1$ continuous correspondence $F$ between the 1-cells $AB$ and $CD$ and their ends in such a way that $A$ corresponds to $D$ and $B$ corresponds to $C$, and then regarding the pairs of points which correspond under $F$ each as a single point of $M_2$. This open manifold is called a *tube* or a *cylindrical surface.* That it satisfies the definition of an open manifold is easily proved by dividing the rectangle into 2-cells by a 1-cell joining a point $P$ of the side $AD$ to a point $Q$ of the side $BC$. It is bounded by the two curves formed from the 1-cells $AD$ and $BC$ respectively.

* We use this term rather than "surface" in order to have a terminology which may be used without confusion in Algebraic Geometry. In the latter science the real and complex points of a surface constitute a four-dimensional manifold.

Let a (1 — 1) continuous correspondence $F^1$ be set up between the 1-cells *AD* and *BC* and their ends in such a way that *A* corresponds to *B*, *P* to *Q*, and *D* to *C*. A closed manifold *T* is

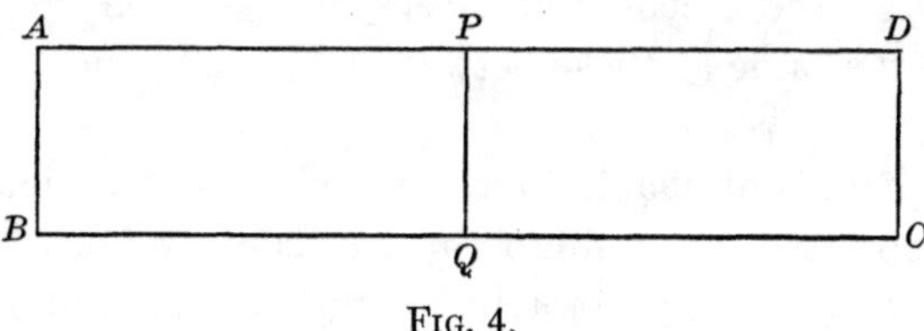


FIG. 4.

defined by regarding as single points of *T* each pair of points which correspond either under *F* or under $F^1$. The four points *A, B, C, D* thus coalesce to one point of *T*. This manifold is called an *anchor ring* or *torus*.

22. If a correspondence *G* between the 1-cells *AB* and *CD* and their ends is set up in such a way that *A* corresponds to *C* and *B* to *D*, an open manifold *M* is obtained by regarding each pair of points which correspond under *G* as a single point of *M*. This open manifold is called the *Möbius band*.* A model is most simply constructed by taking a rectangle, giving it a half-twist and bringing opposite edges together. Thus the rectangle in fig. 4 represents a Möbius band (fig. 5) if we regard as identical

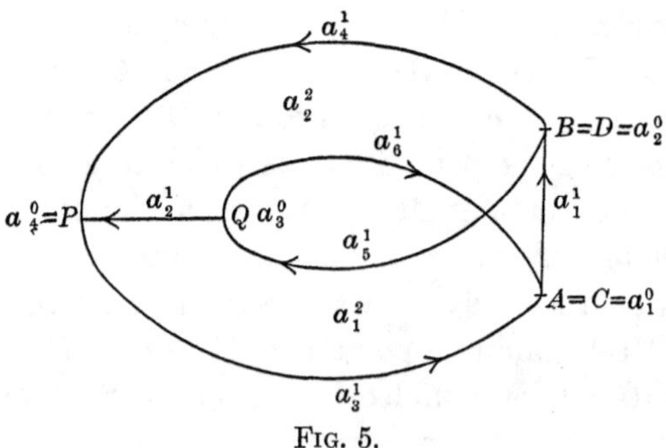


FIG. 5.

the two vertices labelled $a_1^0$, the two edges labelled $a_1^1$ and the two vertices $a_2^0$. If the rectangle be divided into two 2-cells

* Cf. A F. Mobius, Gesammelte Werke, Vol. 2, pages 484 and 519.

by the 1-cell $a_2^1$ joining the two points $a_3^0$ and $a_4^0$ we obtain the following matrices which describe the Mobius band.

$$H_0 = \begin{Vmatrix} 1 & 1 & 1 & 1 \end{Vmatrix},$$

$$H_1 = \begin{Vmatrix} 1 & 0 & 1 & 0 & 0 & 1 \\ 1 & 0 & 0 & 1 & 1 & 0 \\ 0 & 1 & 0 & 0 & 1 & 1 \\ 0 & 1 & 1 & 1 & 0 & 0 \end{Vmatrix}, \qquad H_2 = \begin{Vmatrix} 1 & 1 \\ 1 & 1 \\ 1 & 0 \\ 0 & 1 \\ 1 & 0 \\ 0 & 1 \end{Vmatrix}.$$

23. The Möbius band is bounded by the 1-circuit (0, 0, 1, 1, 1, 1). If a 2-cell be introduced which is bounded by this 1-circuit a complex is obtained whose matrices $H_0$ and $H_1$ are the same as $H_0$ and $H_1$ for the Mobius band, while

$$H_2 = \begin{Vmatrix} 1 & 1 & 0 \\ 1 & 1 & 0 \\ 1 & 0 & 1 \\ 0 & 1 & 1 \\ 1 & 0 & 1 \\ 0 & 1 & 1 \end{Vmatrix}.$$

The set of points on this complex is a manifold homeomorphic with the projective plane. Another set of matrices for the projective plane and some discussion of its Analysis Situs properties will be found in Veblen and Young's Projective Geometry, Vol. II, Chap. IX.

24. The operation of adding two one-dimensional complexes, modulo 2, which was defined in § 15, Chap. I may be extended to two dimensions as follows. Let $C_2$ and $C_2^1$ be two 2-dimensional complexes which have a certain number (which may be zero) of 2-cells in common and have no other common elements except the boundaries of these 2-cells. By

$$C_2 + C_2^1 \quad (\text{mod. } 2)$$

is meant the complex composed of those 2-cells and their boundaries which are in either of $C_2$ and $C_2^1$ but not in both. This operation has the obvious property that if $C_2$ and $C_2^1$ are 2-circuits $C_2 + C_2^1$ (mod. 2) is also a 2-circuit or set of 2-circuits.

25. Let a sphere, $S$, be decomposed into cells by the process described in § 11 and let $s_1^2, s_2^2, \cdots, s_p^2$ be $p$ of the 2-cells so obtained. Let $T^1, T^2, \cdots, T^p$ be $p$ anchor rings no two of which have a point in common and which are such that $s_i^2$ $(i = 1, 2, \cdots, p)$ is a 2-cell of $T^i$ while $T^i$ and $S$ have no other points in common than those of $s_i^2$ and its boundary. The set of all points on the 2-circuit,

$$(1) \qquad M_2 = S + T^1 + T^2 + \cdots + T^p \quad (\text{mod. } 2),$$

is called a *sphere with $p$ handles, or an orientable manifold of genus $p$, or an orientable manifold of connectivity $2p + 1$.* The proof that the set of points on $M_2$ is a manifold is made by subdividing it into 2-cells. By the same device it is easy to prove that a sphere with one handle is an anchor ring.

26. If one of the anchor rings $T^i$ in the last section is replaced by a projective plane, the 2-circuit $M_2$ is easily seen to define a manifold. We shall refer to this as a *one-sided manifold of the first kind of genus $p - 1$,* or *of connectivity $2p$.* It is easy to verify that a projective plane is a one-sided manifold of the first kind of genus zero.

If two of the manifolds $T^i$ are projective planes and the rest are anchor rings the 2-circuit $M_2$ again defines a manifold. This is called a *one-sided manifold of the second kind of genus $p - 2$,* or *of connectivity $2p - 1$.*

In this section and the last one the terms connectivity and genus are used in such a way that

$$R_1 - 1 = 2p + k$$

where $R_1$ is the connectivity, $p$ is the genus, and $k = 0$ for an orientable manifold, $k = 1$ for a one-sided manifold of the first kind, and $k = 2$ for a one-sided manifold of the second kind.

27. The fundamental problem of two-dimensional Analysis Situs is that of classifying all two-dimensional manifolds. The solution of this problem is found by proving: (1) that for every manifold there is an integer $R_1$, the connectivity (cf. § 29), which is an invariant under the group of all homeomorphisms; (2) that

there is an invariant property, that of " orientableness "; and (3) that any two manifolds which have the same connectivity and are both orientable or both non-orientable are homeomorphic. From this it will follow that the examples given in §§ 25 and 26 include all two-dimensional manifolds.

The proof of the propositions (1) and (2) will be given in considerable detail in the following pages because it is the basis of important generalizations to $n$-dimensions. The third proposition is covered more summarily because methods of proving it are well known and there is no possibility of generalizing it directly to $n$-dimensions. There is no known system of invariants or invariant properties of $n$-dimensional manifolds which will characterize a manifold completely even in the three-dimensional case.

### The Connectivity $R_1$

28. The boundary of any of the 2-cells $a_i^2$ which enter into the definition of a complex $C_2$ is given by one of the columns of the matrix $H_2$. The boundary of the complex determined by two of these 2-cells is evidently the sum (mod. 2) of the boundaries of the 2-cells, and therefore is a 1-circuit or set of 1-circuits composed of cells $a_i^0$ and $a_j^1$ of $C_2$. By a repetition of these considerations it follows that the boundary of any two-dimensional complex composed of cells of $C_2$ is a 1-circuit or set of 1-circuits which is the sum (mod. 2) of the boundaries of the 2-cells of the complex. Hence a symbol $(x_1, x_2, \cdots, x_{\alpha_1})$ for such a boundary is linearly dependent (mod. 2) on the columns of $H_2$.

Moreover if any symbol $(x_1, x_2, \cdots, x_{\alpha_1})$ is linearly expressible in terms of the columns of $H_2$ this expression determines a set of 2-cells of $C_2$ such that the sum of their boundaries is $(x_1, x_2, \cdots, x_{\alpha_1})$. Hence *a necessary and sufficient condition that a set of 1-circuits composed of cells of $C_2$ shall bound a complex composed of cells of $C_2$ is that its symbol shall be linearly dependent on the columns of* $H_2$.

29. By § 25, Chap. I the number of solutions of the equations ($H_1$) in a complete set is $\alpha_1 - \rho_1$. So this is the number of 1-circuits in a complete set. If $\rho_2$ is the rank of $H_2$, the 1-circuits

which bound complexes composed of cells of $C_2$ are all linearly dependent on $\rho_2$ such 1-circuits. Hence a complete set of solutions of $(H_1)$ is obtained by adjoining the symbols for $\alpha_1 - \rho_1 - \rho_2$ 1-circuits or sets of 1-circuits to $\rho_2$ linearly independent columns of $H_2$. Let us set

$$(1) \qquad R_1 - 1 = \alpha_1 - \rho_1 - \rho_2.$$

Hence there exist $R_1 - 1$ 1-circuits or sets of 1-circuits $C_1^1$, $C_1^2$, $\cdots$, $C_1^{R_1-1}$ such that every 1-circuit composed of 1-cells of $C_2$ is linearly dependent (mod. 2) on these and on the boundaries of 2-cells of $C_2$.

It can be so arranged that each of $C_1^1, C_1^2, \cdots, C_1^{R_1-1}$ is a single 1-circuit. For if $C_1^1$ represents more than one 1-circuit it is the sum (mod. 2) of these 1-circuits and at least one of these must be linearly independent of $C_1^2, \cdots, C_1^{R_1-1}$ and the bounding circuits, for otherwise $C_1^1$ would itself be linearly dependent on them. Let $C_1^1$ be replaced by this non-bounding 1-circuit. In like manner, there is at least one one among the 1-circuits represented by $C_1^2$ which is linearly independent of $C_1^1, C_1^3, \cdots, C_1^{R_1-1}$ and the bounding 1-circuits, for otherwise $C_1^2$ would be linearly dependent on them. Let $C_1^2$ be replaced by this 1-circuit and let a similar treatment be applied to $C_1^3$, and so on. A set of 1-circuits thus determined is called a *complete set of non-bounding 1-circuits*. It has the properties: (1) There is no two-dimensional complex composed of cells of $C_2$ which is bounded by these 1-circuits or any subset of them. (2) If $C_1$ is any 1-circuit composed of cells of $C_2$ there is a two-dimensional complex composed of cells of $C_2$ which is bounded either by $C_1$ alone or by $C_1$ and some of the circuits $C_1^i$ $(i = 1, 2, \cdots, R_1 - 1)$. The number, $R_1$, is called the *connectivity* of the complex $C_2$, or, when it is necessary to distinguish it from the other connectivities $R_i$ which are defined later, the *linear connectivity*.

30. Now suppose that $C_2$ consists of a single 2-circuit. In this case the sum (modulo 2) of the 1-circuits bounding the 2-cells is $(0, 0, \cdots, 0)$. This constitutes one linear relation among the columns of $H_2$. There cannot be more than one such relation,

for this would imply that a subset of the 2-cells satisfied the definition of a 2-circuit. Hence the rank of $H_2$ is $\alpha_2 - 1$. Thus we have

$$\rho_2 = \alpha_2 - 1, \tag{2}$$

and from § 20, Chap. I we have

$$\rho_1 = \alpha_0 - R_0. \tag{3}$$

But since any 2-circuit is connected, $R_0 = 1$. Hence on combining (2) and (3) with (1) of § 29 we obtain

$$\alpha_0 - \alpha_1 + \alpha_2 = 3 - R_1. \tag{4}$$

This is one of the generalizations of Euler's well-known formula for a polyhedron.

31. Since a two-dimensional closed manifold is the set of points on a particular kind of 2-circuit the formula (4) of § 30, gives the relation between the connectivity $R_1$ and the characteristic of any two-dimensional complex defining a closed manifold. In the case of an open manifold, $M_2$, according to § 19, the boundary consists of a number of curves. Call this number $B_1$. Of these curves, $B_1 - 1$ are linearly independent because otherwise they would be the boundary of a manifold contained in $M_2$, contrary to definition. As in the previous section, a complete set of 1-circuits in the complex $C_2$ defining $M_2$ may be taken to consist of $\rho_2$ bounding 1-circuits and $R_1 - 1$ non-bounding 1-circuits; and of the latter, $B_1 - 1$ may be taken to be circuits of the boundary of $M_2$. Hence if $R_1 - B_1 = \overline{R}_1 - 1$, the non-bounding circuits in the complete set comprise $B_1 - 1$ from the boundary and $\overline{R}_1 - 1$ others.

If $C_2$ be modified by introducing $B_1$ 2-cells each bounded by one of the $B_1$ 1-circuits of the boundary, $C_2$ becomes a 2-circuit $C_2^1$ of $\alpha_2 + B_1$ 2-cells, $\alpha_1$ 1-cells, and $\alpha_0$ 0-cells in which $B_1 - 1$ of the non-bounding circuits of $C_2$ have become bounding circuits. Hence $C_2^1$ has the connectivity $\overline{R}_1$. Hence

$$\alpha_0 - \alpha_1 + \alpha_2 + B_1 = 3 - \overline{R}_1,$$

and

$$\begin{aligned}\alpha_0 - \alpha_1 + \alpha_2 &= 3 - \overline{R}_1 - B_1 \\ &= 2 - R_1\end{aligned}$$

which is the formula for the characteristic of a complex defining an open manifold of two dimensions. The same formula holds for any two-dimensional tree.

## Singular Complexes

32. The cells $a_i^0$, $a_j^1$, $a_k^2$ which enter into the definition of a complex are all non-singular and their boundaries are also non-singular. This restriction was necessary in order to obtain the theorem of § 6 that the matrices $H_0$, $H_1$, $H_2$ fully determine the complex. In many applications, however, it is desirable to drop the restriction that the boundaries of the cells referred to in the matrices $H_i$ shall be non-singular. The results of the theory of matrices can in general be applied whenever it is possible to subdivide the cells having singular boundaries by means of a finite number of 0-cells and 1-cells in such a way as to obtain a complex of non-singular cells with non-singular boundaries.

For example, in § 21 the anchor ring was defined as consisting of one 0-cell, represented by the four vertices of the rectangle, two 1-cells represented by its pairs of opposite edges, and one 2-cell. The matrices of incidence relations of these cells are

$$H_0 = \| 1 \|, \qquad H_1 = \| 0 \quad 0 \|, \qquad H_2 = \left\| \begin{matrix} 0 \\ 0 \end{matrix} \right\|.$$

Thus $\rho_0 = 1$, $\rho_1 = 0$, $\rho_2 = 0$, $\alpha_0 = 1$, $\alpha_1 = 2$, $\alpha_2 = 1$. Hence

$$\begin{aligned} R_1 &= 3 - (\alpha_0 - \alpha_1 + \alpha_2) = 3 \\ &= \alpha_1 - \rho_1 - \rho_2 + 1. \end{aligned}$$

If the rectangle is subdivided into triangles so that a non-singular complex is obtained it will be found that the same value for $R_1$ will be obtained from the non-singular complex as from the singular one.

33. The notion of a singular complex on a one-dimensional complex, as defined in § 8, Chap. I, can be generalized directly to two dimensions as follows:

Let $C_2$ be a two-dimensional complex, $C'$ a generalized complex of zero, one or two dimensions,* and $F$ a correspondence in which

* The definition may be extended so that $C'$ is of any number of dimensions.

each point of $C'$ corresponds to one point of a set of points $[P]$ of $C_2$ while each $P$ is the correspondent of one or more points of $C'$. If $C'$ is of one or two dimensions we require $F$ to be continuous. Under these conditions, any point $X$ of $C'$ associated with the $P$ to which it corresponds under $F$ is called *a point on* $C_2$; it is referred to as the *image* of $X$ under $F$ and is uniquely denoted by $F(X)$; it is said to *coincide* with $P$ and $P$ is said to *coincide* with it. The set of all points $F(X)$ on $C_2$ is in a $(1-1)$ continuous correspondence with the points of $C'$ and thus constitutes a complex $C''$ identical in structure with $C'$. The complex $C''$ is said to be *on* $C_2$. If any of the points $P$ is the correspondent under $F$ of more than one point of $C'$, $C''$ is called a *singular complex on* $C_2$ and the point $P$ in question is called a *singular point.* If $F$ is $(1-1)$, $C''$ is said to be *non-singular.* A cell of $C''$ is said to *coincide with* a cell of $C_2$ if and only if (1) each point of the cell of $C''$ coincides with a point of the cell of $C_2$ and (2) the correspondence thus set up is $(1-1)$.

In case $C''$ is two-dimensional and such that there is at least one point of $C''$ on each point of $C_2$ and if, furthermore, there exists for every point of $C''$ a neighborhood which is a non-singular complex on $C_2$, then $C''$ is said to *cover* $C_2$. In case the number of points of $C''$ on each point of $C_2$ is finite and equal to $n$, $C''$ is said *to cover* $C_2$ *n times* (cf. § 9, Chap. I).

34. Any 2-circuit which is not a manifold can be regarded as a singular manifold. For let $C_2$ be an arbitrary 2-circuit. Each of its edges, $a_i^1$, is incident with an even number, $2n_i$ of 2-cells. These 2-cells may be grouped arbitrarily in $n_i$ pairs no two of which have a 2-cell in common; let these be called the *pairs of 2-cells associated** *with* $a_i^1$. Let $C_2'$ be a 2-circuit on $C_2$ such that (1) there is one and but one 2-cell of $C_2'$ coinciding with each 2-cell of $C_2$, (2) there are $n_i$ 1-cells of $C_2'$ coinciding with each 1-cell $a_i^1$ of $C_2$, each of the $n_i$ 1-cells being incident with a pair of 2-cells of $C_2'$ which coincide with one of the pairs of 2-cells associated with $a_i^1$, and (3) there is one 0-cell of $C_2'$ coincident with each 0-cell $a_i^0$ of $C_2$, this 0-cell being incident with all the

* Cf. § 22, Chap. I.

1-cells of $C_2'$ which coincide with 1-cells of $C_2$ incident with $a_i^0$. Thus $C_2'$ has two 2-cells incident with each of its 1-cells.

The incidence relations of the 1-cells and 2-cells of $C_2'$ which are incident with a vertex $a_i^0$ of $C_2'$ are the same as those of the 0-cells and 1-cells of a linear graph and since there are just two 2-cells incident with each 1-cell this linear graph consists of a number of 1-circuits having no points in common. Let any set of 1-cells and 2-cells of $C_2'$ which are incident with $a_i^0$ and whose incidence relations with one another are those of a 1-circuit be called *a group associated with* $a_i^0$. Let $C_2''$ be a 2-circuit on $C_2'$ such that (1) there is one and but one $i$-cell ($i = 1, 2$) of $C_2''$ coinciding with each $i$-cell of $C_2'$, (2) the incidence relations between the 1-cells and 2-cells of $C_2''$ are the same as those between the cells of $C_2'$ with which they coincide, and (3) there is one 0-cell of $C_2''$ for each group associated with each vertex $a_i^0$ of $C_2'$ and this 0-cell is coincident with $a_i^0$ and incident with those and only those 1-cells and 2-cells of $C_2''$ which coincide with 1-cells and 2-cells of the group. The set of points on the complex $C_2''$ is a two-dimensional manifold, by § 19, and $C_2''$ is a singular complex on $C_2$. Hence $C_2$ may be obtained by coalescing a certain number of 1-cells and 0-cells of a manifold.

### Bounding and Non-bounding 1-Circuits

35. Having defined what is meant by saying that a complex $C_n$ ($n = 0, 1, 2$) is on a complex $C_2$, we can now state and solve the problem of bounding and non-bounding circuits in a perfectly general form: *Given any set of 1-circuits $K_1$ on a complex $C_2$, does there exist a two-dimensional complex $K_2$ on $C_2$ which is bounded by $K_1$?*

In spite of the generality of the complex $K_1$, and because of the generality of $K_2$, this problem is free from many of the difficulties inherent in such point-set theorems as those of Schoenflies and Jordan. This will be illustrated by the simple case considered in the next section.

36. Any closed curve, singular or not, which is on a 2-cell $a^2$ but does not pass through every point of $a^2$ is the boundary of a

2-cell on $a^2$. Let $c$ be the given curve and $O$ a point of $a^2$ not on $c$. Let $OX$ be the straight 1-cell joining $O$ to a variable point $X$ of $c$. Let $O'$ be a point interior to a triangle $t$ of a Euclidean plane and let $X'$ be a variable point of the boundary of this triangle. Let $F$ be a continuous $(1-1)$ correspondence between the set of points $[X']$ and the set of points $[X]$. If we let each point of $O'X'$ correspond to the point of $OX$ which divides it in the same ratio, a continuous correspondence $F'$ is defined in which each point of the interior and boundary of the triangle $t$ corresponds to one point of $a^2$. By § 1 there is thus defined a 2-cell (in general, singular) which is bounded by $c$.

It is not essential that $O$ shall not coincide with a point of $c$, for in case $X$ coincides with $O$ the interval $OX$ may be taken to be a singular one coinciding with $O$. Hence we have without restrictions the theorem that any closed curve on a 2-cell $a$ is the boundary of a 2-cell on $a$.

The theorem may be generalized slightly as follows: *Any curve c on a triangle star* (§ 14) *is the boundary of a 2-cell on the triangle star.* The 2-cell is constructed as above, taking the center of the triangle star as $O$.

### Congruences and Homologies, Modulo 2

37. Before going on to the solution of the problem stated in § 35, let us introduce a notation which is adapted from that of Poincaré. We shall say that a complex $C_n$ $(n = 1, 2)$ is *congruent* (*modulo 2*) to a set of $(n-1)$-circuits $C_{n-1}$ if and only if $C_{n-1}$ is the boundary of $C_n$. This is represented by the notation

$$(1) \qquad C_n \equiv C_{n-1} \pmod{2}.$$

In case $C_{n-1}$ fails to exist, so that $C_n$ is a set of $n$-circuits, $C_n$ is said to be *congruent to zero* (*mod. 2*) and (1) is replaced by

$$(2) \qquad C_n \equiv 0 \pmod{2}.$$

Expressions of the form (1) and (2) are called *congruences* (*mod. 2*). They have been defined thus far only for $n = 1$ and $n = 2$, but these definitions will apply for all values of $n$ as soon as the terms complex, $n$-circuit, and boundary of an $n$-dimensional complex have been defined for all values of $n$.

Both in the one- and two-dimensional cases it is evident that when two complexes are added (mod. 2) the boundary of the sum is the sum (mod. 2) of the boundaries. Hence the sum (mod. 2) of the left-hand members of two congruences is congruent to the sum (mod. 2) of the right-hand members. Or, more generally, *any linear combination (mod. 2) of a number of valid congruences (mod. 2) of the same dimensionality is a valid congruence (mod. 2).*

38. With respect to a complex $C$ a complex $C_{n-1}$ is said to be *homologous* to zero (mod. 2) if and only if it is the right-hand member of a congruence such as (1) in which $C_n$ represents a complex on $C$. This relation is indicated by

(3) $$C_{n-1} \sim 0 \quad (\text{mod. } 2).$$

Thus

$$C_0 \sim 0 \quad (\text{mod. } 2)$$

means that $C_0$ represents a set of 0-circuits which bound a one-dimensional complex on $C$, and

$$C_1 \sim 0 \quad (\text{mod. } 2)$$

means that $C_1$ represents a set of 1-circuits on $C$ which bound a two-dimensional complex on $C$. Thus in every case, (3) implies

(4) $$C_{n-1} \equiv 0 \quad (\text{mod. } 2),$$

but (4) does not imply (3).

From the corresponding proposition in the last section it follows at once that *any linear combination (mod. 2) of a set of valid homologies (mod. 2) is a valid homology (mod. 2).* A homology,

(5) $$C_{n-1} + C_{n-1}' \sim 0 \quad (\text{mod. } 2),$$

is also written

(6) $$C_{n-1} \sim C_{n-1}' \quad (\text{mod. } 2).$$

The homology (6) evidently means that there exists a complex $C_n$ on $C$ which is bounded by $C_{n-1}$ and $C_{n-1}'$.

If $\overline{C}_1$ is a 1-circuit obtained by introducing new vertices in a 1-circuit $C_1$, it is evident that

$$C_1 \sim \overline{C}_1 \quad (\text{mod } 2),$$

because $C_1$ and $\overline{C}_1$ bound a singular two-dimensional complex coincident with them both.

### The Correspondence A

39. The first step toward the solution of the problem of § 35 will be to show that if $\overline{C}_2$ is a regular subdivision of $C_2$, then for any 1-circuit $K_1$ on $C_2$ there is a 1-circuit $K_1'$ *composed of cells of* $\overline{C}_2$ such that

$$K_1 \sim K_1' \quad (\text{mod. } 2). \tag{1}$$

This has the consequence that any homology among 1-circuits can be replaced by one in which each 1-circuit is composed of cells of $\overline{C}_2$; and the problem of § 35 is reduced to that of finding a necessary and sufficient condition that $K_1' \sim 0$ (mod. 2) if $K_1'$ represents a set of 1-circuits composed of cells of $\overline{C}_2$. The next three sections aim at establishing the homology (1).

40. Let $K$ be a one- or two-dimensional complex on a two-dimensional complex $C_2$. Let $\overline{C}_2$ be a regular subdivision of $C_2$. Let a definition of distance and straightness be introduced relative to $\overline{C}_2$, and let $\tilde{C}_2$ be a regular subdivision of $\overline{C}_2$ whose 1-cells are all straight. The triangle stars of $\tilde{C}_2$ constitute a set of overlapping neighborhoods such that every point of $\tilde{C}_2$ is interior to at least one of these neighborhoods. Hence by simple continuity considerations (Heine-Borel theorem) $K$ can be subdivided, by introducing new vertices if it is of one dimension, or by the process of regular subdivision (§ 13) if it is of two dimensions into a complex $\overline{K}$ such that for each 1-cell or 2-cell of $\overline{K}$ there is a triangle star of $\tilde{C}_2$ to which it is interior.

Those of the triangle stars of $\tilde{C}_2$ whose centers are vertices of $\overline{C}_2$ have the property that any point of $\tilde{C}_2$ is either interior to one such triangle star or on the boundaries of 2-cells from two or more such triangle stars. Let us designate as *a correspondence A* any correspondence of the vertices of $\overline{K}$ with those of $\overline{C}_2$ by which each vertex of $\overline{K}$ which is interior to a triangle star of $\tilde{C}_2$ having a vertex of $\overline{C}_2$ as center corresponds to this center, and each vertex of $\overline{K}$ which is on the boundary of two or more such triangle stars corresponds to the center of one of them.* Thus a correspondence $A$ determines a unique vertex of $\bar{C}_2$ for each vertex of $\bar{K}$.

This construction is such that any triangle star of $\tilde{C}_2$ which contains a vertex of $\bar{K}$ has the 0-cell of $\bar{C}_2$ to which this vertex corresponds on its interior or boundary. Moreover any two vertices of $\bar{K}$ which are ends of the same 1-cell of $\bar{K}$ coincide with points of the same triangle star of $\tilde{C}_2$ and hence correspond to points of $\bar{C}_2$ of the interior or boundary of this triangle star. Hence they correspond either to the same vertex of $\bar{C}_2$ or to the two ends of a 1-cell of $\bar{C}_2$ (Cf. § 14). In case $K$ is two-dimensional it follows similarly that any three vertices of $\bar{K}$ incident with the same 2-cell of $\bar{K}$ correspond to one or more vertices of a single 2-cell of $\bar{C}_2$.

41. Let the 0-cells, 1-cells and 2-cells of $\bar{C}_2$ be denoted by $c_1^0, c_2^0, \cdots, c_{\alpha_0}^0$; $c_1^1, c_2^1, \cdots, c_{\alpha_1}^1$; and $c_1^2, c_2^2, \cdots, c_{\alpha_2}^2$ respectively; and those of $\bar{K}$ by $k_1^0, k_2^0, \cdots, k_{\beta_0}^0$; $k_1^1, k_2^1, \cdots, k_{\beta_1}^1$; $k_1^2, k_2^2, \cdots, k_{\beta_2}^2$ respectively. Having fixed on a correspondence $A$ between the vertices of $\bar{K}$ and those of $\bar{C}_2$, let each 0-cell $k_i^0$ be joined by a straight 1-cell $b_i^1$ to the corresponding vertex of $\bar{C}_2$ in case $k_i^0$ does not coincide with its correspondent; and if $k_i^0$ does coincide with its correspondent let it be joined to its correspondent by a singular 1-cell $b_i^1$ coinciding with it.

The two ends of a 1-cell $k_i^1$ are thus joined by two 1-cells $b_j^1$ and $b_k^1$ either to the same vertex of $\bar{C}_2$ or to the two ends of a 1-cell $c_p^1$ of $\bar{C}_2$. In the first case $k_i^1$, $b_j^1$ and $b_k^1$ are the 1-cells of a 1-circuit and in the second case $k_i^1$, $b_j^1$, $b_k^1$ and $c_p^1$ are the 1-cells of a 1-circuit. In either case the 1-circuit is contained in a single triangle star of $\bar{C}_2$ and therefore by § 36 bounds a 2-cell $b_i^2$ on $\bar{C}_2$. *Thus each 1-cell $k_i^1$ of $\bar{K}$ determines a 2-cell $b_i^2$.* The complex composed of the 2-cells $b_i^2$ and their boundaries is called $B_2$.

42. The incidence relations between the 1-cells $b_j^1$ and the

* This is essentially the same as requiring (with Alexander, in the paper cited in our preface) that each vertex of $\bar{K}$ shall correspond to the nearest vertex of $\bar{C}_2$, or to one of the nearest if there are more than one.

2-cells $b_i^2$ of $B_2$ are the same as the incidence relations between the 0-cells and 1-cells of $\overline{K}$. Hence, in particular, if $\overline{K}$ is a 1-circuit or set of 1-circuits, $K_1$, the sum (mod. 2) of the boundaries of the 2-cells $b_i^2$ contains none of the 1-cells $b_j^1$. Hence the boundary of $B_2$ can consist only of cells of $K_1$ and of $\overline{C}_2$. Hence the boundary of $B_2$ is either $K_1$ alone or $K_1$ and a set of 1-circuits composed of cells of $\overline{C}_2$. Let the latter set of 1-circuits be denoted by $K_1'$.

Hence we have the congruence,

$$B_2 \equiv K_1 + K_1' \quad (\text{mod. } 2) \tag{2}$$

in which $K_1'$ is either zero or a set of 1-circuits composed of cells of $\overline{C}_2$. From this there follows the homology

$$K_1 \sim K_1' \quad (\text{mod. } 2) \tag{1}$$

which we have been seeking.

43. If $K_1'$ is zero the question as to whether $K_1$ satisfies a homology

$$K_1 \sim 0 \quad (\text{mod. } 2) \tag{3}$$

is answered in the affirmative. In any other case, since $K_1'$ is composed of cells of $\overline{C}_2$ it is represented by a symbol $(x_1, x_2, \cdots, x_{a_1})$. If this symbol is linearly dependent on the columns of the matrix $\mathrm{H}_2$ for $\overline{C}_2$,

$$K_1' \sim 0 \quad (\text{mod. } 2)$$

according to § 28. Moreover $K_1'$ cannot bound a complex composed of cells of $\overline{C}_2$ unless its symbol $(x_1, x_2, \cdots, x_{a_1})$ is linearly dependent on the columns of $\mathrm{H}_2$. If, therefore, we can prove that $K_1'$ cannot bound any complex on $C_2$ unless it bounds one composed of cells of $\overline{C}_2$, it will follow that (3) is satisfied if and only if $(x_1, x_2, \cdots, x_{a_1})$ is linearly dependent on the columns of $\mathrm{H}_2$. This we proceed to do, thus completing the solution of the problem stated in § 35.

44. Let us return to the notations of §§ 40 and 41 and suppose that $K$ is a two-dimensional complex $K_2$. The three 1-cells $k_i^1$, $k_j^1$, $k_l^1$ of $\overline{K}_2$ incident with a 2-cell $k_p^2$ of $\overline{K}_2$ have been seen to

determine three 2-cells $b_i^2$, $b_j^2$, $b_l^2$. These 2-cells are incident by pairs with the 1-cells joining the three vertices of $k_p^2$ to their correspondents under the correspondence $A$. The vertices of $\overline{C}_2$ to which the vertices of $k_p^2$ correspond are either the three vertices of a 2-cell $c_q^2$ of $\overline{C}_2$ or the two ends of a 1-cell of $\overline{C}_2$ or a single 0-cell of $\overline{C}_2$. In the first case the 2-cells, $k_p^2$, $b_i^2$, $b_j^2$, $b_l^2$ and $c_q^2$ are the 2-cells of a sphere; in the second and third cases the 2-cells $k_p^2$, $b_i^2$, $b_j^2$, and $b_l^2$ are the 2-cells of a sphere. Let the sphere which is thus in every case determined by $k_p^2$ be denoted by $S_2^p$.

A 2-cell $b_i^2$ is in an odd number of these spheres if and only if it is incident with a 1-cell $k_i^1$ of the boundary of $\overline{K}_2$. Hence the result of adding the spheres $S_2^p$ to $\overline{K}_2$ (mod. 2) is either zero or a complex $K_2'$ the 2-cells of which are either 2-cells of $\overline{C}_2$ or 2-cells $b_i^2$ determined by the 1-cells of the boundary of $\overline{K}_2$. In particular, if $\overline{K}_2$ is a 2-circuit, either $\overline{K}_2$ is the sum (mod. 2) of the spheres $S_2^p$ or $K_2'$ is composed entirely of cells of $\overline{C}_2$.

45. If $K_2$ has a boundary, so that

$$\overline{K}_2 \equiv K_1 \pmod{2}, \tag{4}$$

the result of the last section is that by adding a number of congruences,

$$S_2^p \equiv 0 \pmod{2}, \tag{5}$$

to (4) we obtain a congruence,

$$K_2' \equiv K_1 \pmod{2}, \tag{6}$$

such that all 2-cells of $K_2'$ are either 2-cells of $\overline{C}_2$ or 2-cells $b_i^2$ determined by the boundary $K_1$ of $K_2'$. The complex $B_2''$ composed of the latter 2-cells and their boundaries is such that

$$B_2'' \equiv K_1 + K_1'' \pmod{2} \tag{7}$$

where $K_1''$ is composed of 0-cells and 1-cells of $\overline{C}_2$. On adding (6) and (7) we obtain a congruence

$$K_2' + B_2'' \equiv K_1'' \pmod{2} \tag{8}$$

in which the left-hand member represents a complex composed only of cells of $\overline{C}_2$.

46. It is now easy to obtain the result required at the end of § 43, namely that if a set of 1-circuits $K_1'$ is composed of cells of $\overline{C}_2$, then

$$K_1' \sim 0 \quad (\text{mod. } 2)$$

implies that $K_1'$ is the boundary of a complex composed of cells of $\overline{C}_2$. Let $K_1'$ be replaced by a set of 1-circuits $K_1$ which covers it just once (§ 9, Chap. I). Then $K_1' \sim 0$ (mod. 2) implies $K_1 \sim 0$ (mod. 2) and this implies the congruence (4) of the last section. But $K_1''$ as constructed in the last section is identical with $K_1'$. Hence (8) states that $K_1'$ is the boundary of a complex composed of cells of $\overline{C}_2$.

### Invariance of $R_1$

47. An immediate corollary of what has just been proved is that the 1-circuits $C_1^1, C_1^2, \cdots, C_1^{R_1-1}$ of a complete set (§ 29) of non-bounding 1-circuits of $\overline{C}_2$ are not connected by any homology of the form

$$(1) \qquad C_1^{i_1} + C_1^{i_2} + \cdots + C_1^{i_k} \sim 0 \quad (\text{mod. } 2)$$

in which the superscripts are integers less than $R_1$. Moreover if $K_1$ is any 1-circuit on $C_2$ it satisfies a homology of the form

$$(2) \qquad K_1 \sim C_1^{j_1} + C_1^{j_2} + \cdots + C_1^{j_p} \quad (\text{mod. } 2)$$

in which the terms of the right-hand member represent 1-circuits of the complete set. For by § 42

$$(3) \qquad K_1 \sim K_1' \quad (\text{mod. } 2)$$

in which $K_1'$ is zero or a set of 1-circuits composed of cells of $\overline{C}_2$, and by § 29 $K_1'$ is homologous to a combination of 1-circuits of the complete set.

48. But if $K_1^1, K_1^2, \cdots, K_1^N$ is any set of 1-circuits such that (1) any 1-circuit is homologous to a linear combination of them and (2) there is no homology relating them, it is easily proved that $N = R_1 - 1$. For by the properties of the 1-circuits $C_1^1, C_1^2, \cdots, C_1^{R_1-1}$, there are $N$ homologies like (2),

$$(4) \qquad K_1^j \sim C_1^{j_1} + C_1^{j_2} + \cdots + C_1^{j_p} \quad (\text{mod. } 2),$$

one for each value of $j$ from 1 to $N$. If $N > R_1 - 1$ the right-hand members of (4) must satisfy a homology because there are only $R_1 - 1$ $C_1^{i}$'s. But this is contrary to the property (2) of the $K_1^{i}$'s. Hence $N > R_1 - 1$ is impossible. In like manner, inverting the roles of the $K_1^{i}$'s and the $C_1^{i}$'s, it follows that $R_1 - 1 > N$ is impossible. Hence $N = R_1 - 1$.

Any homeomorphism of $C_2$ obviously transforms a set of 1-circuits $K_1^1, K_1^2, \cdots, K_1^N$ satisfying the conditions (1) and (2) into a set of 1-circuits satisfying the same conditions. Since $N = R_1 - 1$ for every such set of 1-circuits, it follows that $R_1$ *is an Analysis Situs invariant of the complex* $C_2$.

49. It was proved in § 16 that the expression in the right-hand member of

$$R_1 - 1 = \alpha_1 - \rho_1 - \rho_2$$

is the same for $C_2$ as for $\overline{C}_2$. Now let $C_2$ be subdivided into any set of cells which form a non-singular complex $K_2$ on $C_2$, and let $\overline{K}_2$ be a regular subdivision of $K_2$. The complex $\overline{K}_2$ can replace $\overline{C}_2$ in the discussion above and hence $\overline{K}_2$ has the same connectivity, $R_1$, as $\overline{C}_2$. Hence $K_2$ and $C_2$ have the same connectivity. In other words any two complexes have the same connectivity if they are identical as sets of points and the cells of each are non-singular on the other.

It should perhaps be remarked that the relation between $K_2$ and $C_2$ may be quite complex in spite of the fact that each cell of $K_2$ is non-singular on $C_2$ and *vice versa*. For any 1-cell of $K_2$ may intersect any number of 1-cells of $C_2$ in an infinite set of points, and any 2-cell of $K_2$ may have an infinite set of regions in common with any 2-cell of $C_2$.

### Invariance of the 2-circuit.

50. If $K_2$ and $C_2$ are related as described in the last section, $K_2$ *is a 2-circuit if and only if* $C_2$ *is a 2-circuit.* Since the relation between $C_2$ and $K_2$ is reciprocal this theorem will be established if we prove that if $K_2$ is a 2-circuit then $C_2$ is one. Also it is evident that $C_2$ or $K_2$ is a 2-circuit if and only if a regular subdivision of it is a 2-circuit. Hence we replace $C_2$ by its reg-

ular subdivision $\overline{C}_2$ as in § 40 and construct the spheres $S_2^p$ as in § 44. By § 44 the result of adding the spheres $S_2^p$ to $\overline{K}_2$ (mod. 2) is either zero or a 2-circuit composed of cells of $\overline{C}_2$. If it were zero the 2-circuit $\overline{K}_2$ would be the sum (mod. 2) of the spheres $S_2^p$. But this is impossible, as shown by the following theorem.

51. *There is no set of 2-circuits $K_2^i$ on a 2-circuit $C_2$ such that* (1) *for each 2-circuit $K_2^i$ there is a 2-cell of $C_2$ on which there is no point of $K_2^i$ and* (2) *the sum (mod.* 2) *of the 2-circuits $K_2^i$ is $C_2$.*

To prove this theorem, we suppose that there is a set of 2-circuits $K_2^i$ having the property (1). We let these 2-circuits take the place of $K$ in § 40, make the regular subdivision of $C_2$ into $\overline{C}_2$ and $K_2^i$ into $\overline{K}_2^i$, construct a correspondence $A$ and obtain a set of spheres $S_2^p$ (which, of course, must not be confused with those in § 50). When the spheres having 2-cells in common with one of the 2-circuits $\overline{K}_2^i$ are added to this $\overline{K}_2^i$ the result is either zero or a non-singular 2-circuit composed of cells of $\overline{C}_2$. But since $\overline{C}_2$ is a 2-circuit the only 2-circuit composed of its cells is $\overline{C}_2$ itself. Since there is one 2-cell of $C_2$ which contains no point of $K_2^i$ it follows that the sum of $\overline{K}_2^i$ and the spheres $S_2^p$ determined by its 2-cells is zero.

Obviously if each of two 2-circuits is such that the sum (mod. 2) of it and the spheres $S_2^p$ determined by its 2-cells is zero the same is true of the sum (mod. 2) of the two 2-circuits. Hence the sum of all the 2-circuits $K_2^i$ has this property. On the other hand the 2-circuit $\overline{C}_2$ is such that the sum of the spheres $S_2^p$ determined by its 2-cells is $\overline{C}_2$ itself. Hence the 2-circuits $K_2^i$ do not have the property (2).

52. Letting the 2-circuit $\overline{K}_2$ and the spheres $S_2^p$ of § 50 take the place of the 2-circuit $C_2$ and the 2-circuits $K_2^i$ of § 51 it follows from the theorem of § 51 that $\overline{K}_2$ is not the sum (mod. 2) of the spheres $S_2^p$. Hence the sum (mod. 2) of $\overline{K}_2$ and the spheres $S_2^p$ is a 2-circuit composed of cells of $\overline{C}_2$. If this 2-circuit is $\overline{C}_2$ itself the theorem of § 50 is verified. If not, let this 2-circuit be denoted by $C_2'$, let $c_j^2$ be one of the 2-cells of $\overline{C}_2$ which is not on $C_2'$, and let $\overline{K}_2$ be regularly subdivided into a complex $K_2'$ which has at least one 2-cell, which is interior to $c_j^2$.

The complex $C_2'$ is composed of non-singular cells on $K_2'$ and hence $C_2'$ and $K_2'$ can replace $\bar{K}_2$ and $\bar{C}_2$ respectively in the construction used in § 50 for the spheres $S_2^p$. Thus a set of spheres can be found which when added to a regular subdivision of $C_2'$ give a 2-circuit $C_2''$ composed of cells of a regular subdivision of $K_2'$. But as $\bar{K}_2$ and its regular subdivisions are 2-circuits, $C_2''$ must be identical with the regular subdivision of $K_2'$. This is not possible unless there is a point of $C_2'$ on each 2-cell of $K_2'$. But this implies that there is a point of $C_2'$ on $c_j^2$, contrary to the hypothesis that $c_j^2$ is not a cell of $C_2'$. Hence $C_2'$ coincides with $\bar{C}_2$, and the proof of the theorem of § 50 is complete.

53. It is an obvious corollary of this theorem that the property of a two-dimensional complex, of being a 2-circuit, is an Analysis Situs invariant. For if $C_2$ and $G_2$ are two complexes which are homeomorphic, the homeomorphism defines a non-singular complex $K_2$ on $C_2$ such that each cell of $K_2$ is the image of a cell of $G_2$. By definition, $K_2$ is a 2-circuit if and only if $G_2$ is a 2-circuit, and by the theorem of § 50 $K_2$ is a 2-circuit if and only if $C_2$ is a 2-circuit.

It is an obvious corollary of this result that the property of a complex, that it defines a manifold, is also an Analysis Situs invariant. In other words, any complex into which a manifold can be subdivided, satisfies the conditions laid down in § 19.

## Matrices of Orientation.

54. Let us now convert the 1-dimensional complex composed of the 0-cells and 1-cells of $C_2$ into an oriented one-dimensional complex in the fashion described in §§ 33 to 40 of Chap. I. The oriented 0-cells are

$$\sigma_1^0, \sigma_2^0, \cdots, \sigma_{\alpha_0}^0,$$

the 1-cells are

$$\sigma_1^1, \sigma_2^1, \cdots, \sigma_{\alpha_0}^1,$$

and the relations between them are given by the matrices $E_0$, $E_1$ satisfying the relation

$$E_0 \cdot E_1 = 0.$$

Each of the columns of $H_2$ is the symbol for a 1-circuit which, according to § 35, Chap. 1, determines two oriented 1-circuits. The symbol for either of these oriented 1-circuits may be obtained from the corresponding column of $H_2$ by changing some of the 1's to $-$ 1's. Hence by changing some of the 1's in $H_2$ to $-$ 1's there is determined a matrix

$$E_2 = \|\epsilon_{ij}^2\| \qquad (i = 1, 2, \cdots, \alpha_1;\ j = 1, 2, \cdots, \alpha_2)$$

each column of which represents an oriented 1-circuit and is therefore a solution of the equations ($E_1$), § 42, Chap. 1. Hence

$$E_1 \cdot E_2 = 0.$$

As an example, the matrix $E_2$ for the tetrahedron in fig. 1, page 3, is (cf. $H_2$ in § 4)

$$E_2 = \left\|\begin{array}{rrrr} 0 & -1 & 1 & 0 \\ 1 & 0 & -1 & 0 \\ -1 & 1 & 0 & 0 \\ 1 & 0 & 0 & -1 \\ 0 & 1 & 0 & -1 \\ 0 & 0 & 1 & -1 \end{array}\right\|.$$

A further example is furnished by the projective plane, for which (cf. §§ 22, 23)

$$E_1 = \left\|\begin{array}{rrrrrr} -1 & 0 & 1 & 0 & 0 & 1 \\ 1 & 0 & 0 & -1 & -1 & 0 \\ 0 & -1 & 0 & 0 & 1 & -1 \\ 0 & 1 & -1 & 1 & 0 & 0 \end{array}\right\|, \qquad E_2 = \left\|\begin{array}{rrr} 1 & 1 & 0 \\ 1 & -1 & 0 \\ 1 & 0 & -1 \\ 0 & 1 & -1 \\ 1 & 0 & 1 \\ 0 & 1 & 1 \end{array}\right\|.$$

Note that the rank of $E_2$ for the tetrahedron is 3, or $\alpha_2 - 1$, and for the projective plane is 3, or $\alpha_2$.

55. Let us denote the ranks of $E_0, E_1, E_2$ by $r_0, r_1, r_2$ respectively. We have seen that

$$r_0 = R_0 = \rho_0$$
$$r_1 = \rho_1$$

and that in case $C_2$ is a 2-circuit,

$$\rho_2 = \alpha_2 - 1$$

It is impossible that $r_2$ should be less than $\alpha_2 - 1$ because this would imply that at least two of the columns of $E_2$ were expressible linearly in terms of the others and hence on reducing modulo 2, that the same statement was true of the columns of $H_2$, contrary to § 30. Hence there remain two possibilities

$$r_2 = \alpha_2 - 1$$

and

$$r_2 = \alpha_2$$

for any $C_2$ which is a 2-circuit. The examples in the last section show that both possibilities can be realized.

56. A 2-circuit $C_2$ such that $r_2 = \alpha_2 - 1$ has the property that the boundaries of its 2-cells can be converted into oriented 1-circuits in such a way that their sum is zero. For the columns of $E_2$ represent a set of oriented 1-circuits, one bounding each 2-cell, and since $r_2 = \alpha_2 - 1$ they are subject to one linear relation,

$$(1) \qquad b_1c_1 + b_2c_2 + \cdots + b_{\alpha_2}c_{\alpha_2} = 0$$

in which the $c$'s represent the columns of $E_2$ and the $b$'s are positive or negative integers or zero. When reduced modulo 2 this relation must state that the sum of the columns of $H_2$ is zero. Hence the relation must involve all columns of $E_2$. In case $C_2$ defines a manifold each 1-cell is incident with two and only two 2-cells. Hence if an oriented 1-cell $\sigma_i^1$ is to cancel out, the two oriented 1-circuits formed from the boundaries of the 2-cells incident with $a_i^1$ must appear in (1) with numerically equal coefficients. It follows that the coefficients of (1) are numerically equal and therefore that by removing a common factor (1) can be reduced to a form in which $b_i = \pm 1$.

Hence by multiplying some of the columns by $-1$, $E_2$ can be reduced to a form in which the sum of the columns is zero. The columns of $E_2$ then represent a set of oriented 1-circuits such that if $\sigma^1$ is any oriented 1-cell formed from a 1-cell of $C_2$, one of these 1-circuits contains $\sigma^1$ and another one contains $-\sigma^1$.

It is obvious in view of § 34 that this result applies to all 2-circuits and not merely to those defining manifolds.

## Orientable Complexes

57. The theorem of the last section is equivalent to the statement that if $r_2 = \alpha_2 - 1$ for a 2-circuit $C_2$ the boundaries of the 2-cells of $C_2$ can be converted into oriented 1-circuits in such a way that their sum is zero. If $r_2 = \alpha_2$ the boundaries of the 2-cells evidently cannot be thus oriented. In the first case $C_2$ is said to be *two-sided* or *orientable* and in the second case to be *one-sided* or *non-orientable*. A manifold is said to be *orientable* or *non-orientable* according as the complex defining it is or is not orientable. This extension of the term is justified by the theorems of §§ 58–60 below according to which the complexes defining a given manifold $M_2$ are all orientable or all non-orientable.

This definition is equivalent to the one given in 1865 by A. F. Möbius, Ueber die Bestimmung des Inhaltes eines Polyëders, Werke, Vol. 2, p. 475; see also p. 519. The term "orientable" was suggested by J. W. Alexander as preferable to "two-sided" because the latter term connotes the separation of a three-dimensional manifold into two parts, the two "sides," by the two-dimensional manifold, whereas the property which we are dealing with is an internal property of the two-dimensional manifold.*

The intuitional significance of orientableness is perhaps best grasped by experiments with the well-known Möbius paper strip described in the article referred to above. These experiments can also be used to verify the theorems on deformation and on the indicatrix in Chap. V.

58. Suppose that a 2-cell $a_i^2$ of a complex $C_2$, the cells of which have been oriented in the manner described above, is separated into two 2-cells by a 1-cell $a^1$. The two new 2-cells are bounded

* On the relation between orientableness and two-sidedness, see E. Steinitz, Sitzungsberichte der Berliner Math. Ges., Vol. 7 (1908), p. 35; and D. König, Archiv. der Math. u. Phys., 3d Ser., Vol. 19 (1912), p. 214. The term orientable (orientierbar) has also been used by H. Tietze in an article in the Jahresbericht der Deutschen Math. Ver., Vol. 29 (1920), p. 95, which came to my attention while these lectures were in proof-sheets. This article contains a general discussion of orientability covering a number of the questions referred to in the beginning of Chap. V below, and also a useful collection of references.

by two 1-circuits which have $a^1$ in common. It is easily seen that if $\sigma^1$ is either of the oriented 1-cells formed from $a^1$, two oriented 1-circuits can be formed from the boundaries of the two new 2-cells in such a way that one of them contains $\sigma^1$ and the other contains $-\sigma^1$. Hence the sum of these oriented 1-circuits is one of the two oriented 1-circuits which can be formed from the boundary of $a_i^2$.

The complex $C_2$ is converted into a new complex $C_2'$ by introducing the new 1-cell $a^1$ and subdividing $a_i^2$. The matrix $\mathrm{E}_2$ of $C_2'$ has one row and one column more than the matrix $\mathrm{E}_2$ of $C_2$, and by the paragraph above can be converted into the matrix $\mathrm{E}_2$ for $C_2$ by adding the two columns corresponding to the two new 2-cells and striking out the row corresponding to $a^1$. These operations evidently reduce the rank by 1. Hence the rank of $\mathrm{E}_2$ for $C_2'$ is equal to the number of 2-cells of $C_2'$ if and only if the rank of $\mathrm{E}_2$ for $C_2$ is equal to the number of 2-cells of $C_2$.

Since a regular subdivision of $C_2$ can be effected by the two operations of introducing new 0-cells on the 1-cells of $C_2$ and separating the 2-cells into new 2-cells by 1-cells, it follows from the theorem just proved that any regular subdivision of $C_2$ is such that

$$r_2 = \alpha_2 - 1$$

if and only if $C_2$ has this property.

59. If $C_2$ is a 2-circuit and $G_2$ is any 2-circuit homeomorphic with $C_2$, let $K_2$ be the 2-circuit on $C_2$ whose cells are respectively homeomorphic with the cells of $G_2$. As in § 50 $C_2$ and $K_2$ may be regularly subdivided into $\overline{C}_2$ and $\overline{K}_2$ and a set of spheres $S_2^p$ constructed such that the sum (mod. 2) of $\overline{K}_2$ and the 2-circuits defining these spheres is $\overline{C}_2$. For each 2-cell $k_p^2$ of $\overline{K}_2$ there is one and only one sphere $S_2^p$ which has $k_p^2$ as one of its -cells.

If $K_2$ is such that $r_2 = \alpha_2 - 1$, $\overline{K}_2$ has the same property, that is to say, the boundaries of its 2-cells can be so oriented that the sum of the oriented 1-circuits thus formed is zero. Each of the spheres $S_2^p$ obviously has this property also. The set of oriented 1-circuits which can be formed from the boundaries of the 2-cells of $\overline{K}_2$ and of the spheres $S_2^p$ is therefore subject to one linear relation involving the oriented 1-circuits of $\overline{K}_2$ and one analogous linear relation for each of the spheres $S_2^p$. Since each $S_2^p$ has just one 2-cell in common with $\overline{K}_2$, the linear relations corresponding to the spheres $S_2^p$ can be multiplied by $\pm 1$ and added to the linear relation corresponding to $\overline{K}_2$ in such a way that all terms involving oriented 1-circuits of $\overline{K}_2$ cancel out, thus giving a linear relation, $R$, among oriented 1-circuits bounding 2-cells of the spheres $S_2^p$ which does not involve any oriented 1-circuit bounding a 2-cell of $\overline{K}_2$.

Among the 2-cells of the spheres $S_2^p$ are the 2-cells $b_i^2$ each determined as explained in § 41 by a 1-cell $k_i^1$ of $\overline{K}_2$. Each such 2-cell is in two and only two spheres $S_2^p$ and since the two oriented circuits bounding 2-cells of $\overline{K}_2$ which are incident with $k_i^1$ were cancelled out in forming $R$, the oriented 1-circuit formed from the boundary of $b_i^2$ is also cancelled out. Hence $R$ contains none of the oriented 1-circuits formed from the boundaries of the 2-cells $b_i^2$. Hence $R$ can only contain oriented 1-circuits formed from the boundaries of 2-cells of $\overline{C}_2$. It must contain some of these, for otherwise each 2-cell of $\overline{C}_2$ would be in an even number of spheres $S_2^p$ and hence the sum (mod. 2) of these spheres $S_2^p$ and the complex $\overline{K}_2$ would be zero contrary to § 51.

Hence the set of oriented 1-circuits formed from the boundaries of the 2-cells of $\overline{C}_2$ is subject to one linear condition. Hence by § 55 $r_2 = \alpha_2 - 1$ for $\overline{C}_2$. Hence by § 58 $r_2 = \alpha_2 - 1$ for $C_2$.

60. The theorem of § 53 was that if $C_2$ is a 2-circuit any complex homeomorphic with $C_2$ is a 2-circuit. The theorem of the last section adds to this result the theorem that *if $C_2$ is orientable so is also any complex homeomorphic with $C_2$*. It follows that if one of the complexes into which a manifold can be decomposed is orientable so are all the complexes into which it can be decomposed. Thus the property of orientability or non-orientability is a property of a manifold and is invariant under the group of homeomorphisms.

As a corollary of this it follows that any complex defining a sphere is orientable. The same follows for any sphere with $p$ handles on observing that the particular complexes used in defining these manifolds are orientable. In like manner, the manifolds defined in § 26 are non-orientable.

## Normal Forms for Manifolds

61. It has now been proved that any two homeomorphic manifolds are both orientable or both one-sided, and have the same connectivity. Conversely it can be proved that *if two closed manifolds are both orientable (or both one-sided) and have the same connectivity they are homeomorphic.* In other words, $R_1$ and the orientableness of a closed manifold characterize it completely from the point of view of Analysis Situs.

62. By way of establishing this theorem we shall outline a method of reducing any manifold to a normal form. This reduction is related to that given in § 31, Chap. I for the matrix $H_1$. It was there found that there are two matrices $A_0$ and $B_1$ such that

$$A_0^{-1} \cdot H_1 \cdot B_1 = H_1^*$$

where $H_1^*$ is a matrix of unitary type.

In the case of a single manifold, which we are now considering, $R_0 = 1$ and

$$\mu = \alpha_1 - \rho_1 = R_1 - 1 + \rho_2.$$

The matrix $B_1$ is such that its first $\rho_1$ columns are the symbols for the 1-cells of a tree, $T_1$, and its last $\alpha_1 - \rho_1$ columns are the symbols for a complete set of 1-circuits $C_1^1, C_1^2, \cdots, C_1^\mu$. The 1-cells not in the tree $T_1$ were denoted (§ 26, Chap. 1) by $a_p^1$ $(p = j_1, j_2, \cdots, j_\mu)$ and are such that the circuits $C_1^1, C_1^2, \cdots,$ $C_1^\mu$ could be formed by adjoining $a_{j_1}^1, a_{j_2}^1, \cdots$ successively to $T_1$.

By reference to § 27, Chap. 1 it is clear that $C_1^1$ may be taken to be a bounding circuit and $a_{j_1}^1$ to be a 1-cell of $C_1^1$. Similarly, if $\rho_2 \geq 2$, $C_1^2$ may be taken as bounding; and by repeating the argument it is found that $a_p^1$ $(p = j_1, j_2, \cdots, j_{\rho_2})$ may be chosen so that $C_1^1, C_1^2, \cdots, C_1^{\rho_2}$ are all bounding circuits. The remaining circuits $C_1^{\rho_2+1}, \cdots, C_1^\mu$ are necessarily non-bounding since the number of bounding circuits in a complete set is $\rho_2$.

63. The tree $T_1$ and the $R_1 - 1$ 1-cells $a_p^1$ $(p = j_{\rho_2+1} \cdots, j_\mu)$

constitute a one-dimensional complex $U_1$ which is such that none of its circuits or sets of circuits bounds. For suppose that it contained a set of bounding circuits $K_1$. This would mean

$$(1) \qquad K_1 = \sum_{r=\rho_2+1}^{\mu} b_r C_1^r \quad (\text{mod. } 2)$$

But since $K_1$ is bounding it is linearly dependent on $C_1^1, \cdots, C^{\rho_2}$ i.e.

$$(2) \qquad K_1 = \sum_{r=1}^{\rho_2} b_r C_1^r \quad (\text{mod. } 2)$$

Combining (1) and (2) we should have a linear relation among the circuits $C_1^r$ $(r = 1, 2, \cdots, \mu)$ contrary to hypothesis.

64. Since the points on $C_2$ constitute a manifold $M_2$, $\rho_2 = \alpha_2 - 1$. Hence the number of 1-cells in the complex $U_1$ is $\alpha_1 - \alpha_2 + 1 = \alpha_0 + R_1 - 2$ and the number of 1-cells not in $U_1$ is $\alpha_2 - 1$. Any of the 1-cells not in $U_1$ is incident with two of the 2-cells $a_i^2$ and with them, by § 9, constitutes a 2-cell, $b_2^2$. The boundary of this 2-cell may be singular because pairs of its edges may coincide with 1-cells of $C_2$. But if $\alpha_2 > 2$, $b_2^2$ must have on its boundary at least one of the 1-cells not in $U_1$ and this 1-cell must be incident with another of the 2-cells $a_i^2$; for otherwise $b_2^2$ and its boundary would be either a 2-circuit or a complex bounded by 1-circuits of $U_1$. The 2-cell $b_2^2$, this 1-cell of its boundary, and the 2-cell $a_i^2$ incident with this 1-cell constitute a 2-cell $b_3^2$ which may be treated in the same manner as $b_2^2$. The process may be continued until we arrive at a 2-cell $b_{\alpha_2}^2$ which is made up of all the 2-cells $a_i^2$ $(i = 1, 2, \cdots, \alpha_2)$ and of $\alpha_2 - 1$ 1-cells. Each of the latter is a 1-cell not in $U_1$. Hence the remaining 1-cells of $C_2$ are all in $U_1$. Hence the boundary of $b_{\alpha_2}^2$ contains $2(\alpha_0 + R_1 - 2)$ 1-cells which coincide by pairs with the 1-cells of $U_1$.

65. The result of the last section may be stated in the following form: Any closed manifold $M_2$ can be set into continuous correspondence with the points of a convex polygon of $2(\alpha_0 + R_1 - 2)$ edges in a Euclidean plane in such a way that (1) each interior

point of the polygon corresponds to and is the correspondent of one point of the manifold; (2) each interior point of an edge of the polygon determines an interior point of another edge such that these two points of the polygon correspond to one point of the manifold, and this point of the manifold corresponds only to these two points of the polygon; (3) each vertex of the polygon determines a set of vertices of the polygon all of which correspond to a single point of the manifold, and this point of the manifold corresponds to these vertices and these only.

66. By a series of transformations on this polygon which involve cutting it by 1-cells running from one vertex to another and piecing it together along corresponding edges, it can be changed into a polygon of $2\ (R_1 - 1)$ sides all of whose vertices correspond to a single 0-cell of $M_2$. This polygon in turn can be transformed into one of three normal forms. If the polygon reduces to the first of these forms the manifold is a sphere with $p$ handles; if the polygon takes the second form, the manifold is a one-sided manifold of the first kind; and if the polygon takes the third form, the manifold is a one-sided manifold of the second kind. Thus, every closed manifold $M_2$ is of one of the three types described in §§ 25 and 26.

A proof of this theorem which follows the line of argument outlined above is to be found in a paper by H. R. Brahana which is to be published in the Annals of Mathematics, Vol. 23.

# CHAPTER III

## COMPLEXES AND MANIFOLDS OF $N$ DIMENSIONS

### Fundamental Definitions

1. In a Euclidean three-space, four non-coplanar points together with the one- and two-dimensional simplexes (§ 1, Chap. I and § 1, Chap. II) of which they are vertices constitute the boundary of a finite region, called a *three-dimensional simplex* or *tetrahedral region,* of which the four given points are called the *vertices.* The points of the boundary are not regarded as points of the simplex.

A set of $n + 1$ points, no $n$ of which are in the same $(n - 1)$ space, together with the one-, two-, $\cdots$, $(n - 1)$-dimensional simplexes of which they are vertices constitute the boundary of a finite region in the $n$-space containing the $n + 1$ points. This region is called an *$n$-dimensional simplex* and the $n + 1$ given points are called its vertices. The points of the boundary are not regarded as points of the simplex.

Consider any set of objects in (1–1) correspondence with the points of an $n$-dimensional simplex $(n > 0)$ and its boundary. The objects corresponding to the points of the simplex constitute what is called an *$n$-dimensional cell* or *$n$-cell,* and those corresponding to the boundary of the simplex what is called the *boundary of the cell.*

The remarks of § 2, Chap. I are now to be applied without change to the $n$-dimensional case.

2. An $n$-dimensional complex is defined by the following recursive statements:

An *$n$-dimensional complex* $C_n$ consists of an $(n - 1)$-dimensional complex $C_{n-1}$ together with a number, $\alpha_n$, of $n$-cells whose boundaries are circuits of $C_{n-1}$, such that no $n$-cell has a point in common with another $n$-cell or with $C_{n-1}$ and such that each $(n - 1)$-cell of $C_{n-1}$ is on the boundary of at least one $n$-cell.

The order relations of the points of the boundary of each $n$-cell coincide with the order relations among these points regarded as belonging to the $(n-1)$-dimensional circuit.* The $(n-k)$-cells $(k = 1, 2, \cdots, n)$ on the boundary of an $n$-cell of $C_n$ are said to be *incident* with it and it is said to be *incident* with them.

An *n-dimensional circuit* or *n-circuit* or generalized $n$-dimensional polyhedron is an $n$-dimensional complex $C_n$ such that (1) each $(n-1)$-cell of $C_n$ is incident with an even number of $n$-cells and (2) no subset of the cells which constitute $C_n$ satisfies (1).

The definition of *homeomorphism* and the remarks in § 3, Chap. II generalize directly to $n$ dimensions. In particular, *any theorem about an n-dimensional complex which remains valid if the complex is subjected to any* (1–1) *continuous transformation is a theorem of Analysis Situs.*

An arbitrary subset of the cells of an $n$-dimensional complex is sometimes referred to as a *generalized n-dimensional complex*, provided it contains at least one $n$-cell.

3. The definition of a singular or non-singular generalized complex $C_k$ on a complex $C_n$ is a direct generalization of that given in § 33, Chap. II. It is obtained from the definition in Chap. II by substituting $C_k$ for $C'$, $C_n$ for $C_2$ and making corresponding substitutions wherever the dimensionality of cells or complexes is mentioned. The number $k$ may be greater than, equal to, or less than $n$.

It is important to notice that in the fundamental definitions in the two sections above all the cells and the circuits bounding them are non-singular. This insures that the representation by matrices given below shall be unique. It does not, however,

* This statement can also be put in the following form: Suppose that an $i$-cell $a^i$ appears on the boundaries of two $(i+k)$-cells, $a_1^{i+k}$ and $a_2^{i+k}$. Then $a_1^{i+k}$ and $a_2^{i+k}$ and their boundaries are, by definition, in (1–1) correspondences $T_1$ and $T_2$ with two $(i+k)$-dimensional simplexes, $b$ and $c$ and their boundaries. In the correspondence $T_1$ $a^i$ corresponds to an $i$-dimensional cell $b^i$ of the boundary of $b$ while in the correspondence $T_2$ it corresponds to an $i$-dimensional cell $c^i$ of the boundary of $c$. The resultant of the correspondences effected by $T_1^{-1}$ and $T_2$ on $b^i$ and $a^i$ respectively is a correspondence in which $b^i$ corresponds to $c^i$. *This correspondence must be continuous.*

exclude the possibility of extending the use of the matrices to cases where, as in § 32, Chap. II, the cells have singular boundaries. But in proving our general theorems we stick to the case of non-singular cells with non-singular boundaries.

## Matrices of Incidence

4. Let $\alpha_k$ $(k = 0, 1, \cdots, n)$ denote the number of $k$-cells in a complex $C_n$. The $k$-cells themselves may be denoted by $a_1^k$, $a_2^k$, $\cdots$, $a_{\alpha_k}^k$. The incidence relations between the $(k - 1)$-cells and the $k$-cells are represented by a matrix

$$\| \eta_{ij}^k \| = \text{H}_k \quad (k = 1, 2, \cdots, n)$$

in which $\eta_{ij}^k = 1$ if $a_i^{k-1}$ is incident with $a_j^k$ and $\eta_{ij}^k = 0$ if $a_i^{k-1}$ is not incident with $a_j^k$. The matrix $\text{H}_k$ has $\alpha_{k-1}$ rows and $\alpha_k$ columns.

An $n$-dimensional complex is completely described by the set of matrices,

$$\text{H}_1, \text{H}_2, \cdots, \text{H}_n,$$

for, as can be shown by an obvious argument (cf. § 6, Chap. II) any two complexes having the same set of matrices are in (1–1) continuous correspondence.

The elements of the matrices are combined as integers reduced modulo 2, just as in Chap. I. The ranks of the matrices are denoted by $\rho_1, \rho_2, \cdots, \rho_n$ respectively.

By the general theory of such matrices, there exists for each $\text{H}_k$ a pair of square matrices $A_{k-1}$, $B_k$, of $\alpha_{k-1}$ and $\alpha_k$ rows respectively, each having its determinant equal to 1, such that

$$A_{k-1}^{-1} \cdot \text{H}_k \cdot B_k = \text{H}_k^*,$$

where $\text{H}_k^*$ is a matrix of $\alpha_{k-1}$ rows and $\alpha_k$ columns in which the first $\rho_k$ elements of the main diagonal are unity and all the rest of the elements are zero. Thus the theory of the $n$-dimensional complex will involve the matrices $\text{H}_i$, $A_{i-1}$, $B_i$, $\text{H}_i^*$, $(i = 1, 2, \cdots, n)$.

5. Special cases to illustrate the incidence matrices are easily constructed. For example the matrices for a complex obtained

by subdividing a projective 3-space into cells are given in Chap. IX, Vol. II of the Veblen and Young Projective Geometry. The following definition gives another example.

By an *n-dimensional sphere* or a *simple closed manifold of n dimensions* is meant the set of points on a complex whose matrices of incidence are

$$H_1 = H_2 = \cdots = H_n = \begin{Vmatrix} 1 & 1 \\ 1 & 1 \end{Vmatrix}.$$

The $n$-dimensional sphere is easily seen to be homeomorphic with the boundary of an $(n + 1)$-cell. Since it has two 0-cells, two 1-cells, $\cdots$, two $n$-cells, its *characteristic*,

$$\alpha_0 - \alpha_1 + \alpha_2 - \cdots + (-1)^n \alpha_n,$$

is 0 if $n$ is odd and 2 if $n$ is even.

6. Any set of the $k$-cells, $a_1^k$, $a_2^k$, $\cdots$, $a_{\alpha_k}^k$, and also the $k$-dimensional complex consisting of a set of $k$-cells and their boundaries, may be denoted by a symbol $(x_1, x_2, \cdots, x_{\alpha_k})$, in which $x_i = 1$ if $a_i^k$ is in the set and $x_i = 0$ if $a_i^k$ is not in the set.

These symbols can be added (mod. 2) by precisely the rule given in §§ 14 and 15, Chap. I, for the 0- and 1-dimensional cases. Corresponding to this we have a rule for the addition of two $k$-dimensional complexes consisting each of a set of $k$-cells and their boundaries. The *sum*, modulo 2, of two $n$-dimensional complexes $C_n'$ and $C_n''$ which have a certain number (which may be zero) of $n$-cells in common and have no other common elements except the boundaries of these $n$-cells is the complex determined by the set of all $k$-cells in $C_n'$ or $C_n''$ but not in both $C_n'$ and $C_n''$; it is denoted by $C_n' + C_n''$ (mod. 2). It has the obvious property that if $C_n'$ and $C_n''$ are $n$-circuits, $C_n' + C_n''$ (mod. 2) is also an $n$-circuit or a set of $n$-circuits.

7. The *boundary* of a $k$-dimensional complex $C_k$ is the $(k - 1)$-dimensional complex consisting of the $(k - 1)$-cells of the complex $C_n$ which are incident each with an odd number of $k$-cells of $C_k$, and the boundaries of these $(k - 1)$-cells. Thus a $k$-dimensional complex is a $k$-circuit if and only if it has no boundary.

By precisely the same reasoning as that used in the 0- and 1-dimensional cases (cf. § 28, Chap. II) the boundary of a $C_k$ is a $(k-1)$-dimensional circuit or a set of $(k-1)$-dimensional circuits having at most a $(k-2)$-dimensional complex in common. From this reasoning it also follows that every bounding $(k-1)$-circuit is a sum (mod. 2) of a set of $(k-1)$-circuits which bound $k$-cells, i.e., which are represented by columns of $\text{H}_k$. Hence all bounding $(k-1)$-circuits are linearly expressible in terms of those corresponding to a linearly independent set of $\rho_k$ columns of $\text{H}_k$, where $\rho_k$ is the rank of $\text{H}_k$.

8. As in the 0-, 1-, and 2-dimensional cases (cf. § 24, Chap. 1),

$$\eta_{i1}{}^k x_1 + \eta_{i2}{}^k x_2 + \cdots + \eta_{i\alpha_k}{}^k x_{\alpha_k}$$

is 1 or 0 according as there are an odd or an even number of $k$-cells incident with the $(k-1)$-cell $a_i^{k-1}$. Hence if

$$\text{(1)} \qquad \text{H}_k \cdot \left\| \begin{matrix} x_1 \\ x_2 \\ \cdot \\ \cdot \\ \cdot \\ x_{\alpha_k} \end{matrix} \right\| = \left\| \begin{matrix} y_1 \\ y_2 \\ \cdot \\ \cdot \\ \cdot \\ y_{\alpha_{k-1}} \end{matrix} \right\| ,$$

$(y_1, y_2, \cdots, y_{\alpha_{k-1}})$ represents the boundary of $(x_1, x_2, \cdots, x_{\alpha_k})$.

As a corollary it follows that the $k$-circuits are the solutions of the equations

$$(\text{H}_k) \qquad \sum_{j=1}^{\alpha_k} \eta_{ij}{}^k x_j = 0 \qquad (i = 1, 2, \cdots, \alpha_{k-1})$$

Since the columns of the matrix $\text{H}_k$ represent $(k-1)$-circuits they represent solutions of the equations

$$(\text{H}_{k-1}) \qquad \sum_{j=1}^{\alpha_{k-1}} \eta_{ij}{}^{k-1} x_j = 0 \qquad (i = 1, 2, \cdots, \alpha_{k-2})$$

and hence

$$\text{(2)} \qquad \text{H}_{k-1} \cdot \text{H}_k = 0 \qquad (k = 1, 2, \cdots, n).$$

### The Connectivities $\text{R}_i$

9. If $\rho_k$ denotes the rank of $\text{H}_k$ (mod. 2) the number of solutions of the linear homogeneous equations $(\text{H}_k)$ in a complete

set is $\alpha_k - \rho_k$ (cf. § 25, Chap. I). According to § 8, the columns of $H_{k+1}$ are solutions of the equations ($H_k$) and hence $\rho_{k+1}$ of these columns can enter in a complete set of solutions of ($H_k$).

Let $R_k - 1$ be the smallest number of non-bounding $k$-circuits which it is necessary to adjoin to a set of $\rho_{k+1}$ linearly independent bounding $k$-circuits in order to have a set of $k$-circuits on which all others are linearly dependent.

Then for an $n$-dimensional complex $C_n$ the number of solutions of ($H_k$) in a complete set is $\rho_{k+1} + R_k - 1$ if $0 < k < n$. Hence

$$\alpha_k - \rho_k = \rho_{k+1} + R_k - 1 \qquad (0 < k < n)$$

and

$$\alpha_n - \rho_n = R_n - 1.$$

By § 20, Chap. I

$$\alpha_0 - \rho_1 = R_0.$$

Hence we have the series of equations

$$(1) \qquad \begin{aligned} R_0 \quad - 1 &= \alpha_0 \quad - \rho_1 \quad - 1, \\ R_1 \quad - 1 &= \alpha_1 \quad - \rho_1 \quad - \rho_2, \\ R_2 \quad - 1 &= \alpha_2 \quad - \rho_2 \quad - \rho_3, \\ &\cdot \\ &\cdot \\ &\cdot \\ R_{n-1} - 1 &= \alpha_{n-1} - \rho_{n-1} - \rho_n, \\ R_n \quad - 1 &= \alpha_n - \rho_n. \end{aligned}$$

On multiplying these equations alternately by $+ 1$ and $- 1$ and adding we obtain

$$(2) \qquad \sum_{i=0}^{n} (-1)^i \alpha_i = 1 + \sum_{i=0}^{n} (-1)^i (R_i - 1).$$

In case the complex $C_n$ is an $n$-circuit, $R_0 = 1$, $R_n = 2$ and (2) becomes

$$(3) \qquad \sum_{i=0}^{n} (-1)^i \alpha_i = 1 + (-1)^n + \sum_{i=1}^{n-1} (-1)^i (R_i - 1).$$

This is a generalization of Euler's formula (§ 30, Chap. II) to $n$ dimensions. If $n$ is even it reduces to

$$(4) \qquad \alpha_0 - \alpha_1 + \alpha_2 - \cdots + \alpha_n = 3 - R_1 + R_2 - \cdots - R_{n-1}.$$

If $n$ is odd (3) when combined with a result obtained in § 30 below reduces to

(5) $$\alpha_0 - \alpha_1 + \alpha_2 - \cdots - \alpha_n = 0.$$

10. The number $\alpha_0 - \alpha_1 + \cdots + (-1)^n\alpha_n$ is called the *characteristic* of the complex $C_n$. The number $R_i$ ($i = 0, 1, 2, \cdots, n$) is called the *connectivity of the ith order.*

It will presently be proved that the connectivity numbers $R_0, R_1, \cdots, R_n$ are Analysis Situs invariants. From this it will follow that the characteristic is also an invariant.

## Reduction of the Matrices $\mathrm{H}_k$ to Normal Form

11. Let us now consider the matrices $A_{k-1}$ and $B_k$ by which $\mathrm{H}_k$ is reduced to its normal form, i.e., the square matrices of determinant 1 such that

(1) $$A_{k-1}^{-1}\cdot\mathrm{H}_k\cdot B_k = \mathrm{H}_k^*$$

where the first $\rho_k$ elements of the main diagonal of $\mathrm{H}_k^*$ are 1 and all the other elements of $\mathrm{H}_k^*$ are 0. The existence of these matrices follows from the general theory of matrices (cf. § 49, Chap. I) and we shall show that they can be so chosen as to satisfy certain additional conditions analogous to those found in §§ 30–32, Chap. I.

Writing (1) in the form

(2) $$\mathrm{H}_k\cdot B_k = A_{k-1}\cdot\mathrm{H}_k^*$$

it follows from § 8 that each of the first $\rho_k$ columns of $B_k$ represents a $k$-dimensional complex bounded by the $(k-1)$-dimensional complex represented by the corresponding column of $A_{k-1}$. Each of the remaining $\alpha_k - \rho_k$ columns of $B_k$ represents a $k$-dimensional complex which has no boundary, i.e., a $k$-dimensional circuit or set of circuits.

Since $B_k$ is a square matrix of $\alpha_k$ rows whose determinant is 1, every symbol of the form $(x_1, x_2, \cdots, x_{\alpha_k})$ in which the elements are reduced modulo 2 is expressible as a linear combination of the columns of $B_k$. Hence the symbol for any $k$-dimensional complex determined by $k$-cells of $C_n$ is expressible in terms of the columns of $B_k$. Moreover since the last $\alpha_k - \rho_k$ columns of $B_k$ are linearly independent and the symbols for all $k$-circuits are linearly dependent on $\alpha_k - \rho_k$ of them, the last $\alpha_k - \rho_k$ columns of $B_k$ are a complete set of $k$-circuits or sets of $k$-circuits.

12. The equation (2) remains valid if we add a given column of $B_k$ to another column of $B_k$ and perform the corresponding operation on the columns of $A_{k-1} \cdot \mathrm{H}_k^*$. Hence in particular we may replace any one of the last $\alpha_k - \rho_k$ columns of $B_k$ by any linear combination of these columns without modifying the right member of (2) since all the last $\alpha_k - \rho_k$ columns of $A_{k-1} \cdot \mathrm{H}_k^*$ are composed of zeros.

This enables us to modify $B_k$ so that each of its last $\alpha_k - \rho_k$ columns represents a *single* $k$-circuit. For suppose such a column, say the $j$th column, represented more than one $k$-circuit. At least one of these $k$-circuits must be linearly independent of the sets of $k$-circuits represented by the rest of the last $\alpha_k - \rho_k$ columns, as otherwise the $j$th column would be linearly dependent on the others. This $k$-circuit is however expressible linearly in terms of all the last $\alpha_k - \rho_k$ columns and hence may replace the $j$th column of $B_k$ without affecting the validity of (2). By applying this reasoning to each of the last $\alpha_k - \rho_k$ columns we see that $B_k$ may be so chosen that each of these columns represents a singe $k$-circuit. Let this be done for all values of $k$ from 0 to $n$.

13. Each of the first $\rho_k$ columns of $A_{k-1}$ represents a bounding $(k - 1)$-circuit or set of circuits and is therefore linearly dependent on the last $\alpha_{k-1} - \rho_{k-1}$ columns of $B_{k-1}$. Hence $B_{k-1}$ may be further modified so that its last $\rho_k$ columns are identical with the first $\rho_k$ columns of $A_{k-1}$. Let this be done for all values of $k$ from 1 to $n$. The last $\rho_k$ columns of $B_{k-1}$ then represent bounding sets of $(k - 1)$-circuits and the $P_{k-1} - 1$ columns preceding these represent non-bounding $(k - 1)$-circuits.

Since all columns of $\mathrm{H}_k^*$ after the $\rho_k$th contain only zeros the last $\alpha_{k-1} - \rho_k$ columns of $A_{k-1}$ are arbitrary subject to the condition that the determinant of $A_{k-1}$ shall be 1. Hence these columns of $A_{k-1}$ may be taken as identical with the first

$\rho_{k-1} + P_{k-1} - 1$ columns of $B_{k-1}$. Let this be done for all values of $k$ from 1 to $n$.

14. By this process it is brought about that the matrices $A_k$ are identical with the matrices $B_k$ except for a permutation of columns. The columns of each matrix $B_k$ fall into three blocks. The first $\rho_k$ columns represent $k$-dimensional complexes bounded by sets of $(k-1)$-circuits. Each of the next $R_k - 1$ columns represents a non-bounding $k$-circuit. The last $\rho_{k-1}$ columns represent sets of bounding $k$-circuits. Thus the reduction of the incidence matrices to normal form affords an explicit method of determining the bounding and non-bounding circuits of all dimensionalities.

## Congruences and Homologies, Modulo 2

15. The definition of congruences and homologies modulo 2 which was made in §§ 37, 38, Chap. II, applies without change to the $n$-dimensional case. Thus

$$C_k \equiv C_{k-1} \pmod{2} \tag{1}$$

means that $C_{k-1}$ is the boundary of $C_k$; and with reference to a complex $C_n$

$$C_{k-1} \sim 0 \pmod{2} \tag{2}$$

means that there exists a complex $C_k$ on $C_n$ which satisfies the congruence (1). The remarks about linear combination of congruences and complexes made in Chap. II apply here without change.

All the relations stated above by means of the matrices $\mathrm{H}_k$ can also be expressed in terms of congruences and homologies. For if we let $a_j^k$ $(j = 1, 2, \cdots, \alpha_k;\ k = 1, 2, \cdots, n)$ represent the cell $a_j^k$ and its boundary, instead of the cell alone as in the notation heretofore used, we have the congruences*

$$a_j^k \equiv \sum_{i=1}^{\alpha_{k-1}} \eta_{ij}{}^k a_i^{k-1} \pmod{2} \tag{3}$$

* We are here making the obvious convention that $\eta\, a_i^{k-1} = a_i^{k-1}$ if $\eta = 1$ and $\eta a_i^{k-1} = 0$ if $\eta = 0$.

in which $\eta_{ij}^k$ are the elements of the matrix $\mathrm{H}_k$. These congruences, which state the incidence relations of the complex $C_n$, are called the *fundamental congruences* (*mod.* 2).

16. If $C_k$ is the complex represented by $(x_1, x_2, \cdots, x_{\alpha_k})$ and $C_{k-1}$ the set of $(k-1)$-circuits represented by $(y_1, y_2, \cdots, y_{\alpha_{k-1}})$, the congruence (1) is equivalent to the matrix equation (1) of § 8. The result of reducing the incidence matrices to normal form as summarized in § 14 therefore amounts to the statement that the fundamental congruences are equivalent to the following set of congruences and homologies

$$
\begin{array}{ll}
K_k^1 & \equiv C_{k-1}^{R_{k-1}} \\
\cdot & \cdot \\
\cdot & \cdot \\
\cdot & \cdot \\
K_k^{\ k} & \equiv C_{k-1}^{R_{k-1}+\rho_k-1} \\
C_k^1 & \equiv 0 \\
\cdot & \cdot \\
\cdot & \cdot \\
\cdot & \cdot \\
C_k^{R_k-1} & \equiv 0 \\
C_k^{R_k} & \sim 0 \\
\cdot & \\
\cdot & \\
\cdot & \\
C_k^{R_k+\rho_{k-1}-1} & \sim 0.
\end{array}
\qquad (\text{mod. } 2) \tag{4}
$$

The further study of these congruences and homologies will involve proving (1) that the $k$-circuits $C_k^1, C_k^2, \cdots, C_k^{R_k-1}$ are not homologous to zero (mod. 2) and (2) that every $k$-circuit on $C_n$ is homologous to a combination of them. With regard to the statement (1) the discussion up to the present shows that no combination of these $k$-circuits bounds any complex composed of cells of $C_n$. And with regard to (2) we know that every $k$-circuit composed of cells of $C_n$ is homologous to a combination of $C_k^1, C_k^2, \cdots, C_k^{R_k-1}$. To bring complexes on $C_n$ which are not composed of cells of $C_n$ into consideration it will be necessary to go beyond the combinatorial properties of $C_n$ and make use of the geometrical properties of the cells.

### Theory of the n-cell

17. The combinatorial properties of a complex $C_n$ which have been discussed above have an elementary application in the theory of the subdivision of a Euclidean space by generalized polyhedra. A system of $(n-1)$-spaces in an $n$-space subdivide the $n$-space into a set of $n$-dimensional convex regions. They intersect in a number of $(n-2)$-spaces which subdivide each $(n-1)$-space into a set of $(n-1)$-dimensional convex regions which bound the $n$-dimensional convex regions. The $(n-2)$-spaces have $(n-3)$-spaces in common which divide the $(n-2)$-spaces into convex regions, and so on. Thus the set of $(n-1)$-spaces defines a subdivision of the $n$-space into a set of cells which can be treated by the methods described above. Any $k$-circuit formed from the $k$-dimensional convex regions is a generalized polyhedron. Any such $k$-circuit bounds a $(k+1)$-dimensional complex composed of convex $(k+1)$-cells.

A treatment of the theory of polyhedra from this point of view by the author is to be found in the Transactions of the American Math. Soc., Vol. 14 (1913), p. 65. (See also the correction Vol. 15, p. 506.) Earlier and later treatments without the machinery used here are to be found in the papers by N. J. Lennes, Am. Journ. of Math., Vol. 33 (1911), p. 37, and Lilly Hahn, Monatshefte fur Math. u. Phys., Vol. 25 (1914), p. 303. Since an $n$-cell is homeomorphic with a Euclidean space all this is the most elementary part of the theory of the $n$-cell.

18. As in § 8, Chap. II, we can define a system of curves in any $n$-cell $a_i^n$ $(i = 1, 2, \cdots, \alpha_n)$ which have the properties of the system of straight lines interior to a simplex in a Euclidean space. It is only necessary to set up a (1–1) continuous correspondence $F_i$ between the interior and boundary of the $n$-cell and the interior and boundary of a simplex and to regard as *straight* those curves in the $n$-cell which are images of straight lines in the simplex.

Under these definitions any two points of an $n$-cell or its boundary determine a straight 1-cell joining them; any three determine a straight 2-cell bounded by them and the three straight 1-cells which they determine by pairs; in general, any $i + 1$ points ($i = 1, 2, \cdots, n$) determine a straight $i$-dimensional simplex bounded by the straight $j$ dimensional simplexes ($j = 0, 1, 2, \cdots, i$) determined by subsets of the $i$ points.

19. From the separation theorems on Euclidean polyhedra (§ 17) there follow at once the following important corollaries, which are all to be understood as referring to complexes composed of "straight" cells:

If $S_{n-2}$ is an $(n - 2)$-dimensional sphere on the boundary of an $n$-cell $a^n$ the boundary of $a^n$ consists of $S_{n-2}$ and two $(n - 1)$-cells $a_1^{n-1}$ and $a_2^{n-1}$. Any $(n - 1)$-cell $a_3^{n-1}$ contained in $a^n$ and bounded by $S_{n-2}$ separates $a^n$ into two $n$-cells, one bounded by $a_1^{n-1}$, $S_{n-2}$, and $a_3^{n-1}$ and the other bounded by $a_2^{n-1}$, $S_{n-2}$, and $a_3^{n-1}$. There are an infinity of non-singular $(n - 1)$-cells contained in $a^n$ and bounded by $S_{n-2}$.

If two $n$-cells $a_1^n$, $a_2^n$ are incident with an $(n - 1)$-cell $a^{n-1}$ and have no common point they and $a^{n-1}$ constitute an $n$-cell $b^n$. If their boundaries have nothing in common except $a^{n-1}$ and its boundary the boundary of $b^n$ is the sum (mod. 2) of their boundaries.

This proposition is a special case of the following theorem: If a set of $n$-cells, $(n + 1)$-cells, $\cdots$, $(n + p)$-cells are all incident with an $(n - 1)$-cell $a^{n-1}$ and are such that the incidence relations between the $(n + i)$-cells ($i = 0, 1, 2, \cdots, p - 1$) and the $(n + i + 1)$ cells are the same as those between the $i$-cells and $(i + 1)$-cells of a $p$-dimensional sphere, the set of all points on $a^{n-1}$ and the cells incident with it constitute an $n$-cell.

The set of all cells of a complex $C_n$ which are incident with an $i$-cell $a^i$ and of higher dimensionality than $a^i$ constitute, with $a^i$ itself, what is called a *star of cells*. If the incidence relations among the cells of a star satisfy the conditions described in the paragraph above the star is said to be *simply connected*. If $a^{i+p}$ is one cell of a star, $a^{i+p}$ and all cells of the star of dimensionality greater than $i+p$ which are incident with $a^{i+p}$ constitute a star of cells.

These theorems all remain valid if the restriction to straight cells is dropped. In this more general form they depend on the generalizations to $n$ dimensions of the Jordan and Schoenflies theorems quoted in § 10, Chap. II. The generalized Jordan theorem has been proved by L. E. J. Brouwer, Math. Ann., Vol. 71 (1911), p. 37 but the generalized Schoenflies theorem is still unproved. As in the two-dimensional case, we shall get along with the restricted form of these theorems.

## Regular Complexes

20. Just as in Chap. II it was found convenient to decompose a complex into generalized triangles, here it will be found convenient to consider complexes whose $n$-cells are generalized simplexes. A complex is said to be *regular* if (1) each $n$-cell $a_j^n$ is in such a (1–1) continuous correspondence with a simplex that each 0-cell incident with $a_j^n$ corresponds to a vertex of the simplex, each 1-cell incident with $a_j^n$ to an edge of the simplex, and in general each $i$-cell ($i = 1, 2, \cdots, n-1$) incident with $a_j^n$ corresponds to an $i$-dimensional simplex of the boundary of the simplex and (2) no set of $i+1$ 0-cells are the vertices of more than one $i$-cell of the complex.

It has been shown in Chap. II how to decompose any 2-dimensional complex $C_2$ into a regular complex $\overline{C}_2$. This process will now be generalized as follows:

For convenience in phraseology, let a definition of straightness be introduced for all the 2-cells of $C_n$ in the fashion of § 18. Then let a definition of straightness be introduced for all the 3-cells, which definition may be entirely unrelated to the one used for the 2-cells. And in general let a definition of straightness be introduced for each $i$-cell ($i = 2, 3, \cdots, n$) quite independently of that used for all other cells.

Let $P_j^0 = a_j^0$ ($j = 1, 2, \cdots, \alpha_0$) and let $P_j^i$ be an arbitrary point interior to the cell $a_j^i$ ($i = 1, 2, \cdots, n$; $j = 1, 2, \cdots, \alpha_i$). The points $P_j^i$ ($i = 0, 1, 2, \cdots, n$; $j = 1, 2, \cdots, \alpha_i$) are the vertices of $\overline{C}_n$. The 1-cells of $\overline{C}_n$ are the straight 1-cells joining every point $P_j^i$ $(i = 1, 2, \cdots, n;\ j = 1, 2, \cdots \alpha_i)$ to every vertex of $\overline{C}_n$ on the boundary of $a_j^i$. A 2-cell of $C_n$ is the set of points on all straight 1-cells joining a point $P_j^i$ $(i = 2, 3, \cdots, n; j = 1, 2, \cdots, \alpha_i)$ to the points of a 1-cell of $C_n$ on the boundary of $a_j^i$. Each of these 2-cells is bounded by just three 1-cells of $\overline{C}_n$.

Continuing this process step by step we obtain the 3-cells, 4-cells, $\cdots$, $n$-cells of $\overline{C}_n$. A $k$-cell of $\overline{C}_n$ is the set of points on all straight 1-cells joining a point $P_j^i$ $(i = k, k + 1, \cdots, n;\ j = 1, 2, \cdots, \alpha_i)$ to the points of a $(k - 1)$-cell of $\overline{C}_n$ on the boundary of $a_j^i$. Each $k$-cell so defined is evidently bounded by $k + 1$, $(k - 1)$-cells.

The complex $\overline{C}_n$ thus defined is called a *regular subdivision* of $C_n$.

21. No two 0-cells of $\overline{C}_n$ are joined by more than one 1-cell. Hence any 1-cell of $\overline{C}_n$ may be denoted by $P_k^i\ P_l^j$ $(i < j)$. In like manner no $m$ 0-cells $(2 \leqq m \leqq n + 1)$ are vertices of more than one $(m - 1)$-cell of $\overline{C}_n$. Hence any such cell may be denoted by its vertices $P_q^i\ P_r^j \cdots P_v^m$. These vertices are by construction all on cells of $C_n$ of different dimensionality. Hence they may always be taken in such an order that $i < j < \cdots < m$.

Incidentally it may be remarked here that on account of the properties just referred to, $\overline{C}_n$ may be described by means of a matrix giving the incidence relations between its $n$-cells and 0-cells. Also, it can be set into (1–1) continuous correspondence with a set of cells of a simplex in a Euclidean space of a sufficiently high number of dimensions. For these propositions, see the Annals of Mathematics, Vol. 14 (1913), pp. 175–177. The correspondence with cells of a Euclidean simplex can be used to introduce such a definition of distance and straightness in $\overline{C}_n$ that the straightness and distance of any cell is in agreement with the straightness and distance of any cell with which it is incident.

22. The relationship between the complexes $C_n$ and $\overline{C}_n$ may be stated as follows:

(1) Each $n$-cell of $C_n$, $a_i^n$, is the sum (mod. 2) of all $n$-cells $P_a^0\ P_b^1 \cdots P_i^n$ of $\overline{C}_n$ having $P_i^n$ as a vertex.

.

.

.

$(n - k)$ Each $k$-cell of $C_n$, $a_i^k$, is the sum (mod. 2) of all $k$-cells $P_a^0 P_b^1 \cdots P_i^k$ of $\overline{C}_n$ which have $P_i^k$ as a vertex (the superscripts are all less than or equal to $k$).

.

.

.

$(n)$ Each 0-cell of $C_n$, $a_i^0$ is the 0-cell $P_i^0$.

23. *The values of $R_1$, $R_2$, $\cdots$, $R_n$ determined from $C_n$ are the same as those determined from $\overline{C}_n$.* In order to prove this, consider any $i$-circuit $K_i$ of $\overline{C}_n$ which is not a circuit of $C_n$ and which therefore contains at least one of the points $P_j^n$. The $i$-cells of $K_i$ which are incident with $P_j^n$ are incident with $(i - 1)$-cells of the boundary of the cell $a_j^n$ of $C_n$. These $(i - 1)$-cells of $a_j^n$ constitute one or more $(i - 1)$-circuits $K_{i-1}^a$ because the $(i - 1)$-cells of $K_i$ which are incident with $P_j^n$ and with $(i - 2)$-cells of the boundary of $a_j^n$ are incident each with an even number of $i$-cells of $K_i$. Each of these $(i - 1)$-circuits on the boundary of $a_j^n$ bounds at least one $i$-dimensional complex $C_i^a$ composed of cells of $\overline{C}_n$ on the boundary of $a_j^n$, as follows easily from § 17. By its definition it also bounds a complex composed of $i$-cells of $K_i$ which are incident with $P_j^n$. These two complexes constitute an $i$-circuit, or set of $i$-circuits $K_i^a$, which bounds the complex composed of the $(i + 1)$-cells of $\overline{C}^n$ which are incident with $P_j^n$ and the $i$-cells of $C_i^a$. If all the $i$-circuits $K_i^a$ determined by $P_j^n$ and $K_i$ are added (mod. 2) to $K_i$ the resulting $i$-circuit $K_i'$ does not pass through $P_j^n$. Repeating this argument for all the vertices $P_k^n$ of $C^n$ on $K_i$ it follows that by adding bounding circuits to $K_i$ it can be converted into an $i$-circuit which does not pass through any of the vertices $P_k^n$ of $\overline{C}_n$. Such an $i$-circuit is composed of cells of $C_n$.

From this it follows that all $i$-circuits of $\overline{C}_n$ are linearly dependent on bounding circuits and the circuit $C_i^p$ $(p = 1, 2 \ldots, R_i - 1)$ of the complete set of non-bounding $i$-circuits of $C_n$ determined in § 16. Hence the value of $R_i$ determined by $\overline{C}_n$ is not greater than that determined by $C_n$. It also cannot be less, for if so there would be a linear relation among the $i$-circuits $C_i^p$ $(p = 1, 2, \ldots, R_i - 1)$ regarded as circuits of $\overline{C}_n$. But this would mean that there was a complex $K_{i+1}$ composed of cells of $\overline{C}_n$ and bounded by some or all of the circuits $C_i^p$. By an argument like that in the paragraph above $K_{i+1}$ could be replaced by a complex $K'_{i+1}$ which contains none of the vertices $P_{jn}$ of $\overline{C}_n$ and which therefore is composed of cells of $C_n$. But the existence of $K'_{i+2}$ would mean a linear relation among the $i$-circuits of $C_i^p$ regarded as $i$-circuits of $C_n$. Hence the value of $R_i$ determined by $\overline{C}_n$ is not less than that determined by $C_n$.

## Manifolds

24. By a *neighborhood* of any $i$-cell $a^i$ on a complex $C_n$ is meant any set $S$ of non-singular cells on $C_n$ such that any set of points of $C_n$ having a limit point on $a^i$ contains points on the cells of $S$.

If $C_n$ is an $n$-circuit such that every point on it has a neighborhood which is an $n$-cell the set of points on $C_n$ is called a *closed n-dimensional manifold.* A set of points obtainable by removing a finite number of $n$-cells and their boundaries from a closed manifold is called an *open* manifold of $n$ dimensions.

If $P$ is an arbitrary point of a complex $C_n$ it can be taken as one of the points $P_j^i$ in a regular subdivision of $C_n$. The set of cells of $\overline{C}_n$ which are incident with $P$ determines a neighborhood of $P$. Hence the process of regular sub-division gives an explicit method of determining whether the set of points on $C_n$ is or is not a manifold.

## Dual Complexes

25. A complex $C_n'$ is said to be *dual* to a complex $C_n$ if the incidence relations between the $k$-cells and $(k - 1)$-cells of $C_n'$ are the same as those between the $(n - k)$-cells and $(n - k + 1)$-cells of $C_n$ for $k = 1, 2, \cdots, n$. In case $C_n$ defines a manifold, a complex $C_n'$ dual to $C_n$ can be constructed by first making a regular subdivision of $C_n$ into $\overline{C}_n$, then defining as an $n$-cell of $C_n'$ the set of all points on each star of cells of $\overline{C}_n$ having a vertex of

$C_n$ as center, next defining as an $(n-1)$-cell of $C_n'$ the set of all points on each star of cells of dimensionality $n-1$ and less which are incident with the point $P_i^1$ on a 1-cell of $C_n$, and so on, finally defining as the 0-cells of $C_n'$ the points $P_i^n$ on the $n$-cells of $C_n$.

This process is illustrated in fig. 3, page 41 for the two-dimensional case. In this figure the vertices of $C_2'$ are the points $P_i^2$, the 1-cells of $C_2'$ are made up of the pairs of 1-cells $P_i^2\,P_j^2$, $P_i^1\,P_k^2$ of $\overline{C}_2$, and the 2-cells of $C_2'$ are the triangle stars at the vertices of $C_2$.

26. The construction for $C_n'$ may be stated a little more explicitly in terms of our notations (cf. § 22) as follows:

(1) Each 0-cell of $C_n'$ is the 0-cell $P_i^n$.

.

.

.

$(n-k)$ Each $(n-k)$-cell of $C_n'$, $b_i^{n-k}$, is the sum (mod. 2) of all $(n-k)$-cells, $P_i^k\,P_j^{k+1}\cdots P_p^n$ of $\overline{C}_n$ which have $P_i^k$ as a vertex.

.

.

.

$(n)$ Each $n$-cell of $C_n'$, $b_i^n$, is the sum (mod. 2) of all $n$-cells $P_i^0\,P_j^1\cdots P_t^n$ of $\overline{C}_n$ which have $P_i^0$ as a vertex.

In order to make sure that this actually defines a complex dual to $C_n$ it must be proved first that each of the statements (1) $\cdots$ $(n)$ defines a cell and second that the set of cells has the properties required of a dual complex.

27. Consider first the statement $(n)$. The 0-cell $P_i^0$ is a vertex $a_i^0$ of $C_n$. Since we are dealing with a manifold, $a_i^0$, and the set of all cells of $\overline{C}_n$ incident with it form a simply connected star, and the set of points on this star form an $n$-cell. This $n$-cell we have called $b_i^n$.

No two of the $n$-cells $b_i^n$ have a point in common because no $n$-cell of $\overline{C}_n$ is incident with more than one vertex of $C_n$ (in the notation $P_i^0\,P_j^1\cdots P_q^n$ only one superscript is zero). Moreover every point on a cell of $C_n$ is on the interior or boundary of one of the cells $b_i^n$ because each $n$-cell of $\overline{C}_n$ is incident with at least one vertex of $C_n$ (the superscript zero always appears once in the notation $P_i^0 P_j^1 \cdots P_q^n$).

Next consider the statement $(n - k)$. The point $P_i^k$ is on the $k$-cell $a_i^k$ of $C_n$ and this $k$-cell contains a $k$-cell $P_a^0 P_b^1 \cdots P_i^k$ of $\overline{C}_n$. Since the set of all points on $\overline{C}_n$ form a manifold, $P_a^0 P_b^1 \cdots P_i^k$ and the set of all cells of $\overline{C}_n$ of dimensionality $k + 1$ or greater which are incident with it form a simply connected star (§§ 19, 24); and the set of all points on the cells of the star forms a single cell which is the sum (mod. 2) of the $n$-dimensional cells of the star. The $n$-dimensional cells of the star are all $n$-cells of $\overline{C}_n$ which can be denoted by $P_a^0 P_b^1 \cdots P_i^k P_j^{k+1} \cdots P_p^n$ in which the first $k + 1$ of the $P$'s are fixed and the rest are variable. The incidence relations among the cells of this star are by § 19 those of an $(n - k - 1)$-dimensional sphere. These incidence relations are however the same as those among the $(n - k)$-cells $P_i^k P_j^{k+1} \cdots P_p^n$ described in the statement $(n - k)$ and the cells of lower dimensionality with which they are incident by pairs. Hence the sum, (mod. 2) of the cells $P_i^k P_j^{k+1} \cdots P_p^n$ described in the statement $(n - k)$ is an $(n - k)$-cell. This $(n - k)$-cell we call $b_i^{n-k}$. It obviously has the point $P_i^k$, and this point only, in common with $a_i^k$.

28. Let us next find the incidence relations among the $b$'s. If $a_i^k$ is incident with $a_j^{k+1}$, there is a $k$-cell, $P_a^0 P_b^1 \cdots P_i^k$, of $\overline{C}_n$ contained in $a_i^k$ which is incident with the $(k + 1)$-cell, $P_a^0 P_b^1 \cdots P_i^k P_j^{k+1}$, contained in $a_j^{k+1}$. The cell $b_i^{n-k}$ dual to $a_i^k$ is the sum (mod. 2) of all the $(n - k)$-cells $P_i^k P_j^{k+1} P_l^{k+2} \cdots P_s^n$ for the given value of $i$. The cell $b_j^{n-k-1}$ dual to $a_j^{k+1}$ is the sum (mod. 2) of all the $(n - k - 1)$-cells $P_j^{k+1} P_l^{k+2} \cdots P_s^n$ for the given value of $j$. Since each of the $(n - k)$-cells of $\overline{C}_n$ which enter into $b_i^{n-k}$ is incident with an $(n - k - 1)$-cell of $\overline{C}_n$ contained in $b_j^{n-k-1}$ it follows that $b_i^{n-k}$ is incident with $b_j^{n-k-1}$.

Hence if $a_i^k$ is incident with $a_j^{k+1}$, $b_j^{n-k}$ is incident with $b_i^{n-k-1}$. The converse proposition is proved in exactly the same way.

Hence $a_i^k$ is incident with $a_j^{k+1}$ if and only if $b_i^{n-k}$ is incident with $b_j^{n-k-1}$.

**Duality of the Connectivities $R_i$**

29. Stating this result for the case $k = n - 1$, we have that $a_i^{n-1}$ is incident with $a_j^n$ if and only if $b_i^1$ is incident with $b_j^0$. Hence the matrix of incidence relations between the 0-cells and 1-cells of the complex $C_n'$ is the matrix $H_n'$ obtained from the matrix $H_n$ of the complex $C_n$ by interchanging rows and columns. In like manner it is seen that, in general, the matrix of incidence relations between the $(n - k - 1)$-cells and $(n - k)$-cells of the complex $C_n'$ is the transposed matrix $H_k'$ of the matrix $H_k$ of the complex $C_n$. Hence the matrices of incidence $H_1, H_2, \cdots, H_n$ of $C_n'$ are the matrices $H_n', H_{n-1}', \cdots, H_1'$ of $C_n$.

The ranks of these matrices are $\rho_n, \rho_{n-1}, \cdots, \rho_1$ respectively. Moreover the numbers of 0-cells, 1-cells, $\cdots$ $n$-cells of $C_n'$ are $\alpha_n, \alpha_{n-1}, \cdots, \alpha_1, \alpha_0$ respectively. Hence by the formula for the $i$-dimensional connectivity $R_i$, it follows that the 1-, $\cdots$, $(n - 1)$-dimensional connectivities of $C_n'$ are $R_{n-1}, \cdots, R_1$ respectively.

It was shown in § 23 that the connectivity $R_i$ of a complex $\overline{C}_n$ obtained by a regular subdivision of $C_n$ is the same as that of $C_n$. But by comparing § 22 with § 26 it is seen that $\overline{C}_n$ is a regular subdivision both of $C_n$ and of $C_n'$. Hence the connectivity $R_i$ of $C_n'$ is the same as that of $C_n$. Hence $R_{n-1}, R_{n-2}, \cdots, R_1$ are the same as $R_1, R_2, \cdots, R_{n-1}$, respectively. That is

$$R_{n-k} = R_k \quad (k = 1, 2, \cdots, n - 1).$$

It should be noted that this duality relation does not apply to $R_0$ and $R_n$. In the case of a manifold, which we are considering here, $R_0 = 1$ and $R_n = 2$.

30. An important corollary of this result is that for a manifold of an odd number of dimensions the characteristic is zero. For the equations

$$\alpha_0 - \alpha_1 + \cdots + (-1)^n\alpha_n = 1 + (-1)^n + \sum_{i=1}^{n-1}(-1)^i(R_i - 1)$$

and

$$R_i = R_{n-i} \quad (i = 1, 2, \cdots, n - 1)$$

give

$$\alpha_0 - \alpha_1 + \alpha_2 - \cdots - \alpha_n = 0,$$

as already noted in § 9.

## Generalized Manifolds

31. It follows from § 24 that the cells of higher dimensionality incident with any cell of a complex defining a manifold constitute a simply connected star. This property could in fact be taken as the definition of a manifold. It is the basis of the following generalization.

A *generalized manifold* of $n$ dimensions is the set of all points on an $n$-circuit $C_n$ such that if $a^{i-1}$ is any cell of $C_n$ the incidence relations among the $(i)$-cells, $(i + 1)$-cells, $\cdots$, $(i + k)$-cells (where $i + k = n$) incident with $a^{i-1}$ are the same as the incidence relations among the 0-cells, 1-cells, $\cdots$, $k$-cells of a complex defining a generalized manifold of $k$ dimensions; a generalized manifold of zero dimensions is a 0-circuit.

This definition is obviously invariant under the group of all homeomorphisms. For $n = 0, 1, 2$, a generalized manifold is the same as a manifold. But for $n \geq 3$ it includes sets of points which are not manifolds in the narrow sense.

32. To bring this out let us consider the following example given in the article on Analysis Situs by Dehn and Heegaard in the Encyclopädie. Let $S_4$ be a Euclidean space of four dimensions, $a^0$ a point in $S_4$, $S_3$ a three-space in $S_4$ but not on $a^0$, and $M_2$ an arbitrary two-dimensional manifold (e.g., an anchor ring) in $S_3$. Let $M_2$ be decomposed into 0-cells, 1-cells and 2-cells constituting a two-dimensional complex, $B_2$. The segment joining any 0-cell of $B_2$ to $a^0$ is a 1-cell, the points on the segments joining the points of a 1-cell of $B_2$ to $a^0$ constitute a 2-cell, and the points on the segment joining the points of a 2-cell of $B_2$ to $a^0$ constitute a 3-cell. The complex $C_3$ composed of all the 1-cells, 2-cells and 3-cells found by this process, together with $a^0$ and the cells of $B_2$, is such that the boundary of an arbitrarily small neighborhood of $a^0$ is of the same structure as $B_2$. Hence the set of points on each such boundary is a surface like $M_2$ (e.g., an anchor ring).

It is obvious that a generalized three-dimensional manifold can be constructed which has any number of points with neighborhoods which are not spherical. A generalized four-dimensional manifold can have both 0-cells and 1-cells whose neighborhoods are not simply connected, and so on.

33. It was shown in Chap. II that any 2 circuit can be regarded as a singular manifold. The generalization of this theorem is that any $n$-circuit is a *singular* (cf. § 3) *generalized manifold.* We shall repeat the process of § 34, Chap. II, for the three-dimensional case, because one new point enters, but shall leave the formal generalization to the reader.

Let $C_3$ be an arbitrary 3-circuit. Each of its 2-cells $a_i^2$ is incident with an even number $2n_i$ of 3-cells. These may be grouped in $n_i$ pairs of 3-cells associated with $a_i^2$, and the method used in § 34, Chap. II, may be used to obtain a 3-circuit $C_3'$ whose cells coincide with those of $C_3$ and which is such that each of its 2-cells is incident with two and only two of its 3-cells.

The incidence relations between the 2-cells and 3-cells of $C_3'$ which are incident with a 1-cell $a_j^1$ of $C_3'$ are the same as those of a linear graph in which each 0-cell is incident with just two 1-cells. Since such a linear graph is a set of 1-circuits having no points in common, the 2-cells and 3-cells incident with $a_j^1$ fall into a number, $n_j$, of *groups associated with* $a_j^1$ such that the incidence relations among the cells of a group are those of a 1-circuit. With the aid of these groups, by the method of § 34, Chap. II, a complex $C_3''$ is defined whose cells coincide with those of $C_3'$ and which is such that all of its cells of dimensionality greater than $i$ which are incident with any one of its $i$-cells ($i = 2, 1$) are related among themselves by a set of incidence relations identical with those of an $(i - 1)$-circuit.

The incidence relations between the 1-cells, 2-cells and 3-cells incident with a 0-cell $a_k^0$ of $C_3''$ now satisfy the same conditions as those between the 0-cells, 1-cells and 2-cells of a number, $n_k$, of two-dimensional manifolds which have no points in common. Hence they fall into $n_k$ *groups associated with* $a_k^0$ such that the incidence relations among the 1-cells, 2-cells and 3-cells of a group are the same as those among the 0-cells, 1-cells and 2-cells of a two-dimensional manifold. Hence a complex $C_3'''$ can be defined whose cells coincide with those of $C_3''$ and which satisfies the definition of a generalized manifold.

$C_3'''$ will be a manifold in the narrow sense only in the case where each of the groups associated with each vertex $a_k^0$ has the incidence relations of the cells of a sphere.

34. Since the boundary of any complex consists of one or more circuits, it consists of one or more generalized manifolds any or all of which may be singular.

### Bounding and Non-bounding k-circuits

35. Let us now take up the problem: Given a $k$-circuit, $C_k$ on a complex $C_n$, *to determine whether or not there exists a* $(k + 1)$-*dimensional complex, singular or not, on* $C_n$ *which is bounded by* $C_k$. This is the problem solved in Chap. II (cf. § 35) for the case where $n = 2$ and $k = 1$. As the problem is now formulated $k$ may be less than, equal to, or greater than $n$, and $C_k$ may have singularities of any degree of complexity compatible with the definition in § 3.

The solution of the problem in the simplest case is contained in the following obvious theorem which is a direct generalization of that given in § 36, Chap. II: *Any sphere of k dimensions on an n-cell* $a^n$ *is the boundary of a* $(k + 1)$-*cell on* $a^n$. The $(k + 1)$-cell can be constructed by joining an arbitrary point, $P$, of $a^n$ to all the points of the $k$-dimensional sphere by straight 1-cells or, in case of points of the sphere which coincide with $P$, by singular 1-cells coincident with $P$. The solution of our problem for the general case which we shall now develop is entirely parallel to that carried out in §§ 39 to 46, Chap. II.

36. Let $K_i$ be an $i$-dimensional complex on $C_n$. Let $\overline{C}_n$ be a regular sub-division of $C_n$. Let a definition of distance and straightness be introduced relative to $\overline{C}_n$ and let all references to distance and straightness in the rest of this argument be understood to refer to this definition. Let $\tilde{C}_n$ be a regular sub-division of $\overline{C}_n$. By simple continuity considerations it can be

proved that $K_i$ can be regularly subdivided into a complex $\overline{K}_i$ such that for each $j$-cell of $K_i$ there is a star of cells of $\tilde{C}_n$ to which it is interior. *A correspondence A* is now defined as a correspondence between the vertices of $\overline{K}_i$ and those of $\overline{C}_n$ by which each vertex of $\overline{K}_i$ which is interior to a star of cells of $\tilde{C}_n$ having a vertex of $\overline{C}_n$ as center corresponds to that vertex of $\overline{C}_n$, and by which each vertex of $\overline{K}_i$ which is on the boundary of two or more stars of cells of $\tilde{C}_n$ having vertices of $\overline{C}_n$ as centers corresponds to one of these vertices of $\overline{C}_n$.

Since every point of $C_n$ is on or on the boundary of some star of cells of $\tilde{C}_n$ with center at a vertex of $\overline{C}_n$, a correspondence $A$ determines a unique vertex of $\overline{C}_n$ for each vertex of $\overline{K}_i$. Moreover since any cell of $\overline{K}_i$ is on a star of cells of $\tilde{C}_n$ *its vertices correspond to vertices of a single cell of* $\overline{C}_n$. Hence the correspondence $A$ makes each cell of $\overline{K}_i$ correspond to a cell of $\overline{C}_n$ of the same or lower dimensionality.

37. Let the $r$-cells of $\overline{C}_n$ be denoted by $c_j^r$ $(r = 0, 1, 2, \cdots, n;$ $j = 1, 2, \cdots \alpha_r)$ and those of $\overline{K}_i$ by $k_j^r$ $(r = 0, 1, 2, \cdots, i;$ $j = 1, 2, \cdots \beta_r)$. Each 0-cell $k_j^0$ of $\overline{K}_i$ can be joined to the 0-cell of $\overline{C}_n$ to which it corresponds under the correspondence $A$ by a straight 1-cell $b_j^1$; or, if $k_j^0$ coincides with the point to which it corresponds, by a singular 1-cell $b_j^1$ coinciding with $k_j^0$. Similarly, for each 1-cell $k_j^1$ of $\overline{K}_i$, a 2-cell $b_j^2$ can be constructed by joining each point of $k_j^1$ to a point of the corresponding cell of $\overline{C}_n$ by a 1-cell which is either straight or coincident with a point. By a similar construction there is determined for every cell $k_j^r$ of $\overline{K}_i$ a cell $b_j^{r+1}$ composed of 1-cells joining points of $k_j^r$ to points of the cell of $\overline{C}_n$ to which $k_j^r$ corresponds under the correspondence $A$. The $(i + 1)$ dimensional complex composed of the cells $b_j^{i+1}$ and their boundaries is denoted by $B_{i+1}$. It is such that the incidence relations of $b_p^{r+1}$ and $b_q^r$ are the same as those of $k_p^r$ and $k_q^{r-1}$.

38. If $K_i$ is an $i$-circuit, all $i$-cells $b_j^i$ $(j = 1, 2, \cdots, \beta_{i-1})$ must cancel out when the boundaries of the $(i + 1)$-cells $b_j^{i+1}$ $(j = 1, 2, \cdots, \beta_i)$ are added together (mod. 2). Hence the boundary of $B_{i+1}$ consists either of $\overline{K}_i$ alone or of $\overline{K}_i$ and a set of $i$-circuits $K_i'$ composed of cells of $\overline{C}_n$. That is to say

(1) $$B_{i+1} \equiv \overline{K}_i + K_i' \quad (\text{mod. } 2)$$
and
$$\overline{K}_i \sim K_i' \quad (\text{mod. } 2)$$
where $K_i'$ is either zero or a set of $i$-circuits composed of cells of $\overline{C}_n$.

There is no difficulty in seeing that any $i$-circuit is homologous (mod. 2) to any regular sub-division of itself. Hence
$$K_i \sim \overline{K}_i$$
and therefore

(2) $$K_i \sim K_i'$$

It is obvious that $K_i' = 0$ if $i > n$. Hence

(3) $$K_{n+r} \sim 0 \quad (\text{mod. } 2)$$
whenever $r > 0$.

39. From the homology (2) it follows that $K_i \sim 0$ if and only if $K_i' \sim 0$. By § 7, $K_i'$ bounds a complex composed of cells of $\overline{C}_n$ if and only if it is represented by a symbol $(x_1, x_2, \cdots, x_{\alpha_i})$ which is linearly dependent on the columns of the matrix $\mathrm{H}_{i+1}$ for $\overline{C}_n$. We shall now prove that if $K_i' \sim 0$, $K_i'$ bounds a complex composed of cells of $C_n$, from which result it obviously follows that $K_i \sim 0$ if and only if the symbol $(x_1, x_2, \cdots, x_{\alpha_i})$ for $K_i'$ is linearly dependent on the columns of $\mathrm{H}_{i+1}$.

40. Given that $K_i' \sim 0$ and that $K_i'$ is composed of cells of $\overline{C}_n$, let $K_i''$ be a non-singular set of $i$-circuits which coincides with $K_i'$, each cell of $K_i''$ coinciding with one and only one cell of $K_i'$ and *vice versa*. Obviously $K_i''$ is the boundary of a complex on $C_n$ because $K_i'$ is bounded by such a complex. Letting $K_{i+1}$ denote the complex bounded by $K_i''$ we have

(4) $$K_{i+1} \equiv K_i'' \quad (\text{mod. } 2)$$

Moreover there is a singular complex, $G_{i+1}$, obtained by joining each point of $K_i''$ to the point of $K_i'$ with which it coincides by a singular 1-cell coincident with it. This gives the congruence

(5) $$G_{i+1} \equiv K_i' + K_i'' \quad (\text{mod. } 2)$$

Let us construct a correspondence $A$ for $K_{i+1}$ exactly as in § 36 and by means of it construct a complex $B_{i+2}$ analogous to the complex $B_{i+1}$ of § 37. When the boundaries of the $(i+2)$-cells of $B_{i+2}$ are added to $K_{i+1}$ (mod. 2), all the $(i+1)$-cells of $B_{i+2}$ cancel except those determined by cells $k_j^i$ of the boundary of $K_{i+1}$. But the $(i+1)$-cells of the complex $G_{i+1}$ of the paragraph above can evidently be taken to be identical with these $(i+1)$-cells. Under this convention, the boundary of $B_{i+2}$ is composed of $K_{i+1}$, $G_{i+1}$, and a complex $K_{i+1}'$ composed of certain cells of $\overline{C}_n$. The latter cells must exist because the sum of $K_{i+1}$ and $G_{i+1}$, being bounded by $K_i'$, is not an $(i+1)$-circuit and hence cannot by itself bound $B_{i+2}$. This gives the congruence

$$B_{i+2} \equiv K_{i+1} + G_{i+1} + K_{i+1}' \pmod{2} \tag{6}$$

or the homology

$$K_{i+1} + G_{i+1} + K_{i+1}' \sim 0 \pmod{2} \tag{7}$$

which implies the congruence

$$K_{i+1} + G_{i+1} + K_{i+1}' \equiv 0 \pmod{2}. \tag{8}$$

On adding (4), (5) and (8) we obtain

$$K_{i+1}' \equiv K_i', \tag{9}$$

which states that $K_i'$ bounds a complex composed of cells of $\overline{C}_n$ which is the theorem stated in § 39.

41. We now have an explicit method for determining whether a set of $i$-circuits $K_i$ on $C_n$ does or does not bound. For a construction has been given to determine the homology (2) of § 38 and $K_i \sim 0$ if and only if $K_i'$ bounds a complex composed of cells of $\overline{C}_n$.

It is a corollary that no $n$-circuit composed of cells of $C_n$ can satisfy a homology $K_n \sim 0$. For there are no $(n+1)$-cells in $\overline{C}_n$. Hence, in particular, an $n$-circuit $C_n$ cannot bound a singular complex on $C_n$. On the other hand, every $(n+k)$-circuit $(k > 0)$ on $C_n$ bounds an $(n+k+1)$ dimensional complex on $C_n$ as stated in (3), § 38.

## Invariance of the Connectivities $R_i$

42. We are now ready to prove the invariance of the connectivities $R_0, R_1, \cdots, R_n$ under the group of all homeomorphisms. This invariance is obvious for $R_0$ because $R_0$ is the number of connected complexes which compose $C_n$. To prove the invariance of $R_i$ $(i > 0)$ for any complex $C_n$, we first observe that according to § 23, $R_i$ is the same for $C_n$ as for any regular subdivision of $C_n$. We therefore fix attention on a regular subdivision $\bar{C}_n$.

By § 9 there exists* a set of $i$-circuits $C_i^j$ $(j = 1, 2, \cdots, R_i - 1)$ such that (1) there is no $(i + 1)$-dimensional complex composed of cells of $\bar{C}_n$ which is bounded by any combination of the circuits $C_i^j$ and (2) if $C_i'$ is any other $i$-circuit composed of cells of $\bar{C}_n$ it is homologous to the sum (mod. 2) of some or all of the $i$-circuits $C_i^j$. By combining (1) with the theorem of § 39 we have at once that: (*a*) *there is no* $(i + 1)$*-dimensional complex of any sort on* $C_n$ *which is bounded by any combination of the circuits* $C_i^j$. From (2) and § 38 it follows that: (*b*) *if* $C_i$ *is any* $i$*-circuit on* $\bar{C}_n$ *it is homologous to a linear combination* (*mod.* 2) *of the* $i$*-circuits* $C_i^j$ $(j = 1, 2, \cdots, R_i - 1)$. For $C_i$ is homologous either to zero or to an $i$-circuit $C_i'$ which is composed of cells of $\bar{C}_n$, and by (2) $C_i'$ is homologous to a combination of the $i$-circuits $C_i^j$.

From the properties (*a*) and (*b*) it follows by a mere repetition of the argument in § 48, Chap. II that $R_i$ *is an Analysis Situs invariant of the complex* $C_n$.

43. It should perhaps be pointed out explicitly that the proof which has just been completed applies as well for $i = n$ as for other values of $i$. If $C_n$ is a single $n$-circuit, $R_n = 2$, and since $R_n$ is an invariant, any complex $C_n'$ homeomorphic with $C_n$ contains just one $n$-circuit. By a repetition of the argument in § 52, Chap. II, it follows that this $n$-circuit contains all points of $C_n'$. *Hence any complex homeomorphic with an* $n$*-circuit is an* $n$*-circuit.*

* This is not intended to exclude the case in which $R_i - 1 = 0$, in which the set of $i$-circuits $C_i^j$ is a null-set.

It is a simple corollary of this that any complex $C_n$ homeomorphic with a manifold $M_n$ defines a manifold. In other words the definition of a manifold is invariant under the group of homeomorphisms. The same is true of the definition of a generalized manifold.

# CHAPTER IV

## ORIENTABLE MANIFOLDS

### Oriented n-cells

1. Let us now take up the orientation of $n$-dimensional complexes. The first problem is to give a definition of the term "oriented $n$-cell." We shall give a definition here which suffices for the elementary part of the matrix theory and shall postpone to the next chapter the theorems on deformation which give the full intuitional content of the notion of orientation. The definition will be made as a part of a process of mathematical induction in which we prove that if certain theorems are true and certain terms defined for all complexes $C_i$ for which $i < n$, then the theorems are true and the terms can be defined for any complex $C_n$. Since the theorems and definitions in question have already been established for all linear graphs, $C_1$, this process will establish them for all complexes $C_n$.

The terms which we assume to be defined are: oriented $i$-cell of a complex $C_j$ $(i, j < n)$ orientable $i$-circuit $(i < n)$, oriented $i$-circuit $(i < n)$, oriented $i$-dimensional complex $(i < n)$, sum of oriented $i$-dimensional complexes $(i < n)$ in case this sum is an $i$-dimensional complex. The theorems are: (1) *any i-circuit* $(i < n)$ *which is homeomorphic with an orientable i-circuit is orientable*; (2) *any i-circuit defining an i-dimensional sphere* $(i < n)$ *is orientable.*

2. The proof that these theorems hold for any $C_n$ if they hold for all $C_i$ $(i < n)$ is a direct generalization of the proof given in §§ 58 to 60, Chap. II for the case $n = 2$. Before establishing the theorems we state the definitions which, it will be noted, derive their content from the theorems for the cases $i < n$.

An *oriented n-cell* of a complex $C_n$ is the object obtained by associating a cell $a_i^n$ $(i = 1, 2, \cdots, \alpha_n)$ of $C_n$ with one of the oriented $(n - 1)$-circuits which can be formed from its boundary according to the theorem (2) of the last section. One of the oriented $n$-cells formed from $a_i^n$ is denoted by $\sigma_i^n$ and the other by $-\sigma_i^n$. Any set of oriented $n$-cells of $C_n$ is called *an oriented n-dimensional complex* and may be denoted by a symbol $(x_1, x_2, \cdots, x_{\alpha_n})$ in which $x_i = +1$ $(i = 1, 2, \cdots, \alpha_n)$ if $\sigma_i^n$ is in the set, $x_i = -1$ if $-\sigma_i^n$ is in the set and $x_i = 0$ if neither of them is in the set. The *sum* of two such symbols is defined as in § 45, Chap. 1; and if the sum of the symbols for two oriented complexes, $\Gamma_n'$, $\Gamma_n''$ is the symbol for an oriented complex $\Gamma_n'''$, the complex $\Gamma_n'''$ is called the *sum** of $\Gamma_n'$ and $\Gamma_n''$ and denoted by $\Gamma_n' + \Gamma_n''$.

Now suppose that $C_n$ is an $n$-circuit and let one of the two oriented $(n-1)$-circuits into which the boundary of $a_i^n$ $(i = 1, 2, \cdots, \alpha_n)$ can be converted be denoted by $\Gamma_{n-1}^i$. Since each $(n-1)$-cell of $C_n$ is incident with an even number of $n$-cells of $C_n$, the number of oriented $(n-1)$-circuits $\Gamma_{n-1}^i$ which contain a given oriented $(n-1)$-cell $\sigma_j^{n-1}$ or its negative is even. If the oriented $(n-1)$-circuits $\Gamma_{n-1}^i$ $(i = 1, 2, \cdots, \alpha_n)$ can be so chosen that for each $j$ $(j = 1, 2, \cdots, \alpha_{n-1})$, $\sigma_j^{n-1}$ and $-\sigma_j^{n-1}$ appear in equal numbers of them, $C_n$ is said to be *orientable.* In other words, $C_n$ is orientable if and only if the oriented $(n-1)$-circuits $\Gamma_{n-1}^i$ $(i = 1, 2, \cdots, \alpha_n)$ can be so chosen that their sum is zero.

A set of oriented $n$-cells formed from the $n$-cells of an orientable $n$-circuit in such a way that the sum of the oriented $(n-1)$-circuits associated with the $n$-cells is zero is called an *oriented n-circuit.* Thus an oriented $n$-circuit is an oriented $n$-dimensional complex formed from an orientable $n$-circuit in a particular way.

3. By reference to § 22, Chap. III, it is obvious that the boundaries of the $n$-cells into which an $n$-cell $a_i^n$ of $C_n$ is decomposed by a regular subdivision can be converted into a set of oriented $(n-1)$-circuits whose sum is the oriented $(n-1)$-circuit $\Gamma_{n-1}^i$ formed from the boundary of $a_i^n$. Hence an $n$-circuit $C_n$ is orientable if and only if a regular sub-division $\overline{C}_n$ of it is orientable.

It can now be proved by exactly the method used in §§ 58, 59, Chap. II that *if $G_n$ is any n-circuit homeomorphic with $C_n$, $G_n$ is*

* This term is given a more extensive significance in § 9 below.

*orientable if and only if $C_n$ is orientable.* In outline, the proof is as follows:

Let $K_n$ be the $n$-circuit on $C_n$ whose cells are the images under the homeomorphism of the cells of $G_n$. Let $\overline{C}_n$ be a regular subdivision of $C_n$ and $\overline{K}_n$ a complex obtained from $K_n$ by regular subdivisions as in § 36, Chap. III. Also let a correspondence $A$ and a set of $(n + 1)$-cells $b_j^{n+1}$ $(j = 1, 2, \cdots, \beta_n)$ be defined as in § 36. Each $b_j^{n+1}$ is bounded by an $n$-circuit $S_n^j$ which is evidently orientable because it is obtainable by subdividing the complex used in § 5, Chap. III, to define an $n$-sphere.

If $K_n$ is orientable there can be formed from the $(n - 1)$-circuits bounding the $n$-cells of $\overline{K}_n$ a set of oriented $(n - 1)$-circuits $\Gamma_{n-1}^i$ $(i = 1, 2, \cdots, \beta_{n-1})$ which are such that their sum is zero. From the $(n - 1)$-circuits bounding the $n$-cells of each $S_n^j$ is formed a set of oriented $(n - 1)$-circuits whose sum is zero which contains one oriented $(n - 1)$-circuit which is the negative of one of the $\Gamma_{n-1}^i$'s. On adding all the oriented $(n - 1)$-circuits thus obtained from $\overline{K}_n$ and the spheres $S_n^j$, all the oriented $(n - 1)$-cells cancel out except some formed from the boundaries of the $n$-cells of $\overline{C}_n$. The latter are present because otherwise $\overline{K}_n$ would bound an $(n + 1)$-dimensional complex on $\overline{K}_n$. These oriented $(n - 1)$-circuits of $\overline{C}_n$ are subject to the one linear relation obtained by adding the linear relation among the $\Gamma_{n-1}^i$'s and the ones obtained from the spheres $S_n^j$.

By an argument just like that given in § 56, Chap. II this linear relation involves all the $(n - 1)$-circuits which can be formed from the boundaries of $n$-cells of $\overline{C}_n$, and hence $\overline{C}_n$ and $C_n$ are orientable $n$-circuits. Therefore, if $G_n$ is orientable, so is $C_n$. The relation between $C_n$ and $G_n$ being reciprocal, it follows at once that if $C_n$ is orientable, so is $G_n$.

4. The complex used to define an $n$-dimensional sphere in § 5, Chap. III, is obviously orientable. By the last section, any complex homeomorphic with this one is orientable. Hence any $n$-circuit which defines an $n$-dimensional sphere is orientable. As a corollary, any $n$-circuit bounding an $(n + 1)$-cell is orientable.

This completes the proof that the two theorems (1) and (2) of § 1 are true for $C_n$ if they are true for all $C_i$ $(i < n)$ and thus establishes the cycle of theorems and definitions in § 1 for all values of $n$.

## Matrices of Orientation

5. Each column of the matrix $H_k$ $(k = 1, 2, \cdots, n)$ for $C_n$ is the symbol in the sense of § 2 for a $(k - 1)$-circuit bounding a $k$-cell. This $(k - 1)$-circuit is orientable because the set of points on it is a $(k - 1)$-dimensional sphere. Hence by changing some of the 1's in the symbol $(x_1, x_2, \cdots, x_{\alpha_k})$ for the $k$-circuit into $- 1$'s this symbol is converted into the symbol in the sense of § 2 for one of the two oriented $(k - 1)$-circuits which can be formed from the $k$-dimensional circuit. Hence by changing some of the 1's of $H_k$ into $- 1$'s $H_k$ can be converted into a matrix,

$$E_k = ||\epsilon_{ij}^k|| \quad (i = 1, 2, \cdots, \alpha_k; j = 1, 2, \cdots, \alpha_{k-1})$$

the $j$th column of which represents the $(k - 1)$-circuit which is associated with $a_j^k$ to form the oriented $i$-cell $\sigma_j^k$.

The oriented $(k - 1)$-cells which enter into this $(k - 1)$-circuit are said to be *positively related* to $\sigma_j^k$ and *negatively related* to $- \sigma_j^k$, while their negatives are said to be *negatively related* to $\sigma_j^k$ and *positively related* to $- \sigma_j^k$. Hence the matrix $E_k$ is such that $\epsilon_{ij}^k = 1$ if $\sigma_i^{k-1}$ is positively related to $\sigma_j^k$, $\epsilon_{ij}^k = - 1$ if $\sigma_i^{k-1}$ is negatively related to $\sigma_j^k$ and $\epsilon_{ij}^k = 0$ if $\sigma_i^{k-1}$ is neither positively nor negatively related to $\sigma_j^k$. If the notation is changed so as to interchange the meanings of $\sigma_j^k$ and $- \sigma_j^k$, the elements of the $j$th column of $E_k$ and of the $j$th row of $E_{k+1}$ must be multiplied by $- 1$.

6. In case $C_n$ is an $n$-circuit the rank of $E_n$ determines whether $C_n$ is orientable or not. For if $C_n$ is orientable each orientable $(n - 1)$-cell is positively and negatively related to equal numbers of orientable $n$-cells and hence each column of $E_n$ contains equal numbers of $+ 1$'s and $- 1$'s. Hence the rank of $E_n$ is at most $\alpha_n - 1$. It cannot be less than $\alpha_n - 1$ because then the rank of $H_n$ would be less than $\alpha_n - 1$ (Cf. § 55, Chap. II).

On the other hand if the rank of $E_n$ is $\alpha_n - 1$ there must be a linear relation among its rows, and by the reasoning used in § 56, Chap. II it follows that the rows can be multiplied by + 1 and − 1 in such a way as to reduce $E_n$ to a form in which there are equal numbers of + 1's and − 1's in each column. Hence $C_n$ is orientable if the rank of $E_n$ is $\alpha_n - 1$. Thus *$C_n$ is orientable if the rank of $E_n$ is $\alpha_n - 1$ and it is not orientable if the rank of $E_n$ is $\alpha_n$.*

7. In consequence of the theorem (1) of § 1, if one complex defining a manifold $M_n$ is orientable so are all complexes defining $M_n$. It is therefore justifiable to call a manifold orientable or one-sided according as a particular complex into which it can be decomposed is orientable or not. Hence the criterion given in the last section will determine by a finite number of steps whether a manifold is orientable or not.

Thus for example, it is quite easy to write down a set of matrices defining a real projective space of $n$ dimensions and prove the theorem that a real projective space is orientable if $n$ is odd and not orientable if $n$ is even. A proof of this theorem which makes use of combinatorial ideas but not of the matrix notation is given by Dénes König in the Proceedings of the International Congress of Mathematicians at Cambridge in 1912, Vol. 2, p. 129.

## Covering Oriented Complexes

8. As in § 9, Chap. I and § 33, Chap. II, a generalized complex $C_n'$ which is on a complex $C_n$ is said to *cover* $C_n$ if there is at least one point of $C_n'$ on each point of $C_n$ and there exists for every point of $C_n'$ a neighborhood (§ 24, Chap. III) which is a non-singular complex on $C_n$. In case the number of points of $C_n'$ which coincide with a given point of $C_n$ is finite and equal to $m$ for every point of $C_n$, $C_n'$ is said to *cover* $C_n$ *m times.*

In order to extend the notion of covering to oriented complexes we find it necessary to introduce the conception of cells coinciding both as sets of points and in orientation. Let $C_k$ be a complex on $C_n$ and such that each cell of $C_k$ covers a cell of $C_n$ just once. If the cells of both complexes are oriented, an oriented cell $\bar{\sigma}_p^i$ of $C_k$ will be said to *coincide* with an oriented cell $\sigma_q^i$ of $C_n$ if and only if (1) $\bar{\sigma}_p^i$ is formed from an $i$-cell $\bar{a}_p^i$ which covers $a_q^i$ and (2) the oriented $(i-1)$-cells formed from $(i-1)$-cells of $C_k$ and positively related to $\bar{\sigma}_p^i$ coincide with oriented $(i-1)$-cells formed from $(i-1)$-cells of $C_n$ and positively related to $\sigma_q^i$. This definition must be taken in the inductive sense. That is, since the meaning of "coincide" as applied to oriented 1-cells has already been established (§ 43, Chap. 1), this statement when read with $i = 2$ defines it for oriented 2-cells, and so on.

9. The symbol $(x_1, x_2, \cdots, x_{\alpha_k})$ in which the $x$'s are positive or negative integers will be used to denote a set of oriented $k$-cells in which there are $|x_i|$ $(i = 1, 2, \cdots, \alpha_k)$ oriented $k$-cells coincident with $\sigma_i^k$ if $x_i$ is positive or zero, and with $-\sigma_i^k$ if $x_i$ is negative or zero.

If two oriented complexes $C_k$ and $C_k'$ are formed from complexes whose cells have no common points unless they coincide, the two complexes can be regarded as on a third complex, and the two oriented complexes may be denoted by $(x_1, x_2, \cdots, x_{\alpha_k})$ and $(y_1, y_2, \cdots, y_{\alpha_k})$ respectively, the $x$'s and $y$'s being positive or negative integers or zero. An oriented complex which can be denoted by $(x_1 + y_1, x_2 + y_2, \cdots, x_{\alpha_k} + y_{\alpha_k})$ is called the *sum* of $C_k$ and $C_k'$ and is denoted by $C_k + C_k'$.

In case the numbers $x_1, x_2, \cdots, x_{\alpha_k}$ have a common factor, so that

$$(x_1, x_2, \cdots, x_{\alpha_k}) = (pz_1, pz_2, \cdots, pz_{\alpha_k}),$$

the oriented complex $(z_1, z_2, \cdots, z_{\alpha_k})$ is said to be *covered p times* by $(x_1, x_2, \cdots, x_{\alpha_k})$. It is evident that $(x_1, x_2, \cdots, x_{\alpha_k})$ can be formed by orienting the cells of a complex covering (in the sense of § 8) a complex which can be oriented so as to give $(z_1, z_2, \cdots, z_{\alpha_k})$.

## Boundary of an Oriented Complex

10. By the *boundary* of an oriented $i$-cell $\sigma_p^i$ is meant the set of all oriented $(i-1)$-cells $\sigma_q^{i-1}$ positively related to $\sigma_p^i$. Hence the $p$th column of the matrix $E_i$ is the symbol $(y_1, y_2, \cdots, y_{\alpha_{i-1}})$

for the boundary of $\sigma_p{}^i$. The symbol for $\sigma_p{}^i$ itself is $(x_1, x_2, \cdots, x_{\alpha_i})$ provided that $x_p = 1$ and $x_j = 0$ if $j \neq p$. Hence if

$$\text{(1)} \qquad \mathrm{E}_i \cdot \left\| \begin{matrix} x_1 \\ x_2 \\ \cdot \\ \cdot \\ \cdot \\ x_{\alpha_i} \end{matrix} \right\| = \left\| \begin{matrix} y_1 \\ y_2 \\ \cdot \\ \cdot \\ \cdot \\ y_{\alpha_{i-1}} \end{matrix} \right\| ,$$

where $(x_1, x_2, \cdots, x_{\alpha_i})$ is the symbol for $\sigma_p{}^i$, then $(y_1, y_2, \cdots, y_{\alpha_{i-1}})$ is the symbol for the boundary of $\sigma_p{}^i$.

By the *boundary* of any oriented $i$-dimensional complex we mean the sum of the boundaries of the oriented $i$-cells which compose it. Hence, from the identity,

$$\text{(2)} \qquad \mathrm{E}_i \cdot \left\| \begin{matrix} x_1 + x_1' \\ x_2 + x_2' \\ \cdot \\ \cdot \\ \cdot \\ x_{\alpha_i} + x_{\alpha_i} \end{matrix} \right\| = \mathrm{E}_i \cdot \left\| \begin{matrix} x_1 \\ x_2 \\ \cdot \\ \cdot \\ \cdot \\ x_{\alpha_i} \end{matrix} \right\| + \mathrm{E}_i \cdot \left\| \begin{matrix} x_1' \\ x_2' \\ \cdot \\ \cdot \\ \cdot \\ x_{\alpha_i}' \end{matrix} \right\|$$

it follows that if in the equation (1) $(x_1, x_2, \cdots, x_{\alpha_i})$ represents any $i$-dimensional complex, $(y_1, y_2, \cdots, y_{\alpha_{i-1}})$ represents its boundary.

11. In case the numbers $y_1, y_2, \cdots, y_{\alpha_{i-1}}$, in Equation (1) have a common factor, so that

$$(y_1, y_2, \cdots, y_{\alpha_{i-1}}) = (kz_1, kz_2, \cdots, kz_{\alpha_{i-1}}),$$

the equation (1) signifies that the boundary of $(x_1, x_2, \cdots, x_{\alpha_1})$ is an oriented complex which covers the oriented complex denoted by $(z_1, z_2, \cdots, z_{\alpha_{i-1}})$ $k$ times. An example of what this signifies geometrically may be constructed as follows:

Let $S$ be the interior of a circle $c$ in a Euclidean plane. Let $F_n$ be a correspondence in which each point of $c$ corresponds to the point obtained by rotating it about the center of $c$ in a fixed sense through an angle of $2\pi/n$. The points of $c$ are thereby arranged in sets of $n$ such that each point of a set is carried by $F_n$ into another point of the same set. All points in a set will be said to be "congruent." Let $S_n$ be the set of objects consisting of the points of $S$ and the sets of $n$ points determined by $F_n$, each set of $n$ congruent points being regarded as one object.

The set of points $S_n$ can be decomposed into a complex $C_2$ by the straight 1-cells joining the center of $c$ to the $2n$ points of $c$ in two of the sets of $n$ congruent points. It is thus easily verified that the 2-cells of $C_2$ may be so oriented that their boundary is an oriented 1-circuit of $2n$ oriented 1-cells which covers an oriented circuit composed of two oriented 1-cells $n$ times.

In case $n = 2$, the sets of $n$ points are the diametrically opposite pairs of points of $c$, and $S_n$ is homeomorphic with the projective plane.

## Oriented k–circuits

12. An oriented $k$-circuit (§ 2) has no boundary. Hence the symbol $(x_1, x_2, \cdots, x_{\alpha_k})$ for any oriented $k$-circuit satisfies the set of linear equations

$$(\mathrm{E}_k) \qquad \sum_{j=1}^{\alpha_k} \epsilon_{ij}{}^k x_j = 0 \quad (i = 1, 2, \cdots, \alpha_{k-1})$$

which are equivalent to the matrix equation

$$(3) \qquad \mathrm{E}_k \cdot \left\| \begin{matrix} x_1 \\ x_2 \\ \cdot \\ \cdot \\ \cdot \\ x_{\alpha_k} \end{matrix} \right\| = 0.$$

Conversely, it is easily seen, that any solution of these equations in integers represents a set of oriented $k$-circuits of $C_n$.

13. Since each column of $\mathrm{E}_{k+1}$ is the symbol $(x_1, x_2, \cdots, x_{\alpha_k})$ for an oriented $k$-circuit, it satisfies the condition (3). Hence

$$(4) \qquad \mathrm{E}_k \cdot \mathrm{E}_{k+1} = 0 \quad (k = 0, 1, \cdots, n-1).$$

Let us notice that the process by which the matrices $\mathrm{E}_k$ were defined in § 5 amounts merely to introducing minus signs in the matrices $\mathrm{H}_k$ in such a way that the equations (4) should be satisfied.

## Normal Form of $E_k$

14. Let the rank of $E_k$ $(k = 0, 1, \cdots, n)$ be denoted by $r_k$. By the theory of matrices whose elements are integers (cf. § 49, Chap. 1) there exist square matrices $C_{k-1}$ and $D_k$ with integer elements and determinants $\pm 1$, of $\alpha_{k-1}$ and $\alpha_k$ rows respectively, such that

$$C_{k-1}^{-1} \cdot E_k \cdot D_k = E_k^* \tag{5}$$

where $E_k^*$ is a matrix of $\alpha_{k-1}$ rows and $\alpha_k$ columns all the elements of which are zero except the first $r_k$ elements of the main diagonal, which are the invariant factors of $E_k$. We shall denote the elements of the main diagonal of $E_k^*$ by $d_j^k$. and understand that $d_j^k = 0$ if $j > r_k$.

Equation (5) is equivalent to

$$E_k \cdot D_k = C_{k-1} \cdot E_k^*, \tag{6}$$

and (6) may be regarded as a set of $\alpha_k$ equations of the form,

$$E_k \cdot \left\| \begin{matrix} x_{1j} \\ x_{2j} \\ \cdot \\ \cdot \\ \cdot \\ x_{\alpha_k j} \end{matrix} \right\| = \left\| \begin{matrix} d_j^k \, y_{1j} \\ d_j^k \, y_{2j} \\ \cdot \\ \cdot \\ \cdot \\ d_j^k \, y_{\alpha_{k-1} j} \end{matrix} \right\|, \tag{7}$$

in which $x_{1j}, x_{2j}, \cdots, x_{\alpha_k j}$ are the elements of the $j$th column of $D_k$ and $y_{1j}, y_{2j}, \cdots, y_{\alpha_{k-1} j}$ those of the $j$th column of $C_{k-1}$. By § 11, this means that the $j$th column of $D_k$ represents an oriented complex the boundary of which covers the oriented complex represented by the $j$th column of $C_{k-1}$ a number of times equal to the $j$th element of the main diagonal of $E_k^*$.

15. Since the last $\alpha_k - r_k$ columns of $E_k^*$ are composed entirely of zeros, the last $\alpha_k - r_k$ columns of $D_k$ represent a complete set of $k$-circuits or sets of $k$-circuits. As in § 12, Chap. III, these columns may be modified without affecting the equations (6) so that each column represents a single $k$-circuit. Let this be done for all values of $k$, $k = 0, 1, 2, \cdots, n$.

Next we observe that in

$$E_{k+1} \cdot D_{k+1} = C_k \cdot E_{k+1}^*$$

each of the first $r_{k+1}$ columns of $C_k$, say the $j$th column, represents an oriented $k$-circuit or set of oriented $k$-circuits covered a certain number, $d_j^{k+1}$, of times by the boundary of the oriented complex represented by the $j$th column of $D_{k+1}$. Each such column of $C_k$ is linearly expressible with coefficients which are relatively prime in terms of the last $\alpha_k - r_k$ columns of $D_k$. Hence $D_k$ may be further modified so that its last $r_{k+1}$ columns are identical with the first $r_{k+1}$ columns of $C_k$. The remaining $\alpha_k - r_k - r_{k+1}$ of the last $\alpha_k - r_k$ columns of $D_k$ then represent a set of oriented $k$-circuits which it is necessary to add to those linearly expressible in terms of the bounding oriented $k$-circuits to obtain a complete set.

16. Thus we have determined $D_k$ in such a way that: (1) each of its first $r_k$ columns represents an oriented $k$-dimensional complex having a boundary which covers a set of oriented $(k - 1)$-circuits a certain number $d_i^k$, of times; (2) each of the next $\alpha_k - r_k - r_{k+1}$ columns represents a single oriented $k$-circuit which is not linearly dependent on bounding $k$-circuits; (3) each of the last $r_{k+1}$ columns represents a set of oriented $k$-circuits covered a certain number, $d_i^{k+1}$, of times by the boundary of an oriented $(k + 1)$-dimensional complex.

Since all but the first $r_{k+1}$ columns of $E_{k+1}^*$ consist of zeros the last $\alpha_k - r_{k+1}$ columns of $C_k$ are arbitrary, subject to the condition that the determinant of $C_k$ is to be $\pm 1$. We arrange that these columns of $C_k$ shall be identical with the first $\alpha_k - r_{k+1}$ columns of $D_k$. Thus $C_k$ is obtainable from $D_k$ by interchanging the blocks of columns (1) and (3).

## The Betti Numbers

17. The last $\alpha_k - r_k$ columns of $D_k$ are a complete set of solutions of the equations $(E_k)$ of § 12, in integers. For since the last $\alpha_k - r_k$ columns of $E_k^*$ consist entirely of zeros, the last $\alpha_k - r_k$ columns of $D_k$ are solutions of $(E_k)$; and since the

determinant of $D_k$ is $\pm 1$ they are linearly independent, and the numbers in any column are relatively prime.

On the other hand, every column of $E_{k+1}$ represents a solution of $(E_k)$ since it represents an oriented $k$-circuit bounding a $k$-cell. The number of these in a complete set is $r_{k+1}$. Hence $\alpha_k - r_k - r_{k+1}$ is the number of oriented $k$-circuits which must be added to those which bound $(k+1)$-cells in order to obtain a complete set of oriented $k$-circuits or sets of oriented $k$-circuits. Such a set of $\alpha_k - r_k - r_{k+1}$ oriented $k$-circuits is given explicitly by the second block of columns of $D_k$ described in § 16. It may be referred to as a *complete set of oriented k-circuits not linearly dependent on bounding k circuits.* The number of oriented $k$-circuits in such a set is denoted by $P_k - 1$ so that

$$P_k - 1 = \alpha_k - r_k - r_{k+1}. \tag{8}$$

The number $P_k$ is called by Poincaré the $k$th *Betti number.*

18. It was shown in §39, Chap. I, that

$$P_0 = \alpha_0 - r_1.$$

By the definition in the last section,

$$P_k - 1 = \alpha_k - r_k - r_{k+1}$$

if $0 < k < n$, and

$$P_n - 1 = \alpha_n - r_n.$$

Multiplying these equations alternately by $+1$ and $-1$ and adding, we obtain

$$P_0 + \sum_{k=1}^{n} (-1)^k (P_k - 1) = \sum_{k=0}^{n} (-1)^k \alpha_k \tag{9}$$

which may also be written

$$\sum_{k=0}^{n} (-1)^k \alpha_k = \tfrac{1}{2}(1 - (-1)^n) + \sum_{k=0}^{n} (-1)^k P_k \tag{10}$$

The expression on the left is the characteristic, and the formula is a generalization of Euler's formula. If $C_n$ is connected, $P_0 = 1$. If further, $C_n$ is an orientable $n$-circuit, there is one and but one solution of the equations $(E_n)$ and hence $P_n - 1 = 1$. In this case, therefore,

$$(11)\quad \sum_{k=0}^{n}(-1)^k\alpha_k = 1 + (-1)^n + \sum_{k=1}^{n-1}(-1)^k(P_k - 1),$$

$$= \tfrac{3}{2}(1 + (-1)^n) + \sum_{k=1}^{n-1}(-1)^k P_k.$$

Finally if $C_n$ is a one-sided $n$-circuit, there is no solution of the equations ($E_n$) and hence $P_n - 1 = 0$ and

$$(12)\qquad \sum_{k=0}^{n}(-1)^k\alpha_k = 1 + \sum_{k=1}^{n-1}(-1)^k(P_k - 1)$$

$$= \tfrac{1}{2}(3 + (-1)^n) + \sum_{k=1}^{n-1}(-1)^k P_k.$$

19. Using the fact (§ 30, Chap. III) that the characteristic is zero if $n$ is odd the equation (11) reduces to

$$(13)\qquad P_1 - P_2 + \cdots - P_{n-1} = 0 \quad (n = 2m + 1)$$

if $C_n$ is an orientable $n$-circuit and (12) reduces to

$$(14)\qquad P_1 - P_2 + \cdots - P_{n-1} = 1 \quad (n = 2m + 1)$$

if $C_n$ is a non-orientable $n$-circuit.

In the three-dimensional case (13) and (14) have the corollary that $P_1 = P_2$ for an orientable 3-circuit and $P_1 = P_2 + 1$ for a non-orientable 3-circuit. The first of these formulas is a special case of the duality formula obtained in § 40, below.

### The Coefficients of Torsion

20. The numbers $d_1^k, d_2^k, \cdots, d_{r_k}^k$ defined in § 14 are such that the boundary of the complex represented by the $i$th column $(i = 1, 2, \cdots, r_k)$ of $D_k$ covers the $(k - 1)$-circuit represented by the $i$th column of $C_{k-1}$ $d_i^k$ times.

Let us denote the absolute values of those of the numbers $d_1^k, d_2^k, \cdots, d_{r_k}^k$ which are not equal to $\pm 1$ by

$$t_1^{k-1}, t_2^{k-1}, \cdots, t_{\tau_{k-1}}^{k-1}$$

the $t$'s being arranged in such an order that each of them is the highest common factor of itself and all the $t$'s which follow it.

The numbers $t_1^{k-1}, t_2^{k-1}, \cdots, t_{\tau_k-1}^{k-1}$ are known as the *coefficients of torsion of dimensionality* $k-1$.

Each coefficient of torsion of dimensionality $k$ is associated with a definite column of $C_k$ which represents a set of oriented $k$-circuits such that the boundary of a $(k+1)$-dimensional complex covers them a number of times equal to the coefficient of torsion. Moreover there is no $(k+1)$-dimensional complex composed of cells coincident with cells of the complex $C_n$ which can be converted into an oriented complex whose boundary coincides with the given set of oriented $k$-circuits a less number of times than the coefficient of torsion, because this would imply that the column of the matrix $C_k$ which corresponds to this coefficient of torsion would be linearly dependent on previous columns of $C_k$.

It will be proved (§ 38) that the coefficients of torsion are topological invariants, and also that in case $C_n$ defines an orientable manifold they satisfy a duality relation (§ 39).

21. It has been seen in § 48, Chap. I, that the invariant factors of the matrix $E_1$ are $\pm 1$. Hence *there are no zero-dimensional coefficients of torsion.*

The matrix $E_n$ in the case of an orientable manifold must have one $+1$ and one $-1$ in each column. But any such matrix can be regarded as the matrix $E_1$ of a linear graph (§§ 17 and 38, Chap. I) and therefore has no invariant factors* except $\pm 1$. Hence *an orientable manifold of n-dimensions has no* $(n-1)$-*dimensional coefficients of torsion.*

22. *The matrix* $E_n$ *for a one-sided manifold* $M_n$ *has one coefficient of torsion, and the value of this coefficient is* 2. To prove this let $\Gamma_n$ be any oriented $n$-dimensional complex formed by orienting the cells of a subdivision of $M_n$. Also let $D_n$ be a matrix whose first $\alpha_n - 1$ columns are the symbols $(x_1, x_2, \cdots, x_{\alpha_n})$ for $\alpha_n - 1$ of the oriented $n$-cells of $\Gamma_n$, and whose last column is composed entirely of 1's. The determinant of $D_n$ is obviously $\pm 1$.

The product $E_n \cdot D_n$ is a matrix whose first $\alpha_n - 1$ columns are

* This theorem is also proved algebraically in the Annals article referred to in § 49, Chap. 1.

symbols for the boundaries of the oriented $n$-cells of $\Gamma_n$ and whose last column is the sum of the columns of $E_n$. Since each column of $E_n$ contains either two $+1$'s, two $-1$'s or one $+1$ and one $-1$, the elements of the last column of $E_n \cdot D_n$ are either 0 or $\pm 2$. They cannot all be 0 because the rank of $E_n$ is $\alpha_n$. Hence

$$E_n \cdot D_n = C_{n-1}^{-1} \cdot E_n^*$$

where $C_{n-1}^{-1}$ is a square matrix of determinant unity and $E_n^*$ is a matrix all of whose elements are zero except those of the main diagonal. The elements of the main diagonal are all $\pm 1$ except the last which is $\pm 2$.

## Relation between the Betti Numbers and the Connectivities

23. The matrices $E_k$ reduce to the matrices $H_k$ if all elements are reduced modulo 2. Hence if $\delta_k$ denote the number of even $k$-dimensional coefficients of torsion, the ranks of $E_k$ and $H_k$ are connected by the relation

$$r_k - \rho_k = \delta_{k-1}.$$

Since

$$R_k - 1 = \alpha_k - \rho_k - \rho_{k+1}$$

and

$$P_k - 1 = \alpha_k - r_k - r_{k+1}$$

it follows that

$$R_k - P_k = \delta_{k-1} + \delta_k \tag{15}$$

which is the formula for the connectivities in terms of the Betti numbers and the coefficients of torsion.

24. In the Monatshefte für Math. und Physik, Vol. 19 (1908), p. 49, a set of numbers, $Q_k$ $(k = 0, 1, 2, \cdots, n)$, are defined by H. Tietze in terms which are very similar to our definition of the numbers $R_k$. But Tietze finds the formula (p. 56):

$$Q_k = P_k + \delta_{k-1}$$

which shows that the $Q_k$'s as he used them are distinct from the $R_k$'s.

## Congruences and Homologies

25. The results obtained from the reduction of the matrices $E_k$ to normal form will perhaps be clearer if they are restated in terms of another notation. Following Poincaré, we shall say that an oriented $n$-dimensional complex, $\Gamma_n$, is *congruent* to a set of oriented $(n-1)$-circuits, $\Gamma_{n-1}$, if $\Gamma_{n-1}$ is the boundary of $\Gamma_n$, and shall denote this relation by the symbols

(1) $$\Gamma_n \equiv \Gamma_{n-1}.$$

In case $\Gamma_n$ has no boundary (i.e., is a set of $n$-circuits) $\Gamma_n$ is said to be congruent to zero, and this is indicated by

(2) $$\Gamma_n \equiv 0.$$

The expressions (1) and (2) are called *congruences* and (2) is regarded as a special case of (1).

From § 10 it is evident that the sum of the left hand members of the two congruences is congruent to the sum of the right hand members. Moreover if both members of a congruence are multiplied by an integer, $m$, the resulting congruence,

(3) $$m\Gamma_n \equiv m\Gamma_{n-1}$$

has a meaning and is a consequence of (1) if we understand that $m\Gamma_n$ is an oriented complex which covers $\Gamma_n$ $m$ times. If we understand that $-\Gamma_n$ stands for the oriented complex obtained from $\Gamma_n$ by reversing the orientation of each of its cells, this statement can be extended to cover the cases in which $m$ is negative. Hence *any congruence derived from a set of valid congruences of the same dimensionality by forming a linear homogeneous combination of them with integral coefficients is a valid congruence.*

26. Whenever the congruence

(4) $$\Gamma_k \equiv \Gamma_{k-1}$$

is satisfied by an oriented complex $\Gamma_k$ on $C_n$, $\Gamma_{k-1}$ is said to be *homologous to zero,*

(5) $$\Gamma_{k-1} \sim 0.$$

The relation

$$\Gamma_{n-1} - \Gamma_{n-1}' \sim 0$$

is also written

(6) $$\Gamma_{n-1} \sim \Gamma_{n-1}'$$

and expressed in words by saying that $\Gamma_{n-1}$ is homologous to $\Gamma_{n-1}'$. Since a homology can always be reduced to a congruence it follows that homologies can be combined linearly according to the rules that hold for the linear combination of congruences. Since the boundary of an oriented $k$-dimensional complex is a set of oriented $k$-circuits, the homology (5) implies the congruence

(7) $$\Gamma_{k-1} \equiv 0.$$

It should be noted that these definitions do not permit the operation of dividing the terms of a homology by an integer which is a common factor of the coefficients. In other words,

(8) $$p\Gamma_{k-1} \sim 0$$

does not necessarily imply (7). Thus we are dealing with what Poincaré calls "homologies without division."

### The Fundamental Congruences and Homologies

27. The relations between the $k$-cells and the $(k-1)$-cells given by the matrix $E_k$ are equivalent to the system of congruences

$[E_k']$ $$\sigma_j^k \equiv \sum_{i=1}^{\alpha_{k-1}} \epsilon_{ij}^k \sigma_i^{k-1} \qquad (j = 1, 2, \cdots, \alpha_k)$$

The matrix of this system of congruences is obtained from $E_k$ by interchanging rows and columns. The symbol $(x_1, x_2, \cdots, x_{\alpha_k})$ was used in § 9 to denote an oriented $k$-dimensional complex

$$x_1\sigma_1^k + x_2\sigma_2^k + \cdots + x_{\alpha_k}\sigma_{\alpha_k}^k$$

Hence any matrix equation,

(9) $$E_k \cdot \left\| \begin{matrix} x_1 \\ x_2 \\ \cdot \\ \cdot \\ \cdot \\ x_{\alpha_k} \end{matrix} \right\| = p \left\| \begin{matrix} y_1 \\ y_2 \\ \cdot \\ \cdot \\ \cdot \\ y_{\alpha_{k-1}} \end{matrix} \right\|$$

is equivalent to the congruence

$$(10)\quad x_1\sigma_1{}^k + x_2\sigma_2{}^k + \cdots + x_{\alpha_k}\sigma_{\alpha_k}{}^k \equiv p(y_1\sigma_1{}^{k-1} + y_2\sigma_2{}^{k-1} + \cdots + y_{\alpha_{k-1}}\sigma_{\alpha_{k-1}}{}^{k-1}).$$

28. The fundamental congruences $[\mathrm{E}_k']$ give rise to the fundamental homologies

$$\{\mathrm{E}_k'\} \qquad \sum_{i=1}^{\alpha_{k-1}} \epsilon_{ij}{}^k \sigma_i{}^{k-1} \sim 0 \qquad (j = 1, 2, \cdots, \alpha_k)$$

and the matrix equation (9) corresponds to the homology

$$(11)\qquad p(y_1\sigma_1{}^{k-1} + y_2\sigma_2{}^{k-1} + \cdots + y_{\alpha_{k-1}}\sigma_{\alpha_{k-1}}{}^{k-1}) \sim 0.$$

29. The reduction of $\mathrm{E}_k$ to normal form, as interpreted in §§ 15 and 16, gives rise to the following congruences and homologies:

$$(K_1)\quad \Gamma_k{}^i \equiv \Gamma_{k-1}{}^i \qquad (i = 1, 2, \cdots, r_k - \tau_{k-1}),$$
$$(K_2)\quad \Gamma_k{}^i \equiv t^{k-1}_{i-r_k+\tau_{k-1}}\Gamma_{k-1}{}^i \qquad (i = r_k - \tau_{k-1}+1, \cdots, r_k),$$
$$(K_3)\quad \Gamma_k{}^i \equiv 0 \qquad (i = r_k + 1, \cdots, r_k + P_k - 1),$$
$$(K_4)\quad \Gamma_k{}^i \sim 0 \qquad (i = \alpha_k - r_{k+1} + 1, \cdots, \alpha_k - \tau_k),$$
$$(K_5)\quad t^k_{i-\alpha_k+\tau_k}\Gamma_k{}^i \sim 0 \qquad (i = \alpha_k - \tau^k + 1, \cdots, \alpha_k)$$

in which $\Gamma_k{}^i$ is the oriented $k$-dimensional complex represented by the $i$th column of $D_k$, $\Gamma_{k-1}{}^i$ the oriented $(k-1)$-circuit represented by the $i$th column of $C_{k-1}$.

The congruences $(K_1)$ correspond to the columns of $D_k$ in the class (1) of § 16 for which the corresponding values of $d_i{}^k$ are $\pm 1$.

The congruences $(K_2)$ correspond to the columns of $D_k$ in the first block for which the values of $d_i{}^k$ are different from $\pm 1$. Thus $t_i{}^{k-1}$ is the $i$th $(k-1)$-dimensional coefficient of torsion.

The congruences $(K_3)$ correspond to the second block of columns of $D_k$ enumerated in § 16. The oriented $k$-circuits $\Gamma_k{}^i$ $(i = r_k + 1, \cdots, r_k + P_k - 1)$ constitute a *complete set of non-bounding k-circuits.* They have the property that no linear combination of them coincides with the boundary of any oriented $(k-1)$-dimensional complex composed of oriented cells of $C_n$.

The oriented $k$-circuits in the homologies $(K_4)$ correspond to those of the last $r_{k+1}$ columns of $D_k$ which are identical with the first $r_{k+1} - \tau_k$ columns of $C_k$. They therefore appear in the right-hand members of the congruences analogous to $(K_1)$ which are determined by the matrix $E_{k+1}$.

The oriented $k$-circuits in the homologies $(K_5)$ correspond to the last $\tau_k$ columns of $D_k$ and also to the set of columns of $C_k$ which correspond to the coefficients of torsion $t_i^k$ and thus appear in the right-hand members of the congruences analogous to $(K_2)$ which are determined by the matrix $E_{k+1}$.

30. All symbols $(x_1, x_2, \cdots, x_{\alpha_k})$ in which the $x$'s are integers are linearly dependent on $\alpha_k$ such symbols. Since the determinant of $D_k$ is unity its columns are a set of linearly independent symbols $(x_1, x_2, \cdots, x_{\alpha_k})$ the $x$'s of no one of which have a common factor different from unity. Hence all symbols $(x_1, x_2, \cdots, x_{\alpha_k})$ are linearly expressible with integral coefficients in terms of the columns of $D_k$. Of these, the ones which represent sets of oriented $k$-circuits are expressible (§ 16) with integral coefficients in terms of the last $\alpha_k - r_k$ columns of $D_k$. Hence if $\Gamma_k$ is any oriented $k$-circuit composed of oriented $k$-cells of $C_n$ it satisfies a homology,

$$\Gamma_k \sim \sum_{i=1}^{\alpha_k - r_k} a_i \Gamma_k^{r_k+i}, \tag{1}$$

in which the coefficients $a_i$ are integers and the $\Gamma_k^{r_k+1}$'s are the oriented $k$-circuits which appear in the congruences and homologies $(K_3)$, $(K_4)$, $(K_5)$. But by means of the homologies $(K_4)$ and $(K_5)$ this reduces to

$$\Gamma_k \sim \sum_{i=1}^{P_k-1} a_i \Gamma_k^{r_k+i} + \sum_{i=1}^{\tau_k} b_i \Gamma_k^{\alpha_k - \tau_k + i} \tag{2}$$

in which the $a_i$'s are integers and each $b_i$ is an integer whose absolute value is less than the coefficient of torsion, $t_i^k$.

With a slight change of notation this result may be stated as follows: *There exists a set of* $P_k - 1$ *k-circuits* $\Gamma_k^1, \Gamma_k^2, \cdots, \Gamma_k^{P_k+1}$ *and a set of* $\tau_k$ *sets of k-circuits,* $\Gamma_k^{P_k}, \Gamma_k^{P_k+1}, \cdots, \Gamma_k^{P_k+\tau_k-1}$ *such that if* $\Gamma_k$ *is any oriented k-circuit composed of oriented k-cells of* $C_n$ *it satisfies a homology,*

$$\Gamma_k \sim \sum_{i=1}^{P_k-1} a_i \Gamma_k^i + \sum_{i=1}^{\tau_k} b_i \Gamma^{P_k-1+i} \tag{3}$$

*in which the $a_i$'s and $b_i$'s are integers and each $b_i$ is less in absolute value than the coefficient of torsion $t_i^k$. The k-circuits $\Gamma_k^1, \Gamma_k^2, \cdots, \Gamma_k^{P_k+\tau_k-1}$ satisfy the $\tau_k$ homologies*

$$(4) \qquad t_i^k \Gamma_k^{P_k-1+i} \sim 0 \qquad (i = 1, 2, \cdots, \tau_k).$$

### Bounding k-circuits

31. The results which have just been derived from the matrices apply only to complexes composed of cells of $C_n$. But they can be proved to be valid for all complexes on $C_n$ by an argument which is closely analogous to that used in Chap. III for the modulo 2 case. This argument centers about the following problem: *Given a set of oriented i-circuits $\Gamma_i$ on $C_n$, does there exist on $C_n$ an oriented $(i+1)$-dimensional complex of which $\Gamma_i$ is the boundary?* It is of course understood that $\Gamma_i$ may have any singularities compatible with its being on $C_n$.

32. This problem is solved by the means employed for the corresponding problem in Chap. III for complexes without orientation. The oriented $i$-circuits $\Gamma_i$ are obtained by properly orienting the cells of a set of $i$-circuits $K_i$ on $C_n$. For the $i$-circuits $K_i$ we make the regular subdivisions and define the correspondence $A$ and the complex $B_{i+1}$ as in §§ 36, 37, Chap. III. The complex $\overline{K}_i$ which is obtained from $K_i$ by regular subdivisions may by § 3 be converted into a set of orientable $i$-circuits $\overline{\Gamma}_i$.

The complex $B_{i+1}$ has one and only one $(i+1)$-cell $b_j^{i+1}$ incident with each $i$-cell of $\overline{K}_i$ and the $(i+1)$-cells and $i$-cells of $B_{i+1}$ are subject to the same incidence relations as the $i$-cells and $(i-1)$-cells of $\overline{K}_i$. Hence if $B_{i+1}$ is converted into an oriented complex $\Gamma_{i+1}$ by orienting each $(i+1)$-cell of $B_{i+1}$ so as to be positively related to one and only one $i$-cell of $\overline{\Gamma}_i$, each of the $i$-cells $b_j^i$ of $B_{i+1}$ will be so oriented as to be positively and negatively related to equal numbers of oriented $(i+1)$-cells of $\Gamma_{i+1}$. Hence none of the oriented $i$-cells formed from $b_j^i$ will appear in the boundary of $\Gamma_{i+1}$. This boundary is the sum of the boundaries of the oriented $(i+1)$-cells of $\Gamma_{i+1}$ and therefore consists either of $\overline{\Gamma}_i$ alone or of $\overline{\Gamma}_i$ and an oriented $i$-dimensional complex, which we shall call $\Gamma_i'$, each oriented cell of which coincides with a cell of $\overline{C}_n$. Thus

$$(1) \qquad \Gamma_{i+1} \equiv \overline{\Gamma}_i + \Gamma_i'$$

and hence

$$(2) \qquad \overline{\Gamma}_i \sim \Gamma_i'$$

where $\Gamma_i'$ is either 0 or such that each of its cells coincides with a cell of $\overline{C}_n$.

Now $\overline{\Gamma}_i$ is formed by orienting a regular subdivision of the complex $K_i$ from which $\Gamma_i$ is obtained by a process of orientation. It is therefore obvious that

$$(3) \qquad \Gamma_i \sim \overline{\Gamma}_i$$

and hence that

$$(4) \qquad \Gamma_i \sim \Gamma_i'.$$

33. From the homology (4), in case $\Gamma_i^1$ is not zero, it follows that if $m$ is an integer different from zero

$$(5) \qquad m\Gamma_i \sim 0$$

if and only if

$$(6) \qquad m\Gamma_i' \sim 0.$$

The homology (6) means that there is an oriented complex $\Lambda_{i+1}$ on $C_n$ whose boundary, $\Lambda_i$, covers $\Gamma_i'$ $m$ times. We shall now prove that if this is the case there is an oriented complex $\Gamma_{i+1}$, *composed of oriented cells which coincide with cells of* $C_n$, such that its boundary covers $\Gamma_i'$ $m$ times. To begin with we have

$$(7) \qquad \Lambda_{i+1} \equiv m\Gamma_i'.$$

Let $K_{i+1}$ be the complex from which $\Lambda_{i+1}$ is obtained by orienting its cells, and let $B_{i+2}$ be constructed as in § 37, Chap. III, by joining each point of $K_{i+1}$ by a 1-cell to a point of $\overline{C}_n$.

If the $(i+2)$-cells of $B_{i+2}$ are oriented so that each shall be positively related to an $(i+1)$-cell of $\Lambda_{i+1}$, $B_{i+2}$ is converted into an oriented complex $\Gamma_{i+2}$. The boundary of this oriented complex consists of $\Lambda_{i+1}$, of the set of oriented $(i+1)$-cells* of $B_{i+2}$ which are positively related to the oriented $i$-cells of $\Gamma_i'$,

* These are analogous to the cells of the complex $G_{i+1}$ of § 40, Chap. III.

and of an oriented complex $\Gamma_{i+1}$ whose cells coincide with cells of the same dimensionality of $\overline{C}_n$. The complex $\Gamma_{i+1}$ must exist because the other two classes of oriented $(i+1)$-cells of the boundary of $\Gamma_{i+2}$ cannot constitute an oriented $(i+1)$-circuit. But by construction the boundary of $\Gamma_{i+1}$ covers $\Gamma_i'$ $m$ times,

$$\Gamma_{i+1} \equiv m\Gamma_i', \tag{8}$$

which proves the theorem.

34. We now have the solution of the problem of § 31. For a method has been given by which if $\Gamma_i$ is any set of oriented $i$-circuits on a complex $C_n$ and $\overline{C}_n$ is a regular subdivision of $C_n$, one can find an oriented $i$-circuit $\Gamma_i'$ whose oriented cells coincide with cells of the same dimensionality of $\overline{C}_n$, such that $\Gamma_i' \sim \Gamma_i$ and, moreover, we have proved that if $\Gamma_i'$ satisfies any homology $m\Gamma_i' \sim 0$ it satisfies a congruence $\Gamma_{i+1} \equiv m\Gamma_i'$ in which $\Gamma_{i+1}$ is an oriented complex composed of oriented cells which coincide with cells of $\overline{C}_n$. From this it follows that if the oriented $k$-circuits $\Gamma_k^1, \Gamma_k^2, \cdots, \Gamma_k^{P_k+\tau_k-1}$ are defined as in § 30 every oriented $k$-circuit $\Gamma_k$ satisfies a homology like (3) of § 30 and all homologies are linearly dependent on the homologies (4) of § 30.

## Invariance of the Coefficients of Torsion

35. Let us now suppose that

$$\Lambda_k^i \equiv 0 \qquad (i = 1, 2, \cdots, \mu), \tag{9}$$

is a finite set of $k$-dimensional congruences such that: (1) if

$$\Lambda_k \equiv 0$$

is any $k$-dimensional congruence, $\Lambda_k$ satisfies the homology

$$\Lambda_k \sim \sum_{i=1}^{\mu} \lambda_i \Lambda_k^i, \tag{10}$$

in which the coefficients $\lambda_i$ are integers; and (2) there is no homology

$$\sum_{i=1}^{\mu} \gamma_i \Lambda_k^i \sim 0,$$

in which the coefficients $\gamma_i$ are integers having no common factor different from unity. We shall prove (a) that $\mu = P_k - 1 + \tau_k$ and (b) that there are $\tau_k$ homologies of the form

$$(11) \qquad t_j^k\left(\sum_{i=1}^{\mu} \delta_{ij}\Lambda_k^i\right) \sim 0 \qquad (j = 1, 2, \cdots, \tau_k).$$

36. By §§ 30 and 34

$$(12) \qquad \Lambda_k^j \sim \sum_{p=1}^{P_k-1+\tau_k} \alpha^j{}_p \Gamma_k{}^p \qquad (j = 1, 2, \cdots, \mu).$$

The matrix of the coefficients $\alpha^j{}_p$ has $\mu$ rows and $P_k - 1 + \tau_k$ columns. If the rank of this matrix were less than $\mu$ there would be a linear relation among the rows of the form

$$\sum_{j=1}^{\mu} q_j \alpha^j{}_p = 0 \quad (p = 1, 2, \cdots, P_k - 1 + \tau_k),$$

in which the integers $q_j$ are relatively prime. From this and the homologies (12) we could infer

$$\sum_{j=1}^{\mu} q_j \Lambda^j{}_k \sim 0,$$

contrary to (2) in the definition of the $\Lambda^j{}_k$'s.

If the rank of the matrix of the coefficients $\alpha^j{}_i$ were less than $P_k - 1 + \tau_k$, we could find a set of integers

$$\alpha_1, \alpha_2, \cdots, \alpha_{P_k-1+\tau_k},$$

which is linearly independent of the rows of this matrix. Defining $\Lambda_k{}^{\mu+1}$ by the equation

$$\Lambda_k{}^{\mu+1} = \sum_{p=1}^{P_k-1+\tau_k} \alpha_p \Gamma_k{}^p$$

it would follow that $\Lambda_k^{\mu+1}$ is linearly independent of $\Lambda_k^1, \Lambda_k^2, \cdots, \Lambda_k^{\mu}$ contrary to (1) of the definition of the $\Lambda_k^j$'s. Hence the rank of the matrix is not less than $P_k - 1 + \tau_k$.

Hence the rank of the matrix is not less than the number of its rows nor than the number of its columns. This is possible only for a square matrix of determinant different from zero. Hence

$$\mu = P_k - 1 + \tau_k$$

and the determinant $|\alpha^j{}_i| \neq 0$.

9

37. By the definition of the $\Lambda_k^{j}$'s there exists a set of homologies

$$(13) \qquad \Gamma_k^{i} \sim \sum_{j=1}^{\mu} \beta^i{}_j \Lambda_k^{j} \qquad (i = 1, 2, \cdots, \mu).$$

If we substitute (12) in (13) we obtain

$$(14) \qquad \Gamma_k^{i} \sim \sum_{j=1}^{\mu} \sum_{p=1}^{\mu} \beta^1{}_j \alpha^j{}_p \Gamma_k^{p} \qquad (i - 1, 2, \cdots, \mu).$$

For $i = 1$ this gives the homology

$$(14_1) \quad (\sum_{j=1}^{\mu} \beta^1{}_j \alpha^j{}_1 - 1)\Gamma_k^{1} + (\sum_{j=1}^{\mu} \beta^1{}_j \alpha^j{}_2)\Gamma_k^{2} + \cdots + (\sum_{j=1}^{\mu} \beta^1{}_j \alpha^j{}_\mu)\Gamma_k^{\mu} \sim 0.$$

If this homology is multiplied by the last coefficient of torsion all the last $\tau_k$ terms drop out in virtue of the homologies (4) of § 30, since all the $k$-dimensional coefficients of torsion are factors of $t_{\tau_k}{}^k$. The remaining terms would give a homology connecting $\Gamma_k^1, \Gamma_k^2, \cdots, \Gamma_k{}^{P_k-1}$, contrary to §§ 30 and 34, unless the first $P_k - 1$ coefficients in $(14_1)$ were zero. Hence these coefficients are zero. If $(14_1)$ is multiplied by the coefficient of torsion $t_{\tau_k-1}{}^k$ all terms of $(14_1)$ drop out except the last. Hence the last coefficient of $(14_1)$ is zero. If $(14_1)$ is multiplied by $t_{\tau_k-2}{}^k$, all terms of $(14_1)$ except the next to the last drop out. Hence the next to the last coefficient of $(14_1)$ is zero. And by a similar argument all the rest of the coefficients of (14) are zero.

The same reasoning can be applied for all values of $i$ ($i = 1, 2, \cdots, \mu$) to show that the coefficient of every $\Gamma_k^p$ in (14) is zero. Hence

$$(15) \qquad \|\beta^i{}_j\| \cdot \|\alpha^j{}_p\| = I,$$

where $I$ is the identity matrix of $\mu$ rows and columns. Hence the determinant of $\|\alpha^j{}_p\|$ is unity and $\|\beta^i{}_j\|$ is the inverse of $\|\alpha^i{}_p\|$.

From this it follows in an obvious way that all homologies among the $\Lambda_k^{j}$'s are linearly dependent on the $t_k$ homologies,

$$(16) \qquad t_i^k(\sum_{j=1}^{\mu} \beta^{Pk-1+i}{}_j \Lambda_k^{j}) \sim 0 \qquad (i = 1, 2, \cdots, \tau_k),$$

which are obtained from (4) of § 30 by the transformation (13).

38. It has thus been proved that the coefficients of torsion $t_1^k, t_2^k, \cdots, t_{\tau_k}^k$ are uniquely determined and are the same for all sets of congruences

$$\Lambda_j^i \equiv 0$$

defined as in § 35. Since $P_k - 1 = \mu - \tau_k$ it follows that the Betti number $P_k$ is also the same for all these sets of congruences. But since congruences and homologies are obviously transformed into congruences and homologies by any homeomorphism, it follows that *the Betti numbers and the coefficients of torsion are Analysis Situs invariants.*

There is no difficulty in seeing that the Betti numbers and coefficients of torsion of $\overline{C}_n$ and of $C_n$ are the same. Hence these numbers are the same for all complexes into which $C_n$ can be decomposed.

### Duality of the Coefficients of Torsion

39. The duality relation,

$$R_{n-i} = R_i \qquad (i = 0, 1, \cdots, n-1)$$

was proved (§ 29, Chap. III) by showing that if $\mathrm{H}_k$ $(k = 1, \cdots, n)$ are the incidence matrices of $C_n$ and $\overline{\mathrm{H}}_k$ $(k = 1, 2, \cdots, n)$ those of a matrix $C_n'$ dual to $C_n$, then

$$\mathrm{H}_{n-i} = \mathrm{H}_{i+1}' \qquad (i = 0, 1, \cdots, n-i),$$

where $\mathrm{H}_{i+1}'$ is the matrix obtained by interchanging the rows and columns of $\mathrm{H}_{i+1}$.

Now if $C_n$ is an orientable manifold the matrices $\mathrm{E}_k$ $(k = 1, 2, \cdots, n)$ can be formed from $\mathrm{H}_k$ in such a way that the matrix $\mathrm{H}_n$ has one $+1$ and one $-1$ in each row. Moreover the equation

$$\mathrm{E}_k \cdot \mathrm{E}_{k+1} = 0$$

is equivalent to

$$\mathrm{E}_{k+1}' \cdot \mathrm{E}_k' = 0.$$

Hence if we introduce $-$ signs in the matrix $\overline{\mathrm{H}}_k$ to define $\overline{\mathrm{E}}_k$ so that

$$\overline{\mathrm{E}}_{n-i} = \mathrm{E}_{i+1}'$$

we have

$$\bar{E}_i \cdot \bar{E}_{i+1} = 0$$

and therefore the matrices $\bar{E}_1, \bar{E}_2, \cdots, \bar{E}_n$ satisfy the conditions required of the matrices of orientation of $C_n'$.

Since the invariant factors of $E_{k+1}'$ are the same as those of $E_{k+1}$ and $\bar{E}_{n-k} = E_{k+1}'$ it follows that the invariant factors of $\bar{E}_{n-k}$ and of $E_{k+1}$ are the same. Hence *the* $(n - k - 1)$*-dimensional coefficients of torsion of an oriented manifold are the same as the k-dimensional ones.* In other words

$$t_j^k = t_j^{n-k-1} \qquad (k = 1, 2, \cdots, n - 1;\ j = 1, 2, \cdots, \tau_k).$$

40. In view of the equation (§ 23),

$$R_k - P_k = \delta_{k-1} + \delta_k$$

and the equation $R_{n-k} = R_k$ it follows from this that the Betti numbers of an orientable manifold satisfy the condition

$$P_{n-k} = P_k.$$

It should be noted particularly that while the relation $R_{n-k} = R_k$ is satisfied by the connectivities of any manifold the relation $P_{n-k} = P_k$ is restricted to the orientable manifolds.

# CHAPTER V

## THE FUNDAMENTAL GROUP AND CERTAIN UNSOLVED PROBLEMS

### Homotopic and Isotopic Deformations

1. Let $K_i$ be a generalized complex on a generalized complex $C_n$. A set of transformations $F_x$ $(0 \leqq x \leqq 1)$ is called a *one-parameter continuous family of transformations* if each $F_x$ for each number $x$ $(0 \leqq x \leqq 1)$ is a transformation of $K_i$ and if for each point $P$ of $K_i$ the set of points $[F_x(P)]$ for which $0 < x < 1$, constitutes a 1-cell whose ends are $F_0(P)$ and $F_1(P)$. A (1–1)-continuous transformation $F$ of $K_i$ into a generalized complex $K'$ on $C$ is called a *deformation on* $C_n$ if there exists a continuous family of (1–1) continuous transformations $F_x$ $(0 \leqq x \leqq 1)$ such that $F_0$ is the identity, $F_1 = F$, and each $F_x$ transforms $K_i$ into a complex on $C_n$.

For example, $C_n$ may be taken to be a 2-cell and $K_i$ to be a single point. The points $F_x(P)$ then constitute a 1-cell with its ends, the 1-cell being singular or not according to the properties of $F_x$. As another example, $K_i$ may be taken to be a 1-cell with its ends, the complexes into which $K_i$ is deformed then are all 1-cells and constitute a 2-cell and its boundary.

Under the conditions described above, the complex $K_i$ is said to be *deformed* into the complex $K'$ and the complexes into which $K_i$ is transformed by the functions $F_x$ $(0 < x < 1)$ are called the *intermediate positions* of $K_i$.

It is an obvious consequence of the definitions made that if $F_1$ is a deformation on $C_n$ which carries $K_i$ to a generalized complex $K'$ on $C_n$ and $F_2$ a deformation on $C_n$ of $K'$ and if $F_3$ is the resultant of $F_1$ and $F_2$, then $F_3$ is a deformation on $C_n$.

2. Following the nomenclature introduced in the Dehn-Heegaard article on Analysis Situs in the Encyklopädie we shall distinguish between isotopic and homotopic deformations. A deformation is called an *isotopy* or an *isotopic deformation* if it is

the resultant of a finite number of deformations each of which satisfies the following conditions: (1) It is a deformation of a non-singular generalized complex $K_i$ ($i = 0, 1, \cdots, n$) through a set of intermediate positions which are non-singular and homeomorphic with $K_i$ into a non-singular generalized complex $K_i'$ which is homeomorphic with $K_i$; (2) Each $i$-cell $a^i$ of $K_i$ either coincides* with the corresponding cell of $K_i'$ and all its intermediate positions, or else the $(i + 1)$ cell composed of the intermediate positions of $a^i$ is non-singular. A non-singular generalized complex is said to be *isotopic* with any complex into which it can be carried by an isotopy.

The term *homotopy* will be used to designate a deformation in the general sense of § 1, and two generalized complexes $C'$ and $C''$ will be said to be *homotopic* if one can be carried into the other by means of a homotopy.

For example, consider two pairs of distinct points $A\ B$ and $C\ D$ of an open curve. It is always possible to find a one-parameter continuous family of transformations carrying $A$ and $B$ into $C$ and $D$ respectively, but it is not always possible to find one in which all intermediate positions of $A\ B$ are pairs of distinct points. In particular, it is not possible to interchange $A$ and $B$ by an isotopy.

## Isotopy and Order Relations

3. We shall now state without proof a series of theorems which establish the relation between the order relations and the isotopic deformations. Let us agree that if a deformation $F$ carries a 0-cell $a^0$ into a 0-cell $\bar{a}^0$ and if $\sigma^0$ and $\bar{\sigma}^0$ are the oriented 0-cells obtained by associating $a^0$ and $\bar{a}^0$ respectively with $+ 1$, then $\sigma^0$ is said to be carried by $F$ into $\bar{\sigma}^0$, and $- \sigma^0$ to be carried by $F$ into $- \bar{\sigma}^0$. This determines fully what is meant by the deformation of an oriented $n$-cell.

4. The following propositions hold for the non-singular 1-cells of either an open or a closed curve. Any two 1-cells are isotopic and any two oriented 1-cells are homotopic. But the oriented

* Note that this does not require individual points of $a^i$ to remain fixed.

1-cells fall into two classes such that two oriented 1-cells of the same class are isotopic, whereas two oriented 1-cells of different classes are not isotopic. Either of these classes may be called a *sense class,* or an *orientation* class or a *sense of description of the curve.* All oriented 1-cells of a sense-class are said to be *similarly sensed* or *oriented* and *to have the same sense.* All the oriented 1-cells of an oriented 1-circuit, as defined in § 35, Chap. I, are in the same sense-class. If two oriented 1-cells of a curve are both positively related to the same 0-cell, one of the 1-cells is contained in the other. If of two oriented 1-cells one is positively and the other negatively related to the same oriented 0-cell, either of the 1-cells can be deformed by an isotopy which leaves the 0-cell invariant so as to have no points in common with the other.

5. Any transformation of a closed curve into itself which transforms a sense-class into itself is said to preserve sense; otherwise it alters sense. A (1–1) continuous transformation which preserves sense is an isotopic deformation. The isotopic deformations of a curve into itself form a self-conjugate sub-group of index two of the group of homeomorphisms of the curve into itself. A (1–1) continuous transformation which alters sense has at least two invariant points.

6. At the beginning of Chap. IV, an oriented 2-cell of a complex $C_2$ was defined by associating a 2-cell with a particular oriented 1-circuit of its boundary, i.e., with a particular set of oriented 1-cells. This definition was sufficient for the combinatorial theory in which it was used but is manifestly not flexible enough to correspond fully to the intuitional idea of an element of surface with a sensed boundary. A definition which satisfies this requirement is the following:

An *oriented 2-cell* is a 2-cell associated with a sense-class of its boundary. If we recall that all the oriented 1-cells of an oriented 1-circuit belong to the same sense-class it is clear that the present definition can be substituted for the one used in Chap. IV without changing any of the theorems there obtained. From this point onward we shall use the term oriented 2-cell according to its new definition.

7. The fundamental theorems on deformation of oriented 2-cells are closely related to the theorem of § 60, Chap. II, on the invariance of orientableness. They may be stated, without proof, as follows: Any two oriented 2-cells on the same complex are homotopic. The non-singular oriented 2-cells on an orientable two-dimensional manifold fall into two classes called *sense-classes,* such that any two oriented 2-cells of the same sense-class are isotopic, and no two oriented 2-cells of different sense-classes are isotopic. Any oriented 2-cell and its negative belong to opposite sense-classes. Two isotopic oriented 2-cells are said to be *similarly oriented.* Two oriented 2-cells which have no point in common and are one positively and one negatively related to an oriented 1-cell are similarly oriented. Any two oriented 2-cells of a one-sided manifold are similarly oriented. Any one-sided manifold contains a Möbius strip.

The theorems in § 5 have been generalized to two dimensions by L. E. J. Brouwer, H. Tietze, and J. Nielsen, who have obtained a number of interesting theorems on the continuous transformations of two-dimensional manifolds and have also uncovered a number of interesting problems. The work of Brouwer and Nielsen can be found in recent volumes of the Mathematische Annalen, and further references to the literature can be found in an article on the subject of orientation by Tietze in the Jahresbericht der Deutschen Math. Ver., Vol. 29 (1920), p. 95.

8. It is obvious that the theorems in the first paragraph of § 7 form the basis for a generalization to $n$ dimensions. An oriented 3-cell is defined as a 3-cell associated with a sense-class of its boundary. A set of theorems analogous to those just quoted for 2-cells hold for oriented 3-cells and form the basis of a definition of an oriented 4-cell, and so on.

9. In a regular complex an oriented $n$-cell may be denoted by the order in which its vertices $P_0, P_1, \cdots, P_n$, are written, with the convention that any even permutation of the vertices represents the same oriented $n$-cell and any odd permutation represents its negative. We have not had to use this notation, and mention

it only because it is useful in applications. Its significance may be said to depend on the following theorem:

The complex composed of an $n$-dimensional simplex (§ 1, Chap. III) and the $k$-dimensional simplexes determined by sets of $k + 1$ ($k < n$) of its vertices can be isotopically deformed into itself in such a way that each of the $k$-dimensional simplexes goes into a $k$-dimensional simplex and the vertices are subjected to an arbitrary even permutation. This complex cannot be isotopically deformed into itself in such a way that each of its $k$-cells goes into one of its $k$-cells and so that the vertices are subjected to an odd permutation.

### The Indicatrix

10. Another point of view from which the orientable manifolds may be considered is the following: Let $A$ be a point of a manifold $M_n$ and consider the set of all non-singular oriented $n$-cells on $M_n$ which contain $A$. It can be proved that any such oriented $n$-cell can be deformed into any other such $n$-cell or into its negative through a set of intermediate positions which are all non-singular oriented $n$-cells containing $A$. Moreover, no such oriented $n$-cell can be thus deformed into its negative. Each of the two classes of oriented $n$-cells thus determined for the point $A$ is called an *indicatrix*, and the two indicatrices are called *negatives* of each other.

Now consider an isotopic deformation of a point $A$ and its indicatrices. This carries $A$ along a curve to a point $A'$ and also a given indicatrix of $A$ into an indicatrix of $A'$. If there is any closed curve along which $A$ can be carried in such a way that one of the indicatrices at $A$ is deformed into its negative, then $M_n$ is one-sided. If not, $M_n$ is orientable.

Another way of stating this result is as follows: Let a point associated with one of its indicatrices be called an indicatrix-point. In the case of an orientable manifold $M_n$ the indicatrix-points consist of two manifolds, each of which covers $M_n$ once. In case $M_n$ is one-sided the indicatrix-points constitute a single manifold which covers $M_n$ twice.

A rather full discussion of the indicatrix, together with references to the literature is given by E. Steinitz, Sitzungsberichte der Berliner Mathematischen Gesellschaft, 7 Jahrgang (1908), p. 29. (Cf. footnote on page 67 above.)

11. These covering manifolds can also be obtained directly from the cellular structure of the complex $C_n$ defining $M_n$. Let us form a complex $C_n$ by the following rule: The $i$-cells $(i = n - 1, n)$ of $C_n$ are to be the $2\alpha_i$ oriented $i$-cells $\sigma_j{}^i$ and $-\sigma_j{}^i$ $(j = 1, 2, \cdots, \alpha_i)$. For each oriented $(n - 1)$-cell $\sigma_j{}^{n-1}$, there are four oriented $n$-cells, $\sigma_p{}^n$, $\sigma_q{}^n$, $-\sigma_p{}^n$, $-\sigma_q{}^n$, which are positively or negatively related to it. These fall into two pairs, one pair containing $\sigma_p{}^n$ and the other containing $-\sigma_p{}^n$, such that one of the oriented $n$-cells of a pair is positively related while the other is negatively related to $\sigma_j{}^{n-1}$. Let both oriented $n$-cells of one pair be incident with $\sigma_j{}^{n-1}$ and let both the oriented $n$-cells of the other pair be incident with $-\sigma_j{}^{n-1}$ in the set of incidence relations defining $C_n$. A singular $n$-circuit which is thus defined on $M_n$ can be converted by the method of § 33, Chap. III, into either one or two manifolds, each of which covers $M_n$.

If there are two of these manifolds, $M_n$ is orientable; and if there is only one, $M_n$ is one-sided or non-orientable. Moreover, each oriented $(n - 1)$-cell of $C_n$ is positively related to one oriented $n$-cell of $C_n$ and negatively related to one other. Hence the covering manifold or manifolds are orientable.

12. The covering manifolds which are referred to above must be distinguished clearly from Riemann surfaces. The latter are surfaces on a sphere which have the properties of covering surfaces except at a finite number of points, the branch points. It would be easy to develop the topological part of the theory of Riemann surfaces at this point by the methods which we have been using, and this would doubtless be done in a more extensive treatise.

It is well known that any orientable two-dimensional manifold can be regarded as a Riemann surface. The definition of a Riemann surface has been generalized to $n$ dimensions by P. Heegaard and it has been proved by J. W. Alexander (Bull.

Amer. Math. Soc., Vol. 26 (1920), p. 370) that any orientable manifold can be regarded as a Riemann manifold.

## Theorems on Homotopy

13. By a slight modification of the argument in §§ 35 to 45, Chap. III, it can be proved that *any k-dimensional complex* $C_k$ *on a regular n-dimensional complex* $\overline{C}_n$ *is homotopic with a complex* $C_k'$ *consisting of cells each of which covers (§ 8, Chap. IV) a cell of* $\overline{C}_n$. The nature of the modification needed will be sufficiently indicated by a consideration of the case of a 1-circuit $K_1$ on a regular complex $\overline{C}_n$. Let the definition of the 1-cell $b_i^1$ in § 37, Chap. III, be modified so that $b_i^1$ stands in each case for a 1-cell joining a vertex of $\overline{K}_1$ not to a vertex of $\overline{C}_n$ but to a point coincident with a vertex of $\overline{C}_n$. Likewise let the boundary of each $b_i^2$ be the same as in Chap. III except that if it contains a cell of $\overline{C}_n$ this cell is replaced by one coincident with it. Thus when the boundaries of the 2-cells $b_i^2$ are added (mod. 2) the only 1-cells cancelled are the 1-cells $b_i^1$. Hence the boundary of $B_2$ is the 1-circuit $\overline{K}_1$ and a 1-circuit or set of 1-circuit $K_1'$ composed of 0-cells and 1-cells each covering a cell of $C_n$.

It is obvious that $K_1$ is homotopic with $K_1'$. For a definition of straightness and distance on $B_2$ can be made in such a way that each cell of $B_2$ is a square with one side on $K_1$ and one on $K_1'$ or a triangle with one side on $K_1$ and the opposite vertex on $K_1'$. Each point $X$ of $K_1$ may then be joined to a point of $K_1'$ by a straight 1-cell $x$ in such a way that every interior point of $B_2$ is on one and only one of these 1-cells. A transformation $F_t$ may be defined as that transformation which carries each point $X$ of $K_1$ to the point $P$ of the 1-cell $x$ whose distance along $x$ from $X$ is to the length of the 1-cell $x$ in the ratio $t$. The transformations $F_t$ evidently give a one-parameter continuous family which define a deformation of $K_1$ into $K_1'$.

14. A fundamental theorem of homotopy is the following: *If* $K_n$ *is a non-singular n-circuit on an n-circuit* $C_n$, *then* $K_n$ *cannot be deformed into a single point on* $C_n$. For if such a deformation of $K_n$ were possible $K_n$ would bound a singular

$(n+1)$-dimensional complex on $C_n$ composed of $K_n$, the point into which $K_n$ was deformed, and all intermediate positions of $K_n$. This would be contrary to the first theorem in the second paragraph of § 41, Chap. III.

### The Fundamental Group

15. The theory of the homotopy of curves on a complex leads to the important concept of the fundamental group. Let $O$ be an arbitrary point of a complex $C_n$ and consider all oriented 1-cells on $C_n$ whose initial and final points coincide with $O$. These 1-cells may be singular in any way whatever.

Two of these oriented 1-cells which are such that one of them can be deformed into the other through a set of intermediate positions, all of which are oriented 1-cells of the set, are said to be *equivalent*. Let us denote oriented 1-cells of the set by $g$'s with subscripts, as $g_1$, $g_2$, $g_i$, $g_x$, etc., with the convention that any two equivalent $g$'s may be denoted by the same symbol. Hence by the usual convention on the equality sign, $g_1 = g_2$ means that any oriented 1-cell denoted by $g_1$ is equivalent to any one denoted by $g_2$. Also let any 1-cell which is the negative of one denoted by $g_1$ be denoted by $g_1^{-1}$. Finally let any 1-cell of the set which may be deformed into the point $O$ through a set of intermediate positions which are all $g$'s be denoted by 1. Thus the equation

$$g_x = 1$$

means that $g_x$ may be deformed into coincidence with $O$ through a set of $g$'s.

16. If the terminal point of an oriented 1-cell $g_1$ is identical with the initial point of an oriented 1-cell $g_2$, the oriented 1-cell $g_3$ containing all points of $g_1$ and $g_2$ and having the same initial point as $g_1$ and terminal point as $g_2$ is denoted by $g_1 \cdot g_2$, and $g_3$ is called the *product* of $g_1$ and $g_2$.

This definition holds whether the initial and terminal points of $g_1$ coincide with the same point of $C_n$ or not. For any $g_1$ and $g_2$ whose terminal and initial points respectively coincide with the same point of $C_m$ there exists a $g_3$ such that

$$g_3 = g_1 \cdot g_2$$

because there always exists one of the oriented 1-cells denoted by $g_2$ which has the terminal point of $g_1$ as its initial point. It is also clear that, in general,

$$g_1 \cdot g_2 \neq g_2 \cdot g_1,$$

whereas

$$g_1 \cdot g_1^{-1} = 1,$$

and

$$g_1 \cdot (g_2 \cdot g_3) = (g_1 \cdot g_2) \cdot g_3.$$

17. The symbols $g$ defined in § 15 can be regarded as the operations of a group. For there is a single valued definition of multiplication, they satisfy the associative law, they include among themselves an identity operation, and there is a unique inverse in the set for each operation. This group is known as the *fundamental group* of the complex $C_n$.

The fundamental group of any complex $C_n$ is independent of the choice of the point $O$. For let $O'$ be any other point of $C_n$ and let $g_1$ be an oriented 1-cell whose initial point coincides with $O'$ and whose terminal point coincides with $O$. If $g_x$ is any oriented 1-cell whose initial and terminal points coincide with $O$,

$$\bar{g}_x = g_1 \cdot g_x \cdot g_1^{-1}$$

is one whose initial and terminal points coincide with $O'$. The operations $\bar{g}_x$ form a group which is isomorphic with that formed by the operations $g_x$ because

$$\begin{aligned} \bar{g}_x \cdot \bar{g}_y &= g_1 \cdot g_x \cdot g_1^{-1} \cdot g_1 \cdot g_y \cdot g_1^{-1} \\ &= g_1 \cdot g_x \cdot g_y \cdot g_1^{-1}. \end{aligned}$$

## The Group of a Linear Graph

18. The groups of two particular linear graphs should be noticed:

(1) In case $C_1$ is an open curve its group contains only one operation, the identity. For every closed curve on $C_1$ can be deformed into coincidence with $O$.

(2) In case $C_1$ is a simple closed curve its group contains an operation $g$ which represents an oriented 1-cell which has just

one point coincident with each point of $C_1$ except $O$. The complete set of operations may be represented by

$$\begin{array}{llllll} 1, & g, & g^2, & \cdots, & g^n, & \cdots \\ & g^{-1}, & g^{-2}, & \cdots, & g^{-n}, & \cdots \end{array}$$

where

$$g^2 = g \cdot g, \quad g^3 = g^2 \cdot g, \quad \text{etc.}$$

and

$$g^{-n} = (g^{-1})^n.$$

The operations are all distinct in consequence of the theorem of § 14.

19. In case $C_1$ is an arbitrary linear graph and $a_i^1$ a 1-cell joining two distinct 0-cells of $C_1$, the operation of *shrinking* $a_i^1$ *to a point* will be taken to mean the operation of replacing $C_1$ by a complex $C_1'$ which is identical with $C_1$ except that $a_i^1$ and its ends have been replaced by a single 0-cell which is incident with every 1-cell with which either of the ends of $a_i^1$ was incident.

The operation of shrinking $a_i^1$ to a point does not change the characteristic of $C_1$. For it decreases $\alpha_1$ and $\alpha_0$ each by 1 and hence leaves $\alpha_0 - \alpha_1$ invariant. The operation may make the boundaries of certain 1-cells singular by bringing their ends into coincidence. But by introducing a new 0-cell in the interior of each such 1-cell, the graph may be restored to a form in which each 1-cell has distinct ends. The operation of shrinking a 1-cell to a point obviously leaves $R_0$ invariant. Hence, by the formula,

$$\alpha_0 - \alpha_1 = R_0 - R_1$$

it leaves $R_1$ invariant. This is obvious also because the operation neither produces nor destroys 1-circuits.

The operation may be repeated so long as there are two distinct 0-cells joined by a 1-cell. In case $C_1$ has no 1-circuits, i.e., in case it consists of $R_0$ trees, the operation reduces $C_1$ to a set of $R_0$ 0-cells.

In case $C$ is not a tree and $R_0 = 1$, the result of repeating the operation of shrinking to a point $\alpha_0 - 1$ times is a linear graph consisting of $R_1$ closed curves having a single point in common. In case $R_0 > 1$ the result is $R_0$ such graphs.

20. The operation of shrinking a 1-cell $a_i^1$ of a linear graph $C_1$ to a point changes $C_1$ into a complex $C_1'$ having the same group as $C_1$. This is because: (1) if a closed curve is entirely on $a_i^1$ it can be deformed into coincidence with a single point and (2) if a closed curve $C$ on $C_1$ cannot be deformed into coincidence with a point, the operation of shrinking $a_i^1$ to a point converts $C$ into a curve which cannot be deformed to a point on $C_1'$. From this it follows that: (1) The group of any tree is the identity; (2) the group of any complex which is not a tree is the same as the group of a complex consisting of $R_1 - 1$ 1-cells each having a 0-cell $O$ as its initial and terminal point, and no two having a point in common. This group consists of $R_1 - 1$ operations $g_i$ ($i = 1, 2, \cdots, R_1 - 1$) and all combinations of them. Thus the general expression for an operation of the group is

$$g_1^{a_1} \cdot g_2^{a_2} \cdots g_\mu^{a_\mu} \cdot g_1^{b_1} \cdot g_2^{b_2} \cdots g_\mu^{b_\mu} \cdots g_1^{j_1} \cdot g_2^{j_2} \cdots g_\mu^{j_\mu}$$

where the exponents can be any integers, positive, negative or zero, and $\mu = R_1 - 1$.

21. The operations $g_1, g_2, \cdots, g_\mu$ are called the *generators* of the group of $C_1$. They are absolutely independent of each other, that is to say they satisfy no identities except the laws of combination given in § 16.

In the general theory of discrete groups having a finite number of generators the generators are supposed to satisfy certain identities of the form,

$$g_{i_1}^{m_1} g_{i_2}^{m_2} \cdots g_{i_k}^{m_k} = 1,$$

which are known as *generating relations*. The groups of $n$-dimensional complexes ($n \geq 2$) will be seen usually to have generating relations. The group of a linear graph is thus characterized by the lack of generating relations.

## The Group of a Two-dimensional Complex

22. Let $C_2$ be a two-dimensional complex, $\bar{C}_2$ a regular subdivision of it, and let $C_1$ be the linear graph composed of the

1-cells and 0-cells on the boundaries of the 2-cells of $\overline{C}_2$. Also let the point $O$ which is the common end point of the generators $g$, of the fundamental group be a vertex of $\overline{C}_2$. By § 13 any 1-circuit on $C_2$ may be deformed into (is homotopic with) one composed of 0-cells and non-singular 1-cells coincident with 0-cells and 1-cells of $C_1$. *Hence the generators of the fundamental group of $C_2$ may be taken to be a set of generators of the fundamental group of $C_1$.*

Every 2-cell $a_i^2$ of $\overline{C}_2$ determines a relation among the $g$'s. For let $a$ be an oriented 1-cell whose initial point is $O$ and whose terminal point, $P$, is on the boundary of $a_i^2$ and let $b$ be an oriented 1-cell having $P$ as initial and terminal points and coinciding in a non-singular way with the boundary of $a_i^2$. Then $a \cdot b \cdot a^{-1}$ is one of the $g$'s and is expressible in terms of the generating operation of the fundamental group of $C_1$. Hence

$$a \cdot b \cdot a^{-1} = 1$$

is a relation among the generators of the fundamental group of $C_2$.

If $a_k^2$ is another 2-cell of $C_2$ whose boundary has an oriented 1-cell $m_1$ in common with the boundary of $a_i^2$, the boundaries of $a_k^2$ and $a_i^2$ can be expressed in the forms

$$m_2 \cdot m_1 \text{ and } m_1^{-1} \cdot m_3$$

respectively, where $m_2$ and $m_3$ are oriented 1-cells. The boundary of the 2-cell $b^2$ composed of $a_k^2$ and $a_i^2$ and the points of $m_1$ exclusive of its ends is then

$$m_2 \cdot m_1 \cdot m_1^{-1} \cdot m_3 = m_2 \cdot m_3.$$

Moreover $a$ may be taken to be a 1-cell joining $O$ to an end of $m_1$. The relation determined among the generators of $C_2$ by $a_k^2$ is therefore

(1) $$a \cdot m_2 \cdot m_1 \cdot a^{-1} = 1,$$

that determined by $a_i^2$ is

(2) $$a \cdot m_1^{-1} \cdot m_3 \cdot a^{-1} = 1$$

and that determined by $b^2$ is

(3) $$a \cdot m_2 \cdot m_1 \cdot a^{-1} \cdot a \cdot m_1^{-1} \cdot m_3 \cdot a^{-1} = a \cdot m_2 \cdot m_3 \cdot a^{-1} = 1.$$

The equation (3) is obviously a consequence of (1) and (2). Hence any 2-cell on $\overline{C}_2$ which is composed of cells coincident with the cells $a_i^0$, $a_i^1$, $a_i^2$ gives rise to a relation among the generators of the group which is a consequence of those determined by the 2-cells $a_1^2, a_2^2, \cdots, a_{\alpha_2}^2$.

But any 2-cell on $C_2$ is homotopic with one which is composed of 0-cells and non-singular 1-cells and 2-cells of $\overline{C}_2$. Hence any relation among the generators of the group is expressible in terms of the relations determined by the 2-cells of $\overline{C}_2$. Hence the group has $\alpha_2$ generating relations, some of which, in general, are redundant.

23. In case $C_2$ defines a closed manifold $M_2$, its group $G$ can be obtained in a simple form by considering $C_2$ reduced as in § 64, Chap. II, to a singular 2-cell bounded by a linear graph $C_1$ in which there are $R_1 - 1$ linearly independent circuits. It follows readily that $G$ is generated by $R_1 - 1$ generators connected by one generating relation. If $C_1$ is further normalized as outlined in § 66 this relation may be reduced to one of the following three forms

$$(1) \qquad a_1 \cdot b_1 \cdot a_1^{-1} \cdot b_1^{-1} \cdots a_p \cdot b_p \cdot a_p^{-1} \cdot b_p^{-1} = 1$$

$$(2) \qquad a_1 \cdot b_1 \cdot a_1^{-1} \cdot b_1^{-1} \cdots a_p \cdot b_p \cdot a_p^{-1} \cdot b_p^{-1} \cdot c_1 \cdot c_1 = 1$$

$$(3) \qquad a_1 \cdot b_1 \cdot a_1^{-1} \cdot b_1^{-1} \cdots a_p \cdot b_p \cdot a_p^{-1} \cdot b_p^{-1} \cdot c_1 \cdot c_1 \cdot c_2 \cdot c_2 = 1$$

in which the $a$'s, $b$'s and $c$'s are generating operations and the relation (1) corresponds to a two-sided manifold of genus $p$, (2) to a one-sided manifold of the first kind, and (3) to a one-sided manifold of the second kind. The generating relations (2) and (3) can also be written in the form

$$(4) \qquad c_1^2 \cdot c_2^2 \cdots c_{R_1-1}^2 = 1$$

which is equivalent to (2) if $R_1 - 1 = 4p + 2$ and to (3) if $R_1 - 1 = 4p + 4$.

The fundamental group of a closed manifold is infinite except in the case of the sphere, for which the group is the identity, and of the projective plane, for which it consists of one operation of period two and the identity.

24. An important though obvious consequence of the last sections is that any discrete group with a finite number of generators is the fundamental group of a two-dimensional complex. For, given a group with $n$ generators $g_1, g_2, \cdots, g_n$ and $k$ generating relations, construct a linear graph $C_1$ consisting of a point $O$ and $n$ closed curves having $O$ and no other points in common. Let one of these curves correspond to each generator. The left hand member of each generating relation denotes a closed curve on $C_1$. Introduce a 2-cell (whose boundary is in general singular) bounded by each of these curves. The result is a two-dimensional complex having the given group as its fundamental group.

### The Commutative Group $\bar{G}$

25. Suppose that a group $G$ is determined by $n$ generators $g_1, g_2, \cdots, g_n$ and a number $k$ of generating relations. The latter may be written in the form

$$
(1)\qquad
\begin{array}{l}
g_1^{a_{11}}\cdot g_2^{a_{12}}\cdots g_n^{a_{1n}}\cdot g_1^{b_{11}}\cdot g_2^{b_{12}}\cdots g_n^{b_{1n}}\cdots g_1^{j_{11}}\cdot g_2^{j_{12}}\cdots g_n^{j_{1n}}=1,\\
g_1^{a_{21}}\cdot g_2^{a_{22}}\cdots g_n^{a_{2n}}\cdot g_1^{b_{21}}\cdot g_2^{b_{22}}\cdots g_n^{b_{2n}}\cdots g_1^{j_{21}}\cdot g_2^{j_{22}}\cdots g_n^{j_{2n}}=1,\\
\cdot\quad\cdot\quad\cdot\quad\cdot\quad\cdot\quad\cdot\quad\cdot\quad\cdot\quad\cdot\quad\cdot\\
\cdot\quad\cdot\quad\cdot\quad\cdot\quad\cdot\quad\cdot\quad\cdot\quad\cdot\quad\cdot\quad\cdot\\
\cdot\quad\cdot\quad\cdot\quad\cdot\quad\cdot\quad\cdot\quad\cdot\quad\cdot\quad\cdot\quad\cdot\\
g_1^{a_{k1}}\cdot g_2^{a_{k2}}\cdots g_n^{a_{kn}}\cdot g_1^{b_{k1}}\cdot g_2^{b_{k2}}\cdots g_n^{b_{kn}}\cdots g_1^{j_{k1}}\cdot g_2^{j_{k2}}\cdots g_n^{j_{kn}}=1.
\end{array}
$$

The exponents of the $g$'s are positive or negative integers or zero. The group is characterized by the matrix of the exponents. This matrix has $k$ rows and a number of columns which is a multiple of $n$. It will be called the *matrix of the group*.

If the group $G$ is commutative, that is, if $g_i \cdot g_j = g_j \cdot g_i$ for all values of $i$ and $j$, the left member of each expression in (1) can be written in the form

$$g_1^{a_{r1}}\cdot g_2^{a_{r2}} \cdots g_n^{a_{rn}}.$$

Hence in this case the matrix is one of $k$ rows and $n$ columns.

If $G$ is not commutative there is a unique commutative group $\bar{G}$ associated with it, namely the group generated by $g_1, g_2, \cdots, g_n$ subject to the conditions (1) and the condition that all the operations are commutative. The matrix of $\bar{G}$ is

$$||\gamma_{rs}|| \quad (r = 1, 2, \cdots, k; s = 1, 2, \cdots, n)$$

where

$$\gamma_{rs} = a_{rs} + b_{rs} + \cdots + j_{rs}.$$

26. Regarding $G$ as the group of a two-dimensional complex, the commutative group $\bar{G}$ can be studied by means of the matrix $E_2$. For let the oriented 1-cells $\sigma_i^1$ $(i = 1, 2, \cdots, \alpha_1)$ be denoted by $\sigma_i$, and also, in the present section, denote the number $\alpha_1$ by $\lambda$. Then each of the generators $g_1, g_2, \cdots, g_n$ can be expressed in the form

$$(2) \quad g_i = \sigma_1^{\alpha_{i1}}\sigma_2^{\alpha_{i2}} \cdots \sigma_\lambda^{\alpha_{i\lambda}} \cdots \sigma_1^{\zeta_{i1}}\sigma_2^{\zeta_{i2}} \cdots \sigma^{\zeta_{i\lambda}} \quad (i=1, 2, \cdots n).$$

On substituting these expressions in (1) we find the generating relations of $G$ expressed in terms of the $\sigma$'s. If the group is set up in the manner described in § 22 each of these relations takes the form

$$(3) \qquad l_j\, m_j\, l_j^{-1} = 1$$

where $l_j$ is a set of $\sigma$'s representing a curve from $O$ to a point on the boundary of one of the 2-cells $a_j^2$ and $m_j$ represents the boundary of the 2-cell.

On passing to the group $\bar{G}$ by introducing the condition of commutativity (3) becomes

$$(4) \qquad m_j = 1.$$

Since $m_j$ represents the boundary of the 2-cell $a_j^2$ it is expressible in the form

$$(5) \qquad \sigma_1^{e_{1j}}\sigma_2^{e_{2j}} \cdots \sigma_\lambda^{e_{\lambda j}} = 1 \qquad (j = 1, 2, \cdots, \alpha_2)$$

in which the exponents are the elements of the $j$th column of the matrix $E_2$. Hence *the generating relations of the group $\bar{G}$ when expressed in terms of $\sigma_1, \sigma_2, \cdots, \sigma_{\alpha_1}$, take the form* (5) *in which the matrix of the exponents is $E_2'$, the matrix obtained by interchanging the rows and columns of* $E_2$.

It is worthy of comment that whereas the group $G$ is defined in terms of a definite point $O$ of $C_2$ (an isomorphic group is obtained from any other point $O'$), the group $\tilde{G}$ has no reference to any particular point $O$. This is because the terms $l_j$ and $l_j^{-1}$ in (3) cancel out when the assumption of commutativity is introduced.

27. The fundamental group $G$ is such that

$$g_x = 1$$

signifies that the closed curve represented by $g_x$ bounds a 2-cell on $C_2$. The geometric significance of the group $\tilde{G}$ is equally simple. If $g_y$ is an element of this group

$$g_y = 1 \tag{6}$$

signifies that the closed curve or set of closed curves represented by $g_y$ *bounds a two-dimensional complex on* $C$, or in other words,

$$g_y \sim 0 \tag{7}$$

where we now let $g_y$ stand for the oriented curve obtained by identifying the initial and terminal points of the oriented 1-cell $g_y$. That (6) and (7) have the same geometrical significance is immediately evident if one compares the steps by which (6) is obtained from (5) with those by which (7) is obtained from the fundamental homologies of § 28, Chap. IV.

## Equivalences and Homologies

28. The operation of combining two elements of a group which is called multiplication in the sections above can equally well be denoted by the sign + and called addition. This is done in fact by Poincaré in a number of places. He thereby replaces any relation of the type (1) by

$$a_{i1}g_1 + a_{i2}g_2 + \cdots + a_{in}g_n + \cdots + j_{i1}g_1 + j_i g_2 \cdots + j_{in}g_n \equiv 0 \tag{8}$$

which he calls an *equivalence*. In an equivalence the operation of addition is non-commutative. The equivalence (8) signifies that the elements on the left-hand member constitute the boundary of a 2-cell. To develop the theory of equivalence further would amount merely to repeating the theory of the group $G$ in a different form. Any equivalence can be derived from the corresponding group identity by the formal process of taking logarithms.

Poincaré also makes use of a second class of equivalences which he calls *improper equivalences.* These are obtained from the proper equivalences by dropping the restriction that each 1-cell shall begin and end at $O$ and allowing *cyclic permutation* of the terms of an equivalence. Thus if two 1-cells are properly equivalent they are homotopic by a deformation through intermediate positions each of which is a 1-cell whose ends coincide with $O$. If they are improperly equivalent they are homotopic in the general sense.

It should be noted that the equivalences and congruences (§ 25, Chap. IV) of Poincaré are entirely different notions although they are designated by the same notation.

29. Any equivalence (8) gives rise to a homology

$$\gamma_{i1}g_1 + \gamma_{i2}g_2 + \cdots + \gamma_{in}g_n \sim 0 \tag{9}$$

which is distinguished from (8) by the fact that the commutative law of addition holds good and by the fact that

$$\gamma_{ik} = a_{ik} + b_{ik} + \cdots + j_{ik} \quad (k = 1, 2, \cdots, n).$$

The homologies thus correspond to the identities of the group $\tilde{G}$, which may well be called the homology group.

## The Poincaré Numbers of G

30. Let us consider a set of $n$ operations of $G$, $g_1'$, $g_2'$, $\cdots$, $g_n'$, where

$$\begin{matrix} g_1' = g_1^{a_{11}} \cdot g_2^{a_{12}} \cdots g_n^{a_{1n}} \cdots g_1^{\zeta_{11}} \cdot g_2^{\zeta_{12}} \cdots g_n^{\zeta_{1n}} \\ \cdot \quad \cdot \quad \cdot \quad \cdot \quad \cdot \quad \cdot \quad \cdot \\ \cdot \quad \cdot \quad \cdot \quad \cdot \quad \cdot \quad \cdot \quad \cdot \\ \cdot \quad \cdot \quad \cdot \quad \cdot \quad \cdot \quad \cdot \quad \cdot \\ g_n' = g_1^{a_{n1}} \cdot g_2^{a_{n2}} \cdots g_n^{a_{nn}} \cdots g_1^{\zeta_{n1}} \cdot g_2^{\zeta_{n2}} \cdots g_n^{\zeta_{nn}} \end{matrix} \tag{10}$$

and inquire under what circumstances they can serve as a set of generators for $G$. The necessary and sufficient condition for this is obviously that it shall be possible to solve the equations (10) so as to express $g_1, g_2, \cdots, g_n$ by equations analogous to (10) in terms of $g_1', g_2', \cdots, g_n'$.

The equations (10) determine an analogous set of equations for the commutative group $\tilde{G}$

$$g_i' = g_1^{\mu_{i1}} g_2^{\mu_{i2}} \cdots g_n^{\mu_{in}} \qquad (i = 1, 2, \cdots, n) \tag{11}$$

in which

$$\mu_{ij} = \alpha_{ij} + \beta_{ij} + \cdots + \zeta_{ij}.$$

A solution of the equations (10) must correspond to a solution of the equations (11). But since the elements in (11) are commutative the process of solution is entirely analogous to that of solving the linear equations,

$$x_i' = \mu_{i1}x_1 + \mu_{i2}x_2 + \cdots + \mu_{in}x_n \quad (i = 1, 2, \cdots, n)$$

in terms of integers. The condition that a unique solution in integers shall exist is

$$\left\| \begin{matrix} \mu_{11} & \mu_{12} & \cdots & \mu_{1n} \\ \mu_{21} & \mu_{22} & \cdots & \mu_{2n} \\ \cdot & \cdot & & \cdot \\ \cdot & \cdot & & \cdot \\ \cdot & \cdot & & \cdot \\ \mu_{n1} & \mu_{n2} & \cdots & \mu_{nn} \end{matrix} \right\| = \pm 1. \tag{12}$$

Hence (12) is a *necessary* condition that (10) shall be a transformation to a new set of generators of $G$.

31. If $G$ is to be expressed in terms of the generators $g_1', g_2', \cdots, g_n'$, the expressions for $g_1, g_2, \cdots, g_n$ in terms of $g_1', g_2', \cdots, g_n'$ must be substituted in the generating relations (1) in order to obtain a new set of generating relations in terms of $g_1, g_2, \cdots, g_n$. When this set of generating relations is modified by allowing all elements to be commutative it becomes a new set of generating relations for $\tilde{G}$. This set of generating relations for $\tilde{G}$ could also be obtained by substituting directly the solutions of (11). *This amounts to multiplying the matrix* $||\gamma_{rs}||$ *on the right by a square matrix of n rows and determinant* $\pm 1$.

The generating relations (1) can also be modified by replacing them by equivalent expressions resulting from algebraic combinations. As applied to the matrix $||\gamma_{rs}||$ this means *multiplying it on the left by a square matrix of k rows and determinant* $\pm 1$.

The two operations on $||\gamma_{rs}||$ are the operations required to reduce a matrix to the normal form E* given in § 49, Chap. I, in which all elements are zero except the first $r$ elements of the main diagonal which are denoted by $d_1, d_2, \cdots, d_r$. This reduction of $||\gamma_{rs}||$ to normal form determines one or more transformations of the generators and generating relations of $\tilde{G}$ to such a form that it has $n$ generators subject to $r$ generating relations,

$$\begin{aligned} g_1^{d_1} &= 1 \\ g_2^{d_2} &= 1 \\ &\cdot \\ &\cdot \\ &\cdot \\ g_r^{d_r} &= 1. \end{aligned}$$

In case certain of the numbers $d_1, d_2, \cdots, d_r$ are $\pm 1$ it may happen that certain of the corresponding generators of $\tilde{G}$ are equal to the identity. In this case the symbols for these generators may be omitted, for $\tilde{G}$ is unaffected by introducing or removing a generator $g_i$ which satisfies the condition $g_i = 1$.

32. Those of the numbers $d_1, d_2, \cdots, d_r$ which are not equal to $\pm 1$ have been called by H. Tietze* the *Poincaré numbers* of the discrete group $G$. *They are invariants of G under all transformations to new sets of generators.*

For if two sets of generators are given for $G$ with different numbers of generators, additional generators each equal to the indentity can be introduced in the one set or the other so that both sets have the same number of generators. Then by the argument in § 30 the relation between the two sets of generators must be one which corresponds to a transformation of the generators of $\tilde{G}$ of determinant $\pm 1$. Let one set of generators be expressed in terms of the other set. This will in general

* Monatshefte für Math. u. Physik, Vol. 19 (1908), p. 56.

yield two sets of generating relations in terms of one set of generators. When the condition of commutativity is introduced, this gives two sets of generating relations in terms of one set of generators for $\bar{G}$. But, as in the theory of linear equations, this means that either set of relations is expressible in terms of the other by an operation which amounts to multiplying the matrix on the left by a matrix of determinant $\pm 1$. Hence the only possible transformations of the generators and generating relations of $G$ produce transformations of $G$ which do not change the Poincaré numbers.

33. If $G$ is the fundamental group of a complex $C_n$ it is evident from § 13 that $G$ is the fundamental group of the two-dimensional complex composed of the 0-, 1-, and 2-cells of any regular subdivision of $C_n$. Hence the Poincaré numbers of $G$ are the invariant factors of the matrix $E_2$ for this regular subdivision. Hence *they are the one-dimensional coefficients of torsion of* $C_n$.

Whether there exist generalizations of the fundamental group, and whether, in particular, these generalizations can be made in such a way as to bear a relation like the one just described to the $n$-dimensional Betti numbers and coefficients of torsion is a problem on which nothing has yet been published.

34. The equality of the Poincaré numbers of two discrete groups, $G$ and $G'$, is a necessary condition that the two groups be isomorphic, but it is far from being a sufficient condition. In fact, the problem of determining by a finite number of steps whether two groups, each given by means of a set of generators and a set of generating relations, are or are not isomorphic, seems to be a very difficult one. A clear discussion of this problem as well as of the general theory of discrete groups is given by M. Dehn, Math. Ann., Vol. 71 (1912), p. 116. The isomorphism problem has been solved for the following special case by J. Nielsen, Math. Ann., Vol. 79 (1919), p. 269: Let $G$ be generated by $n$ operations $g_1, g_2, \cdots, g_n$ subject to no relations, and let $g_1', g_2', \cdots, g_n'$ be a set of $n$ operations of $G$ which are subject to no relation; to determine by a finite number of steps whether the second set of operations also generate $G$. Further

accounts of the theory of discrete groups, particularly the groups of two-dimensional manifolds, are to be found in the Kiel dissertation of H. Gieseking.

35. In an earlier paper (Math. Ann., Vol. 78, p. 385), Nielsen solves the isomorphism problem for the case $n = 2$ and applies the results to the study of systems of curves on the anchor ring. In the Math. Ann., Vol. 82 (1920), p. 83, he obtains a formula for the minimum number of fixed points of a homeomorphism of a two-dimensional manifold of genus 1 with itself in terms of the type of the homeomorphism, the type being determined by the isomorphism of the fundamental group which is effected by the given homeomorphism of the manifold. This is one of the papers referred to in § 7.

## Covering Manifolds

36. The fundamental group of a complex $C_n$ determines a covering manifold in the following manner. Let $O$ be an arbitrary fixed point of $C_n$ and let $X$ be a general point. If $\sigma^1$ be any oriented 1-cell joining $O$ to $X$ it determines an infinite set of oriented 1-cells joining $O$ to $X$ which is such that any oriented 1-cell of the set can be deformed into $\sigma^1$ through a set of intermediate positions all of which are oriented 1-cells joining $O$ to $X$. The oriented 1-cells of such a set are said to be *equivalent* to one another. If $g$ is any operation of the fundamental group, which is distinct from the identity, $g \cdot \sigma^1$ is not equivalent to $\sigma^1$. The set of all non-equivalent oriented 1-cells joining $O$ to $X$ may be represented in the form $g \cdot \sigma^1$ where $\sigma^1$ is fixed and $g$ may be any operation of the fundamental group.

A set of points $[Y]$ on $C_2$ may be defined by the convention that each $Y$ is an $X$ associated with the set of all oriented curves equivalent to a certain oriented 1-cell joining $O$ to $X$. Thus for each $X$ there is a set of $Y$'s which is in (1–1) correspondence with the operations of the fundamental group. A 1-cell $a^1$ composed of $X$'s determines a set of 1-cells composed of $Y$'s each of which covers $a^1$, and there is one such 1-cell covering $a^1$ for each operation of the fundamental group. Similarly a $k$-cell $a^k$ $(k = 0, 1, \cdots, n)$ composed of $X$'s determines a set of $k$-cells composed of $Y$'s, each such $k$-cell covering $a^k$, and the totality of $k$-cells which cover $a^k$ being in (1–1) correspondence with the operations of the fundamental group.

37. In case $n = 2$ and $C_2$ is a complex determining a sphere, the set of points $[Y]$ is evidently a sphere covering $C_2$ once, because the fundamental group of $C_2$ is the identity. In case $C_2$ is a projective plane, $[Y]$ is a sphere covering $C_2$ twice. This follows because the group of the projective plane is a cyclic group of order two. The set of points $[Y]$ is essentially the same as the two-sided covering surface of a projective plane considered in § 11.

In general $[Y]$ is a complex of an infinite number of cells. If $C_2$ defines an orientable manifold not a sphere or a projective plane, $[Y]$ is homeomorphic with a single 2-cell. For a proof of this theorem and for a further consideration of covering manifolds, the reader is referred to the book of H. Weyl, Die Idee der Riemannschen Fläche, Leipzig, 1913.

The set of points $[Y]$ is called a *universal covering surface* of $C_2$ in case $C_2$ defines a manifold. If $C_2$ is reduced to a normal form as in § 66, Chap. II, so that $C_2$ has only one 2-cell, the 2-cells of $[Y]$ which cover it may be regarded as constituting a network of regular polygons of $2p$ sides each, in a Euclidean ($p = 1$) or non-Euclidean plane. This is therefore the point at which the well-known applications to Automorphic Functions and the Uniformization theory fit into our outline of Analysis Situs.

### Three-dimensional Manifolds

38. In the case of a two-dimensional manifold the fundamental group determines the orientation and the connectivity and therefore, the manifold, completely. In the three-dimensional case, such invariants as are known can be derived from a consideration of the fundamental group. For it has been shown above that the one-dimensional coefficients of torsion can be obtained from the group and also that $P_1$ is equal to the difference between the number of generators and the rank of the matrix $||\gamma_{ij}||$. Also, by § 19, Chap. III, $P_1 = P_2$ if the manifold is

orientable and $P_1 = P_2 + 1$ if it is one-sided. Hence $P_1$, $P_2$, and the coefficients of torsion are all derivable from the fundamental group.

It is natural to ask whether the fundamental group is determined by $P_1$ and the coefficients of torsion. This question was answered in the negative by Poincaré, who showed that there are manifolds for which $P_1 = 1$ and the coefficients of torsion are absent and for which the group does not reduce to the identity. An infinite class of such manifold has been studied by M. Dehn, Math. Ann., Vol. 69 (1910), p. 137, and called by him the *Poincaré spaces.* The group of a Poincaré space may be either finite or infinite.

It has also been proved that a three-dimensional manifold is not fully determined by its fundamental group. This was established by J. W. Alexander (Trans. Am. Math. Soc., Vol. 20 (1919), p. 339) by setting up two non-homeomorphic three-dimensional manifolds which have the same group, the cyclic group of order 5.

39. The problem still remains unsolved, however, to determine whether there is any three-dimensional manifold other than the three-dimensional sphere the fundamental group of which reduces to the identity.

The group of the covering manifold determined for any manifold $M_n$ by its fundamental group obviously reduces to the identity. Hence in case the covering manifold is closed, the solution of this problem has an important bearing on the study of a manifold by means of its fundamental group.

The problem may be not entirely unrelated to the problem of generalizing the Schoenflies theorem referred to in § 19, Chap. III. The latter theorem has not yet been proved (so far as known to the writer) even for the following special case: Given a non-singular and simply connected two-dimensional polyhedron in a Euclidean space; to prove that the interior region of this polyhedron is homeomorphic with the interior of a tetrahedron.

### The Heegaard Diagram

40. The most direct way of attacking the problem of classifying three-dimensional manifolds is to try to reduce them to normal

form by a process analogous to that outlined in § 62, Chap. II. If we start with a non-singular complex $C_3$ defining an orientable manifold $M_3$ and perform a sequence of operations (1) of coalescing pairs of 3-cell which have a common 2-cell on their boundaries and (2) of shrinking to a point 1-cells which join distinct points, $C_3$ is reduced to a complex $C_3'$ consisting of one 3-cell and one 0-cell and equal numbers, $\alpha$, of 2-cells and 1-cells. Hence $M_3$ may be represented by means of the interior and boundary of a Euclidean sphere, the boundary being a map all the vertices of which represent the same point of $M_3$. The 2-cells of this map fall into $\alpha$ pairs each of which represents a single 2-cell of $C_3'$. The 1-cells of the map fall into $\alpha$ sets such that all 1-cells in the same set represent the same 1-cell of $C_3'$.

41. This representation of a manifold $M_3$ by means of a sphere has not yet proved as fruitful as the related *Heegaard diagram* which may be obtained as follows: Let the 0-cell of $C_3'$ be enclosed by a small 3-cell containing it and let each of the 1-cells of $C_3'$ be enclosed by a small tube containing it. Thus we obtain a three-dimensional open manifold $L_3$ bounded by a two-dimensional manifold $M_2$ consisting of a sphere with $\alpha$ handles. $M_3$ is orientable if and only if $M_2$ is orientable. In case $M_3$ is orientable $L_3$ can be represented as the interior of a sphere with handles having no knots or links in a Euclidean 3-space.

The 2-cells of $C_3'$ meet $M_2$ in a system of $\alpha$ curves no two of which intersect and which bound a set of $\alpha$ 2-cells $a_1^2, a_2^2, \cdots, a_\alpha^2$ contained in the 2-cells of $C_3'$. The points of the 2-cells $a_i^2$ together with the points of the 3-cell of $C_3'$ which are not in $L_3$ or $M_2$ constitute the interior of an open three-dimensional manifold $N_3$ bounded by $M_2$.

Thus $M_3$ consists of two open manifolds $L_3$ and $N_3$ which have a common boundary, $M_2$. It is clear that $M_3$ is fully determined if $L_3$, $M_2$ and the boundaries $c_1, c_2, \cdots, c_\alpha$ of the cells $a_i^2$ are given. For the manifold $M_3$ can be reconstructed by putting in 2-cells bounded by the curves $c_1, c_2, \cdots, c_\alpha$ and a 3-cell bounded by $M_2$ and these 2-cells, each counted twice.

The representation of a manifold by means of $L_3$, $M_2$, and $c_1, c_2, \cdots, c_\alpha$ is called the Heegaard diagram. It is due (in a form which generalizes to $n$ dimensions) to P. Heegaard in his dissertation, Forstudier til en topologisk teori for de algebraiske fladers sammenhaeng, Copenhagen, 1898 (republished in the Bulletin de la Soc. Math. de France, Vol. 44 (1916), p. 161). It is also described very clearly by M. Dehn, Math. Ann., Vol. 69, p. 165. Dehn draws from it the corollary that any $M_3$ can be defined by a non-singular complex having four 3-cells.

42. The curves $c_1, c_2, \cdots, c_\alpha$ are the boundaries of a set of 2-cells which reduce $N_3$ to a single 3-cell. In like manner there is a set of $\alpha$ curves, $d_1, d_2, \cdots, d_\alpha$ no two of which have a point in common and which bound a set of $\alpha$ 2-cells which reduce $L_3$ to a single 3-cell. Moreover $M_2$ and the two sets of curves fully determine $M_3$.

In fact, suppose we have a manifold $M_2$ of genus $\alpha$ and two sets of curves $c_1, c_2, \cdots, c_\alpha$ and $d_1, d_2, \cdots, d_\alpha$, each set being such that no two of its curves have a point in common and such, moreover, that by introducing $\alpha$ 2-cells each bounded by one of the curves, $M_2$ is converted into a complex which can bound a 3-cell if each of the $\alpha$ 2-cells is counted twice. Then if we introduce a set of 2-cells of this sort for the curves $c_1, c_2, \cdots, c_\alpha$ and a 3-cell bounded by the resulting complex we obtain an open manifold $L_3$ bounded by $M_2$. If now we introduce another set of $\alpha$ 2-cells bounded by $d_1, d_2, \cdots, d_\alpha$ and having no points in common with each other or with $L_3$, or $M_2$, we can introduce another 3-cell bounded by $M_2$ and these 2-cells. The resulting three-dimensional complex is clearly a manifold which is homeomorphic with $M_3$ if $M_2$ and the curves were determined from $M_3$ in the manner described in the paragraph above.

43. The problem of three-dimensional manifolds is thus reduced to one regarding systems of curves upon a two-dimensional manifold. The modifications which can be made in the systems of curves of a Heegaard diagram without changing the manifold $M_3$ represented by the diagram have been studied (though not completely) by Heegaard in his dissertation. The most important results thus far obtained on systems of curves are those of Poincaré in his fifth complement, in which he was evidently considering the problem of three-dimensional manifolds from

approximately the point of view outlined in the last section. Reference should also be made in connection with the problem of systems of curves on two-dimensional manifolds to two articles by C. Jordan in the Journal de Mathematique, Ser. 2, Vol. 11 (1866), to an article by Dehn, Math. Ann., Vol. 72 (1912), to the dissertation of J. Nielsen, Kiel, 1913, to the article by Brahana cited in § 66, Chap. II, and to the articles on the group of a two-dimensional manifold already referred to in this chapter.

### The Knot Problem

44. Very closely related to the problem of classifying the three-dimensional manifolds is the problem of classifying the knots in the three-dimensional Euclidean or spherical space. A *knot* may be defined as a non-singular curve in a Euclidean space which is not isotopic with the boundary of a triangular region; and two knots are regarded as of the same type if and only if they are isotopic.

A large number of types of knots have been described by Tait and others and a list of references will be found in the Encyklopädie article on Analysis Situs. But a more important step towards developing a theory of knots was taken by M. Dehn, who introduced the notion of the group of the knot, which is essentially the group of the generalized three-dimensional complex obtained by leaving out the knot from the three-dimensional space. Dehn gave a method for obtaining the group of a knot explicitly and applied it to the construction of the Poincaré spaces already referred to (§ 38). Dehn's work is to be found in his articles in the Math. Ann. in Vols. 69 and 71 to which we have already referred and in an article on the two trefoil knots in Vol. 75 (1914), p. 402.

It is obvious that if a three-dimensional Riemann space of $k$ sheets be found which has a given knot as its only branch curve, the invariants (Betti numbers, etc.) of this space will be invariants of the given knot. This method of studying the invariants of a knot has been developed by J. W. Alexander in a paper read before the National Academy of Sciences in November 1920, but not yet published.

www.ingramcontent.com/pod-product-compliance
Lightning Source LLC
LaVergne TN
LVHW020620110826
845149LV00002B/539

* 9 7 8 1 4 1 8 1 8 2 3 2 8 *